UKRAINE'S REVOLT, RUSSIA'S REVENGE

UKRAINE'S REVOLT, RUSSIA'S REVENGE

CHRISTOPHER M. SMITH

BROOKINGS INSTITUTION PRESS

Washington, D.C.

Library of Congress Control Number: 2021950366

ISBN 9780815739241 (hc)
ISBN 9780815739258 (ebook)

9 8 7 6 5 4 3 2 1

Typeset in Garamond Premier Pro

Composition by Elliott Beard

To Natalya, Andrew, Elena, and the Ukrainian people

CONTENTS

PREFACE

One motivation compelled me to write this book. I was never asked by the State Department to take on this work, and my management and colleagues in the US Foreign Service had mixed reactions when I told them about it, ranging from high enthusiasm to cautious skepticism. In short, I was frustrated by the constant lies and distortions about the work of US Embassy Kyiv during the 2013–2014 Euromaidan Revolution—and these lies were coming from the Russian state apparatus. Russian government statements and high-volume, confident Russian media invective constantly implored publics worldwide to believe that the US Embassy was the secret but decisive force behind the Ukrainian protest movement, plotting to thwart Russia's interests in its own backyard in some sort of geopolitical maneuver. Their distorted mirror presented the Ukrainians as pawns, legitimate Russian interests as innocent targets, and the United States as a hostile interloper with motivations somewhere between a satanic jackal and a cartoonish horror movie villain.

None of this was true, and it congealed into a foundational lie upon which propagandists built fresh new sedimentary layers of deceit. Today in Russia, the falsehood that the United States had some pivotal role in supporting, funding, or even creating Euromaidan as a cynical maneuver against Russia is treated as established truth beyond question. Stacked on top of this were mistruths about Ukraine being run by "fascists," separatists in eastern Ukraine being local and organic, and much, much more. But having served there at the time in US Embassy Kyiv, I was shocked to realize that many people worldwide believed these crude propaganda hooks. I wanted a way to tell the story of what those at the embassy witnessed and what we did during that time. Russian propaganda organs pressed their disinformation lines constantly, but after the events passed into history, the United States largely remained silent. Because of this, the United States started to lose ground to loudly screamed falsehoods from Russia. I felt that someone needed to give voice to the true story.

I then realized that I had a great asset for telling the real story. The vast majority of the narrative in these pages comes from a single source: the unpublished email archive of US Embassy Kyiv. This archive includes hundreds of thousands of unclassified messages of the "KyivTaskForce" group, a sprawling collective that blasted out messages related to nearly every aspect of the crisis and the US government's response. Material in this book that is not otherwise attributed comes from this primary source. As a courtesy, in some cases I have used a pseudonym in place of a person's real name.

While the classified system may also contain a few interesting data points, as the thrust of the US effort in Ukraine was overt, the unclassified archive is the most important way to tell the story in a way that has never been publicly told before. Several other sources were also extremely helpful. My colleague Joseph Rozenshtein's interviews with US Embassy Kyiv staff members following those fateful events were quite valuable. I also interviewed others to gain clarity on what they had experienced.

Turning hundreds of thousands of emails into a readable narrative took time, and in my case, a bit of luck. In between Foreign Service assignments in Washington and Guangzhou, I had six months before my language training began. I approached the State Department's Office of the Historian and asked if they could give me a desk and a computer during that time while I attempted to do something I had never done before and am unlikely to do again—write a book. They gave me what I asked for and so much more, namely the advice of professional historians who helped me to create a useful and engaging narrative out of very raw material. I began in the summer of 2016, and I completed the rough draft by the end of that year. I feel compelled to note that future developments such as US-Ukraine affairs becoming the heart of an American presidential impeachment inquiry would have been completely unbelievable to me as I drafted this text.

Some days, sitting on Navy Hill across the road from the Foggy Bottom State Department "mothership" in the Office of the Historian, I felt as though I was reliving events while reviewing the endless stream of archived emails. I would return to my home and family in suburban Maryland while I was still mentally back on the streets of Kyiv surrounded by tire fires and confusion, armed only with an aging US government–issued BlackBerry and a diplomatic passport. That was the worthwhile price of truthfully recounting what we lived through.

Everyone involved has a story, some certainly better than mine. But mine is the one I had to tell. If this book places into context what the Euromaidan Revolution meant to those Ukrainians who were engaged in it; if it undoes some of the damage done by slanderous propaganda about these events; if it informs people about the actual work of the Foreign Service; and if it explains the injustices inflicted upon Ukraine by its more powerful neighbor after 2013, then I'm humbly honored to be a part of telling this story.

ACKNOWLEDGMENTS

There's no true way to thank those in my life without whom this book would never exist. First, of course, comes my wife, Natalya, and my children, Andrew and Elena, as well as my mother-in-law, Liudmila, who went through these experiences with me every moment of the way. Their adventurousness and love for life inspires me in everything I do. Thank you! My parents, Eddie and Lilla, gave me the most precious gift any parents could give a child—a window into a greater world. As I mention in the book, they stretched far beyond their means to send me to Russia in 1992, giving me inspiration and a life path. I owe them so much. I must thank my sister, Rebecca, her husband, Ryan, and their children, Sienna, Cameron, and Landon, for enriching my life in ways beyond what I can express here. My brothers, Dean and Darin, thank you. And Mike and Jim, you know what you did.

As far as taking this book from a jumbled rough word collage to something that I hoped people would want to read, I need to thank my literary agent, Peter Bernstein, and the incredible work of Dr. Steven Levine. While Peter relentlessly searched for a publisher, Steve was my writing soulmate as we swapped increasingly better edited chapters between North Carolina and Guangzhou, China. Peter and Steve: this book would not exist without you. Steven's expertise and kindness is woven into every sentence.

I must thank Dr. Stephen Randolph and Renee Goings from the State

Department Office of the Historian. I may not have met your high professional standards, but your support and advice made this work possible.

I most specifically need to thank my colleagues at US Embassy Kyiv, many of whom are quoted in the text. To my bosses, David Meale and Elizabeth Horst, you were irreplaceable crisis managers and mentors. To Valentyna Sizaya, my amazing tutor on all things Ukraine, the US government can never repay you for all that you have given. There are so many others who are quoted in the book, and I can only hope that I have quoted you properly, and that if you've read the text, you've enjoyed recalling some incredible days.

As far as my educational mentors, I must mention the contagious intellectual curiosity of professor Thomas Lairson at Rollins College. In graduate school, professor Peter Reddaway immutably shaped my conception of the world in invaluable ways. I owe my moral bearing to my flawed attempts to emulate Professor Reddaway's towering intellectual honesty and bravery. Peter Reddaway's calm steadfastness showed me at an early age that holding tight to your values is its own reward.

I also owe a great debt to Olena Karbovskyy, Iryna MacDonald, and Iryna Shcherbak—the Ukrainian language faculty at the State Department's Foreign Service Institute. As a Russian (not Ukrainian) speaker, I was not qualified to transliterate Ukrainian into English. In their spare time, they did so out of a labor of love. Thank you so much.

Regarding my Foreign Service mentors, I owe Patrick Murphy, Paul Mayer, Dan Kritenbrink, Aubrey Carlson, Chris Castro, Thomas Hodges, Jim Levy, Eric Johnson, and so many others a debt of gratitude for giving me their time and teaching me to better represent America.

There are others I simply must mention, including my Embassy economics, political, and public affairs crew from Lesotho, including the King of Lesotho's right-hand man Thabong Tlalojoe, the irreplaceably skilled Mamosa Makaya, and the amazingly hip Ma-Lord Mefane. Ronald Feng in Guangzhou remains a constant and vital professional. I thank Akram Kelam for the sacrifices he made in his work for the US government before he was forced to leave his homeland.

Lastly, I would like to thank the US Foreign Service. Despite flaws, it is a triumphant moral vehicle for pursuing the interests of the American people worldwide. For young people eager to change the world, this could be your path. It was mine. I celebrate the Foreign Service and thank the institution for giving me a way to share my nation and myself.

POLAND

BELARUS

RUSSIA

Brest
Lublin
Pinsk
Homyel
Mazyr
Voronezh
Kursk
Belgorod
Rostov-na-Donu
Krasnodar
Novorossiysk

Vistula
Bug
Pripyat
Dnieper
Don
Seym
Desna
Dniester
Prut
Kuban

Rzeszów
Uzhhorod
ZAKARPATS'KA
OBLAST'
SLOV.
HUNG.

L'viv
LVIVS'KA
OBLAST'
Ivano-
Frankivs'k
IVANO-FRANKIVS'KA
OBLAST'
Chernivtsi
CHERNIVETS'KA
OBLAST'

Kovel'
Luts'k
VOLYNS'KA
OBLAST'
Rivne
RIVNENS'KA
OBLAST'
Ternopil'
TERNOPIL'S'KA
OBLAST'
Khmel'nyts'ky
KHMEL'NYTS'KA
OBLAST'

Satu Mare
Baia Mare
Suceava
Botoşani
Iaşi
Bacău
ROMANIA
Galaţi
Focşani
Brăila
Bucharest
Constanţa

MOLDOVA
Chişinău
Tiraspol'
Bălţi
Bolhrad

Novohrad-
Volyns'kyy
ZHYTOMYRS'KA
OBLAST'
Zhytomyr
Korosten'
Chornobyl'
(Chërnobyl')
VINNYTS'KA
OBLAST'
Vinnytsya

Chernihiv
CHERNIHIVS'KA
OBLAST'
Hlukhiv
Hluhiv
SUMS'KA
OBLAST'
Sumy
Okhtyrka
KYIVS'KA
OBLAST'
Kyiv
MISTO
KYYIV
Kyiv
Reservoir

RUSSIA

Kharkiv
KHARKIVS'KA
OBLAST'
LUHANS'KA
OBLAST'
Luhans'k
Slov"yans'k
DONETS'KA
OBLAST'
Donets'k

POLTAVS'KA
OBLAST'
Poltava
Pyryatyn
Kremenchuk
Kremenchuk
Reservoir
CHERKAS'KA
OBLAST'
Cherkasy
Uman'

DNIPROPETROVS'KA OBLAST'
Dnipro
Kropyvnyts'kyy
KIROVOHRADS'KA
OBLAST'
Novovorontsovka
Zaporizhzhya
ZAPORIZ'K
OBLAST'
Melitopol'
Berdyans'k
Mariupol'
Sea of Azov

MYKOLAYIVS'KA
OBLAST'
Mykolayiv
Novoodesa
ODES'KA
OBLAST'
Odesa
KHERSONS'KA
OBLAST'
Kherson
Kakhovka
Krasnoperekops'k
Dzhankoy
Yevpatoriya
Simferopol'
CRIMEA
MISTO SEVASTOPOL'
Sevastopol'
Yalta
Kerch
Kerch
Strait
Black Sea

Southern Buh
Southern Buh
Dnieper
Karkinits'ka Zatoka

Dnieper
Dnieper

UKRAINE

⊛ Capital city
⊙ Oblast' or oblast'-level
  center
── International boundary
⋯ Oblast' or oblast'-level
  boundary
── Road

| 0 | 50 | 100 Miles |
| 0 | 50 | 100 Kilometers |

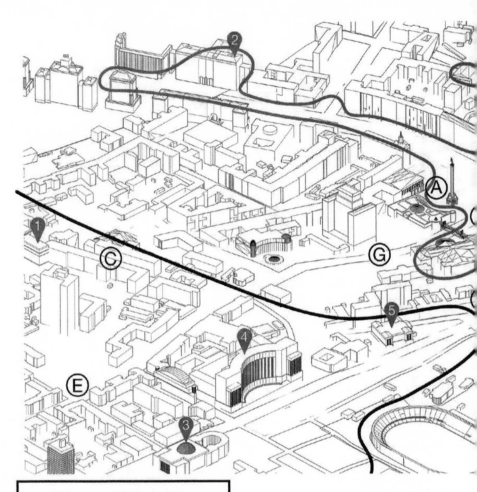

: **GOVERNMENTAL QUARTERS CONTROLLED BY POLICE FORCES**

: **APPROXIMATE TERRITORY OF MAIDAN PROTESTS, DECEMBER – FEBRUARY**

(A) November, 30, 2013: Euromaidan is stormed by Berkut. December, 11, 2013: Police stage another night raid of Maidan.

(B) November, 30, 2013: Protesters shelter here, fleeing from Berkut. February, 18-20, 2014: Monastery is converted into a field hospital and medication bank.

(C) December, 1, 2013: Berkut disperses a picket of the Presidential Administration.

(D) January, 19, 2014: Confrontations begin on Grushevskogo St.

(E) February, 18, 2014: Violent clashes ensue after an attempted march on Parliament. Both sides use firearms.

(F) February, 18-20, 2014: A wall of flaming tires separates the two forces (Maidan/Police).

(G) February, 19, 2014: Sniper fire kills protesters advancing up Institutskaja St., making this the bloodiest day of Maidan.

 PRESIDENTIAL ADMINISTRATION. Built in 1936–1939 for the Central Committee of the Communist Party of Ukraine (architect S. Grigoryev).

 CITY ADMINISTRATION OF KIEV. Built in 1952–1957 (architects A. Vlasov, A. Zavarov, A. Malinovsky). Part of the general complex of Khreschatik Street.

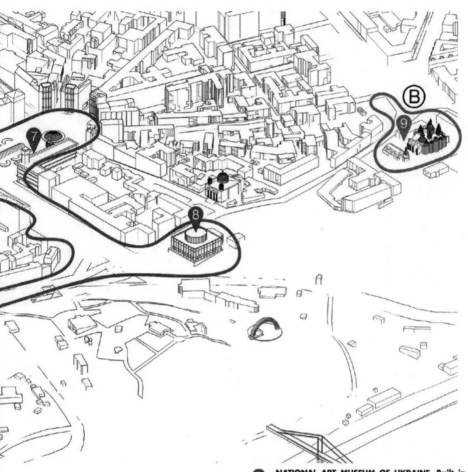

Approximate Territorial Control
As of September 29, 2020

- DPR/LPR control today
- DPR/LPR controlled city
- Formerly DPR/LPR controlled city
- Other Ukraine-controlled city
- Divided or unclear control

Minsk II Ceasefire Lines

— DPR/LPR (Sept. 19, 2014 frontline)
— Ukraine (Feb. 15, 2015 frontline)

UKRAINE
AND SEPARATIST STATELETS

0 km   50
0 mi   50

RUSSIA

Starobilsk

LUHANSK

KHARKHIV

Rubizhne
Severodonetsk
Sloviansk   Trokhizbenka
Lysychansk   Shchastya
Mykolaivka   Zolote   Vesela Hora
Popasna   Stanytsia Luhanska
Kramatorsk   Slavianoserbsk
Pervomaisk   Luhansk
Druzhkivka   Stakhanov
Oleksandrivka   Artemivsk   Alchevsk
Kostiantynivka   Horlivka   Svitlodarsk   Perevalsk   Lutuhyne
Dobropillia   Dzerzhynsk   Debaltseve   Krasnodon
Pivdenne   Vuhlehirsk   Krasnyi Luch
DNIPROPETROVSK   Krasny Partisan   Yenakiieve   Antratsyt
Krasnoarmiisk   Avdiivka   Yasynuvata   Zhdanivka
Karlivka   Piski   Khartsyzk   Rovenky   Sverdlovsk
Krasnohorivka   Torez   Snizhne
Marinka   Makiyivka
Oleksandrivka   Donetsk
Velyka Novosilka   Olenivka   Amvrosiivka   "Lugansk People's Republic" (LPR)
Starobesheve
DONETSK   Bohdanivka   "Donetsk People's Republic" (DPR)
Volnovakha   Novolaspa
Starohnativka   Bila Kamianka
Telmanovo
ZAPORIZHIA   Pavlopol
Pishtevik   Kominternove
Vodyane
Mariupol   Shyrokyne   Novoazovsk

Sea of Azov

BELARUS   RUSSIA
POLAND
Lviv   Kiev   Kharkiv
Luhansk
Dnipropetrovsk   Donetsk
MOLDOVA
TRANSNISTRIA   Kherson   Sea of
ROMANIA   Odessa   Azov
Crimea
Black Sea   Kerch Strait

www.polgeonow.com

Map by Evan Centanni and Djordje Djukic

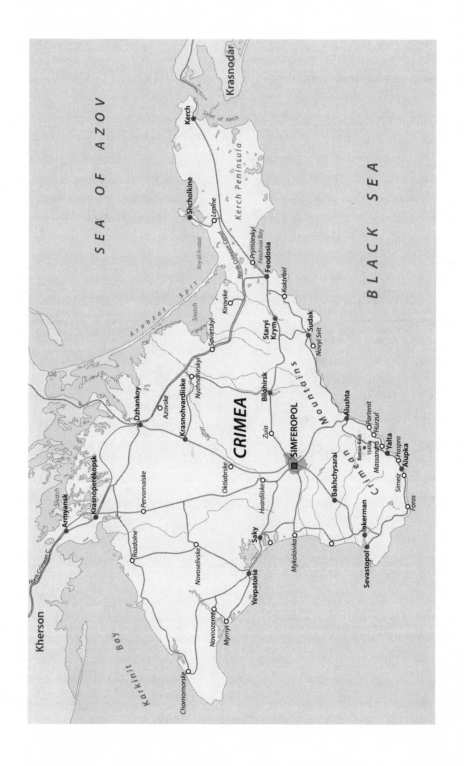

PROLOGUE

February 21, 2014. A cold, tense night in Kyiv, the capital of Ukraine. The main stage in Maidan Square. For three months Maidan has been the epicenter of a popular rebellion against Ukrainian President Viktor Yanukovych, who heads a corrupt and increasingly autocratic government. Arseniy Yatsenyuk, Oleh Tyahnybok, and Vitali Klitschko, the three main leaders of the political opposition, make their way to the stage through a crowd of thousands to announce details of a deal for political reorganization and reform that they have just struck with the embattled president.

Just the day before, the mounting tension inside Kyiv and throughout Ukraine had reached its brutal climax in a massacre relentlessly cheered on by the Russian media and government. Russia's Prime Minister Medvedev crudely questioned Yanukovych's manhood, declaring that he was nothing more than a "foot rag" if he hesitated to spill protester blood. Government forces, including expert riflemen, their guns equipped with sniper sights, backed by thuggish pro-government auxiliaries, fired on demonstrators in Kyiv. Many were shot in the back. Sixty-seven were killed, 184 wounded by gunfire. Now the mood in the capital is blacker than the northern winter night. Justice for the dead and a change of regime is what people in Maidan Square demand, not political compromise with a detested and discredited national leader.

As the opposition leaders mount the stage, they are met by jeers, catcalls, and booing. The crowd passes several open caskets of yesterday's victims overhead, their corpses brought to the stage accompanied by chants that Yanukovych must go. Volodymyr Parasyuk, a commander of the popular self-defense forces, a young man from Lviv in his mid-20s, grabs the microphone and gives an impassioned speech expressing the mood of the crowd. "Our kinsmen have been shot and our leaders shake hands with this killer. This is shameful. Tomorrow, by 10 o'clock, he has to be gone."

Yatsenyuk and Tyahnybok leave the stage, and Klitschko, the six-foot-six-inch former world heavyweight boxing champion turned politician, retakes the microphone. Responding to Parasyuk, he apologizes for shaking Yanukovych's hand after signing the agreement. "If that is the will of Maidan," he says, "I am willing to explore other ways to remove Yanukovych from power." He adds that despite his having sided with the protesters for the past three months, this is the first time they have not listened to him. His attempt at contrition fails. A Hromadske TV journalist confronts the towering Klitschko on stage, calling opposition leaders "betrayers of Euromaidan" and accuses them of signing the agreement without approval of the Maidan Council as previously agreed.

Amid the impassioned screams for Yanukovych's resignation, no one on Maidan or, for that matter in the diplomatic community, yet knows the truth. Yanukovych, the man with a brand new internationally praised agreement that has re-legitimized his rule for the next nine months, is already on the run. He has already been shipping his valuables and cash from Kyiv for days. Yanukovych is not just going, he is gone.

1

MY ROAD TO KYIV

The distance between Orlando, Florida, and Kyiv, the capital of Ukraine, is 5,586 miles. The flight time on the most direct route is 11 hours and 36 minutes. Of course, there are no direct flights between Orlando and Kyiv; one has to change planes at least once, in New York City, Newark, or Philadelphia, or twice, with an additional stop in Frankfurt, Warsaw, or Istanbul.

In my case, the journey from my family home in Orlando to Kyiv, where I served in the US Embassy in 2012–2014, involved a long and circuitous route through Washington, D.C., Moscow, Tallinn (the capital of Estonia), Maseru (the capital of Lesotho), and Beijing. Since this book is largely based on my reporting from Kyiv, as well as that of my embassy colleagues, some personal background is appropriate, though I do not pretend to be a person of any importance in these events.

I grew up in Orlando with my sister, Rebecca, near the fantasy land that is Disney World, and the real world beyond central Florida seemed so distant. But even as a child, I wanted to understand what that world was. The stream of relatives flowing through our house from my mother's native Iceland opened windows to a world beyond Mickey Mouse and the Magic Kingdom. I remember the glossy publications my father, who worked for the US Department of Defense, brought home, with ominous titles like *Soviet Military Power: 1987*. Bold graphics proclaimed that "they" had many more soldiers than "we" did. In my early teens I learned that the United States and the Soviet Union targeted thousands of nuclear missiles at each other. While I was still in grade school, my father took me to see a "boomer" (ballistic missile submarine). Our navy guide escorted us to "the forest"—a large compartment housing floor-to-ceiling vertical cylinders, like the trunks of huge steel trees, each containing a nuclear missile. Threading our way through the forest, I suddenly realized that the destruction of my comfortable world was a real possibility. That feeling has never left me.

As a high school junior in 1992, shortly after the dissolution of the Soviet Union, I received a letter from People-to-People Student Ambassadors announcing a student trip to newly independent Russia. I still thought of the now defunct USSR as the globe-spanning monster I had encountered in my father's Department of Defense magazines. Soviet leader Mikhail Gorbachev's efforts at reform made for some hopeful headlines in the *Orlando Sentinel*, but their actual impact was beyond my suburban teenage grasp. After all, most of official Washington had been suspicious of the new Kremlin boss and inclined to mistrust his sweeping policy declarations. Now both Gorbachev and the Soviet Union were gone. Pundits announced the end of history. We had won the Cold War. Russia, defeated, was lurching toward who knew what, and I wanted to see it with my own eyes. When my fundraising efforts to pay for the trip fell short, my parents dug deep into their limited resources and bailed me out.

The experience changed my life. On this first trip, at age seventeen, I struck up a friendship with the beautiful young girl I would one day marry, and decided what I wanted to do with my life.

In the early 1990s, hope and despair hung in the balance in post-Soviet Russia. Despair soon tipped the scales. In Moscow, I met a furloughed college professor working in a factory after his department had collapsed. The factory owners withheld wages for nearly a year as inflation soared. Most Russians struggled to survive, while ruthless, well-connected insiders amassed vast fortunes by stealing state assets. After a year of IOUs, the professor-turned-proletarian was paid his salary in tampons. "I was very happy," he told me. "At least I could sell the tampons and buy food for my family." What would my family in Orlando have done?

The trip was an eye-opener. Everyone back home was convinced that the hardships in Russia, Ukraine, and other fragments of the former Soviet Union were merely bumps on the road to Westernization, meaning democracy and prosperity. That, or the just penance history was imposing for the decades misspent under godless communism. American academics and think tankers launched the field of "transitology," writing prescriptions for accelerating the recovery of the former Soviet states from the disease of communism. The rampant corruption and criminality shredding the social fabric were largely dismissed as the healing pains of convalescence. Time proved this wrong. It was not a temporary bug—it was the new system.

After high school I stayed close to home, enrolling in Rollins College, a small liberal arts college in Winter Park, Florida, where I majored in international relations and minored in Russian. I spent my junior year in Moscow at the Russian State University of the Humanities, studying Russian history and acquiring some fluency in the language. Then, I spent the first half of my senior year in the Washington Semester Program of American University in Washington, D.C., another strange and exotic capital that captivated me as had Moscow. Continuing on to graduate school at George Washington University, I was fortunate to encounter some great scholars, foremost among them Professor Peter Reddaway, whose profound knowledge of Russian politics, history, and culture enabled him to challenge effectively the transient "truths" of the deluded transitologists. He readily agreed when I suggested spending a semester in Pskov, a medium-sized city in western Russia, to study how ultranationalist Vladimir Zhirinovsky's grotesquely misnamed Liberal Democratic Party had won the regional governorship. I was seriously interested in the topic, but no less so in spending time in the hometown of Natalya, the young woman to whom I soon became engaged and later married.

My M.A. in Russian and East European Studies was not much help in landing a job in the late 1990s. The fragments of the former Soviet empire offered few business opportunities compared to a booming China, and no longer seemed to pose any national security threats to the United States or our allies. When I finally got a job in the Department of Commerce, calculating antidumping duties on foreign firms accused of selling goods in the United States below market value, I was relieved and immensely grateful, in part for travel opportunities to China, Chile, and Latvia. Yet a career in the Foreign Service remained my lodestar.

I had been taking the Foreign Service exam since my undergraduate days at Rollins and had passed the written exam, which was not particularly difficult. The oral exam was another matter entirely. Under the watchful eyes of stone-faced career Foreign Service Officers, it involved negotiating with other equally determined applicants on various issues in a fictional country, "solving" hypothetical problems in challenging scenarios, and drafting memos. Although I had enjoyed my undergraduate and graduate student years, I wanted to practice diplomacy, not teach or write about it. The second time I took the orals, I was already working in the US Department of Commerce and less tense. I was one of only three hopefuls who passed the oral exam that day in early September 2001.

Then came 9/11. I was sitting at my desk in the Commerce Department when the Pentagon was struck. All I heard was a low rumble and never imagined that it was something serious. But that day changed everything. Suddenly, the State Department's Diplomatic Security Service had more urgent business than finishing background checks on new Foreign Service Officers. My security clearance took two-and-a-half years to complete. It wasn't until 2003 that I actually joined the Foreign Service. After going through basic training, I received my first assignment—to Tallinn, the capital of Estonia. After six months of intensive Estonian language instruction in Washington, Natalya and I boarded a flight to Tallinn armed with our newly minted diplomatic passports and visas.

That first tour of duty was followed by another in Maseru, capital of the independent African kingdom of Lesotho, by which time the birth of our infant son, Andrew, had made us a family of three. Then back to Washington for a year of intensive Chinese language training. Meanwhile, Natalya had studied for, and breezed through, her exams to be accepted into the Foreign Service. We were now colleagues as well as husband and wife. Jointly assigned to the US Embassy in Beijing, we immersed ourselves in the life of the Chinese capital and further expanded our family by adopting one-and-a-half-year-old Elena, who looked like a frightened little bird when we first met her. She quickly became an inseparable part of our family.

When Natalya received her second assignment, in the consular section of the US Embassy in Kyiv, I pulled every string I could to get an assignment there, too, so that our family could remain together. Fortunately, Eric Schultz, then the deputy chief of mission in Kyiv, offered me a position in the Embassy's economic section, focusing on trade and intellectual property rights, hot button issues in US-Ukrainian relations. It wasn't quite what I was hoping for—I was not an economic officer—but it meant that the four of us—me,

Natalya , Andrew, and Elena—would be together. Natalya had left Beijing three months before I was able to and preceded me to Kyiv. Our family reunion took place on July 18, 2012, in our new four-bedroom apartment, a twelve-minute ride from Kyiv's central square, officially called Maidan Nezalezhnosti (Independence Square). Everyone just called it Maidan. It was to become the focal point of our tour of duty for the next two momentous years.

2

BUILDING UKRAINE, FROM THE HETMANS TO MAIDAN

Ukraine and I achieved our independence in the same year—1991. Mine came easily when I turned sixteen and held my first driver's license, that affirmation of independence that American teenagers aspire to on their road to recognition as adults. Ukraine's independence as a sovereign country was a very long time in the making. It was officially declared on August 24, 1991, after a nearly unanimous vote by the parliament of the Ukrainian Soviet Socialist Republic, one of sixteen constituent republics of the Union of Soviet Socialist Republics (USSR). When those republics—including Russia—began to declare sovereignty, no one really understood whether they were declaring themselves to be countries, free trade zones, or just mafia-friendly casino venues. But the vote was a critical step in the accelerating disintegration of the Soviet Union. The Ukrainian declaration of independence came just three days after a coup d'état in Moscow by communist hard-liners failed to topple Soviet leader Mikhail S. Gorbachev, who had come to power in 1985. In addition to huge improvements in domestic human rights, his attempts at modernizing the creaky Soviet political and industrial system had produced economic distress, arousing widespread domestic opposition among the privileged Soviet elite and the general public. Shops were empty, and people were feeling the costs much more than the benefits of reform. In the waning months of 1991, the bonds that held the Soviet Union together snapped as the individual components of the supposedly monolithic superpower declared their independence. When Gorbachev announced his resignation on Christmas Day, 1991, both he and the Soviet Union were already irrelevant.

Ukraine's path to independent statehood was tortuous, unfolding over more than a millennium. Geography played an outsize role in its destiny. For many centuries, the diverse lands that constitute contemporary Ukraine were a frontier region where the forests and plains of Eastern Europe shaded into the vast Eurasian steppe, across which nomadic tribes from Central Asia traveled westward. From the Baltic Sea in the north, Vikings from Scandinavia ventured south along the rivers into the forests of what is now central Ukraine. Over the centuries the lands were home to Goths, Huns, Khazars, Vikings, Slavs, Jews, and many other nationalities and tribes.

Contemplating the long arc of their history, Ukrainians often focus on two great eras seen as critical to forming their national identity and asserting their claim to historical continuity. Yet, such a claim belies the kaleidoscopic shifts in the fate of the Ukrainian lands engendered by endemic power struggles among neighboring kingdoms and principalities, population shifts, and frequent wars. The first golden era was Kievan Rus' (ca. A.D. tenth to thirteenth centuries), whose capital was Kyiv. Founded by Vikings and later ruled by Christianized Slavs, Kievan Rus' is claimed by both contemporary Ukrainians and Russians as the historical root of their own nations. Kievan Rus' merchants conducted an extensive trade in slaves and forest products down the Dnieper River to the Crimean peninsula on the Black Sea. Kyiv was oriented eastward toward Constantinople, the Byzantine capital and seat of Eastern Orthodox Christianity, a faith to which the pagan prince Volodymyr converted in A.D. 989 and imposed upon his subjects. This era ended with the Mongol conquest of Kyiv on December 7, 1240, resulting in the occupation of a harsh foreign regime.

The second historical focal point or golden era was the hetmanate, a state centered in the southern and southeastern plains of what is now Ukraine. It was founded by Cossack leader Bohdan Khmelnytsky in 1648 in the Great Revolt that culminated a series of Cossack uprisings against the powerful Polish-Lithuanian Commonwealth. The Cossacks had evolved from rude frontiersmen at the bottom rung of the social ladder into what Serhii Plokhy, a leading historian of Ukraine, calls "members of a cohesive military brother-hood that regarded itself as a distinct social order" comprising an officer elite controlling powerful military forces. On January 8, 1654, Khmelnytsky swore allegiance to Tsar Aleksei Romanov of Muscovy. Russian historians interpret this as Ukraine's incorporation into the fledgling Russian Empire. Ukrainian historians and patriots interpret it as a conditional contract between virtual equals. They laud Khmelnytsky as "the father of the nation, the liberator of his people from the Polish yoke." Either way, Russian tsar Peter I (Peter the Great—1672–1725) abolished the hetmanate in 1722, adding its territory to his own vast empire.

Almost two hundred years passed before the next attempts to establish an independent state in the territories of Ukraine, during which Ukrainian lands were divided among the Romanov (Russian), Habsburg (Austro-Hungarian), and Ottoman (Turkish) empires. Each followed different paths of develop-ment and tried to incorporate the people living in the Ukrainian lands they controlled into their own polities and cultures. Most were peasants with local loyalties devoid of any consciousness of belonging to a Ukrainian nation. The concept of a distinctive Ukrainian nation began to crystallize in the early nine-teenth century, the era of rising national consciousness among many different European elites.

Educated Ukrainians, writing in their own native Ukrainian language rather than in Russian, were creating the cultural foundations on which to assert their claim to a distinctive Ukrainian national identity, one that was neither ancillary nor inferior to Russian identity. Among this intellectual elite were writers, poets, historians, and folklorists, including Taras Shevchenko, Ivan Kotliarevsky, and Mykola Kostomarov. In the second half of the nine-teenth century the advent of the Industrial Revolution, urbanization, and the construction of modern rail and communication networks accelerated the economic and social integration of the diverse, and still politically separated, Ukrainian lands, giving rise to new social classes and new ideas of what it meant to be Ukrainian.

The dawn of the twentieth century heralded Ukraine's political awakening. Political parties ranging from radical socialists on the left, centrist liberals, to monarchists on the right sprang up and addressed their appeals to the literate minority in Ukrainian language publications that were legalized in 1905 after being banned in Russia for more than a generation. That turbulent year of revolution shook the foundations of the tsarist Russian autocracy. Throughout the disparate Ukrainian territories a national movement formed. Gradually, an independent Ukrainian state emerged as the ultimate goal.

In 1914, the clash of competing empires raised the curtain on the First World War; the death of empires in 1917–1918 was its last act. The Romanovs, the Habsburgs, the Hohenzollerns (Germany), and the Ottomans all made their final exits. Amid the carnage and rubble of war, many nationalist movements seized the opportunities presented by the collapse of imperial authority to assert claims to independent statehood. Ukrainian cultural and political independence movements were among them. Instead of a single, unified Ukrainian state emerging from the chaos, however, several aspiring Ukrainian states were established. Centered in different Ukrainian lands and oriented toward, or allied with, different foreign powers, each of these embryonic states had its own military force and administrative structure, its own leadership and ideological orientation, and represented or incorporated different social forces. Brutal conflict ensued. In this complex war—part civil war, part international war—tens of thousands of Jews, long a significant minority, became the primary victims of terrible pogroms carried out by many of the warring forces, a tragic legacy that has not been and should never be forgotten.

From this maelstrom, the party of Ukrainian Bolsheviks, allied with Lenin and Trotsky's Russian communist revolutionaries, emerged victorious. In 1922, the Ukrainian Socialist Soviet Republic, with a population of around 30 million, became a constituent member of the USSR. Throughout the next seven decades, the fate of Ukraine and its multiethnic population was inextricably bound up with that of the Soviet Union.

That meant the implementation in Ukraine of the Kremlin's draconian policies. After initially flirting with support of various national identities, Moscow's policy shifted toward the forcible creation of a new man, Homo Sovieticus—an idealized Marxist citizen free of any ethnic allegiances, yet somehow cognizant that Russian culture was just "objectively" superior. By the end of the great terror of the 1930s, Moscow had little or no tolerance for national differences in any of the Soviet republics and viewed nationalism as a subversive force manipulated by foreign enemies. Determined to transform the Soviet Union into a Eurasian communist superpower, Soviet dictator Joseph Stalin (1878–1953) and his successors centralized authority, further entrenched state control of the economy, obliterated nonparty civil society, and employed a shifting mix of terror, repression, propaganda, and rewards to communist elites to achieve their goals. While they intermittently promoted cultural Ukrainization to attract support within Ukraine, they more often perceived Ukrainian culture, including language, as incipient threats to their power. Such threats might lead to political demands for greater autonomy within the USSR, or even independence. They must therefore be crushed.

The greatest horror that befell Ukraine during the communist era was the massive famine of 1932 to 1934, in Ukrainian known as the Holodomor (death from starvation). It resulted from Stalin's decision in 1929 to impose collectivized agriculture on the resistant peasant population. State demands for compulsory delivery of absurdly high quotas of grain left the Ukrainian countryside almost completely stripped of food. Ukrainian peasants desperately struggled to survive. Accusing the starving peasants of economic sabotage by hiding grain, Moscow dispatched armed communist zealots to scour the villages, confiscating everything edible. Almost 4 million Ukrainians died, one-eighth of the population, and additional thousands were deported to Siberia. Like the Great Famine in China (1958–1960), the Holodomor was not a natural disaster, but a state-caused tragedy. In 2006, independent Ukraine's parliament branded the Holodomor an act of Soviet genocide, an assertion that outraged Russia's President Vladimir Putin. His government preferred to bury hard truths rather than exhume and learn from historical tragedy. The Holodomor left an indelible scar on Ukrainian national consciousness.

There were more scars to come. During 1937–1938, more than a quarter million Ukrainians were arrested, and almost half of those killed, in the Great Terror—the orgy of repression and summary execution that Stalin unleashed. In the years preceding Hitler's attack on the Soviet Union in June 1941, Stalin's secret police deported over 1 million Ukrainians, including members and suspected members of Ukrainian nationalist groups, to Soviet Central Asia.

Ukraine, in the crosshairs of the German invasion, was quickly occupied in the second half of 1941. Hoping to escape Stalin's hell, some Ukrainian nationalists briefly cast their lot with Germany, among them Stepan Bandera, a leader of the Organization of Ukrainian Nationalists (OUN). They were soon disappointed when the Nazis, who perceived all Slavs as an "inferior race," rejected Ukrainian independence, imprisoning Bandera and his followers. (In 1959, a Soviet agent assassinated the exiled Bandera in West Germany.) In Serhii Plokhy's words during World War II, "Ukraine became a graveyard for millions of Ukrainians, Russians, Jews, and Poles. . . . Gone, too, were the German and Mennonite settlers of southern Ukraine and Volhynia."

In the last year of the war, the Soviet Red Army reconquered Ukraine and, advancing westward, occupied, among other places, Poland, Czechoslovakia, and Romania. Stalin redrew national boundaries, incorporating territories largely inhabited by ethnic Ukrainians that had belonged to Poland, Czechoslovakia, and Romania into the Ukrainian SSR. (Poland was "compensated" for its lost eastern territories by formerly German lands to the west.) Large-scale, coerced population transfers accompanied these changes. Stalin's twisted notions of geopolitics determined the fate of millions.

Given the vast scale of wartime death and destruction, the task of postwar reconstruction in Ukraine was enormous. It took place early in the Cold War and was punctuated by another major famine in 1947 in southern Ukraine, claiming almost a million lives. Sporadic Ukrainian nationalist guerrilla resistance to the reimposition of Stalinist rule continued in western Ukraine until the early 1950s. In February 1954, the three-hundredth anniversary of Bohdan Khmelnytsky's pact with Tsar Peter I, Soviet leader Nikita S. Khrushchev, Stalin's successor, transferred the Crimean peninsula from the Russian SSR to Ukraine. This was a rational administrative action that seemed of limited importance. For Khrushchev, it must have felt like moving a coin from one pocket to another. Six decades later, however, it acquired enormous significance when, in March 2014, Vladimir Putin forcibly annexed Crimea and incorporated it into the Russian Federation, in defiance of an international agreement, cosigned by the United States, pledging to respect independent Ukraine's territorial integrity—an agreement he had pledged to uphold. How that happened is detailed later in this book.

Post–World War II Ukraine became an industrial and agricultural powerhouse of the Soviet Union with a high concentration of advanced and heavy industry, mining, space and aeronautics, and grain production. Given its geographic position, even in the nuclear age it possessed outsize strategic significance as Moscow's second line of defense vis-à-vis the NATO alliance behind the Soviet forces stationed in frontline East Central European satellite states.

Once begun, the Soviet Union unraveled with breathtaking speed. Not long after taking power in March 1985, Mikhail S. Gorbachev introduced a new look in Soviet domestic and foreign policy. He tried to rejuvenate the sclerotic communist superpower through a transfusion of economic and political reforms intended to produce prosperity and introduce more democracy within the Communist Party while ending the Cold War. Gorbachev was viewed with considerable skepticism by a West predisposed to view Soviet moves cynically. Domestically, his innovative but questionably implemented reforms evoked opposition from both privileged Soviet communist elites and many ordinary Soviet citizens. For example, an intentional pinch on Russia's vodka supply was never going to win friends. The sagging Soviet economy and democratizing reforms engendered political turmoil as dissidents demanded more. As Marxist-Leninist ideology melted under the heat lamps emitting the truth that outdated leftist extremism obviously wasn't relevant or helpful, the centrifugal forces of born-again nationalism, especially in the Baltic republics (Estonia, Latvia, Lithuania) and Ukraine, as well as in Russia itself, pulled the USSR apart.

The April 1986 Chernobyl nuclear power plant explosion in Ukraine, which the Kremlin initially tried to cover up, fueled an environmental movement that blamed Moscow for the deadly catastrophe. Meanwhile, the political space opened by Gorbachev's liberalizing reforms encouraged Ukrainian intellectuals to revitalize civil society organizations that had been suppressed. For its part, the Ukrainian communist establishment abhorred Gorbachev's reforms, which threatened their power and privileges. Mistrusted by emboldened liberal democrats and reviled by reactionary communists, the small band of Kremlin reformers were like doomed polar bears isolated on thinning ice far from shore. Not orthodox enough for other communists and not radical enough for the dissidents, they pleased no one.

In 1989, Rukh (movement), a mass political reform organization, snowballed rapidly and elected a substantial minority bloc of deputies to the Ukrainian parliament in 1990. That same year, the Ukrainian Catholic Church was legalized and soon became a powerful force in society. On October 2, 1990, the first student political protest took place in Kyiv on October Revolution Square, later renamed Independence Square, or The Maidan, when Ukraine declared its independence just ten months later.

As noted earlier, the Ukrainian parliament officially declared independence on August 24, 1991. This was confirmed in a popular referendum on December 1, in which over 90 percent of those taking part favored independence. Ukrainians in great numbers had collectively signed the death certificate of the Soviet Union.

The end, of course, was also a beginning. But a clean break with the past seldom occurs in real life. Most of the leaders of newly independent Ukraine, including its first president, Leonid Kravchuk, came from within the former communist elite. A smaller number were former dissidents.

The new, or perhaps more accurately, repurposed leadership of Ukraine, faced several pressing issues that had to be addressed simultaneously: (1) disentangling Ukraine from the wreckage of the USSR, establishing its independent identity in the world, charting its own course in international affairs, and managing its relationship with a Russian Federation, which gradually transformed from chaotic but benign to belligerent and revanchist; (2) institutionalizing a democratic and equitable political system accepted as legitimate by the citizens of Ukraine, ensuring peaceful political succession according to constitutional procedures, curbing corruption and other abuses of power, and balancing the disparate interests of different regions; (3) addressing serious economic issues arising from the dissolution of the USSR, halting and then reversing economic collapse, and securing reliable sources of energy, new markets, and international financial and technical assistance; and (4) managing domestic social and cultural issues, including language, education, and minority populations.

While Vladimir Putin especially seemed to view its very existence as a historical anomaly and an affront to Russian pride, post–Soviet Russia's attempts to draw Ukraine back into its orbit started earlier. First through the Moscow-led Commonwealth of Independent States (CIS), and later through the direct application of political, economic, and military pressure, they tried to draw Ukraine into agreements and multilateral organizations to tether it to Russia. Ukraine faced the choice of looking eastward, submitting to Kremlin pressure, and accepting a position of *compromised or attenuated sovereignty* or looking westward to Europe and the European Union. Political, economic, security, and cultural integration into the dynamic family of European nations had long been the hope of progressive Ukrainian democrats, particularly in the western regions of Ukraine.

In the 1990s, Ukraine's first president Leonid Kravchuk, and his successor Leonid Kuchma, rebuffed the Kremlin's attempts to bind Ukraine into Russia's orbit. They secured international, including Russian, guarantees of Ukraine's territorial integrity when it gave up the nuclear weapons that the defunct Soviet Union had stationed there. Yet Kyiv had to make concessions to Moscow, including agreeing to an 82:18 percent division of the former Soviet

Union's naval fleet in the Black Sea and granting Russia a long-term lease of the naval base in Sevastopol on the Crimean peninsula. Simultaneously, Ukraine took initial steps toward integrating into the European economic and security systems. The United States became a major donor of aid to Ukraine. Yet the issue of which was the stronger magnetic force acting upon Ukraine—Russia or the European Union—remained unsettled. Many Ukrainian leaders preferred to straddle the fence and play both sides.

Ukraine's attempt to maintain a democratic political system since 1992 should be viewed in comparative perspective. Transitions from authoritarianism to democracy are seldom, if ever, easy. Old habits and expectations die hard, and backsliding is common. High-ranking leaders often abuse their positions for personal gain or to punish political opponents, facilitated by the absence or weakness of reliable systems of checks and balances. Often an ongoing battle between executive and legislative powers occurs—with the public occasionally intervening to tilt the balance. Peaceful transitions of power, an indicator of maturing democracies, are important mileposts on the path to stable democracy. No less important, of course, is what the political system actually delivers in terms of national security and domestic public goods, including prosperity, health, education, and justice. The US and European democracies developed over hundreds of years. Most of the Western experts who thought they could bottle the secret sauce of liberal democracy and export it were deluding themselves.

In this context, Ukraine's postindependence record is a mixed one, but it is better than many post-Soviet states, including notably Russia, that have reverted to authoritarian rule. Such pseudodemocracies present a facade of democratic institutions while empowering autocratic rulers like Vladimir Putin and privileging a tiny minority of oligarchs enriched by a corrupt system of crony capitalism. Free speech becomes a threat, as does normal civic activism.

Ukraine's first postindependence transfer of power occurred peacefully in 1994 with the election of Leonid Kuchma, who won a second term in 1999 among high hopes of reversing the economic collapse of the 1990s. But bribe-taking and other forms of corruption, Kuchma's repression of political opponents, and his apparent involvement in the grisly murder of an investigative journalist discredited his administration. In the presidential contest of 2004, Kuchma's favored successor, Viktor Yanukovych, tried to steal the election, while his main opponent, Viktor Yushchenko, barely survived an apparent assassination attempt involving his poisoning by dioxin, a potent nerve agent. Public outrage at the blatant attempt to steal the election by falsifying the polling results led to massive demonstrations in Kyiv's central square—Maidan— over a period of weeks in the fall of 2004, an eruption of people power called the Orange Revolution. Responding to domestic and international pressure, Ukraine's Constitutional Court annulled the results and called for new elections in December 2004, which Yushchenko won. Direct action by an aroused public had rescued Ukraine's democracy.

Yushchenko's term in office, likewise conceived in hope, was disappointing in terms of concrete achievements, although the economic recovery that began under Kuchma was well underway. Government and party infighting involving Yushchenko, his prime minister (the charismatic Yuliya Tymoshenko), and others who will appear later in this book, produced another letdown from the high expectations Yushchenko's victory had induced. This letdown was compounded by rampant corruption and the reluctance of major powers in the European Union to accept Ukraine into their ranks, partly from disappointment with Ukraine's own poor reform record and partly from aversion to antagonizing the Kremlin. In February 2010, Kremlin favorite, and loser of the Orange Revolution, Viktor Yanukovych, a native of southeastern Ukraine where the Russian-speaking minority is concentrated, won the presidency. His subsequent attempts to concentrate power in his own hands, enrich himself and his cronies, and give vent to his vindictiveness by imprisoning Yuliya Tymoshenko on politically motivated charges while leaving Ukraine increasingly vulnerable to Russian manipulation, are detailed in the pages that follow.

Like Russia, Ukraine plunged into a colossal economic depression after the dissolution of the USSR as systems of economic supply, production, distribution, regional specialization; networks of energy supplies; and existing markets were disrupted or collapsed. Widespread misery resulted. To a majority of Ukrainians, democracy seemed to spell destitution. From the rubble of state socialism, in a post-Soviet economy still dominated by large, state-owned enterprises, emerged a new class of rough-edged entrepreneurs and financiers—the oligarchs. Like their counterparts in Russia, combining guile, great energy, ruthlessness, disregard for weak existing laws, and access to power, they grabbed state assets, converted them to private property, and amassed great fortunes. Their raw power and disproportionate share of the

new economy became the greatest symbol of the new Ukraine. While Western
transitologists convinced themselves that this was just an unsightly pit stop on
the road to modernity, it actually was the beating heart of a new system that
merged criminal and government power.

During the nearly quarter century from independence to the Euromaidan
Revolution, Ukraine grappled with age-old problems of accommodating, if
not reconciling, regional differences with respect to language, religion, cultural orientation, historical memories, and ideological differences within a
diverse population that was both an asset and a problem. Even in long-existing
democracies like the United States, the United Kingdom, France, Canada,
and Scandinavia, to name just a few, such issues are contentious and must be
managed to avoid the advantages of diversity from turning into destructive
divisiveness. Ukraine is no different. What may be different, however, is the
urgency of addressing all these issues simultaneously in the harsh conditions
of national insecurity brought about by the hostility of Putin's Russia and the
lukewarm support the international community offered Ukraine. All these
challenges were interconnected and had to be addressed by political elites,
nongovernmental organizations, and a public without long experience of managing the friction and frequent conflicts that both disrupt and enrich dynamic
democracies throughout the world.

It may help to think of independent Ukraine as a new sports franchise in a
long-established league. With apologies and a nod to its baseball namesake—
let's call it a new franchise in the International League—comprising a few
well-known veteran players, some cast-offs, and quite a few promising but
untested rookies under a manager with a short-term contract, the renewal of
which depends on success on the field. First place is an impossible dream; last
place a nightmare. Just staying competitive requires a concerted team effort.
Between independence in 1991 and the Euromaidan Revolution of 2013–2014,
Ukraine had an uneven record, passing through good times and bad. Even
now, within the context of an attractive but disinterested Europe, a weak then
hostile Russia, and an international system in flux, Ukraine's future remains
uncertain. Yet compared to most of the other former members of the Soviet
Union, including Russia in the first instance, it has done quite creditably.
Through democratic elections as well as popular protests, it fended off authoritarian leaders wishing to become Ukraine's Vladimir Putin or Alexander
Lukashenko and preserved, not without difficulty, a functioning parliamentary

democracy. From the nausea-inducing depths of the mid-1990s, its economy regained normalcy, and the general welfare of Ukrainians modestly improved. Yet oligarchic power and corruption remained intractable problems. The failure of the Orange Revolution to deliver anything more than a fresh crew of bickering kleptocrats left those who poured their souls into those protests sour and disillusioned with the idea of sacrificing their own sweat and tears to make Ukraine a better place.

This was the Ukraine that I and my family stepped into in the summer of 2012, a country steeped in history, mired in corruption, and disappointed with the lackluster results of trying to make things better. But there were some positive ground truths that were largely taken for granted when I arrived—and would soon change drastically. Ukraine was at peace with its neighbors, and its territorial integrity was unquestioned. No one, from the more nationalist west to the Russian-speaking east, and even down south in Crimea, questioned the fact that they were all part of the Ukrainian nation, for better or worse. There were no serious questions of separatism or casting one's lot with a bigger neighbor rather than one's own country. But all these questions, and the destruction unleashed by them, were artificially imposed upon Ukraine by Russia in the years to come. Those who argue that the theft of Crimea or the war in Ukraine's east are the inevitable results of Ukraine's divisions or the Euromaidan Revolution in Kyiv are either misinformed or purposefully lying. I will expand on all of these points, here just touched upon lightly, in the concluding chapter of this book after the detailed recounting of the dramatic events of 2013 and 2014 that I observed, along with my wife, from our posts in the American Embassy in Kyiv.

3

CORRUPTION 101:
MY INTRODUCTION TO UKRAINIAN REALITIES

Not long before I arrived in Kyiv, the State Department opened a new US Embassy compound surrounded by a park and several residential apartment blocks some distance from downtown. The somewhat inconvenient location was dictated by security concerns. Since 9/11, the State Department mandated increasingly larger setbacks between US Embassies and public roads. This made it almost impossible to build new embassies in city centers. They rarely had sufficient suitable open space. But regardless of the location, the new Kyiv facility was quite beautiful and well designed. I was assigned a fourth floor cube by a window overlooking the gate to the consular section where thousands of visa seekers shuffled in and out every day. The fourth floor also housed our ambassador, John F. Tefft, the Political and Economic sections, our Defense Attaché Office, and our Regional Security Office, responsible for ensuring our safety.

My desk was equipped with classified and unclassified computer systems— our information lifeblood—and a phone. Habitually somewhat disorganized, I quickly amassed mounds of paper on my desk, inadvertently putting myself at risk. Everyone knew that the Marine Security Guards spent hours every night inspecting offices for unsecured classified information. When they spotted a stray classified document, they would note it in your personnel file, where it could block your next promotion or worse. Information hygiene was critical.

Moving into the new compound facilitated cooperation among different sections of the mission that had previously been housed separately. The compound also boasted a small gym, a decent cafeteria serving Ukrainian staples, and a commissary where we could buy essential made in America products like tortillas, peanut butter, and Ben and Jerry's. Despite its imposing dark marble facade, on the inside the place felt friendly.

While David Meale was the chief of our Economic Section, I reported directly to Deputy Chief Elizabeth Horst. When I asked Natalya about Elizabeth, she said, "It's going to be a challenge keeping up with her." When we first met, I understood at once. Elizabeth was hypercompetent and engaged, never at a loss for words or a goal to pursue. Just before running out to meetings, she was always dashing off one last email or making one more phone call. She was constantly maximizing her own impact and coaxing the greatest effort from her colleagues—a great role model.

There were four Ukrainian staff members in our section. Valentyna Sizaya, a grandmother with a kindly smile and an insider's view of the players shaping Ukraine's economy, was assigned to my portfolio. I was lucky to have such a knowledgeable and patient tutor. She immediately began educating me about the major Ukrainian players involved in intellectual property rights (IPR) and trade—the core issues of my own work. Deeply knowledgeable about the corruption infecting Ukraine, Valentyna could not conceal her despondency over the dire state of her homeland that no one expected to improve.

But Valentyna was not my only instructor. Early in my posting at the Embassy, I volunteered to meet an AIDS activist eager to speak with an American diplomat. I had dealt with the fight against AIDS in Lesotho. How different could it really be in Ukraine, I thought naively.

"The first thing you need to know is that the owner of the largest pharmaceutical company in Ukraine is the son of the minister of health," my informant told me, treating me as the innocent I was then. "Of course, he didn't have that position before his mother took over the ministry. The business model is simple—they import the AIDS medications at 0.475 hryvnia per dose, and sell it to the Ukrainian government for 2.06 hryvnia per dose. The state budget for purchasing these medications is almost exhausted. Only one quarter of the doses that were supposed to be purchased will actually be purchased. People will start dying. Likely soon." This was worse than Lesotho.

I quickly learned that procurement was the most efficient way to embezzle public funds. The scams started at the top. In 2010, President Yanukovych signed a procurement law designed to meet world standards on paper. Two years later he signed Draft Law 9634, boring holes in Ukraine's procurement procedures large enough to drive trucks through. Trucks filled with cash.

Minister of Education and Science Dmytro Tabachnyk was another example of pervasive high-level corruption. A fire-breathing politician who insulted many western Ukrainians by indiscriminately branding them as profascists during the Second World War, he also dismissed the Holodomor famine, a foundational trauma of modern Ukraine, as a propaganda invention of hostile Western media. Tabachnyk's scam was a fraternal enterprise, a good cop–bad cop duo.

"Tabachnyk has a brother who runs the criminal side of things," another visitor to the Embassy told us. "While Minister Tabachnyk is the upright public face of the operation, this brother runs a shadow operation that sucks money from the Ministry of Education. Textbook procurement, shady privatization of ministry assets, and diploma sales are probably the most profitable for them right now. Business is good."

Corruption seemed omnipresent. It weighed Ukraine down like a massive anchor and poisoned Ukrainians' feeling about their country. In Kyiv, I had yet to meet anyone expressing pride in their country. Most dismissed the sorry state of affairs with a shrug of the shoulders; some thought of emigrating. Ukraine had a free and often brave press that wrote about public corruption issues regularly, but nothing ever changed.

Like every embassy "reporting officer," my first in-depth view of Ukraine was through the lens of my own portfolio, focusing on IPR and trade issues. Through that lens, I learned about lots more than just IPR and trade. It was my introduction to Ukrainian politics and society, for better and worse.

Consulting my notes from my pre-departure meetings in Washington, I came across the name Ihnat Berezhnyy and asked Valentyna to arrange an appointment. We agreed to meet at a local café. In his late twenties, Ihnat was a friendly and ambitious emissary of the music industry. His thick, dark hair made him look even younger than his age. I immediately sensed we were going to get along well. He was a walking encyclopedia of the IPR scene in Ukraine. I knew I would need many meetings with him to come up to speed.

Ihnat brought a friend—Oleksiy—the head of the Ukrainian Music Rights

League Collecting Society, who tutored me on how the IPR system worked with respect to the musical scene. In Ukraine, like much of Europe, public places such as bars and restaurants are supposed to pay royalties for using recorded music: "The law gives collecting societies the right to request payment from private businesses. Racketeers, of course, are attracted by this. If they took over this sector, they would have legal cover for a wide range of shakedowns. That's why it's so important to keep good actors in this area." Oleksiy explained that the State Intellectual Property Service of Ukraine (SIPSU) had recently revoked the authorization of legitimate collecting societies like Oleksiy's, which were recognized and respected by the US recording industry, and now favored shadier characters. Since SIPSU's mandate was to protect intellectual property in Ukraine, this was an ominous development. "First we just fought pirates," said Oleksiy wearily. "Now we fight the state."

SIPSU's recent past did not inspire confidence. Its last chairman had bolted from Ukraine under a barrage of corruption allegations. While the charges were unproven, the report that he had fled to his Swiss summer home—supposedly purchased on his modest government salary—raised both eyebrows and suspicions. His departure left First Deputy Chairman Henadiy Yanov in charge. Given Yanov's connections to rogue collecting societies and doubtful devotion to SIPSU's mission, that was bad news. Moreover, SIPSU was under the Ministry of Education, and Education Minister Tabachnyk's brother seemed a bit too interested in SIPSU—especially the collecting societies under its control.

Valentyna treated me as her prize pupil. I knew that I had a tremendous amount to learn. "You are arriving at post just in time for the biggest intellectual property event of the year—the SIPSU Yalta conference," Valentyna explained. "Everyone dealing with IPR issues in Ukraine will be there. It's a great excuse to go down to Crimea. People will be eager to meet you. You might not know, but you're scheduled to give opening remarks. It's a tradition of sorts."

It was true. I hadn't heard. But wanting to make the right impression, I quickly dashed off something and asked our staff to translate it into Russian. Though my Russian skills were imperfect, I practiced the speech at home, getting pronunciation pointers from my wife. A few days later, I boarded a small plane for the short flight to Simferopol's tiny airport—Crimea's primary gateway. After we landed, we were met outside by a conference organizer from SIPSU for the one-hour drive from Simferopol to Yalta. We passed some attractive hotels and resorts, but when we arrived at our conference lodging, it was clear that its owners had better uses for their money than upgrading the rusting facilities.

As I entered the hotel, a young woman from SIPSU hastily approached me. "Do you have the money for your room?" she demanded. "Cash only." The rate was $300 per night, about twice that of much better hotels in the area.

"Shouldn't I check in first?" I countered.

"No," she said. "This is urgent. Three days at $300 is $900. I take US cash."

"Thanks, I think I'll check into the conference first."

I detoured around her to the conference registration table and gave them my card. In return, the SIPSU greeters handed me a conference agenda. "Have you paid your upfront cash yet?" they asked, obviously concerned.

A tall man, smiling broadly, walked up to me. "Who do you think is putting the pressure on them—their coke dealer or their bookie?" he joked in a British accent. He introduced himself as the EU representative, whom I'll call Jack Francis. "Nice to meet you," he said. I was delighted to encounter a colleague who had been in country for a while and had some insights into how to deal with the Ukrainian government. But it was time for the conference to start.

Yanov took the podium to kick off the conference. Blond and boyish, he seemed rather young and smirking to be the senior Ukrainian government official at the event. His eyes darted around the room, then he began.

> A Jew was visiting a new town and he was taken late at night by other Jews to the synagogue to drink vodka. When he asked what this was all about, he was told that many years ago a town leader who wanted everyone to pray at the synagogue in the evenings instituted a vodka-drinking session after the prayer to give everyone a good reason to show up. "Now we've forgotten about the praying, but everyone still likes to come and have some vodka in the synagogue," they explained. And in that spirit, here we are in Yalta for this year's annual IPR conference.

Everyone laughed at the jovial acknowledgment that nothing would get done in the coming days.

I delivered my introductory remarks in Russian, careful not to butcher my pronunciation. The first session followed with eight presentations. Five were pro-piracy. This, at a government-funded event on protecting intellectual property. I imagined how doctors at an Ebola conference would react if pro-Ebola speakers dominated the discussion. Yanov just yawned throughout, his gaze frequently shifting to the rocky beach outside.

After the procession of pro-piracy presentations, Dmytro Prykordonnyy, head of the Coalition of Producers and Performers of Ukraine, raised his hand. "You guys drive me crazy," he said, crackling with anger. He described how intellectual piracy had destroyed his livelihood and decimated the Ukrainian film industry. I realized that I had to get to know him.

Then a grizzled, older SIPSU IPR inspector named Klyuk spoke, promising not to take bribes "no matter how little money we make." When he finished, he was verbally attacked by Nikolai Sosnovskiy, the so-called intellectual godfather of the huge pirate website EX.UA. Incensed, Klyuk interrupted him and left the podium with this parting shot: "Sometime I will invite you to a restaurant where they are playing unlicensed music. And I will spit in your face."

Sosnovskiy, sporting a week-old hipster beard and exuding a roguish charm, approached me. "We came today only for the benefit of the US Embassy. We want you to know that we are here and that we are real." He then rejoined the pirate brigade. I knew they were real, and they had friends in high places. Earlier that year, when Ukrainian authorities took the popular pirate website EX.UA offline, there were street demonstrations. One of President Yanukovych's sons, a member of parliament, defended the pirate website, calling downloading of pirated content a "human right." I was in for an interesting few days on my first official visit to Crimea before returning to Kyiv.

Meanwhile, the word from Washington was that Ukraine's behavior was freaking out the World Trade Organization (WTO). WTO Article 28 allowed members to raise certain tariff rates as long as they lowered others in some way that balanced out the transaction. Various countries, including the United States, had used this provision occasionally to adjust a number of tariff rates. But Ukraine had just entered a filing that they wanted to adjust over 350 tariff rates, which would be the biggest such adjustment of any country in the history of the WTO. Moreover—and much worse—Ukraine claimed that the entire system was unfair, and that newer members were forced to accept much lower tariff rates than older members. If Ukraine succeeded with this ploy, every new WTO member would line up to renegotiate thousands of tariff rates. The system might collapse. Washington was worried that Ukraine might single-handedly push the entire international trade system off a cliff.

This was another example of strange Ukrainian behavior that could not be ignored. So Valentyna and I arranged to see Svitlana Zaitseva, director of the Department of WTO Issues in the Ministry of Economic Development and Trade.

With short-cropped hair and the bearing of a hip college professor, Zaitseva certainly knew her brief. "This is our right as a WTO member," she responded after I objected to what her government was proposing. She then plunged into the minutiae of WTO procedures and history, displaying the knowledge she had amassed as one of the guiding hands behind Ukraine's WTO accession. I disagreed with her arguments and was worried about where this was heading, but understood that she was serious about the issues and was committed to the best path forward for Ukraine. Despite our disagreement, she was someone we could work with.

The opposite was true of her counterpart from the trade remedies division, a woman I shall call Tatyana Zimnova. A stout, middle-aged woman with unnaturally jet black hair, she loathed anyone from our Embassy. My colleague Valentyna hated how long it took—weeks or even months—to schedule a meeting with her on antidumping cases. When we finally met, I quickly learned that Zimnova excelled at two things: ignoring anything we said, and launching into bitter diatribes claiming US hypocrisy. But I had one advantage in these conversations. Unlike most arcane areas of trade, I actually knew something about the antidumping calculations, which were her office's focus. During my three years as an antidumping analyst at the Commerce Department, I developed a respect for the US system, which was based on rules and math, not political considerations. Despite some flaws, our system was fair, and it worked.

"Your Commerce Department wants to offer us a training session on antidumping analysis?" she sneered at our first meeting. I had indeed just offered to bring some of our high-level trade officials to Kyiv to present the same type of professional course that we give our own analysts, mainly to show that we could offer her office something useful, something collaborative. "Your American trade remedies system is closed and conspiratorial. All of its decisions are based on your political maneuvering. We've been doing this for twenty-five years. We don't want to take a step backwards. Now if your officials want to come and negotiate a fair end to some of your unfair cases against Ukrainian companies, that might be worthwhile." That was, of course, a nonstarter for my former colleagues. So we got nowhere.

I later asked a Ukrainian economics professor who knew everyone in the trade scene about this rebuff. He just laughed. "What was of value to her in your offer?" he questioned incredulously. "There are a few things you should note about Tatyana. First, those sunglasses that she always wears, even after dark. They cost about $300. Have you seen her car? Nicer than yours, I promise you. She had none of those before she got her big promotion to head that office. At her direction, money can create a trade case, and money can make cases go away. It's true that her analysts don't know how to do a world-standard anti-dumping calculation. But doing things fairly according to world standards isn't going to pay for her Paris vacation this year, is it? I had a Japanese trade delegation come to me in shock over her openness in asking for kickbacks." He smiled at me like he would at a child. "Anyway," he sighed, "check out the sunglasses next time you're fortunate enough to be in her presence. And ask yourself again whether you were actually offering something of value to her or not."

Although my brief was IPR and trade, I also became part of the Embassy's extensive election monitoring effort for the September 2012 parliamentary elections. In that role, I traveled twice to Odesa to report on the political situation. What I saw were hum-drum issues—incumbents using their offices to further their campaigns, using taxpayer money to buy off taxpayers—but nothing headline worthy.

My wife Natalya did her monitoring closer to home in Kyiv. Each of us was paired with a local Embassy staff member who, of course, spoke Ukrainian better than we did and was much better acquainted with local culture. They also had an emotional reaction to seeing the dark underbelly of their own democratic process. We were like the Vulcans from *Star Trek*, rationally observing for posterity while knowing that we would be leaving Ukraine in a few years. They saw these election shenanigans as their own future and the future of their children being betrayed.

After the polls closed, Natalya and her Ukrainian partner observed the ballot counting in one Kyiv polling station. Other observers, mostly from local political parties, watched as well. But an observer from the Party of Regions, an antireformist, Russia-friendly party established as a vehicle for Viktor Yanukovych and his allies, with substantial involvement by American lobbyist, pollster, and future US presidential campaign chief Paul Manafort, was front and center. The middle-aged woman was on especially good terms with the election officials, counting with them and sometimes sitting at their table. As the counting was almost finished, she pulled a sheet of paper with some numbers on it from her jacket, showed it to the election officials, then returned it to her jacket. That was too much for Natalya's Ukrainian team partner.

"I demand to see that paper," she announced to the Party of Regions monitor.

"What paper?" she yelled back.

"The paper you pulled out of your jacket pocket and showed to the election officials. I demand to see it."

Of course, she didn't actually have the right to demand anything. Natalya just watched.

"You're insane," the Party of Regions woman hissed. "There is no paper. You must be hallucinating." She started to walk away down a hallway, and our election team member ran after her, demanding the paper. Natalya heard the two women's yells echo down the hallway. Then the Party of Regions monitor turned and slapped our election team monitor in the face. Hard. She stood there, in shock. It was over. There was no piece of paper.

No one likes to be lectured, least of all by a foreigner. Arguing that Ukrainians should care about the financial fortunes of companies like Disney and Microsoft and pop icons like Rihanna was definitely a hard pitch. But IPR issues ran deeper than that. The world was turning increasingly into an information economy. Without protection for the results of intellectual labor, especially their own, Ukraine would just fall farther behind. Ukraine's software engineers were leaving in droves; the ones who stayed were working mostly for foreign outsourcing firms. Ukraine wasn't going to have its own major software firms or become a real cultural force in music or cinema unless it protected intellectual property. But I knew that I was an imperfect messenger.

Brainstorming with Ihnat and other friends, we hit on an idea. What if we had a competition in which we asked university economics students to predict the hypothetical impact on the Ukrainian economy of the government beginning to protect intellectual property? The State Department granted me $10K for the project. We announced the contest, saying we would bring two winning teams—one from Kyiv, one from outside the capital—to the Embassy for an award ceremony, with iPads as prizes. We would also arrange radio and other media interviews for the winners to discuss their projects. Young Ukrainians would be telling their fellow countrymen how protecting intellectual property was important for their own future.

The project went off flawlessly, and Ambassador Tefft enjoyed meeting the fresh-faced, bright young students. The next day, on the way back from a radio interview, one of the students from the Odesa team told me, "We didn't believe this was a real contest at first, so many of these things are just ways for our senior officials to give awards to their own kids, or to give a particular university a favor in exchange for giving a minister an honorary degree, something like that," she sighed. "But then we saw it was the US Embassy, and thought maybe it was worthwhile. You can see why we are excited about the agreement with the European Union. We just want normal standards here. We want life to be fair. Anyway, thanks for the contest—this has been fun." Her appreciation helped to counteract the bad taste left in my mouth from encounters with the likes of Tatyana Zimnova.

Unfortunately, in the world of IPR, there never seemed to be any good news. Under Yanov, any efforts at reform continued to falter. Deeply frustrated, Microsoft's general manager in Ukraine, Dmytro Shymkiv and antipiracy manager Yuriy Omelchenko informed us about the lack of progress toward a deal under which the Ukrainian government would legalize its own software. If the Ukrainian government itself was using pirated software, what were the chances it would put the rest of the country on the right track? Shymkiv also pointed out the obvious: "Imagine an entire country whose government— including the military, intelligence services, everything—is running computers with intentionally broken operating systems which never get security updates? The spies and bandits know all the old flaws and how to exploit them, but within the Ukrainian government's networks, they're all still there. That's our situation, here in a country with many of the best hackers in the world. It's not just a financial problem. Our entire government's networks might as well put up neon welcome signs for hackers. There's no lock on the door. Maybe even the door has been stolen already," he said bitterly. In other areas, SIPSU's persistent failure to authorize the operation of a legitimate music collecting society continued to benefit Yanov's friends. Ukraine was hosting an increasing share of the world's top pirate websites.

Every year, the US Trade Representative (USTR) published the "Special 301" report on IPR problems around the world, a report card on international trading practices. Ukraine had been on the "Priority Watch List" for years, and given its current trajectory, USTR wanted to downgrade Ukraine to the worst possible designation—"Priority Foreign Country." No countries had been on that list for the past eight years. The last country awarded this dubious distinction in the early 2000s was—you guessed it—Ukraine. Ukraine had managed to negotiate its way off the list and, most recently, in 2010, had agreed to a new IPR action plan to clean up its act. Not only had Kyiv failed to fulfill the terms of that plan, but things had actually gotten worse. USTR felt entirely justified in declaring Ukraine the worst in the world with respect to IPR violations—worse than China, worse than India, worse than every country in sub-Saharan Africa.

In December 2012, Ihnat urgently messaged me that a new SIPSU chairman had just been appointed. Mykola Kovinya, an IPR lawyer with a firm known for doing some business with Yanukovych, was to take over SIPSU. Neither Ihnat nor any of my other contacts knew anything about him. We had not seen him at conferences or heard about any of his positions. In a week, David Meale and I were sitting in his office for our first meeting.

"Our government's use of unlicensed software is a clear embarrassment to us all," Kovinya led off. With a round, friendly face under his graying hair, Kovinya was quite young for his new responsibilities. Always neatly dressed in a tie and jacket, he immediately struck a more professional and personable tone than Yanov. At least he was saying the right things, and I felt inclined to believe him. He seemed to have a plan for software legalization, and he had a desire to move forward on collecting societies and to learn more about the other issues in his portfolio.

As we left, Kovinya stopped David and me for a moment. "Before taking this job, I had to sit down for a meeting with President Yanukovych. He said to me: 'Your instructions are to clean up this area and make real progress quickly.' So that's what I plan to do." We all shook hands. "And my president added one thing: 'If there is any corruption in your organization, I'll deal harshly with you myself.'"

Getting lectured by Yanukovych on fighting corruption struck me like getting a self-righteous lecture on clean sportsmanship from Lance Armstrong. But Kovinya seemed sincere, which was a great improvement. However, if he wanted to run a clean ship, what would he do—what could he do—about his own deputy, Yanov, who was not only gunning for his job but also seemed to have his hand permanently planted in the cookie jar?

After so little progress for such a long time, I was amazed when things started to inch forward. Shortly after Kovinya's appointment, the Ukrainian Rada—the parliament—actually approved money for government software legalization. Microsoft Ukraine had unexpected visitors from Ukrainian intelligence arrive to ensure that there would be no corruption in the expected upcoming deal. But after the initial momentum, things stalled again for the next few months.

During these doldrums, we were introduced to Oleh Voloshyn, senior adviser to Ukraine's consummate diplomat and foreign minister turned Deputy Prime Minister Kostyantyn Hryshchenko. David and I would meet Voloshyn at coffee shops and discuss various IPR issues. We all knew why someone senior like Voloshyn would be brought into IPR issues—the threat of Special 301. Ukraine clearly wanted to avoid being put on the Priority Foreign Country list. Voloshyn explained to us in flawless English what the Ukrainian government was trying to accomplish on these issues, why the failures and delays were not a good measure of Ukraine's intentions, and why his government needed more time. As a former foreign ministry spokesperson, behind his smiles was someone who just might be able to cut through the Ukrainian bureaucracy and get some progress on our issues. He was well liked in Washington during his trips there. He inspired hope.

When it was time to decide whether Ukraine would be the only country placed on the most ignominious Special 301 IPR list, there were no real accomplishments we could cite in Ukraine's defense. Our section and Ambassador Tefft didn't want to list Ukraine, but USTR did. Since they had the White House badges and the eop.gov email addresses (Executive Office of the President), and they were the ones who published the report, not surprisingly they won.

The Special 301 report brought lots of negative press and attention in Ukraine. Newspapers accused the United States of bullying Ukraine on behalf of greedy corporations. The following months were contentious. The feared General Prosecutor's Office launched a case against the only collecting society respected by the US recording industry. Prosecutor Rinat Kuzmin was a controversial political character known for going after former Ukrainian premier Yuliya Tymoshenko and doing Yanukovych's bidding. Like so many things in Ukraine, the players' objectives in this drama were completely opaque. Some said that the prosecution was retaliation against the United States, others that it was to strike at Yanov for exceeding his authority. The more we looked into the matter the less we understood. But everyone knew that the General Prosecutor's Office could throw people in jail for a long time on nothing much more than a whim. Within the Ukrainian ecosystem, they were at the top of the food chain.

We tried to stay creative and active within this unpromising situation. We hit on an idea to spotlight Ukrainians who wanted to protect their own intellectual property rights. Musicians were getting pummeled by pirates, and their fans respected what they said. Why not have a free concert highlighting the fact that IPR protection provides Ukrainian musicians the ability to make Ukrainian music? The more Ihnat and I considered it, the more potentially useful it seemed. We would distribute free tickets to anyone who answered an online questionnaire about legal downloading, and use the best online comments to draft a brochure on why Ukrainians want to defend their own intellectual property. The mood in the IPR sphere was gloomy, but we tried to bolster our spirits with these sorts of plans. I wrote the proposal and asked the State Department for a small amount of money.

When the time came to return to Yalta for the 2013 SIPSU conference I was better prepared than in the previous year. Looking for someone whom all of those techie pirates would actually listen to, I persuaded Public Affairs to bring Richard Bennett, inventor of many of the technologies that made wi-fi possible, to Ukraine to participate in the conference. Bennett, with his scraggly white beard, informal style, and deft grasp of the intersection of IPR and electronica, would be perfect for the occasion.

This time we stayed at the much nicer Intourist hotel, and our payment was collected by the hotel, not by SIPSU in shakedown style. The event felt marginally "cleaner." Bennett's presentation was great. Even the pirates seemed to enjoy getting to interact with an inventor of wi-fi. Despite the criticism and moaning from the podium about Special 301, we seemed to be getting somewhere. Then I noticed that this official government conference was actually sponsored and paid for by two main groups—the pirates' law firm Juscutum (pronounced: "You scoot 'em!"), and a local vodka company.

Juscutum attorneys, generally young, fashionably dressed, and goateed, used all opportunities, including multiple presentations from the podium, questions after others' presentations, and special events, to emphasize the greed of Western corporations and the oppression of less developed nations. While most Juscutum team members appeared polished, one attorney, proficient in Russian criminal slang, claimed during his presentation from the podium, without prompting or provocation, that it was "scientifically proven" that most rapes occur because female victims were "leading men on." One woman in the audience stood up and screamed at him, but was ignored.

Juscutum hosted evening events. The first was a screening of the classic 1957 film *12 Angry Men*, about the tortuous deliberations of a jury considering a murder case against a teenage defendant. "This movie will get us in the right frame of mind for tomorrow's brainstorming session," one young Juscutum guy told me over his well-groomed goatee. "One impassioned and morally correct orator can change minds and get the larger group to realize the errors of its ways," he said. He clearly pictured himself as just that orator, whose brilliance would convince anyone within earshot to immediately chuck all copyright law into the historical dustbin.

He must have been disappointed when the moment for his imagined triumph arrived—the "jazz brainstorming session." The evening jazz session began with a band playing sporadically in between their drummer's delivery of five- to ten-minute lectures on "cooperation" and "collaboration," corporate management seminar boilerplate. After the jazz band finished around 10:00 p.m., Juscutum announced that they were now transitioning to a brainstorming session in which every participant should write down ten problems in the Ukrainian copyright environment. At that point, most of the audience stood up and left immediately. A few drunken participants heckled the event organizers with slurred requests for more music and were escorted out. The few remaining participants were shuffled into groups to reach consensus on the main problems in Ukraine. None did. Pro-piracy folks argued that the main problems were high software prices and rights holders' greed, others strongly disagreed. At 12:30 a.m., I split. The event ended at 2:00 a.m. One goatee announced that the results of this session would be compiled and given to the US Embassy, but there didn't appear to be any result at all. I made a mental note to avoid trying to solve complex issues that I might face in the future through drunken midnight pirate jazz brainstorming.

The conference closed with a final evening party, poolside with a live DJ, multiple rounds of vodka toasts and finger food dispensed by waitresses in cocktail dresses. Pro-piracy and pro-copyright factions huddled separately like boys and girls at middle school dances. The painfully loud dance music stopped at regular intervals at the appearance of a synchronized swimming team in the enormous illuminated pool, alternatively offering energetic movements to dance tunes or tender swaying to romantic ballads. This evoked polite applause and more vodka shots. And then more vodka shots. And then maybe another. And definitely a heavy head on the way to the tiny Simferopol airport in the morning.

In sum, despite our constant efforts, there was not much positive coming out of my portfolio. I was not alone. Our Embassy reports back to Washington lacked the drama or the tragedy that produce headlines and command attention. Rather, they transmitted the low, dull, creaking hum of a country that wasn't going anywhere, a country so weighed down by corruption and inefficiency that US policymakers had largely written it off. The relationship was stalling—no high-level visitors from Washington wanted to come to Kyiv to interact with the Yanukovych administration. There was no point in our Embassy proposing anything ambitious to Washington. There was no animosity toward Ukraine or any active dislike, simply a justifiable lack of enthusiasm in Washington to engage with Ukraine because of disappointment over its chronic underachievement. But there was still some hope that Ukraine might yet take the European path, a path that would lead it westward toward the European Union. It was the hope that the type of world standards laid out in excruciating detail in the EU Association Agreement would eventually lift Ukraine out of its morass and transform it into a real partner with which the United States and other developed Western countries would willingly engage. Among Ukraine's own citizens, the daily grind of corruption and disillusionment drove this hope underground and made it embarrassing to express aloud. Even so, hope turns out to be a surprisingly resilient thing.

4

KYIV'S TUG-OF-WAR:
PUTIN TILTS THE BALANCE

Russian President Vladimir Putin, who, in 2005, publicly declared that the collapse of the USSR in 1991 was "the greatest geopolitical catastrophe of the century," only grudgingly accepted Ukraine's existence as an independent country, despite his having personally signed international agreements recognizing Ukraine's sovereignty and guaranteeing its territorial integrity. Putin's attempts to reassert dominant Russian influence over several independent countries that were historically part of the former Soviet Union have been most direct with respect to Ukraine and Georgia. In Ukraine, they escalated over time from economic blackmail to outright annexation of territory and imposing war on southeast Ukraine, including supplying men and material to fight it. But throughout 2012 and 2013, open conflict between Ukraine and Russia was still unthinkable. The struggle for influence played out through diplomatic negotiations, trade blockages, and parliamentary debates. To suggest at the time that the battle would move to an actual battlefield would beggar belief. I wouldn't have believed it myself.

In charting a course in international affairs, there have always been fundamental questions for Ukrainian leaders: Where does Ukraine fit into Europe? Does its future lie with the European Union or in association with Russia? Can Ukraine prosper and advance its still young democracy by balancing on the fulcrum of European geopolitics, pursuing its advantage by shifting its weight from one side to the other, or must it seat itself firmly on one side? In the period leading up to the Euromaidan Revolution, the concrete expression of this question was whether Ukraine should sign an Association Agreement (AA) with the European Union or bow to Russian pressure to join the Moscow-led Customs Union that aspired to be an alternative to European economic integration. This was the contemporary version of an age-old question in Ukraine, a country that straddles the east-west geographical, cultural, and religious divide in Europe, and has experienced the push and pull of contending forces over many centuries.

In December 2012, Ukrainian journalist Tetyana Shylina published an editorial in the popular newspaper *Dzerkalo Tyzhnya* (*Weekly Mirror*) quoting an expert who had chided her for writing about how life is better in Brussels than in rural Russia. "Just imagine how bored you would be," wrote this expert, "if we joined the EU and you had to write about EU directives and regulations like the types of cucumbers allowed for export and the technical requirements for glass containers." "Honestly," I replied, "it would be much better to write about cucumber regulations than . . . the [Moscow-led] Customs Union! Its ghost has now haunted Ukraine for a decade, gaining strength and becoming almost palpable every time Ukraine is extremely weak or is preparing to take a fateful decision."

Ukraine was again approaching one of those fateful decisions. Ukraine and the EU had been negotiating an agreement since 2008. The technical, painfully detailed negotiations were dragging on. The AA included a large section called the Deep and Comprehensive Free Trade Agreement (DCFTA). According to the EU, the AA sought "political association and economic integration" between the EU and Ukraine.

The EU had no intention of making Ukraine a member any time soon. No one in Europe thought that Ukraine would have made a good partner. Imagining Viktor Yanukovych at EU summits, playing various European leaders against each other to maximize his own kickbacks, rightfully gave European leaders indigestion. The AA was meant to set the EU's Texas-sized neighbor on a better course so that Ukraine could work better, generating solutions instead of problems. Perhaps at the end of a long road, Ukraine would be able to join the EU, but that journey had barely begun.

The draft AA text proposed greater interaction between the EU and

Ukraine, including EU-Ukraine presidential-level summits, parliamentary and judicial exchanges, and regular meetings of technical experts. Fighting corruption, achieving greater governmental transparency, and fostering a healthy civil society were among the major objectives. It was the economic component of the agreement that attracted the most initial attention, and if implemented, could have the greatest immediate impact on the lives of Ukrainians. About 70 percent of the DCFTA concerned technical standards that would facilitate Ukrainian exports of eggs, steel, and many other commodities, thereby integrating Ukraine's economy into that of Europe. "Deep and Comprehensive" was not just an empty phrase. The AA was over 2,100 pages long, most of it highly technical.

There was much more to it than those dry words. In Ukraine, the AA also exerted a powerful emotional appeal, speaking to the fraught question of identity politics and the collective dream of the country's future. Ukrainians knew very well that Europe, for all its flaws, worked far better than their own country. The AA symbolized the possibility of a *European* Ukraine, a democratic and developed country that would deliver for its citizens and provide higher standards of living. A Ukraine whose police were trustworthy rather than solicited bribes. A Ukraine in which ordinary citizens could hold their local elected officials accountable for inefficiency or corruption. If Europe could have it, why not Ukraine?

In emotional terms, the Moscow-backed Eurasian Customs Union was an echo of Ukraine's recent past. Although the Customs Union was not the Soviet Union, it was still a world apart from the EU. Its appeal lay largely in the possibility of re-creating the Soviet-era system in which widgets from Ukraine would have a dependable customer in Russia who would combine them with Kazakh widgets to create an industrial product that delivered social status and benefits for all involved. Such was the economic system whose industrial supply lines had integrated the Soviet Union. The collapse of the Soviet Union disrupted that system, causing huge problems for Ukraine's old economy. The new economy was not advancing quickly enough to compensate. Millions of Ukrainians who had once had faith in the old system were suffering as a result.

Few Westerners seemed to know anything about the Customs Union, partly because it was a rapidly evolving organization that had gone through many name changes. In December 1991, Russian President Boris Yeltsin, Ukrainian President Leonid Kravchuk, and Belarus's parliamentary chairman

Stanislav Shushkevich met in secret to sign the Belavezha Accords, which drove a stake into the heart of the Soviet Union and created a new organization, the Commonwealth of Independent States (CIS), an ill-defined successor that possessed few real powers.

Despite being a founding state of the CIS, Ukraine's parliament never ratified its charter due to a dispute with the Kremlin over whether Russia was the sole successor state to the USSR. In 1993, Ukraine became an "associate" rather than a member of the CIS. Ukraine's presidents often attended CIS summit events, and Ukraine eventually joined the CIS Free Trade Area in 2012. But Ukraine never joined the CIS military alliance or the Collective Security Treaty Organization, and it never participated in its regular training exercises. Ukraine's ambivalence toward the CIS, typical of its relations with everyone, was obvious. On January 1, 2010, after a long period of gestation, the Eurasian Customs Union, later renamed the Eurasian Economic Union, formally came into existence, headquartered in Moscow with a large staff and comprising Russia, Belarus, and Kazakhstan, with Armenia and Kyrgyzstan joining later.

Unlike the EU, the Customs Union did not press Ukraine for political reform or government transparency. If Ukraine joined the Customs Union, its leaders could ignore moralizing lectures from Western leaders on good governance and how to "reform" a system that already suited their personal interests just fine. Yanukovych could attend meetings in his native Russian, and all of the transactions would look and feel familiar, with deals transacted in his familiar native cultural currency. On the economic front, the Customs Union would take the existing CIS Free Trade Area, of which Ukraine was already a member, and expand it into a "common economic space," in theory akin to the EU. But unlike the AA, whose greatest attraction was the prospect of higher long-term growth and perhaps a future invitation to the West, the Customs Union offer came with concrete and immediate sticks and carrots.

Natural gas served as both a carrot and a stick. Russia provided Ukraine with nearly all of its natural gas, a commodity of vital importance in heating the country through its harsh winters. Ukraine-Russia gas pricing deals were always opaque and politically driven. As Ukraine's pipelines carried vital supplies of Russian gas into Western Europe, Russia-Ukraine energy relations were an outsized international issue. When a 2005 crisis involving corrupt, high-level officials in Kyiv and Moscow resulted in diverting gas transiting through Ukraine's pipelines to Europe, the resulting brouhaha roiled international markets. In 2009, a more serious crisis over Russia's gas prices to Ukraine caused a gas shortage in eighteen European countries.

The Ukrainian gas industry was a playground for corruption. Gas could be bought from Russia for one price and sold for different prices, depending on whether it was labeled for Ukrainian domestic consumers or Ukrainian industry, or was shipped out to Europe. The Ukrainian government provided staggering domestic subsidies for gas to keep prices to consumers down. Mislabeling or misdirecting gas could lead to massive instantaneous windfalls. None of the gas sales were direct, but were conducted through byzantine networks of shell companies belonging to the well connected. Russian control of gas prices also meant control of vast corruption networks. They could utilize these opaque networks for their own benefit.

We heard rumors that in exchange for Ukraine joining the Customs Union, Russia would slash the price of natural gas from a punishing $430 per 1,000 cubic meters to $160. This was incredibly important and seductive. The exorbitant $430 rate was not only starving the corruption networks but also threatening to bankrupt the country. But there were other carrots in the basket. Russia also had the discretionary power to approve the free flow of gas to Ukraine from other CIS members through its own pipelines. This meant that if Russian gas was too expensive, Ukraine could buy cheaper gas from Turkmenistan for delivery through Russia, but only if Russia approved. The Kremlin could also open up the Eurasian Economic Community stabilization fund to Ukraine. Another interesting wrinkle was that Russia offered to reimburse Ukraine for an expected whopping bill from World Trade Organization (WTO) members to cover their losses should Ukraine join the Customs Union and raise its external tariffs.

My Ukrainian trade professor friend talked me through what to expect: "So, let's pretend that we in Ukraine join the Customs Union. Every WTO member that trades with Ukraine will seek reimbursement of their losses if we raise our external duties in line with Moscow's Customs Union requirements. Russia has agreed to foot that bill and reimburse us. How would this actually work?" he asked, as we sat in the restaurant of a Kyiv hotel owned by Donetsk billionaire Rinat Akhmetov. He continued:

Of course, Ukraine would ask for the money up front, before committing to join the Customs Union. Why not? Why trust Russia? And why not base your ask on the worst possible case scenario, knowing that you won't actually have to pay out that much in the end? Of course! So this inflated amount of money makes its way to our state coffers from Russia. Of course, the trade cases against Ukraine determining the exact amount of money we owe to other WTO members will take years, many years, to wind their way through WTO arbitration. You've been here in Ukraine for a while now. Do you expect any of the money from Russia to still exist in our treasury when the WTO cases are resolved and it is time for Ukraine to pay up? Come on.

He looked past me, and continued:

The Russians are not dumb about this. They know it all, and they understand these corruption networks better than you or I ever will. But after they've gotten their prize and Ukraine is in the Customs Union, do they have any reason to care that the money's been stolen? It's Ukraine's WTO bill, anyway. This is all just speculation about something that hasn't happened, but it's speculation based on seeing this kind of thing play out so many times.

We in the Embassy figured that Yanukovych wanted to keep Ukraine in the middle for as long as possible—asking for gifts from the EU to stay away from the Customs Union, and asking for gifts from Moscow to back away from the EU. In other words getting paid for doing nothing. That was the perfect position from which Yanukovych could extract profit from Ukraine's "strategic position."

To add to the complexity was the case of Yuliya Tymoshenko. An impassioned, firebrand orator with a signature braided hairdo that led to her nickname of Princess Leia of the Orange Revolution, the postrevolutionary prime minister of Ukraine became an internationally known figure. By the time of the Orange Revolution in 2004, she was already one of the most successful and wealthy businesspersons in Ukraine through her management of United Energy Systems of Ukraine, a primary importer of Russian natural gas. Her other nickname, the Gas Princess of Ukraine, pointed to the fortune she had made in this monumentally corrupt industry. After Yanukovych took office, Ukraine's General Prosecutor's Office opened a case against Tymoshenko for exceeding her legal authority by signing a controversial gas deal with Russia while she was in office. That Yanukovych also signed immensely controversial natural gas deals with Russia was irrelevant. In October 2011, Tymoshenko was sentenced to seven years in prison and fined nearly $200 million. Verdicts against other top officials in her administration were also forthcoming. While not proclaiming Tymoshenko's innocence, the EU and the United States called the case an example of the "selective prosecution" of Yanukovych's political opponents. The prosecution was seen as a horrible precedent. If Ukraine's leaders couldn't leave office without fear of being imprisoned, they would be tempted to cling to power by any means necessary.

Viewing Tymoshenko as a victim of a politically motivated prosecution, the EU was unlikely to sign any agreement with Ukraine as long as she remained behind bars. But despite the EU's hard line, Yanukovych was impervious to any argument on the subject. The charismatic Tymoshenko was a formidable political foe, and he firmly believed that she had unlawfully taken to the streets in 2004's Orange Revolution to steal an election that he had already rightfully stolen for himself.

The rough and tumble competition among Ukrainian political clans and the lure of competing international political alliances provided the background for the Embassy's TechCamp program. The fate of that program turned out to be a harbinger of things to come. TechCamp was run by Assistant Information Officer Luke Schtele. Luke and his partner Ben were a lot of fun—consistently upbeat, great with mixology and parties, and willing to tolerate old married people like me and Natalya. At this time we had no premonition that Luke's seemingly noncontroversial work in Ukraine would be the focus of dark conspiracy theories concocted by propagandists wanting to convince people that the United States was somehow behind the Maidan movement.

TechCamp is a global US program to help civil society activists make full use of social media and other technological resources. Successful TechCamps have been held from Almaty to London to Zanzibar to Taipei. US sponsorship of TechCamp reflects a commitment to supporting development efforts around the world—sometimes successfully, sometimes not. Enthusiastic citizens trying to improve their own communities were indispensable to economic growth in the United States and elsewhere. Civil society is vital because real and lasting improvements in communities rarely come just from the top. People need to make their voices heard. TechCamp empowers civic-minded folks to harness technology effectively. Without such efforts to help people make their own nations and communities better, I always felt that much of our development funding would have been wasted.

In September 2012, Luke and his local staff held a successful TechCamp in Kyiv. Over 120 local community leaders attended, and about a dozen US trainers were flown in. The Ukrainian participants, mostly younger people, came from all walks of life across Ukraine. While some focused on "big picture" issues, such as government transparency, anticorruption, and e-governance, most cared more about smaller issues. Think trash pickup and medicine delivery to the elderly. The common denominator was a desire to help their own communities. The Embassy also invited Ukrainian government officials to attend to pre-empt any misunderstandings about the program or its goals. By the end of the event, the participants were enthused about what they could accomplish and already asking Luke when the next TechCamp would be.

Since the September program was so successful, Luke and the public affairs team organized another smaller event in March 2013, a "regional TechCamp," with about sixty participants in Kyiv. Microsoft Ukraine hosted the event. It would be the last TechCamp in Ukraine to go according to plan. Problems encountered with our subsequent TechCamps foreshadowed the mounting tensions in Ukraine concerning the overall direction of the country. Brussels beckoned, but with conditions unacceptable to Yanukovych. Moscow both beckoned and threatened, possessing the power to reward as well as to punish if denied.

On April 4, the next "regional TechCamp" began in Donetsk in eastern Ukraine. The setting was the lovely Izolyatsia (isolation) Art Center, a former brick factory converted into an art space. Right before Ambassador Tefft arrived to open the event, one of the participants approached Luke to tell him that a well-known local pro–Party of Regions, pro-Russian provocateur was in the front row. Luke alerted the security staff, but the provocateur remained silent during the ambassador's remarks. Shortly after the ambassador left, however, a large crowd, estimated at 100 to 150, surrounded the complex. Police on the scene assured Luke it was a peaceful, registered protest. The "peaceful protesters" then broke down the outer fence and began beating on the windows of the art center. They were well prepared, brandishing signs reading, "No Arab Spring in Ukraine" and "TechCamp = Revolution." After they broke into the building, they didn't physically attack anyone. Instead, they stole all the instructional materials they could find and recorded footage of the event and its participants. When the violent demonstrators broke in and ransacked the place, Luke barricaded himself in the bathroom, e-mailing back to the Embassy regularly with updates. At the Embassy in Kyiv, we all anxiously read Luke's increasingly alarming messages while the Regional Security Office (RSO) repeatedly called local officials in Donetsk for help. When more police arrived one hour later, they let the attackers disperse while lining up all the TechCamp participants as if they were the guilty ones, taking their names and addresses. RSO terminated the event and directed all US Embassy personnel and instructors to return to Kyiv. Later, Ambassador Tefft sent a letter to the Donetsk governor and Ukraine's minister of internal affairs requesting an official investigation, but to no effect.

A second "regional TechCamp" was already planned for Ivano-Frankivsk in western Ukraine, where the security situation seemed much better. The local host of the event, the National Technical University of Oil and Gas, assured the Embassy that the event would proceed smoothly. Given the recent trouble in Donetsk, however, RSO swept the venue. Again, Ambassador Tefft opened the event, and Ukrainian officials were invited to attend. Just before lunch, about forty black-armor-clad police and their dogs stormed into the second floor conference room, announcing that there had been a bomb threat. All participants and instructors were marched outside by police, who oddly evacuated only the second floor of the four-story building, which was supposedly the location of the "bomb." University officials told Luke they were mortified. After the TechCampers were evacuated outside, agents of the Security Service of Ukraine (SBU) took over. They separated the Ukrainians and Americans and interrogated the Ukrainians inside the gymnasium. One agent justified the interrogation to Luke by asserting that their suspect was likely one of the participants. All participants were detained until 5:30 p.m., the scheduled end of TechCamp, and then released slowly in staggered pairs. Once again, RSO instructed the Americans to return to Kyiv.

The frustrated Ukrainian TechCamp participants were not intimidated. Several told Luke they would hold the session, even without American instructors if necessary. They asked if the buses could take them to a downtown park where they could hold their meeting in public. They would show that they had nothing to hide and weren't doing anything wrong. The group, including Luke, boarded their bus, but shortly after its departure, it was pulled over by police who stated there was a new bomb threat and that the bomb could be on the bus. By the time the group finally reached the park, it was filled with "men reading newspapers." Since it was unlikely that Ivano-Frankivsk had such a large SBU office, reinforcements must have been brought in from other provinces. In any case, the TechCamp had been successfully sabotaged.

Over the coming months, the campaign against TechCamp ramped up. Those trying to paint a picture of nefarious Western influence portrayed the relatively banal sessions as dens of traitorous, foreign-backed coup plotting. In late May, a Ukrainian state TV channel aired a slanderous "documentary" railing against TechCamp, much of which used misrepresented and out of context footage shot by the Donetsk hooligans who had attacked TechCamp. In July, an anti-TechCamp, anti-US documentary, using the same Donetsk footage, aired on Russian television. YouTube videos based on this same anodyne footage, with an ominous voice-over claiming that the United States was fostering a "color revolution," began popping up like poisonous toadstools. Many people who didn't know what TechCamp was and didn't understand the US interest in promoting civil society believed these ridiculous charges. The concerted attacks against TechCamp and its participants were an omen of what was to come.

As summer began, I became increasingly worried. Our EU counterparts were confident that the AA signing, scheduled for November, was already a done deal. But the churning swill of anti-EU propaganda, fear of Russia's response if the AA went through, and the Yanukovych administration's notorious eagerness to be bought off were all ominous signs. I pondered how to do something, however small, to inject clarity into the muddled conversation.

When the USSR imploded, the economies of Ukraine and Poland were roughly equal. Poland pursued a successful course of economic reform and joined the EU in May 2004. Its economy prospered, averaging more than 4 percent annual GDP growth from 1995 to 2018. Ukraine's economy stagnated by comparison. By 2012, Poland's per capita wealth was more than three times that of Ukraine. The debate over Ukraine's future course should have hinged on such incontestable data, but it did not. It was far more common to hear people talking about how the EU would make Ukraine "gay" or turn it into an EU colonial dependency. The conversation was off-kilter and irrational. I wrote a proposal to assemble college students from across Ukraine to analyze the impact of EU accession on Poland and the Czech Republic, and compare it to the impact of Customs Union membership on economic growth in Belarus and Kazakhstan. We could invite the Ukrainian press to cover the event. These savvy youngsters would have one day to review the economic data and the various treaties, and then discuss their findings. This event would highlight the practical implications of Ukraine's alternate choices and underline the incredible growth that free trade with Europe had brought two of Ukraine's former communist neighbors. Washington seemed ready to allot a small sum of funding to the project. My Economic Section leadership, David and Elizabeth, approved on condition that the EU mission was on board. I invited Jack Francis at the EU mission to lunch and broached the idea, initially proposing that the students conduct some economic modeling of the effects of the various agreements on Ukraine.

"Well," he said suspiciously, "Economic modeling is the most dismal plank of the dismal science. . . . What if some of the participants came in with some really crazy assumptions which skewed the whole thing? I'm not sure about this."

He had a good point. I told him I would send him a revised proposal, which I did a few weeks later, with the economic modeling component removed. He responded that while the goal of the project was "reasonable," the very different nature of the EU and the Customs Union made the idea problematic. "So, in short, we remain very skeptical about the value of this project," he concluded. I knew that without EU cooperation, the project was dead on arrival. I understood that with regard to the AA, the EU was reluctant to be seen with us in public. So much for my pet project.

Meanwhile, in the main ring of Ukrainian politics, starting in early 2013, the decisive bout between the Customs Union and the EU AA was underway. The bell for round one sounded after a December 2012 EU Foreign Affairs Council meeting set dates for "sequenced engagement" with Ukraine. According to this plan, Ukraine would need to deal with "selective justice" issues (read: free Tymoshenko already!), electoral problems highlighted in the October 2012 election, and other domestic reform issues listed in a so-called Association Agenda. If these conditions were met, the path would be clear for Ukraine to sign the AA in late November 2013 at the forthcoming Eastern Partnership Summit in Vilnius, Lithuania.

In February, Yanukovych was angling for a compromise that would allow him to keep sitting on the fence. The idea of a "partial accession" to the Customs Union was gaining traction in Kyiv. Yanukovych seemed to fantasize that Ukraine could sign only certain provisions of the Customs Union agreement that would not preclude Ukraine from also signing the AA. However, Moscow never approved of this "three plus one" arrangement (Russia, Belarus, and Kazakhstan as full Customs Union members, Ukraine as a partial member). The idea was stillborn. "You cannot be a little bit pregnant," Russian Foreign Ministry official Aleksandr Gorban announced at a news conference—a strange metaphor that left many Ukrainians wondering exactly what Russia wanted to do to their country. Nevertheless, Yanukovych and his foreign minister Leonid Kozhara kept flogging the idea in the press.

On February 25, 2013, Yanukovych attended the EU-Ukraine Summit in Brussels. European leaders put Ukraine on notice that real progress would have to be made by May if Ukraine expected to sign the AA in Vilnius in November. They also agreed to provide Ukraine 610 million euros in financial assistance if Kyiv followed the IMF's reform recommendations. But European Commission president José Manuel Barroso explicitly warned Ukraine: "What we have to be clear about is one country cannot at the same time be a member of a customs union and be in a . . . free trade area with the European Union. This is not possible." Sitting on the fence with one leg dangling on each side— Yanukovych's favorite position—was not an option. Yet, fulfilling International Monetary Fund (IMF) conditionality meant eliminating gas subsidies, doubling or tripling gas prices, and causing Yanukovych to violate one of his election campaign pledges. His popularity already low, he may have calculated that he couldn't afford the risk that entailed.

On May 26, on short notice, Putin and Yanukovych met in Sochi. Five days later, Ukrainian Prime Minister Azarov signed a memorandum declaring Ukraine's willingness to become an observer of the Eurasian Economic Union—the organization that the Customs Union was slated to morph into at the beginning of 2015. This made no sense, as there was no position of "observer" defined within the Customs Union, and the Eurasian Economic Union hadn't yet been formed. It was a pledge to take a role that didn't exist in a body that didn't exist.

"The Customs Union is an economic union on paper, but it functions more like a political animal," one of my contacts explained to me over what passes for sushi in Kyiv. "The Ukrainian government probably sees this display of filial respect as a way of deflecting the onslaught of Russian trade sanctions if they move closer to the European Union. But would it actually have that effect, actually dulling the pain the Russians would inflict? That's a very different question."

To better understand what Ukrainians thought about the choice facing their country I needed to listen to the pro-Russians among them since most of my existing contacts were pro-EU. I pressed Valentyna to track down some authentic pro-Russia, anti-Western types.

Around then I started visiting the CIS Institute in Kyiv to see a man whom I will call Mr. Maksim Maksimov. The CIS Institute was a "think-tank" that supposedly studied problems of the former Soviet countries. Actually, it just represented Moscow's interests and argued that unless Ukraine moved closer to Russia it would inevitably slide into chaos. Pretty self-serving. On what they perceived to be neutral territory, such as China or Africa, Russian diplomats were happy to engage with us. But Russian diplomats rarely engaged with us in Kyiv, so I considered it useful to talk with Maksimov. However, he wasn't from Ukraine, and, like me, he was representing the interests of a foreign nation. I met with him, but kept trying to find real pro-Russia Ukrainian contacts.

Valentyna came up empty-handed, and when I asked again a few days later, and then again soon after, I could tell she was frustrated and a bit irritated by my request.

"There really aren't people like that in the mainstream in Kyiv," she said. "If you want me to go out to the fringe, I will, but be aware that's where you're sending me."

I was aware, and that's just where I sent her.

Of the several appointments she managed to arrange, I best remember meeting Vyacheslav Burtenko, president of the generically named Center for Systemic Analysis and Prognostication. He suggested that we meet for lunch at a local brewpub.

Valentyna and I arrived five minutes early. Burtenko, sandy haired, somewhat heavyset, and looking a bit rumpled, showed up twenty minutes late. We exchanged cards.

"So, what are your government's current plans for Ukraine?" he asked.

That got me started talking about US government anticorruption efforts and the possibility that Secretary of State John Kerry might visit after the AA was signed. Burtenko seemed totally bored.

"You don't get it," he sighed. "Your government goes around the world creating violence and death to meet your goals. We've seen Iraq, we've seen the color revolutions. We know you guys. So tell me what are you *really* up to in Ukraine?"

We went around in circles for an hour. I told him about our actual goals and plans in Ukraine, which didn't interest him at all. He wanted the inside dope and kept pressing me to reveal dark American conspiracies that he was already convinced were our real business. Finally, he'd had enough.

"Ukrainian sovereignty is a historic mistake which must be rectified," he said. "Look at this pathetic excuse for a state. Only the influence of great Russia can do any good around here."

Valentyna was getting visibly uncomfortable and fidgety. When the meal was over and Burtenko went to the bathroom, I took the opportunity to pay the bill. I had invited him, so it was my treat. When he returned, he pulled out his wallet.

"Don't worry about it," I said. "Already taken care of. Great to meet you. You can pick up the bill next time." I held out my hand. He took it very cautiously. The glint of anger in his eyes now seemed directed at me personally rather than at US policy writ large. Then he walked away.

At the Embassy later that day, Valentyna said, "Burtenko thinks you are going to try to blackmail him over paying for lunch. Part of your evil plan, apparently," she said. I asked to see the text that he had sent to her. "No, I can't show you," she said. "The language is too bad. I'm really embarrassed."

He sent her another text that afternoon that read something like: "Your man's country has such a fucking shitty reputation that he should just leave. He can't do anything here." We agreed there would be no next time. Mr. Burtenko would be spared from picking up the next bill.

As an economic officer in the US Embassy, I was seldom in the spotlight. But on August 14, 2013, I felt like the eyes of the US government were focusing on me. Not all of them, but enough to fill my BlackBerry with messages by the time I woke up. What was going on? All goods were stopped on the Russia-Ukraine border. Russia had apparently declared a trade war against Ukraine, so it was going to be a heavy day for the trade guy in Kyiv.

This latest Russian salvo was not entirely unexpected. Russia-Ukraine trade conflicts had been heating up over the last month. On July 9, Russia notified the WTO that it would increase duties on Ukrainian chocolate, sugar, coal, and float glass. On July 24–25, several Ukrainian companies began to report problems exporting to Russia, including frequent customs searches and unusual and seemingly systematic "skepticism" regarding import documentation—a favorite Russian trade weapon because it was not an official action. Immediately after Russian President Vladimir Putin's July 27–28 visit to Kyiv, Russia's chief health inspector Gennadiy Onishchenko announced that Russia would ban the products of Ukrainian confectionery giant Roshen, owned by Petro Poroshenko, from the Russian market, allegedly over safety concerns. Not even Russia's friendly Customs Union partner countries Kazakhstan and Belarus could find the dangerous contaminants that Russia claimed to have diligently discovered, but no matter. On August 9, the Ukrainian press reported that Russia's Customs service had added over forty Ukrainian companies to an "at risk" list as early as July 12, causing serious problems at the border. Being "at risk" meant that those products were sitting, either gathering dust or rotting.

It became increasingly clear throughout the day that all Ukrainian goods, not just those from sources listed as "at risk," were being halted or slow-rolled. A variety of reasons and official excuses were proffered, but the notion that suddenly all Ukrainian goods needed further inspection was hardly credible. This could not have been a local decision made by officials at all border crossings simultaneously. It could only have come from the Kremlin. Suddenly, all food might be poisoned and needed testing, all steel might be mislabeled or adulterated and needed to be verified. Nothing could pass. In a sudden forceful smack, all Ukrainian goods were suspect. The Russian government's Department of Press and Information denied that there was a high-level decision to block Ukrainian imports, releasing a statement saying, "The [Russian] government is concerned with the existing situation because this impacts trade and economic ties. But this is the decision of the customs bodies and no decision to regulate imports from Ukraine has been made at the governmental level." Young children may believe their Christmas toys are made by elves in Santa's workshop at the North Pole rather than in Shenzhen, but Moscow was unlikely to have thought anyone would buy their cock-and-bull story. They probably didn't even want anyone to believe it. Telling a transparent lie without fear that anyone would be in a position to contradict it can project great strength.

On August 16, Putin and Yanukovych discussed the trade problem by phone, after which Ukrainian Prime Minister Azarov and Russian Prime Minister Medvedev spoke on August 18. According to press reports, Medvedev and Azarov agreed to consultations between their customs services, which took place the next day. Russian customs clearance on Ukrainian imports returned to normal almost immediately. Suspect Ukrainian chocolate was now good to eat, suspect Ukrainian steel suddenly reliable.

Moscow's fog machine was switched off a few days later, and the truth slipped out when Kremlin adviser Sergey Glazyev stated that Ukraine would face more such trade actions if it signed the AA with the EU. He told reporters, "The Russian Customs Service conducted preventive measures related to preparations for changes in customs administration in case Ukraine signs the Association Agreement with the EU. . . . If Ukraine signs an Association Agreement with the European Union, the customs control could again be tightened." On August 22, Putin told media that if Ukraine signs the AA, "the countries of the Customs Union will have to think about protective measures. . . . Next week, our Ukrainian colleagues will come to Moscow to analyze on an intergovernmental level all the possible threats related to this situation." Not least the Russian threat, I was sure.

The Russian statements made it crystal clear that the border actions were a threat and a demonstration of Ukraine's vulnerability as it headed toward signing the AA. Point made. So it wasn't a trade war yet, just a trade weapons show.

In August 2013, Ukrainian daily *Dzerkalo Tyzhnya* published a long "leaked document" on Moscow's strategy vis-à-vis Ukraine. It dripped with paranoia about Western intelligence services' supposed massive penetration of Ukraine and exuded heartfelt pining for Ukraine to integrate its economy with that of Russia. Wondering about its authenticity, I called some contacts, who likewise doubted the paper was actually produced by the Kremlin since it wasn't formatted correctly. But they believed that the paper had likely been written by Moscow's paid consultants in Kyiv. Since those consultants knew the Kremlin's thinking, the paper was valuable despite its dubious provenance, and worth analyzing in detail.

Proposing a full mobilization of Russian influence in Ukraine in order to prevent the signing of the AA, the paper set forth a plan to form an influential network of pro-Russian political forces in Ukraine, neutralize the political and public influence of Euro-integration advocates, and create the conditions for Ukraine's accession to the Customs Union in 2015. Underpinning the strong call for action was Russian fear of the impending AA signing in Vilnius and a perception of the general decline of Russia's influence in Ukraine. That Ukraine's movement toward the EU was bad for Russia was stated as self-evident fact: "Ukraine's signing of the Association Agreement with the EU expected in November of this year . . . will close the possibility of Ukraine joining the Customs Union and dramatically intensify its dependence on Brussels." As Yanukovych was increasingly unpopular, the authors worried about Russia's limited options: "The collapse of the Yanukovych regime would leave us in a 'scorched earth' situation without any influential political forces to rely upon." At least on this level, the paper recognized Russia's unpopularity in Ukraine.

The paper then went beyond garden variety paranoid, veering into serious tin foil hat territory. "The bulk of Ukrainian officials have been through long and dense processing by Western intelligence agencies, foundations, and experts with a view to their use for Western interests. Particular attention is paid to foreign ministry officials, intelligence services, the Ministry of Defense, Ministry of Finance, and the Economy Ministry—most of which are in fact agents of Euro-Atlantic influence. Personally discrediting these individuals with a view to excluding them from leading positions in the new Ukrainian government after the [2015] election is a very important task. . . . We will resist the extensive network fostered by Western intelligence services of agents of influence, which has deep roots in all branches of government, the media, the education system, the expert community, and law enforcement."

I could only laugh. If only this were even slightly true, I could relax at work. Solving problems in my portfolio in Ukraine would be a snap rather than the bane of my existence if this "dense processing" was anything more than a KGB agent's fever dream.

The delusions piled up. Rather than recognizing that Yanukovych's failing popularity resulted from his own poor performance and widespread knowledge of his corruption, a more novel explanation was offered. Yanukovych's nosedive in the opinion polls was supposedly due to his "failure to realize pre-election promises of integration with Russia." This must have been comfort food in Moscow—the only thing wrong with a president as flawed as Yanukovych was that he wasn't cozy enough with the Kremlin.

In sum, the document was an early expression of a worldview that we would increasingly confront. The paranoia, dark conspiracy-mongering, and willingness of the Russian Federation to blatantly meddle in their neighbor's affairs were all real enough, whoever had authored or authorized its publication.

Meanwhile, back in the real world, on October 27, Yanukovych flew to Sochi to meet President Putin. According to the Ukrainian side, there were no "concrete decisions" made at the meeting, but the AA and the Customs Union were the focus. The Ukrainian Foreign Ministry's Yevhen Perebyinis told reporters: "The presidents of Ukraine and Russia held a meeting in Sochi, during which they continued discussing the issues that they discussed as part of a meeting of the CIS Council of Heads of State. . . . The sides are continuing to exchange information and their positions on the settlement of many issues. First and foremost, the issue concerns the future signing of the Association Agreement and concerns from Russia in this regard."

Two weeks later, on November 9, President Yanukovych flew to Moscow to continue this conversation. Normally we could request readouts of these sorts of high-level meetings, but no one in the Ukrainian government seemed to know anything this time. Yanukovych traveled with a very small retinue, and no one was authorized to talk to outsiders. In the world of diplomacy this was odd—getting a readout of a head of state's foreign meetings with other heads of state was pretty standard stuff. Using prepared points from Washington, I had delivered many of these kinds of briefings to contacts through the years who were curious about President Obama's and President Bush's travels. But this one was more mysterious. What was really going on? Was Yanukovych explaining to Putin why he needed to sign the AA and why it shouldn't impact his relations with Russia? Or was Putin putting the squeeze on Yanukovych to bring Ukraine into the Customs Union? Or both? I needed to find out.

One man who always seemed well informed was Dr. Ihor Burakovsky of the Institute for Economic Research and Policy Consulting. Tall, with glasses and a prominent gray mustache partially obscuring his mouth, Burakovsky looked every inch the professor and economist he was. We had been meeting occasionally in his office for many months. I was happy to share what I could about US policy in exchange for his in-depth knowledge of the intersection between Ukrainian trade, politics, corruption, and industry.

"Of course the Putin-Yanukovych meeting was all about the EU versus Customs Union situation," he said. "The real question is what were the Russians offering? That's where it gets interesting." Burakovsky said nothing about the sources of his information, but my past experience with him was that he was usually spot on. He continued:

I hear that the offer was a $5 to $10 billion immediate cash infusion into the Ukrainian state budget, plus assistance for Yanukovych during the Ukrainian presidential election in 2015, and, of course, a new gas discount. The money transfer would be $5 to $7 billion if in cash, but maybe up to 10 if it was an 'investment' giving the Russian government equity in some good assets here. Election help to Yanukovych would include positive coverage in the Russian media, which is heavily watched in eastern Ukraine. They would also provide some direct campaign funding and refrain from any actions which could hurt him, like running other candidates on his side of the political spectrum.

He paused, adding, "They also want a cabinet-level guarantor, someone trusted by Russia and possibly placed at the first deputy prime minister level, who could ensure that Yanukovych would not reverse course again and tack towards the EU after receiving these incentives. The EU may not trust our dear president, but the Russians don't either."

If this information was accurate, what Russia offered was much greater in the short term than the EU, and much more tailored to Yanukovych's personal political and venal interests. I was confident my cable to Washington on the subject would attract some attention.

"Oh, and one more thing," Burakovsky added. "You remember the protest a few months back at the Embassy on behalf of the Ukraine-Syria Friendship Committee? Those guys that showed up waving Syrian flags and Assad pics? I saved this to show you. . . . I thought you would like it."

He pulled up a saved website on his computer. It was an electronic classified ad for protesters. There were several requirements: the would-be protesters needed to be between twenty and fifty, and they needed to show up at one of two collection points to be bused in. The ad stipulated that payment, the equivalent of about US$5, would only be given at the end of the event. Burakovsky noted:

You see, they don't want too many pensioners—a crowd of old people with nothing else to do makes the whole ruse too obvious. And you'll notice a few bits of info that are missing from the ad. One is the group organizing the protest. The other is any information about the point of the protest. So none of those people outside the Embassy knew what they were going to protest when they showed up at the collection buses and were handed the signs. Anyway, you should know this so that you can judge the significance of protests around town. And so you will also understand why people are so cynical about demonstrations and politics. I'll send you a link to the website.

Flashing his sly grin, he added: "Maybe you too can make a little extra money on the weekends if you want, exercising your civic rights here in our country."

This educated conjecture on what the Russians might have offered was an eye-opener. But how do we best operate under these circumstances? As a diplomat I sometimes deal with jittery nerves by writing proposals. I felt like things were heading the wrong way, but at the Embassy we had a tendency to assure ourselves that the EU would deal with it. This was a question for the EU and Ukraine to resolve, and, even though the issues involved had a significant impact on US interests, we were not a direct party to the agreement in question. Also, Ukraine's long record of disappointing its supporters in the West meant Washington had little desire to engage.

While US envoys had consistently voiced our official approval of Ukraine's association with the EU, I thought it would be advantageous in the home stretch to emphasize US support directly to the Ukrainian people. I called a Ukrainian marketing firm I had collaborated with previously and asked them to work up an example of a "light board" advertisement that would be displayed around Kyiv. I asked Public Affairs Officer Eric Johnson as well as my section leadership for support, and received tentative approval, pending a green light from the EU mission too. The total cost of the project was small change. The point was to assure the Ukrainian people that the United States supported their aspirations to join Europe.

Meanwhile, the threat of further Russian actions to harm the Ukrainian economy was increasingly effective. In conversations around town, grim talk about the economic damage Russia could cause in Ukraine eclipsed discussion of the potential benefits of the AA. Ukraine needed to fight back against actions like the August trade blockage, and the only venue for such an effort was the WTO. But Ukraine had neither the technical expertise nor the political focus to do so. I drafted another proposal to help pay for legal and technical services necessary to defend Ukraine's export markets in the WTO and the CIS economic court. This would be a serious signal of our intentions.

I also called up Jack Francis at the EU mission about my idea for a light box campaign. He recoiled at the proposal, assuring me the AA agreement was a done deal. "Chris, as I've told you before, the sales job on the Association Agreement is over. It's done, they will sign. All that we are talking about now is how to implement the agreement." Jack's position was clear. Those words, "the sales job is over," would ring in my ears for years.

The next day, David told me, "EU Ambassador Tombinski approached Ambassador Pyatt on this public campaign idea. They are not just against it—they are *really* against it. They think that anything that has the US name attached to it will bring Cold War overtones into this discussion. Anyway, it's gone up to that level now and the reaction was strongly negative, so it's over. We can't do this kind of thing against the EU's wishes. This is their show."

Later that day, I had a secure conference call with USTR about the idea of helping to fund Ukraine's WTO case. "This idea dies today," I was told with typical USTR bluntness and efficiency. "We will not have US trade policy politicized in this way. It's not how we do business, and it is not a precedent we would ever want to set. Ever."

Even at my small scale, I was losing the bureaucratic debate, unable to convince anyone that my ideas had any merit. It felt like the lowest point of my career. Time to go home, maybe play Candy Land with the kids instead of Ukraine with the grown-ups, and get a stiff drink. I was having zero impact. If I needed any further reminder of where things stood, the fate of TechCamp provided it.

By the time of the last TechCamp event in November 2013, this time again in Kyiv, Luke Schtele and the Embassy were under no illusions. It would be rough. Because the Embassy expected trouble, most preparatory work was done quietly, and the RSO asked that the Public Affairs Section not use its normal outside partner for logistics support. The Embassy would only use its own staff and its trusted outside travel agent to book travel for the participants. Nevertheless, the participant list somehow still leaked. Intimidating fliers branding TechCamp participants as "traitors," some with images of gunshot victims with massive head wounds, began appearing in the apartment blocks of many invited participants. About 10 percent of invitees dropped out, but around 100 young civic-minded Ukrainians still planned to show up in Kyiv for the program.

RSO suggested that the event should be on US government property since even enthusiastic and well-meaning partners, such as the Ivano-Frankivsk Oil and Gas University, had been unable to provide proper security. We decided on the "Old Marine House"—an aging US government-owned building containing several apartments for temporary personnel. Public Affairs installed wi-fi, video screens, and everything needed for a high-tech event there. The night before the event, after the participants arrived at their hotel in Kyiv, some began to call Luke. They had received a "welcome packet" at their hotel, ostensibly from the US Embassy. It contained a note reading: "If you care about the safety of your friends and family, do not attend TechCamp." Luke responded by emailing participants that the event was still going forward.

Shortly afterward, participants received another email, over what looked like Luke's signature, announcing that TechCamp had been canceled due to security concerns. Participants should return to their homes, the email read, and they should not contact the Embassy directly. Of course, these artfully crafted emails were fake. Also on the morning of the event, Luke started getting dozens of phone calls to his government BlackBerry—someone had posted advertisements around town for a "security and IT specialist" position at the US Embassy, listing Luke's work cell phone as the point of contact. Luke's local staff members also started to receive dozens of calls to their BlackBerry numbers. When they would pick up, they would hear recordings of old Soviet war songs.

Public Affairs, the Front Office, and RSO decided to move TechCamp to the most highly controlled location available to us, the Embassy itself. No one was told about the venue change, not even the bus drivers, until the last moment as they were leaving the hotel. At 11:00 a.m., two hundred protesters showed up at the Old Marine House, unaware that the young civic-minded Ukrainians they had intended to harass were not there.

Unwittingly, our Embassy had experienced its first encounter with the future pro-Russian Donetsk separatists. One of the future separatist leaders was the individual who registered the provocateurs for the earlier TechCamp session in the east and contacted Embassy staff via Facebook to gather information on TechCamp. The TechCamp tale was also a taste of the clash between civic-minded activism and corrupt thuggery that was about to play out on a much larger stage.

On the heels of the Putin-Yanukovych meeting in Sochi on October 26, the ball that had started rolling at the beginning of the year toward Ukraine's signing of the AA in Vilnius took on an oddly skewed spin. On November 11,

Yuriy Kulyk, head of the Federation of Trade Unions of Ukraine, addressed an open letter to President Yanukovych requesting a meeting to discuss the damage to Ukraine's economy caused by worsening industrial relations with the Russian Federation. Anatoliy Kinah of the Ukrainian Union of Industrialists and Entrepreneurs also wrote an open letter requesting an urgent meeting. The suspension of Russian Federation certifications necessary to import products from Ukraine was impacting his members, he said, and similar problems were hurting the confectionery and chemical industries. A member of parliament from Yanukovych's Party of Regions announced that he had met with these organizations and proposed a one-year delay in signing the AA to give Ukrainian industry "more time to prepare" and to make the investments necessary to stay competitive.

In concert with these efforts, Prime Minister Azarov opened a cabinet meeting on November 13 stating that "the first question of our national policy is the normalization of relations with Russia. . . . I want everyone in Ukraine to realize that no one offered us and will not offer us compensation for the loss of this market. We cannot afford to shut down businesses, leaving our people without salaries and pensions."

On the same day, Foreign Minister Kozhara tried to project continuity in Ukraine's trajectory toward Europe, telling local press, "I believe that today we have met all preconditions for signing of the Association Agreement. . . . In our opinion, on the background of relations between 46 million Ukrainians and 500 million Europeans, the outstanding issues do not have defining political importance." Despite this bravado, or perhaps attempt at subterfuge, it was clear that Ukraine had not fulfilled the EU's requirements—not on Tymoshenko, not on reform, and not on transparency. Bills on all of these issues were tied up in the Verkhovna Rada, Ukraine's parliament. The Foreign Ministry seemed to be signaling that there might not be any more progress.

That day I was assigned to attend the daily 9:15 a.m. meeting with Ambassador Pyatt, who asked the Economic Section to find out what was going on with the "industrialists' revolt." We all started working the phones. Our contacts were sounding alarm bells. Jorge Zukoski, the bright and well-connected head of the American Chamber of Commerce in Kyiv, felt that the die had now been cast. Under his leadership, Kyiv's AmCham had become an eloquent voice for economic reform and transparency in Ukraine—not just for American companies but for many different foreign firms. AmCham was convinced that the AA would codify many of the reforms they'd been promoting for so many years. Jorge was unequivocal: "This is the day we lost Ukraine," he told us in an email. He speculated that the deciding factor was the EU's insistence on Tymoshenko's release, a deal breaker for Yanukovych. "Uncle Vlad put his checkbook on the table, and he pulled the strings at this decisive moment. . . . Years ago we all sat down and thought about what might happen if this goes south. We will all look back and lament the day we lost Ukraine. We are at that day now."

But elsewhere in Kyiv, Ukraine's zombie-like progress toward signing the AA was still proceeding, with officials and bureaucrats still following yesterday's marching orders. On November 18, Yanukovych's chief of staff, Serhiy Lyovochkin, ordered Foreign Minister Kozhara to have his Ministry prepare in final form all necessary documents so that Yanukovych could sign the AA in Vilnius in ten days' time. As late as November 20, Prime Minister Azarov told the press that the AA signing was still on: "Planned preparations for the Vilnius summit are finished, and in my opinion, everything is okay. . . . No, our plans have not changed."

The intensifying swirl of events was keeping us at work late most days. Everyone in the section, including me, spent our days talking to contacts on the phone, running around the city to meetings, and writing up any tidbits that seemed to shed light on the state of play to send back to Washington. The complex choreography of simultaneous steps toward and away from the AA was hard to follow. Throughout this period, those I spoke with in the Economic Section felt a sense of creeping pessimism. But honestly, we couldn't say what was coming. We had front row seats, but the complexity of the movements on stage kept anyone from knowing what was really transpiring in front of their own eyes.

Meanwhile, the IMF was no longer willing to hide their frustration with Ukraine. Unfortunately, their consternation came at the worst possible time. The Ukrainian economy was in huge trouble and likely heading for a crash. From Yanukovych's perspective, that crash must not happen before the planned presidential elections in 2015, which he expected to return him to office. Ukraine's foreign exchange reserves had fallen precipitously to around $19 billion; all the major economists predicted that if they fell below $15 billion, foreign investors would start to panic. Such predictions are often self-fulfilling. Russia's trade actions against Ukraine were beginning to bite, contributing to Ukraine's growing balance-of-payments problem. Also, Ukraine was facing large debt-servicing payments to external creditors, such as to the IMF, for its past financing. All of this was compounded by the amazing fact that an estimated 15 percent of the entire state budget was lost to procurement fraud. That's right—just stolen. Deputy Central Bank of Ukraine governor Mykola Udovychenko had told the US Embassy that Ukraine had "sixty to ninety days" until a huge crash if neither of its two prospective white knights—the EU/IMF or the Russian government—came to the rescue. Reuters analysts concluded that Ukraine would need $17 billion in the short term to avoid calamity. Russia was apparently offering $7 to $10 billion, plus more in gas discounts. In comparison, the EU was offering about $800 million in direct budget support. The serious money connected to the EU AA was supposed to come not from the EU directly but from the IMF. However, the IMF was a separate and independent organization that attached conditions to its funding—tough conditions intended to put countries back on the right economic footing. By now IMF officials felt increasingly burned and used by Ukraine, a country that rarely fulfilled its promises. Whereas an earnest pledge from other countries to shore up problematic aspects of their finances might suffice to free up some IMF cash, this was no longer the case for Ukraine. Burned and feeling duped, the IMF was not going to take Ukraine at its word anymore.

Negotiations with the IMF were led on the Ukrainian side by Deputy Prime Minister Arbuzov, a round-faced man from Donetsk in his thirties who had rocketed to the top since fellow Donetsk native Viktor Yanukovych became president. Arbuzov's mother, Valentyna Arbuzova, was a long-time banking and finance corporate leader and served as chair of Ukraine Business Bank. The younger Arbuzov followed in her footsteps. In December 2012, Arbuzov was made first deputy prime minister with a portfolio including integration with the EU and talks with the IMF.

During the ongoing dialogue between Ukraine and the IMF, the IMF made it clear that it was unwilling to loosen its purse strings unless Ukraine took immediate measures to put its own finances in order. This included ditching the exchange rate peg under which Ukraine had spent billions to prop up the hryvnia, ending the massive natural gas subsidies for households, improving the business climate, and starting "ambitious fiscal consolidation." Arbuzov had just traveled to Brussels and Washington, pleading that it was the wrong time for Ukraine's government to push hard on this list of demands as the Ukrainian economy was in jeopardy and could not survive such a shock. They could make some modest changes now, but these would inevitably fall far short of IMF demands. But Ukraine needed the money now, if not yesterday, of course. Such arguments likely sounded self-serving and disingenuous to IMF officials. In Ukraine, it was never the right time for tough reforms but always the right time for more cash.

On November 19, the answer to Arbuzov's entreaties arrived in a letter from IMF European Department director Reza Moghadam. Responding to Arbuzov's request for a "stand-in arrangement" under which Ukraine might get money to tide it over before meeting the IMF's conditions, Moghadam, condescendingly addressing the deputy prime minister as "Mr. Arbuzov," summarily dispatched the deputy prime minister's appeals: "In our view, overall the proposals still fall short of the decisive and comprehensive policy turnaround that is needed to reduce Ukraine's macroeconomic imbalances." In other words, stop whining. If further translation was required, "No new cash."

November 21, 2013, was a Thursday. I was representing the Econ section at the regular morning huddle, as David and Elizabeth were out. At these daily meetings, a local staff member would first deliver a briefing on the day's top news items, then leave the room before the detailed, and sometimes classified, discussion began. The ambassador, or the deputy chief of mission (DCM) if he was out, would kick off with a few thoughts or questions for the day, then each person around the circle would say what their section was focused on or anything mission leadership should know. There was nothing unusual that morning, and I returned to my desk after the meeting. The Ukrainian parliament had just passed a law amending Ukraine's parliamentary election law to meet EU standards. They were also still wrangling over Tymoshenko's fate, but that seemed par for the course. Nothing appeared more amiss than usual.

When dark news started to trickle in about the impending AA signing, our new ambassador, Geoffrey Pyatt, was visiting Dnipropetrovsk on one of his first major trips outside the capital after presenting his credentials to President Yanukovych on August 15. Elizabeth and fellow Economic Section officer Chris Greller were accompanying him. He met local leaders, students, civil society representatives, and business leaders, ending his visit at the city's iconic rocket design and manufacturing plant. His hosts, some brilliant Ukrainian rocket scientists and engineering company representatives, were enthusiastic about what a European future might hold and clearly explained to the ambassador how they planned to succeed in a European Ukraine. That was worth noting. Dnipropetrovsk had been a closed city in the Soviet era due to the sensitivity of nuclear ICBM and other defense manufacturing in the area. An outside observer might think that the predominantly Russian-speaking city leaned more to the east, toward Moscow, but that didn't seem to be true on the ground.

During a working lunch with Ukrainian aerospace company executives, Chris Greller's phone rang for the third time in rapid succession. It was Political Section Deputy Brad Parker. "Where is the ambassador?" he asked urgently. "You need to tell him right away that Yanu's not going to sign. Have him call us ASAP, and we'll give him the details. He needs to know; Yanu is not going to sign. Pull him out of whatever he's doing and let him know." Chris walked back in the conference room and quietly whispered Brad's message to the ambassador.

Ambassador Pyatt told the aerospace execs what he had just heard. Confused looks spread around the table. If this was true, the presentation they had just delivered a few minutes ago on their company's long-term planning should be trashed. The final portion of the tour was anticlimactic to say the least. The Embassy group quickly ended the tour and said their goodbyes, and the ambassador immediately started working his BlackBerry on the way to the airport. The short plane ride back to Kyiv would be the most peace and quiet they would get for a long time.

My own phone rang. "Yanu's not going to sign," said Elizabeth, calling in from her trip. "He's going to Vilnius but is supposedly delaying the signature. Find out what you can, we're putting together a report to send home to the mothership in the next few hours."

An avalanche of emails followed. I started calling friends and contacts. More confusion. He said he would delay? Until when? Can he do that? Yanukovych apparently had said that he still planned to sign eventually. Could that be true, or was it just a ruse? Would the Europeans simply give up in frustration or would they still accept Yanukovych's signature later? No one could answer any of these questions. It was like trying to predict the exact splat pattern of a watermelon dropped from the top of a ten-story building. All you know is that it is going to be a mess. The sinking feeling in the pit of my stomach mirrored my depressing thought that nothing will ever improve in Ukraine. There is no hope.

The order then appeared on the government's website: "[This decree is] to suspend the process of preparations for the conclusion of the Association Agreement between Ukraine, on the one part, and the European Union, the European Atomic Energy Community and its Member States, on the other part, and to suspend the decision of the Cabinet of Ministers of Ukraine dated September 18, 2013, on the preparation for the signing of the draft association agreement between Ukraine, on the one part, and the European Union and its member states, on the other part." Just to drive home the point, the order then decreed that Ukraine work with "CIS member states . . . in order to preserve jobs and settle other social issues on the basis of increasing the economic stability of state." The Ukrainian seesaw had just tilted toward Moscow. After the Putin-Yanukovych meetings in Sochi, it was not hard to guess whose weight had shifted the balance.

More details soon leaked out. On his way to the airport to fly to Vienna to meet with Austrian President Heinz Fischer, Yanukovych signed Cabinet Instruction 905-R ordering his government to stop all work on the AA for "reasons of national security." His national security adviser, Andriy Klyuyev, then rushed the document back to the Cabinet of Ministers. In Austria, standing next to the visibly shocked Austrian president, Yanukovych acknowledged that he signed the order but somehow also claimed that, "Ukraine has been and will continue to pursue the path of European integration. . . . We are carrying on our course." Really?

According to the Russian newspaper *Vedomosti* (*The Record*), Moscow officials were ecstatic and traced their "victory" back to the mysterious Putin-Yanukovych meeting earlier in the month: "It turned out beautifully—like stealing the bride at the altar. Everything changed after the meeting," they crowed. At the Embassy we speculated on what leverage Putin might have used to secure this outcome. Dirt on Yanukovych's criminal background? Threats to the Ukrainian economy? Most likely, we thought, there were threats to Yanukovych's personal income streams. That was a lever that Putin had in hand and would not hesitate to pull. But, of course, we didn't know.

The next day, our Public Affairs Section issued an official statement on Yanukovych's U-turn. "The United States joins the European Union in its disappointment with the decision of the Government of Ukraine to delay preparations for signature of an Association Agreement and Deep and Comprehensive Free Trade Agreement with the EU. The EU has offered Ukraine an historic opportunity to cement a European future for its people and demonstrate to international financial institutions and investors its unwavering commitment to democratic reform. . . . We stand with the vast majority of Ukrainians who want to see this future for their country, and we commend the EU for keeping the door open. The United States is convinced Ukraine's integration with Europe is the surest course to economic prosperity and democracy."

That was all we could do. We thought it was the wrong call for Ukraine, but it was the Ukrainian government's call to make, not ours. The US government would continue making the case for Ukraine's European future, but we could not undo Yanukovych's fait accompli. We were not at all surprised when Washington canceled Secretary of State Kerry's proposed trip. Just one more disappointment.

On Thursday night and into Friday morning, our local staff began noticing an increasing number of calls for a protest downtown on Saturday. It started when Mustafa Nayem, a young Kyiv-based journalist born in Kabul, wrote on his Facebook page, "Come on guys, let's be serious, don't just 'like' this post. Write that you are ready and we can try to start something." Receiving an overwhelming response, he suggested that young people upset with Yanukovych's abrupt U-turn meet downtown at Maidan. This is when I read the word *Euromaidan* for the first time in Facebook messages our staff forwarded to let us know what was circulating on social media. Its meaning was immediately clear—a pro-European version of the frequent protests on Kyiv's most important square. While the word *Maidan* literally just meant "the square," it was frequently associated with political protest. Protests there in 1989 and 2001 preceded the massive Orange Revolution protests on Maidan in 2004.

Valentyna told me that she wasn't familiar with any organization called Euromaidan. "It just seems to have sprung up after Yanukovych's announcement on the Association Agreement," she said. "The internet organizers are predicting a huge turnout, of course. We'll see what happens."

On Friday, RSO circulated a security notice on the demonstration, as they did routinely for all major demonstrations:

Rallies are expected to occur on Saturday and Sunday, November 23–24 at various locations in central Kyiv. The locations may include Shevchenko Park, European and Independence [Maidan] Squares. At this time, projected numbers of attendees range from ten to thirty thousand; attendance may fluctuate throughout the day and evening. If this occurs, there will likely be numerous unexpected road closures in and around the city center. RSO highly recommends that you be aware of your surroundings this weekend and avoid large groups, rallies, and demonstrations. Police presence may be significant.

In other words, stay away.

The Political Section was planning to send observers, but everyone else was supposed to avoid downtown. This was very standard advice from RSO—avoid crowds and trouble if at all possible. The same notice was then sent to American citizens registered as being in Ukraine. Stay away, have a quiet weekend.

Local press reports of 100,000 protesters were likely inflated, but it was definitely a large protest with tens of thousands of participants. I stayed glued to my BlackBerry, eager for the reports of our observers. Tim Piergalski, my colleague from the Political Section, sent an early message from downtown:

European Square is full of shoulder-to-shoulder people, with overflow onto the surrounding hillsides. The crowd is carrying opposition party, Ukrainian, and EU flags. The emphasis is much more for EU integra-tion than for Tymoshenko's freedom. . . . Police presence is relaxed, but busloads of Berkut riot police and "titushky" [hired thugs] are present in case of trouble. . . . Authorities appear concerned about the rally and are using a variety of tricks to suppress turnout and effectiveness. Halyna Fomenchenko of the European People's Party reported on Twitter that Ukrainian Democratic Alliance for Reforms (UDAR) leader Vitali Klitschko's plane was not allowed to land in Kyiv today to prevent his participation in the protest. Intercity buses are not being allowed to enter Kyiv. . . . Approximately 2,500 people (most of whom were bused in) are participating in the pro-GOU [government of Ukraine] counterprotest nearby. Our observers report that the [pro-government] crowd is not paying much attention to the band on stage, and the demonstrators appear to be just passing the time. The energy appears to be negative, unlike the positive energy among oppo-sition protesters. Another, smaller (a few hundred people) anti-LGBT protest is also taking place, with the crowd carrying signs saying that "EU = homosexuality."

Later in the evening, he added,

> Several thousand pro-EU protesters remain at European and Independence Squares. Opposition contacts expect 500 to 1,000 of them to camp out through the night in tents. All has been peaceful apart from earlier reports of tear gas near CabMin [Cabinet of Ministers] and one journalist from Fifth Channel reporting all of his equipment damaged after being dragged through CabMin yard. The atmosphere has remained mostly festive with music, open mic, etc.

That day I heard several terms for the first time. I learned that the Berkut (Eagles) was an elite group of riot police within the Interior Ministry who succeeded the feared OMON (special police) force of the Soviet era. While many members of the force that Ukraine's Interior Ministry had deployed on the streets were young, minimally trained conscripts, the Berkut were hardened, well-trained professionals. Titushky, on the other hand—named after the Ukrainian martial arts specialist Vadym Titushko—were hired street thugs, athletic young men who provided muscle for cash. Their calling cards were track or exercise clothes, leather jackets reeking of tobacco, and a penchant for violence.

That same day, on Moscow's Channel One TV, Ukrainian Prime Minister Azarov blamed Ukraine's about-face on the IMF letter: "The straw which broke the camel's back when we were weighing pro and con arguments was a letter from the International Monetary Fund link[ing] the granting of a credit—simply as part of servicing our debt—to a whole number of conditions that were absolutely unacceptable to Ukraine such as raising the tariffs for housing and utility services, freezing wages and pensions, abolishing agricultural subsidies, etc. . . . we could not accept these conditions."

Most of us at the Embassy didn't believe this. The IMF letter was a convenient excuse, a way to blame the whole debacle on the West. My colleagues seemed convinced that the turning point was the opaque Putin-Yanukovych meeting in Sochi on November 9, not the IMF letter.

The weekend's protests were remarkable enough that the international press, which rarely focused on Ukraine, took notice. By Monday, however, the crowds were dwindling even though student leaders had called for "strikes" to continue through the Vilnius summit on November 29. Kyiv's residents had made their point. Many were deeply upset, but by then the majority felt it was time to get back to work and move on. The majority of those remaining on the street were of the younger generation, including many students. Their elders, those with more responsibilities, returned to work and their regular lives. As the week progressed, a few protesters clashed with police. On Monday, a strange procession arrived in Maidan—a group of dour, scowling, darkly dressed people carrying LGBT rainbow flags and pro-European symbols. The Embassy's real LGBT contacts didn't recognize any of them, and pointed out that obviously someone was trying to "taint" the Euromaidan protesters by associating them with the gay community. Scrutinizing the miserable faces under the rainbow flags, I hoped that they were paid a lot more than the standard fee for hired demonstrators featured on the website Dr. Burakovsky had shown me in order to take on this particular assignment.

Later that day, we all gathered around a TV in the Embassy to watch Yanukovych address the nation:

> Nobody will steal our dream about a Ukraine of equal opportunities, a European Ukraine. Nobody will bring us away from the righteous way to this dream. . . . Economic problems have always existed and will always be our most difficult issue. But I would have been dishonest and unfair if I hadn't taken care of the most disadvantaged and vulnerable who are the first to suffer from the burden of the transition period. To put it mildly, I would have been wrong if I hadn't done everything necessary for people not to lose their jobs, receive salaries, pensions and scholarships.

Zhenya Vostrikova, who was among those watching, was our youngest Ukrainian staff member in the Economic Section and the most in touch with the feeling of students and others out on the square. After Yanukovych finished, I asked her, "So, do you think Yanukovych's message will work?" "No," she answered plainly. There was really nothing else to say.

Soon after, Valentyna told me, "There's an article you really should read. It's called 'The Authoritarian Government: The Path to Ruin,' by former parliamentarian and economic analyst Volodymyr Lanovyi, who writes for *Ekonomichna Pravda* [*Economic Truth*]. He traces a lot of the corruption patterns in Ukraine in the article and names names. A lot of people are talking about it. We should set up a meeting and talk to him."

We did so. When we met Lanovyi in a small café and bakery, he was full of facts and figures, names and dates. A virtual encyclopedia of corruption, he was fascinating to talk with. Toward the end of our conversation, his voice darkened. "You should know that our country right now is in a pre-revolutionary phase. The social fabric is loose, and there will be consequences. There are social forces right now, already unleashed, which will lead to major social upheaval. What is coming is probably more serious than the Orange Revolution. Society is more fed up."

Valentyna and I returned to the Embassy where I had to write up the meeting. Should I include Lanovyi's apocalyptic prediction that a revolution was in the immediate offing? I was afraid that if I included it, that would likely discredit a lot of the rest of what he said. I decided to leave it out. After following my issues closely for a year-and-a-half, I thought that Ukraine's choice of its future path was a matter to be hashed out in the economic and diplomatic space. Talk about revolutions, military actions, and other hardcore security stuff would make us and Lanovyi sound like hyperventilating alarmists or conspiracy theorists. Despite all that was going on, the notion that things were progressing to the point of revolution or foreign military intervention was impossible to imagine.

With Thanksgiving a day away, Valentyna and I visited the CIS Institute to check in with Maksim Maksimov. He was in a great mood, visibly elated over Ukraine's turn away from the AA. "Of course Russia was very happy to hear of the Ukrainian government's suspension of EU integration," he began. "Putin instructed his government and our media to stop criticizing Ukraine and Yanukovych in particular. You might have noticed that our Ukraine-related rhetoric became neutral and 'loyal' in recent days."

He waved away my question of how Russia turned the tide on this question. "Only one person, President Yanukovych, was behind this decision. People very close to him say he was very upset about how European leaders have been treating him . . . he never forgives insults. He is a vindictive, vengeful person. He decided that it was EU disrespect which drove them to keep pestering him on the Tymoshenko issue. He felt that Europe placed their bets on Tymoshenko and didn't see him as being president anymore after 2015. This is what really made him take a step back on the Association Agreement. What your newspapers print about Russian pressure is an exaggeration and a myth."

"Assuming that Yanukovych doesn't sign in Vilnius tomorrow, Russia can begin to supply Ukraine with significant financial support," he noted. "You realize that we already have enough Russian capital in Ukraine so that we could have collapsed the country's banking system if they would have signed the EU agreement? That was the plan. But we're in a better place now. No need for punishments," he concluded triumphantly.

I just leaned back and smiled, taking it all in. The day before, Putin had claimed publicly that Ukrainian governmental organizations and private firms owed $28 billion to Russia. Now Maksimov was blithely mentioning the weaponization of Russian capital to shiv Ukraine's banking system. And he had the audacity to assert that pressure from Moscow was an exaggeration and a myth? All I could do was just smile and keep listening.

The protests that began in Kyiv spread. Large Euromaidan protests broke out in Lviv and Ivano-Frankivsk in Western Ukraine; another was dispersed by police in the eastern city of Dnipropetrovsk. In the southern city of Mykolaiv, protests were banned. A fifth-grade teacher reportedly distributed leaflets to her students saying they would be taken from their parents and killed to harvest their organs or gifted to same-sex couples in Europe if Ukraine signed the AA. Odesa banned protests and locked all outdoor toilets as a "precaution." Meanwhile back in Kyiv, Euromaidan activists told newspapers about their phones being hacked and blocked, their home phones jammed, and opposition political party websites being "pwned" and used to send out misleading messages about the end of Euromaidan.

Nevertheless, the EU still had not abandoned hope that the mercurial Yanukovych might make yet another radical U-turn, maybe this time in their direction. Usually well-informed members of Yanukovych's delegation apparently did not know what was going to happen. Why was Yanukovych still going to Vilnius, anyway? If he intended to do nothing, engage in no negotiation, then why not just stay home and avoid angry confrontations with the people he had recently betrayed? Wasn't there still hope?

EU Commission president José Manuel Barroso brought one last surprise to the meeting with Yanukovych: he said that the EU was ready to drop its insistence on the release of Yuliya Tymoshenko as a condition for signing the AA. This concession was facilitated by Tymoshenko herself, who, one week earlier, had said that the EU should not block the AA due to her imprisonment. But Yanukovych was unmoved. That die had already been cast. There had been some speculation that Yanukovych might sign a face-saving document in Vilnius setting out a new schedule for the AA. Instead, he signed nothing.

In Kyiv, news that Vilnius had ended in failure heightened tensions. During the afternoon and evening of Friday, November 29, about 10,000 protesters were in the square, hemmed in on all sides by police. The Embassy received an email that journalists from Hromadske.tv and Channel 5 were attacked by titushky. Opposition leaders, back from a trip to Vilnius to make what turned out to be a futile, last-minute appeal to Yanukovych, were blocked by police as they tried to return to the square. By this time, Ukraine's three main opposition leaders—Arseniy Yatsenyuk, heading Yuliya Tymoshenko's Batkivshchyna (Fatherland) party during her imprisonment, former boxer and UDAR Party leader Vitali Klitschko, and the nationalist party Svoboda's leader Oleh Tyahnybok—were apparently on the periphery of the demonstrations. Their parties supported the demonstrations, but they had not been responsible for calling them and did not seem to be in any position to control them. By around 2:00 a.m. the following morning, only around four hundred protesters, mostly youth, remained encamped on the square.

Earlier that night, I turned to an American colleague at the Embassy who I thought was uniquely qualified to peer into the opaque future. John Bush, who had joined our Economic Section a few months earlier, was assigned the vital energy portfolio. Ever since Ukraine's tussle with Russia over natural gas had threatened Europe's energy supplies a few years earlier, the energy beat was seen as a crucial and high-pressure assignment. John was no stranger to high-pressure situations, as could be seen by the fact that he brought his wife and five sons with him to Kyiv. Most important, he was the only American at the Embassy who had been in Ukraine at the time of the Orange Revolution during his days as a missionary when he had camped in a tent on the Maidan. Our section was empty apart from us, and it was a good opportunity to talk.

"John," I asked, on that fateful Friday after Thanksgiving, "You think this protest on the AA will lead to anything?" "No," he replied. "The Ukrainians are too accustomed to being sold out at this point. They almost expect it. They are still too burned out by the failure of the Orange Revolution. I'm sure these kids who are sleeping in tents are disappointed, but they'll just go home sooner or later. Probably sooner."

It made sense to me. I nodded, and agreed. All the apathy I had encountered in Ukraine led me to believe that folks would soon return to their more typical state of indifference. Had President Yanukovych and his cronies not made a brutally ham-fisted blunder, John and I likely would have been right.

5

BLOOD-STAINED GRANITE

Blood on the granite paving stones of Maidan; blood at the foot of St. Michael's Cathedral. Overnight, everything changed.

At about 4:00 a.m. an estimated two thousand riot police entered Maidan to forcibly evict the several hundred protesters still camped out on the square. Despite Ambassador Pyatt's strong messages to Yanukovych urging him not to use violence, Berkut, carrying shields and wielding truncheons, bore down on the sleeping protesters—the majority of them college kids. Police and security officials cut off the cell phone network downtown to prevent calls for help or reinforcements. By morning, disturbing videos circulated on the internet of unarmed youth huddled together to protect themselves from Yanukovych's centurions who were beating them mercilessly with batons. We all knew that during the Orange Revolution in 2004, Yanukovych implored then president Kuchma to use force against protesters. Now with the reins of power in his own hands, Yanukovych followed his own advice.

Pop singer Ruslana, a young musical hero in Ukraine with long dark hair, was running for cover and sending out desperate text messages while huddled with injured students that night. She had won the 2004 Eurovision song competition with her rendition of "Wild Dances," and she remained a tremendously popular figure in Ukraine. Ruslana led a group of about two hundred students fleeing from the Maidan that was under attack by Yanukovych's marching battalions the few hundred yards to seek sanctuary in St. Michael's Cathedral. Who would have thought that the medieval tradition of seeking sanctuary in churches would be needed again in the twenty-first century? Police later attempted to break down the cathedral doors to arrest the students. Police spokesperson Olha Bilyk tried to justify this breach of a centuries-old tradition by telling journalists that the action was necessary because the protesters were interfering with the city's Christmas preparations on the square. The imperative of installing an oversize fake Christmas tree and setting up an ice rink was the public justification for the vicious assault on students.

I had heard that Oleh Voloshyn, the sandy-haired adviser to the deputy prime minister who had given us some hope regarding intellectual property rights issues, had left government about a month earlier. Since I had known him to be a faithful and effective member of the Yanukovych team, I was astonished to read his email that morning: "Last night the Yanukovych government effectively crossed all red lines. He used violence against peaceful protesters. We count on the world community to put as much pressure on this government as possible. You know I was working for that government thinking I served my country. Now I have no doubt this government has lost its moral right to represent my country in international relations. We'll fight for our rights here. Support us worldwide. They must feel their isolation and full loss of perspectives. Freedom will survive." It was an anguished cry and a clarion call.

As the hours passed, about five thousand protesters gathered outside St. Michael's Cathedral while Kyiv's regular police stood by calmly at a respectful distance. Our Embassy quickly issued a statement: "The United States condemns the violence against protesters on Independence Square early this morning. We urge the government of Ukraine to respect the rights of civil society and the principles of freedom of speech and freedom of assembly which are fundamental to the democratic values that are the bedrock of our strategic partnership." Condemnations of the government's violence rolled in from the EU, Patriarch Filaret of the Kyiv Patriarchy of the Ukrainian Orthodox Church, and even Viktor Medvedchuk—head of the pro-Russian Ukraine's Choice party, whose daughter's godfather was none other than Vladimir Putin. We heard that Yanukovych's chief of staff Serhiy Lyovochkin had offered his resignation, though it was not accepted.

Political Section deputy Brad Parker sent out an email to political and economic officers:

> First off thanks to everyone who braved the cold to observe goings-on at St. Michaels, Maidan, and points in between. Ops [The State Department Operations Center] has been well fed with info today. For tonight and tomorrow, Ambo and DCM [deputy chief of mission] have asked that we coordinate our observation effort: we go out in pairs, check in periodically on whereabouts, and space out our coverage, in shifts. . . . For tomorrow, I propose that we set up a schedule of two-person teams going out for two hour shifts, starting at 11, to cover Maidan and St. Mike's. Doug and I can take the first shift. Email me with your preferred shift time and partner. I will fill in the slots and send out a schedule later this evening. For tonight, please let me know if and when you head out and when you are back home.

I quickly responded to Brad. My Economic Section colleague John Bush, who had witnessed the Orange Revolution, and I would head out at 7:00 p.m. the following night to observe. Now I would have an opportunity to see things with my own eyes.

Early that Sunday morning my cell phone rang, cutting through my heavy sleep. It was a recording of a man giving a speech in Ukrainian to a crowd. Between the early hour and the language issue, I didn't get much of it, but it ended with loud chants of "Ukraine to Europe!" repeated after each cry by a crowd. Was Euromaidan now doing robocalls? It sounded like someone was planning for a big day.

On Sunday, December 1, some protesters commandeered a bulldozer that was parked on Maidan and drove it to the Presidential Administration building on Bankova Street to attempt to pull down its barricades. A street fight between riot police, protesters, and possibly government-paid provocateurs on Bankova got ugly fast. All day, our email was flooded with reports of huge protest movements. One thousand people here, two thousand there. Journalists beaten and injured at Bankova. Fifty-three protesters injured with thirteen hospitalized, while the press reported thirty-five police wounded. Elizabeth wrote to everyone in our section: "The situation is very fluid and getting dangerous around city hall and Bankova. Please do not venture there at the moment. Is everyone at home and accounted for?" I was actually at the mall with my two children, aged eight and four, where everything seemed conspicuously normal. Throughout the protests, events in Kyiv stayed extremely localized within a radius of several city blocks. Outside that small perimeter, it was difficult to tell that this was a city being torn apart. Nevertheless, my mind was constantly grinding on what was going on downtown, especially as I knew I was heading there that night. I thought about the fear, stress, chaos, and desperation I expected to see that night. I spent the late afternoon hours at the Embassy reading the latest news, then climbed into the silver family Saturn Vue for Maidan. John and I had agreed to meet at the McDonald's in the northwest corner of Maidan. What more logical place for Americans to rendezvous?

Walking toward Maidan, I saw protesters on St. Michael's Square hauling in and stacking up firewood. That cold night I would be sleeping in my warm bed; they would be sleeping on freezing granite paving stones. A young man with a makeshift Ukrainian yellow and blue ribbon around his arm, a serious expression on his face, and armed only with a whistle, was managing the flow of cars and pedestrians. He didn't look like a police officer. I met John a few minutes later and mentioned the young traffic guard.

"I saw the same thing during the Orange Revolution," John said. "If someone gets hit by a car or if things look too disorderly, that gives authorities the excuse to intervene. So they police themselves. Avoiding 'provocations' is a key part of this for them."

Provocations (*provokatsiya*) became the topic of the night, a word on the lips of all the protesters. We spoke to some young women outside the Maidan McDonald's, decked out in Ukrainian colors and EU ribbons. "Did you see those videos from Bankova today?" they asked. "There were some protesters there, but who the hell were the guys throwing rocks? Swinging chains? Wearing bandanas over their faces? That's not us. That's *provokatsiya*." As we were walking through the square, another young man handed us a flyer in Ukrainian emphasizing nonviolence and avoiding *provokatsiya*.

We walked across the square, past young men repairing tents torn during the Berkut assault, over to where Institutska Street heads from the square up a hill toward Bankova and the presidential administration. Someone had hacked the massive Jumbotron over the square, which had only yesterday shown images of a smiling Kyiv mayor Oleksandr Popov planting trees. Now, there were only images of waving Ukrainian and EU flags glowing blue and yellow down on the square. That the Ukrainian and EU flags were the same two basic colors made for some great visuals. We went to talk with a group of young men pushing pallets together and binding them with wire. "We're from UDAR," they said, referring to the Ukrainian Democratic Alliance for Reforms, the political party of boxer Vitali Klitschko. "Lots of the provocateurs are still up on Bankova, and we have to keep them off the square. They'll start fights with police from inside the square like they did up there, and that can't happen."

Suddenly the wailing sound of an approaching ambulance was growing louder. The men swung into action, clearing a way through the barricades for the ambulance to drive down onto the Maidan. As soon as it had passed, they swung back into motion, replacing that section of barricade. Smiling broadly, the young man we were speaking with came back over to me. "Less than sixty seconds to take down a serious obstacle and put back up," he noted proudly. "Now tell me, what do you think of these guys? The best, right?"

Walking down Khreshchatyk Street, we heard a number of loud bangs— maybe fireworks, maybe flash grenades. No one seemed alarmed. John and I walked all the way down to Besarabska Square where a statue of Lenin loomed as a reminder of the not-too-distant past. People on the street were talking about provocations around the Lenin statue, saying that masked people had attacked it and fought the Berkut. When we arrived, there was no fighting. A single row of Berkut circled the statue, a threatening contingent fitting for a Bolshevik leader who never hesitated ordering violence. But now, the pedestal on which Lenin's feet were planted was spray-painted with the words "Slava Ukraini" (glory to Ukraine). For the time being Lenin still stood there impassive.

As we walked up Institutska toward the scene of earlier clashes that day at the Presidential Administration building, we saw an instantly recognizable figure standing on the back of a pickup truck. It was Vitali Klitschko, the towering boxer-turned-politician, arguing passionately with a group of young men. We heard him imploring the young men to return to Maidan. Most were respectful, but one kid was heckling him from the back. "Go back to your million dollar home, Klitschko," he yelled. "Look at you, you corrupted politician. How do you even understand what we're fighting for here?"

Klitschko jumped down and sprinted toward the heckler, the crowd parting like sheep before a predator. Suddenly, they were yelling at each other, inches away from each other's faces, spittle flying. It was easy to distinguish

Klitschko, about a foot taller than anyone else, from the rest of the crowd. Klitschko was not afraid of engaging in crisis politics at the retail level. I probably wouldn't be either if I had his stature and street skills. But the confusion of the evening was underlined by the fact that he was imploring these guys to return to Maidan even as his own political party was building barricades around the square to keep people like them out.

Meanwhile, a strange, beatific calm prevailed on Maidan. The feel of this crowd was entirely different from those gathered just one block away. College girls, draped in Ukrainian flags like capes, circulated through the crowd, handing out paper cups of hot tea. Somewhere in the distance an unseen Ukrainian band played folk music. Stickers in Ukrainian announced, "No one pays me to be here" and "I'm not leaving Maidan." The orange-helmeted men of the Self-Defense Force (SDF) were objects of evident respect. I had expected to overhear conversations about when the next assault on the square would come. Instead, the conversations were much more philosophical. "What is Ukraine?" "Who are we, what makes us unique?" "How did we get to this point, and what now?"

Certain slogans heralded the rapidly developing culture of Maidan. One constant refrain was "Bandu Het" (out with the bandits). When someone greeted you with the words, "Slava Ukraini" (glory to Ukraine), you were supposed to respond, "Heroyam Slava" (glory to the heroes). These greetings could be heard constantly on the square.

Suddenly, there was a great honking cacophony from the direction of Khreshchatyk Street. The crescendo of car horns was met with cheers from the denizens of Maidan, or Maidanivtsi. Hot-footing it over toward the revelry, I witnessed "Automaidan" for the first time. Dozens of cars drove down Kreshchatyk, festooned with Ukrainian colors and EU ribbons. People were leaning out the rear windows of the cars, waving flags and trying to work up the crowd, which seemed to know them already.

"They can take our protest anywhere in the city at a moment's notice," one young man who was cheering by the roadside told us. "Without Automaidan, Yanukovych could just make Maidan into a little ghetto and try to forget about us. With them, we can be anywhere. Did you know," he said with suppressed pride and a sly smile, "they took a little drive up to Mezhyhirya?"

Mezhyhirya, Yanukovych's 350-acre luxury estate on the banks of the Dniepro River, was a symbol of mystery, corruption, and shameless opulence. This prime real estate was government property until 2007, when firms related to Yanukovych purchased it for an undisclosed price during a privatization deal. An investigative report in the newspaper *Ukrayinska Pravda* revealed the dirty details of the shady transaction, as well as highlighting the property's amenities including a yacht pier, hunting grounds, equestrian club, and other facilities. The rare sports car collection was said to be really impressive. It all smacked of a monarchy rather than a democratic republic.

Our observation shift was over. It was time to go home. "So, what's your take, John?" I asked. "Sustainable protest movement or intellectualized antigovernment-themed street party?"

"Both," he slowly answered. "Maybe both."

It was only the beginning.

Driving home, I realized that my expectations of the mood on the square—fear and stress—were completely wrong. True, the scene around Institutska was tense, but on the square, there were more warm smiles and friendly conversation among strangers than I had ever seen in Ukraine. It was a unique feeling. Despite everything that had happened during the day and the certainty of more hardships to come, people were not hunkering down. It was more like they were getting reacquainted with each other as a nation and a people after a period of internal estrangement. Early December was an unusual time to find warmth outdoors in Kyiv, but there it was, in spades.

There would be no business as usual as a new work week began. More than 10,000 protesters remained on Maidan. Washington's demands for information increased exponentially as did the need for note takers at the ambassador's endless meetings around town. The information overload from social media and other sources, much of it flawed, biased, or irrelevant, was crushing. To channel the deluge, a "Kyiv Task Force" was established in the Embassy on Monday. From 8:00 a.m. to 10:00 p.m., an experienced officer would serve as "editor" of our regular updates to Washington. A public affairs officer would look at global press reports, another from the US Agency for International Development (USAID) and someone from the consular section would cover their basket of issues, and a local staff member would monitor local press and provide translations as needed. Monday's schedule only ran until Thursday, with Thursday's assignments marked "if necessary." We all thought that the current situation would be over soon, but we could only guess at how it would end. Maybe Yanukovych would agree to some concessions and diffuse the situation. Maybe he would strike a true deal with the opposition. Or maybe he would clear the square violently, and we would be living in a new, openly authoritarian version of Ukraine, filing reports on the slow, creeping repression of the Maidanivtsi. When the Kyiv Task Force hit send on the situation report, "Kyiv SitRep #1," that Monday, none of us would have believed that seven months later we would be issuing "Kyiv SitRep #304." We were doubtful there would still be a need for the Task Force that Thursday.

Shortly after the Task Force was established, an email distribution list was created that became the shortcut for all crisis-related communications. Blasted out through the list were dozens of small news developments each hour, observation reports from downtown, task force updates, requests from the ambassador, questions from Washington, and answers to Washington and the ambassador. The distribution list ballooned as additional people were added, not just nearly everyone at the Embassy, the Ukraine desk, and the European Bureau chain of command but also from throughout the US government. "KyivTaskForce" quickly became both the focus and the bane of our existence as we struggled to sort through and comprehend the hundreds of daily messages.

Meanwhile, Maidan was changing physically. Protesters continued to construct ramshackle barricades all around the Maidan, which is at the confluence of six streets. Defending it wasn't simple, and more tents were cropping up hourly. The protesters had brought in a large stage and sound system that generated new traditions, such as frequent singing of the national anthem. Leaders of the political opposition occasionally spoke from the stage but didn't control access to it. That was the power of Maidan's informal leaders, and they decided who used the stage and for what purpose. Local clergy increasingly ascended the stage to lead the crowds in prayer and deliver sermons. The half-assembled, multistory, artificial Christmas tree on Maidan was a special target of protester attention after police spokesmen invoked the need to erect the tree and a small ice rink as an excuse for the initial assault against protesters. After retaking the square, Maidanivtsi began hanging flags and slogans on the skeleton of the metal tree, transforming it into an early symbol of Euromaidan. Pieces of the unassembled ice rink were repurposed as barricades. Protesters were now operating out of two buildings, Kyiv's city hall and the large Trade Unions Building on Maidan that we referred to as the TUB. The Federation of Trade Unions of Ukraine willingly permitted protesters to use their building, but their presence at city hall was more contentious. During the Orange Revolution, Kyiv's city hall had been a protest headquarters. Although seizing it was not legal, that precedent conferred an aura of legitimacy as a venue for large protests in the city.

Meanwhile, a few blocks away from Maidan, an "anti-Maidan" counter-demonstration in Mariinsky Park attracted from several hundred to as many as five thousand people. Other parts of the city were also becoming sites of protest. Students picketed the Ministry of Education to oppose its efforts to identify students involved in Euromaidan; protesters congregated outside courts, which issued orders for them to vacate government buildings. Demonstrations also took place at the Prosecutor General's Office to oppose its numerous cases against protesters. The suburb of Vasylkiv was yet another site of confrontation as protesters attempted to block the gates of a barracks housing troops they believed had been ordered to assault Maidan, though no one seemed clear on the source of the information.

Embassy Public Affairs Officer Eric Johnson, one of my first Foreign Service bosses years before in Estonia, lived close to Maidan and was a frequent and keen observer of downtown developments. That week he wrote,

> The organic world that is Occupy Maidan [OM, another name for Euromaidan] continues to grow, diversify, and evolve. Its tent city has spread into the streets as OM adds more permanent residents thanks to a steady influx of new immigrants from across Ukraine. The tent city has its own UDAR, Batkivshchyna, and Svoboda neighborhoods as well as those devoted to Ukraine's many regions. There is even an inner "volunteers only" sanctum. City hall and the Trade Union Building are hives of activity. As OM has demarcated its borders with lines painted on the pavement, it now has its first suburb set up by the Democratic Alliance flying its own banners—with OM but not of OM. OM's almost forgotten outpost at St. Michael's still hangs on by a thread with perhaps a hundred citizens inside and outside of the monastery's walls. Those outside the walls are huddled around two oil drums for warmth. They watch as about a hundred visiting students appear to be re-enacting events of days past near Olha's statue for a student documentary film. Back at the heart of OM, a small chapel has appeared with clergy administering to the faithful. Commercial food trucks compete with soup kitchens to feed the growing masses.

The field hospital sends its medics out on patrol to make sure that all of OM's citizens and visitors are doing well. Tonight, the specialization reached new levels as I watched volunteer garbage men hauling trash to a waiting city garbage truck. Although I expected everyone in OM to be somber and depressed after today's earlier political debacle, the mood was impressively positive and upbeat. In front of the stage, there must have been over ten thousand (if not more) OM visitors and residents enjoying the latest free concert by yet another popular Ukrainian musician. The self-organizing world that is OM lives on following a parallel trajectory to its self-proclaimed leaders. I wonder what new discoveries tomorrow will bring.

Euromaidan was a multidimensional phenomenon. Underground, the multistory Globus shopping mall ran beneath the length of Maidan, which made the Euromaidan demonstrations perhaps the most important political event ever to take place on the roof of a shopping mall. Strange as it seems, the mall stayed open throughout these events. Protesters sometimes descended underground into the mall to warm up in the restaurants or spend a few minutes chatting while walking through racks of designer clothes. Surreally, nothing that happened above ground seemed to impact subterranean shoe or gelato sales.

Meanwhile, even as the new world of Euromaidan was taking shape in and around the square, the old world of Ukrainian politics continued to revolve around its wobbly axis. For the time being these two worlds coexisted uneasily in parallel orbits. While a no confidence vote against his government was in the process of failing in the Verhovna Rada, Yanukovych himself gave TV interviews. He vowed to investigate the November 30 attack on the square but also said he would hold the political opposition responsible for recently using students as "human shields." To project a semblance of business as usual, he said he would not cancel his upcoming trip to China. Media reported that the feared Prosecutor General's Office had asked prestigious Shevchenko National University to provide information on students and professors who haven't attended classes during the protests. The hacker collective "Anonymous" announced that it would start leaking stolen Ukrainian government documents. New flyers on Maidan advocated a boycott against companies owned by members of Yanukovych's Party of Regions. Protesters remained in Kyiv's city hall, but they allowed municipal civil servants back inside to work in an uncomfortable sharing of space.

New political fault lines across Ukraine surfaced as regional capitals reacted differently to the developing situation in Kyiv. Ivano-Frankivsk voluntarily opened its city hall to protesters while the city council in Sevastopol, Crimea, passed a resolution stating that Ukraine should join the Russian-backed Customs Union. But there were small Euromaidan rallies even in the eastern cities of Donetsk and Lugansk. Donetsk's Automaidan was especially active. In Crimea, the "Mejlis of the Crimean Tatar People," the most important body representing the Crimean Tatars, issued a statement of solidarity with Euromaidan and demanded the immediate resignation of Ukraine's Cabinet of Ministers.

As always playing both sides, Yanukovych dispatched one deputy prime minister to negotiate with the EU and another to negotiate with Moscow. As we all expected, Yanukovych's ballyhooed trip to China was a bust. Agreements signed were said to be worth $8 billion to Ukraine, but most of these so-called agreements were just innocuous memoranda of understanding with no binding power. The Chinese remained noncommittal regarding any new loans.

Meanwhile, the Kremlin made its position increasingly clear. Before Yanukovych's meeting with Putin in Sochi on December 6, the Russian media's critical stance on the Kyiv protests was hardening. Russian conspiracy theorists were having a field day. Moscow's NTV ran an "exposé" blaming our Embassy's TechCamp and "foreign activism" for the Euromaidan protests. During a trip earlier that week to Armenia, Putin himself said that "outside actors" played a large role in the demonstrations in Ukraine and called Euromaidan "more of a pogrom [a violent riot] than a revolution." Even more menacingly, the most prominent of the Kremlin's surrogate politicians in Ukraine, Viktor Medvedchuk, the leader of Ukraine's Choice, stated that it was now a "fact" that "Ukraine is splintering."

Late in the week, a corpse was found on Maidan near the entrance to the Globus underground shopping mall. After an autopsy, health officials announced that the man had died from a virulent form of antibiotic-resistant tuberculosis. Ukraine's deputy minister of health quickly warned about the possible spread of infectious diseases on Maidan. The message was clear—you or your children can get sick and die at Maidan. Protest organizers claimed that the man had been dropped at the square near death or already dead as a scare tactic, and that they had not seen him at any protest activities. The truth of the matter was beyond us.

Despite the deepening instability in Kyiv, Ukraine was still scheduled to host a major international diplomatic event—the Twentieth Organization for Security and Co-operation in Europe (OSCE) Ministerial. After the November 30 attacks on Maidan, Secretary of State Kerry and many other high-level officials had canceled their own participation. In Kerry's place, Assistant Secretary of State for the European Bureau Victoria (Toria) Nuland headed the US delegation. Especially as so few high-level visitors came to Ukraine now, her visit was a big deal. During her short time in Kyiv, she met top Ukrainian government officials and opposition leaders, urging compromise on all sides, and promised to return soon. As a young woman in 1982, she had worked at a summer camp in Ukraine outside of Odesa. The rank and file at our Embassy were about to get to know our assistant secretary a lot better.

Even as events were unfolding on Maidan, there was routine Embassy work to attend to. Since our last encounter, Maksim Maksimov had hounded me to attend an event at his CIS Institute. I willingly agreed since the conference was supposed to focus on the Shanghai Cooperation Organization, a fascinating organization I had become interested in during my tour of duty in Beijing because of its importance to the Russia-China relationship. I remember mentioning my interest to Maksim, and, voilà, here was an event.

It was the first major snowfall of the year, and traffic on the way to the Commonwealth of Independent States (CIS) Institute was horrendous. Arriving about fifteen minutes late, Valentyna and I rushed into a dimly lit meeting room in which tables had been set up in a large rectangle with name plates for each speaker. An older gentleman was speaking. I eased into my seat and glanced around the room at the sparse attendees: a few elderly professors with stodgy fashion senses (judging from their baggy suits, which were clearly vestiges of the Soviet era) and a handful of diplomats from post-Soviet embassies—Russia, Armenia, Kazakhstan. There were fewer than a dozen in all. I listened to their desultory presentations, which included some anti-American diatribes whose expiration dates should have long since passed along with the Cold War. Several times Maksimov offered me the chance to speak, but I had come just to listen. I thanked him but declined the invitation.

After an hour-and-a-half of tedium and tired anti-American conspiracy theories, Maksimov invited everyone into his office. Unlike the dingy conference room, it was a large, wood-paneled, inviting space. After making sure each of us was supplied with a glass of Moldovan wine, Maksimov offered an anodyne toast: "To friendship and new beginnings," to which we all raised our glasses. At that point the Russian Embassy official standing next to me handed me his card. An older gentleman who spoke flawless English, he was listed as a "Senior Counselor" to the Russian ambassador in Kyiv—a prestigious title that meant nothing, only vaguely hinting at his likely affiliation with the FSB [Federal Security Service], Russia's successor to the notorious Soviet KGB—the training ground where Vladimir Putin had learned his craft. Real diplomats generally are assigned to real embassy sections. But that wasn't the case here.

"It is very nice to meet you," he opened. "You know, I've spent quite a bit of time in the United States. Quite a nice country—I enjoyed it a lot." As he continued describing his time in the United States, complimenting the American people while throwing in occasional barbs at the US government, we seemed increasingly isolated in Maksimov's large office as others migrated to the other side of the room. One participant ensnared Valentyna in a lengthy conversation.

"So, have you spent much time in Russia? What are some of your impressions? Do you have Russian friends?" my interlocutor fired a salvo of questions at me. "Yes—I spent time there in college," I responded. As I spoke, I noticed other participants in the room darting glances at us. It suddenly occurred to me that our conversation was the main event and possibly the real reason why everyone had been assembled.

"So, a lot is happening in Ukraine right now," the Russian continued, finally getting more to the point. "What really interests me is this—does your government seek the removal of Yanukovych? Is that a US goal?" "No," I responded, unequivocally. "We've had our share of issues with the Yanukovych government, and are very concerned about the corruption in his team. But he was democratically elected, and he should leave according to the ballot box as well. We're not in the business of seeking the ouster of democratically elected leaders."

I said this because it was true. While the lengthy record of US interventions in Latin America will forever be cited by those seeking to label the United States a serial meddler, I wasn't working for the Eisenhower administration. I had seen no evidence that anyone in the US government was interested in taking heavy-handed actions of any sort in Ukraine. On the contrary, Yanukovych's corruption caused a disappointed Washington to step back from the relationship and increasingly ignore Ukraine. No one wanted to get more involved. We didn't want to break it; we didn't want to buy it. Wishing the Ukrainian people well, we just wanted the Ukrainian government to get its act together at last.

The Russian diplomat and I spoke for about a half hour. No one interrupted us or attempted to join the conversation. Even assuming that my every word would be quickly reported back to Moscow, I didn't find it difficult to engage him, but nothing I said even mildly dented his paranoid conviction that the United States was somehow driving Euromaidan. I knew that was not the case. Our truthful message to Moscow and everyone else was one and the same. When our inconclusive conversation finished, Maksimov brought everyone together for one more toast, then broke up the event.

As the Embassy driver took us back to the office, Valentyna leaned over. "You know who you were probably talking to?" she asked. "Yes." "OK, just as long as you know," she said. "Let's try not to make another appointment there for a while. It's a bit disturbing."

For my previous assignment in Beijing, I had invested a lot of my life studying Chinese. Now, to keep up my rapidly rusting Mandarin, I tried to make appointments regularly with the Chinese trade mission in Kyiv. Despite the injuries I unintentionally inflicted on his language, the trade counselor seemed pleased to speak in his own language with a struggling foreigner.

Our conversations were more than language study as the Ukraine-China connection was of professional and personal interest. Despite turmoil at home, Yanukovych had kept a previously scheduled three-day trip to Beijing, which started on December 3. Ukrainian newspapers, and even some observers in the United States, expected that the cash-rich Chinese would jump in and rescue the Ukrainians from their self-inflicted fiscal calamities, and that China would supplement, and maybe even surpass, Russia as Ukraine's partner. But in 2013, this was nonsense. To be sure, the Chinese had just signed over $7 billion in deals with Ukraine which sounds impressive, but only $80 million of that was likely to be realized. The rest was tied up in corruption hell. China had given Ukraine about $1.5 billion at the start of a massive "Loans for Corn" arrangement under which China would provide Ukraine massive financing in exchange for regular shipments of corn. The large Chinese down payment was transferred into the Ukrainian pension fund, where it vanished. One Ukrainian official told me, "The deal allowed the Ukrainian side to pick a partner in China for the corn imports, so our guys went around China trying to find out who would give them the biggest kickback in exchange for the contract. They found a pretty good deal for themselves, but after they got the kickback cash from the Chinese, they demanded a still bigger cut. Then the Chinese company balked, and kind of entered a Mexican standoff with the Ukrainian side. So nothing has moved, and the $1.5 billion and the kickback cash are gone. Everyone cheated everyone, so they say." This was prologue to an incident in which a group of Chinese investors were detained at Kyiv's Boryspil Airport for twelve hours with no explanation and offered only $50 loaves of bread to eat before being sent back to Beijing on another plane. In the aftermath of this debacle, when a member of Ukraine's presidential think tank asked the head of the Chinese trade mission what could be done to increase investment, he shot back, "You could start by treating us like human beings." The notion that the Chinese were going to ride in on a white horse and bail out Ukraine at that moment seemed as likely as an extraterrestrial attack.

There were no grand revelations from my tête-à-tête with the Chinese trade counselor. We discussed Yanukovych's visit, but mostly he conveyed the same information I could have downloaded from the PRC Foreign Ministry website. President Xi and Yanukovych had signed a lot and smiled a lot, and Yanukovych was coming back to Kyiv with enough happy paper to claim a victory. But we all knew that a signed paper and real cash were very different things.

"So, these protests," he asked, "when will it stop? Do you think that this is a serious phenomenon which we should pay attention to?" Obviously the Chinese trade delegation did not spend much time in the protest camp. "Yes," I told him. "I would watch it quite closely."

After a few shifts as task force editors, our kids—four-year-old Elena and eight-year-old Andrew—were getting more accustomed to the fact that "Daddy and Mommy work on weekends now."

Elena's school was just blocks from Maidan. Delivering or fetching her, it became impossible not to notice signs of Maidan—people trekking toward the square with firewood or trays of pastries, Maidanivtsi leaving the square with that campfire smell, or sometimes titushky (thuggish young men) walking sullenly down the street avoiding eye contact with anyone. My son's school, Kyiv International School, was far from the city center, but if roads were blocked and his school bus could not get through, his situation could get precarious. The Embassy's Regional Security Office (RSO) staff worked hard to keep us all safe, but even so there was cause for worry. RSO newly mandated that all Americans carry their large black radios at all times. At every embassy where I worked, I was issued such a radio for emergencies—but this was the first time in my ten-year career that I actually had to lug the bulky thing around.

On Saturday, Task Force members were all trying to get information about what was going on downtown. There were many leads to track. I was interested in what Putin had offered Yanukovych in Sochi. Edward Lucas, editor of *The Economist*, reported that they had reached a deal whereby Russia would provide Ukraine with $5 billion in cash in the coming weeks, halve Ukraine's gas price, and provide up to $15 billion sometime later in exchange for Ukraine joining the Customs Union. Neither the Ukrainian nor the Russian government confirmed this information. Russian presidential press secretary Dmitriy Peskov claimed that Putin and Yanukovych had only discussed energy issues. The facts were pretty hazy. Also, Vladimir Putin's least favorite human being, former Georgian President Mikheil Saakashvili, was coming to speak on the Maidan stage. In a particularly Soviet move, Berkut had just surrounded Kyiv's largest TV tower. Finally, the political opposition announced three demands before they would be willing to meet with Yanukovych: release arrested protesters, prosecute Berkut involved in clashes, and remove the Minister of Internal Affairs Zakharchenko. It promised to be another busy shift.

December 8, Sunday evening, I had downtown observation duty. After an early dinner with Natasha and the kids, I drove down close to the north end of Maidan and parked. By this time, our embassy BlackBerries were an information lifeline and an obsession. In the last week I hadn't let more than ten minutes pass without checking my email. Like junkies, we all needed our information fix.

I was exiting my car when I saw initial reports that something was happening at the Lenin statue. This particular statue, an obvious symbol of Ukraine's Soviet past, was unique. While innumerable Lenins populated every city throughout the Soviet Union, Kyiv's eleven-foot-tall Lenin was carved from a rare crystalline basalt—a deep red stone—and had been shipped to New York for the 1939–1940 World's Fair, joining over 44 million tourists who attended.

Only in 1946 did this Lenin take up residence in Kyiv. In June 2009, several right-wing Ukrainian nationalists had attacked the statue with sledgehammers and defaced it, but it was subsequently repaired. Now, just a week ago, as Euromaidan was getting in gear, a group of masked men who tried to attack the statue had been driven away by Berkut riot police. We were sure they would be back.

My phone rang. Tim Piergalski, an on-duty political officer heading up the Task Force, was on the line. "Chris, can you get over to the Lenin statue now? We're hearing reports of some action over there." I quickly hoofed it a few blocks over to Besarabska to take a look.

I got there just as some rough-looking characters, not your typical Maidan protesters, were walking away from the statue. They carried heavy tools and wore awkward homemade body armor. As I approached, I saw that Lenin had been toppled from his pedestal and was lying on the ground. A crowd was watching an intense, short-bearded young man lay into Lenin's head repeatedly with a sledgehammer. I got closer to take some pictures for the Task Force, and felt flecks of the red stone hit my face as he swung again and again. Regular Kyiv police were standing at the edge of the crowd, looking somewhat bemused, clearly not intending to get involved. Apparently, if the Berkut weren't around, no one was prepared to defend Lenin. "One man down, identified as Vladimir Ilich," I typed quickly.

"Yanukovych is next," the middle-aged man next to me yelled as he watched the sledgehammer repeatedly rise and fall. I glanced at my phone. A message from Elizabeth. "Thanks, Chris. Now get out of there. Now."

As I abandoned the basalt Bolshevik to his beating, my email was bulging with information: rumors of Yanukovych preparing for a state of emergency that night, protesters detaining a man from Ukrainian intelligence trying to provoke police, State Ops back in Washington asking someone to review their situation report for the secretary, rightist Svoboda and Pravyi Sektor seizing buildings closer to the presidential administration, Cossack cavalry on the square, UN Secretary General Ban Ki-Moon calls Yanukovych, parliamentarian Tsaryov accuses US of fomenting revolution in Ukraine. There was far too much to absorb all at once.

At the edge of Besarabska, I caught sight of Elizabeth and her husband, J. P. Gresh. J. P., a US Army lieutenant colonel who worked in the Defense Attaché Office and was an incredibly nice guy, understood the evolving security situation in Kyiv much better than I and my fellow civilians. Elizabeth was just coming off her own two-hour observation shift. She and J. P. lived barely one block away and had been watching the action for some time. Euromaidan denied they had anything to do with Lenin's smackdown and blamed the action on far-right groups. But the three of us agreed that the hundreds of folks standing around the battered Lenin statue were jubilant, no matter who was responsible.

Elizabeth knew that I disliked the prominent Soviet symbols in Kyiv, which seemed to shackle Ukraine to its past instead of looking forward to a better future. "You don't need to smile so much," she chided me. My smile was not due to elation, though, but to a nervous adrenaline rush. Given its history and acknowledged artistic merit, this particular Lenin probably deserved a dignified museum retirement, not a sledgehammer. But we were just observers; it was for the Ukrainians to decide his fate as well as that of their present leaders.

I then walked down Khreshchatyk toward the protest city on Maidan, past the swanky shops and restaurants. Barricades surrounded Maidan, but getting inside was never a problem. The barricades were made of whatever random materials were at hand, including wooden pallets, wire, tires, trash cans, broken metal fencing, advertising signboards. They looked simultaneously ramshackle and formidable. Whenever I saw them they seemed to have grown higher. Large gaps enabled people to wander in and out freely even though rumors were circulating that government forces would come at any moment to smash the square's defenses. Overhearing snippets of conversations, I collected shards of life on Maidan as I walked. Two men speculated that Ukrainian intelligence had brought down the Lenin statue to justify a crackdown. SDF huddled around a radio to get more information on a possible state of emergency. Everyone knew of a Kyiv court ruling that all protesters must vacate public buildings by morning. Speakers held court from the main stage, but they were hard to hear among the tens of thousands of people on the square weaving through the chilly night air dense with campfire smoke. I could sense the nervous tension, but there was no palpable fear. Against all odds, the Maidanivtsi projected confidence.

Walking out the other end of Maidan protest city, I proceeded up Hrushevskoho Street toward the Cabinet of Ministers Building. On the south side of the building, inside a small version of the opposition's familiar makeshift barricades, a group of Maidan supporters blared rock and pop songs from a powerful speaker system. Further up the street, nine heavily vandalized buses were parked sideways across the street to serve as the government's barricade. Behind the buses stood about a hundred Berkut riot police in all-black armor, helmets, batons, and shields. An old man stood next to the Berkut, passionately trying to persuade them not to stand up for Yanukovych. They ignored him. The entrance to the building was guarded by another Berkut contingent, but the hundreds of flowers placed by Maidan protesters all around them, mostly carnations sticking out of every crack in the wall or sidewalk, imparted a retro 1960s feel to the scene. Over the hill was Mariinsky Park, which I knew well from weekend family visits to let the kids practice rollerblading. Old-fashioned Soviet orchestral music wafted over from the park, a stronghold of the anti-Maidan Party of Regions.

The difference between the Maidan and anti-Maidan was stark. Entering Mariinsky Park from Maidan, one first had to negotiate a series of barricades and roadblocks. I walked as closely as possible to the anti-Maidan, which was an impromptu fortress in the middle of the park. Inside was a row of Jersey barriers—those slanted concrete slabs used to separate lanes during highway construction. Surrounding the entire perimeter of the waist-high concrete slabs was a taller wall of shoulder-to-shoulder Berkut. The figures I could distinguish inside the fortress were huddled over a campfire, ignoring an onstage speaker busy attacking Yuliya Tymoshenko for signing a gas deal that "sold Ukraine out to the Russians." Since stirring the nationalist pot was working well for those on Maidan, Yanukovych loyalists were giving it a try as well. But the huddled figures inside seemed oblivious to the speeches. No wonder. It was really cold, and time for me to return home and pray for a peaceful night, knowing that tens of thousands would be sleeping out in the cold waiting for what seemed like an inevitable assault.

As a new work week began, cyberspace became another battle front. Frightening ads claiming that multi–drug resistant tuberculosis would kill you on Maidan popped up on popular Ukrainian websites. The website of the Interior Ministry was hacked, and suddenly featured a prominent message that all Ukrainians should go to Maidan. Regional news outlets posting favorable views on Euromaidan, such as the Kharkiv Online Review, also started suffering regular denial of service attacks. While the website of Ukraine's intelligence service, the Security Service of Ukraine (SBU), announced that they were considering charges against opposition politicians for a "coup attempt," protester websites announced that several people engaging in provocations were actually working for the intelligence body. This included a man detained on the Maidan by SDF for picking fights with police and a group of young thugs who entered the parliament with SBU credentials to interrupt Batkivshchyna leader Yatsenyuk's call for a no confidence motion against Yanukovych.

Then our Embassy was targeted. Party of Regions Parliamentarian Oleh Tsaryov, whom we knew as a ringleader behind the defamation campaign against TechCamp, posted a message on his Facebook page:

> I got a call from a journalist who is a staunch opponent of the regime. What is happening now is contrary to his convictions. He claims that the protest actions and activities of the opposition leadership have been coordinated by American citizen Brian Fink. He moves between the office of "Batkivshchyna," "UDAR," and the United States Embassy. In addition to the protests, Brian Fink is part of a group of Americans of Serbian origin. This opposition called themselves "the Georgians" because they did the last revolution in Georgia. The total number of foreigners in the headquarters of the opposition is about thirty people. My friend asked me to publish this information because Brian Fink is now pushing for the seizure of ninety buildings and insists that their capture take place in the most severe way, preferably with victims. I drove to the border guards, and it turned out that this man really exists.

The posting then included Brian's actual birth date and diplomatic passport number.

We all knew Brian and were shocked that he would be targeted for such vicious slander. Brian was a tall, collegial guy we all worked with daily. As an acting office director at USAID, his main responsibilities were organizing aid programs, not running around town to Ukrainian political parties. In addition to the lunatic suggestion that he was inciting violent building seizures, everything else about the post was also wrong. As he wasn't part of the observation teams, he hadn't been on Maidan since the start of demonstrations. He hadn't been to any Ukrainian political party headquarters and had no Serbian or Georgian connections. Now, however, he certainly had to worry about his and his wife's safety. We all asked ourselves, why Brian? Since there was no obvious answer, I concluded it was probably random and that any one of us could have been targeted. They probably just had to pick a name. After all, when inventing a conspiracy theory, truth is superfluous. We knew how absurd the accusations against Brian were, but most Ukrainians, of course, had never been inside the US Embassy or had any understanding of our real day-to-day work. For some of them, such outlandish accusations might have the ring of truth. If so, then Oleh Tsaryov would have accomplished his mission.

Throughout the day on Tuesday, December 9, government security personnel were on the move in Kyiv. They took positions in the building next to city hall, which unleashed a flood of social media speculation that they were on the verge of storming the building. Then Berkut closed off both ends of Khreshchatyk Street as a show of force around Maidan. Priests on the Maidan stage offered a *molében*, a special religious service to ask for the protection of the Virgin Mary. Several hours later Interior Ministry forces completely encircled Maidan. Then rows of troops and buses as well as army vehicles packed with men in full riot gear arrived at St. Michael's cathedral.

Natalya messaged me: "I am worried about Elena." Of course, so was I. Our daughter's preschool was about one block away from St. Michael's. I asked David if I could run out, and dashed to the car. Twenty-five minutes later, I returned to the Embassy with Elena in her car seat. The rest of the day she played on the floor in the office, stapling paper hearts together and drawing. While she played at our feet, we could focus on our work. It would have been nice to go home at a reasonable time, but I had task force duty again that night. One way or another, I told myself, this will end soon. It has to. But it did not.

There was no major government move against Maidan during daylight hours, and the police seemed content to lay siege to the protest encampment. But that night, Ukrainian government forces raided the offices of the Batkivshyna political party, drawing quick international condemnation. On the low-rent intimidation front, titushky twice visited opposition-friendly TV Channel 5 to offer "protection." Similar intimidation tactics were employed at the EU mission as "strange men" with signs in well-written English blocked the front and rear doors that Tuesday. Unlike the US Embassy, with its tall fence and significant setback from the street, the new EU mission was a standard office building with no setbacks. When Elizabeth invited Jack Francis to a meeting the next day, he replied with classic British understatement: "Of course, I cannot rule out changes to my schedule tomorrow . . . e.g., EU del. is currently surrounded by men in ski-masks etc. preventing us from leaving the building. Only three police have arrived so far."

Yanukovych agreed to meet with the three ex-presidents of Ukraine in an attempt to find a solution to the crisis. A fresh opinion poll revealed that only 10 percent of Ukrainians were willing to tell pollsters that they trusted Yanukovych. Events of the coming days would only deepen that mistrust. No one was backing down.

We were not in the least surprised that Moscow was furiously spinning developments in Kyiv. That night another "exposé" of Euromaidan appeared on Moscow's Center TV. Slick Russian propagandists were developing several clear attack lines. First, that the protesters in Kyiv were all radical nationalists, direct successors to the World War II–era Ukrainian Insurgent Army and the vilified Ukrainian nationalist leader Stepan Bandera who had briefly collaborated with the Germans before being imprisoned in a Nazi concentration camp. In other words, Euromaidan protesters were fascists, or "Banderovtsy." This was guaranteed to get Russian audiences riled up. Second, that Maidan protesters were bought and paid for by foreigners, citing the words of a Ukrainian parliamentarian: "I've talked to people from Dnipropetrovsk who attended a meeting of the TechCamp organization. It is an NGO, funded from the USA. They train people to stage color revolutions. . . . About three hundred people were trained. They then saw many graduates working and organizing things in Euromaidan." Numerous other false claims spewed forth about Euromaidan: people were prohibited from speaking Russian on the square, protesters were hungry and only there for free food, Ukraine was falling apart. Most menacingly, the narrator asked, "Will the country survive another Maidan?"

Russian media attacks were not lost on the Maidanivtsi, who frequently watched as Russian TV reporters did scathingly negative, and sometimes completely fictitious, stand-ups from the Maidan. During one of my own wanderings across the Maidan, I watched a Russian reporter and cameraman walking through the square, describing everyone within earshot as starving fascist alcoholics or drug addicts paid in food by Western intelligence services for their participation. Had Maidan not maintained such a peace-and-love vibe in those early days, things could have gotten ugly for such "reporters." But mostly the Maidanivtsi tried to respond with wit and humor. At one point on live Russian TV, one protester walked up to one of these reporters with a small metal statuette, announcing, "Please pass this Oscar to the Rossiya One Channel and to [propagandistic Russian news anchor] Dmitry Kiselev for the lies and nonsense you are telling people about Maidan."

On December 10, Assistant Secretary of State Victoria Nuland arrived back in Kyiv. Unlike her visit less than a week before, during which she attended a major multilateral event, this visit focused solely on Ukraine. EU high representative and foreign policy chief Catherine Ashton was also in town, enabling the two to coordinate their messages in key meetings. The Political Section had arranged a top-level schedule of meetings for Nuland with Ukraine's leaders, including Yanukovych, as well as with opposition leaders, business elite, and key religious figures. Her message was consistent—the Ukrainian government should take the protesters' concerns seriously and work cooperatively with them to deescalate the security situation peacefully. Further violence was not acceptable and would meet with the swift condemnation of the international community. Both Yanukovych and protest leaders should back away from their maximalist positions. The time for real dialogue and compromise was now. It was a simple and powerful message delivered during a whirlwind round of diplomacy intended to forestall any further violence. But while our assistant secretary was still on the ground, some in the Ukrainian government had already hatched other plans.

They came that night. Berkut and other Interior Ministry troops with riot shields began a coordinated push from multiple directions onto the square, attempting to force the protesters away from their barricades and pen them tightly into the middle of the square. Presumably, beatings, mass arrests, or both would follow. What happened next looked like a giant desperate rugby scrum. Protesters locked arms and used their muscle power to push back the government forces. Recent snow made it impossible for either side to secure a solid footing on the granite paving stones or on the street, imparting a recklessly fluid undulation to the pushing match as shoes and boots skidded back and forth across the snow-covered square. Firing canisters of tear gas, government forces broke through the Institutska barricade. The advancing troops ripped apart the makeshift barricades and marched forward. Where the protest camp's barricades were breached, titushky quickly moved in to destroy tents, chairs, camp stoves, or anything else.

After seizing the Institutska barricade, Interior Ministry troops retook the Trade Unions Building, reportedly ransacking the offices the Maidanivtsi had set up inside with permission of the building's owners. But their assault on city hall failed. Hour after hour, the Maidan SDF repelled government forces trying to enter the building. In a reminder that Kyiv is a medieval city, the church bells at St. Michael's monastery, where priests a few weeks before had given protesters refuge from the Berkut's batons, began ringing around 1:00 a.m. to sound the alarm. The church had taken the protesters' side again. Most Kyiv residents had never heard church bells at night, and it was easy to guess what must be going on. During the all-night struggle, additional thousands of protesters poured onto the square. Maidan wasn't shrinking from the fight—it was expanding. By dawn an estimated ten thousand Maidanivtsi were on the square. Secretary of State John Kerry's statement denouncing the violence was read to cheers on the Maidan stage.

After failing to retake city hall and still encountering massive resistance on the square, the Berkut and Interior Ministry forces began pulling back around 10:00 a.m. the next morning. By 11:00, there was almost no police presence anywhere around the protest zone. The Maidanivtsi immediately began rebuilding their barricades, learning what worked and what didn't, and placing stronger makeshift fortifications in new positions. Local press reported that fifteen people were hospitalized due to injuries that night.

A massive pushing match seemed an unusual form of political struggle, like using a game of tug-of-war to determine the fate of the country. Both sides desperately wanted to avoid being seen as responsible for escalating the violence. That was a sure political loser. By using only shields, and not batons, government forces appeared to be in defensive mode. During the struggle for city hall, someone had thrown Molotov cocktails out a second-story window onto Berkut troops below. The Maidanivtsi and the political opposition said it was a paid provocateur whom they identified and expelled. Most naively hoped that the confrontation would stay at the level of the scrum, knowing full well that the government had much more lethal force available if it chose to use it.

After the unsuccessful effort to physically push the Maidanivtsi from the square, Assistant Secretary Nuland and Ambassador Pyatt visited Maidan in the morning. After a full day of high-level diplomacy aimed at securing Ukraine's commitment to avoid violence and begin real dialogue between the government and opposition, the "scrum" represented the Yanukovych government's largest show of force against Maidan since November 30. It was done while both Nuland and Ashton were still on the ground, which couldn't have been a coincidence. The action was an undiplomatic slap in the face, demonstrating that the Yanukovych administration would do whatever it wanted whenever it wanted.

Assistant Secretary Nuland felt she should go to the square as a way of acknowledging the night's events. Our RSO team emphasized that the security situation there was fluid and that they couldn't guarantee her safety. She wasn't dissuaded. In Eastern European culture, guests never arrive empty-handed. En route to the square, my colleague Eric Andersen quickly put together a plan for her visit, including that she hand out bread and cookies to the Ukrainians who had faced the overnight onslaught. It was a small but expressive gesture. Russian media immediately featured pictures of her handing out cookies in the square to assert that the United States was propping up the Maidan movement. Of course, they omitted mentioning that she had also handed out bread to black-helmeted Interior Ministry security troops that same day as an indication Washington was not taking sides. We at the Embassy needed no explanation. Just hours earlier, the people on the square had been engaged in a life-threatening struggle, and the timing of the police raid was likely due to Toria Nuland's presence in the city. The bread and cookies were symbolic; it was the least that she, or we collectively as Americans, could do. She wrote an email with the subject line "Historic Times" to the entire Embassy staff on her departure: "As many of you know, I have been doing this work for almost thirty years. I want you to know that I have never been more proud to serve on a team than I am to serve with all of you during these vital times for Ukraine. . . . Take care of each other and continue to take care of this essential relationship." No matter how many times the Russian propaganda machine uses those photos of Toria Nuland handing out cookies as some sort of talismanic evidence of something evil, I can't help but look at the images and see what was a simple, compassionate, humane gesture.

Meanwhile, in a move clearly designed to turn older Ukrainians against the mostly younger protesters, Prime Minister Azarov announced that due to the ongoing protests no pension payments would be made through the end of the year. Around this same time, opposition parties, finally publicly acknowledging that they were not in command, stated that they would no longer negotiate with the government without a mandate from Euromaidan. The Batkivshchyna party revealed that the Interior Ministry threatened to fire any security personnel who allowed trucks to enter the protest area with food, medical supplies, or firewood. Despite the danger to reporters, Ukraine's intrepid journalists continued to investigate all aspects of the ongoing situation. The newspaper *Economicheska Pravda* estimated that the cost of sustaining Euromaidan for one month was 242 million hryvnia, or about $30 million, for food, medical care, beds, and other services. This money came from many small sources, it stated. But there was no need to cover one large expense that the anti-Maidan counterprotest required—direct payment to the protesters for their presence. According to website censor.net's reporting, the average anti-Maidan protester received a stipend of about $25 per day. *Ukrayinska Pravda* reported that the Yanukovych administration required regional and district governments to provide lists of 250 employees who would take leave without pay and travel to Kyiv to beef up the numbers at the anti-Maidan rally. Odesa Law Academy students also reported being forced onto trains to attend the anti-Maidan under threat of failing their classes. Meanwhile, the Ukrainian press reported numerous protest-related transportation movements in the country—possibly 100,000 protesters coming from Lviv to Kyiv to join Euromaidan, eight buses of Berkut coming from Mykhailov, and a rumored government order to stop selling train tickets from Kharkiv to Kyiv.

In the dead of winter, Maidan continued to blossom and bear fruit. "Open Maidan University" brought many of the country's greatest minds to the square to lecture on various topics, TED Talk style. Politics and economics lecturers were represented, but so were leading figures from such diverse fields as philosophy, art history, and the hard sciences. Like the meals and sleeping space, the lectures were free. The students who dominated the protest at the beginning were still present in force, but the numbers of protesters were swelling with priests, middle-aged working class folks, and Cossacks in full, colorful traditional outfits, occasionally on horseback. Sections of the Maidan tent and barricade city that were washed away by the flood of security forces were rapidly rebuilt. In the freezing weather, ice bags became the new barricade construction material of choice. Just after midnight on December 12, our Embassy observers estimated that there were 25,000 to 30,000 people on the square. From the main Maidan stage, pop singer and civic activist leader Ruslana urged those present to stay for the next six days—at least through Yanukovych's planned trip to Moscow on December 17.

Embassy observers began noticing a strange, white "Iveco" van sporting a nearly three-story tall antenna array parked in different places around the square. The antenna was formidable, its cables as thick as a bodybuilder's arm snaking down from the shrouded equipment at the top of a long pole. Obviously someone's ears were pointed at the Maidan. In reference to J.R.R. Tolkien, Embassy observers named it the Eye of Sauron truck. After the recent clashes, our observers were now all from the Defense Attaché Office. The Embassy now needed observers who could distinguish between the sound of a firecracker and a gunshot, who knew the difference between a new group of security forces arriving in the area and a regular rotation of troops. These observers would now be the Embassy's regular eyes and ears on the square, not Foreign Service Officers like me.

The evolving community that was Euromaidan had its own distinctive colors. Its primary colors were always blue and yellow—not by accident the colors of both the Ukrainian and EU flags. Occasionally, one spied a red-and-black flag. At first I hadn't recognized it, but it was a familiar banner, particularly to older Ukrainians. The red-and-black flag was the World War II battle standard of the nationalist Ukrainian Insurgent Army (UIA), the group that fought Soviet and Polish troops, while at times collaborating with German Nazi forces. Despite the UIA's association with atrocities such as the ethnic cleansing of Polish nationals from Volhynia and Galicia in 1943–1944, its flag was still a recognized symbol of Ukrainian nationalism. One colleague put it to me this way: "It's a little like the Confederate flag in the US. . . . Kind of embarrassing and associated with some nasty stuff, but that doesn't mean that you won't see it if you drive around the South because it means something different and prideful to some white Southerners." In Russia, carrying UIA flags would be viewed no differently than carrying around a Nazi swastika. But Ukraine was not Russia.

I had seen one or two red-and-black flags on the square, but they were just a couple of drops in the vast ocean of colors, sounds, and action. They were certainly not among the predominant symbols in those early days of Maidan, and if you weren't actively searching for them, you might miss them entirely. But on the evening of December 12, one of our Embassy observers saw something quite different—a group of fifty persons, carrying red-and-black flags and tiki torches and wearing arm bands, marching onto Maidan. One person cradled a prop guillotine. All the right-wing, World War II–era iconography guaranteed to make the average Russian's blood boil was there, all present within a single camera frame. Most interesting was that the group was filmed by a professional camera crew from multiple angles as they marched. The footage appeared on Russian television almost instantly. Real Maidanivtsi had no idea who these guys were, but there was no doubt about their utility to the Kremlin propaganda machine, which was now running in overdrive. Such appearances occurred intermittently during the coming months, and the video footage was used in Russia to paint the entire Maidan as fascist to the core. Abraham Lincoln reportedly said, "You can fool all the people some of the time, and some of the people all the time, but you cannot fool all the people all the time." The first two of Lincoln's observations served the Russian propaganda machine's purposes well enough. They could safely ignore the final caveat. Only the unidentified professional cameramen, these groups' constant companions, seemed to know in advance when these goose-stepping oddities would appear around the protest area.

At the Embassy, seven of us, including me, received a message from Katherine Munchmeyer, our management counselor. After the giant shoving match in the middle of the night, it was clear that some of the most important breaking news was likely to occur in the wee hours. The implication was obvious—those of us working the Task Force were about to lose a lot more sleep. Her message read,

> We are revising the Task Force staffing on a twenty-four-hour basis for the near future. We will have a senior watch position, an editor on six-hour shifts. During the day (9:00 a.m.–9:00 p.m.), an additional American will be added as swing capacity (watching news tickers). I am writing you because you have been serving regularly in the Task Force and have experienced how it should best run. We need you to serve as senior watch officer (SWO). This function will no longer be expected to write the SitRep, but will review it before issuing, and will be primarily responsible for overseeing the entire operation, including monitoring all email traffic, coordinating responses to the ambassador's (and others') taskers, calling the overnight duty deputy (Elizabeth Horst) as needed, and generally ensuring that folks are actively monitoring media, etc.

To this point in my career, I had avoided shift work, because I never thought I would be very good at it. But we were now living through an unforeseen crisis, and shift work found me.

While we were shuffling assignments, Ukrainian politicians were at least pretending to look for a peaceful way out of the mess they had created. In a nationally broadcast "roundtable," with the ostensible goal of finding a political solution to the ongoing crisis, Yanukovych sat in the middle of an oblong table, flanked by Ukraine's former presidents alongside the country's religious leaders. Opposition politicians were relegated to the cold end of the long table. It was hardly a real dialogue, rather it was serial monologues that failed to connect. One of the participants, Dmytro Levin, a young man introduced as a "student leader," asked those on the Maidan to return home. Within minutes, he was outed on the internet as an assistant to a Party of Regions parliamentarian. Yanukovych's show closed after bombing on opening night.

Then Ihnat called me. We both agreed it would be best to delay the intellectual property rights (IPR) concert that we were planning to hold in December. Launching the concert during a time of national emergency would definitely seem tone deaf.

"You know," Ihnat said, "Dmytro Prykordonnyy, whom you met from the music producer's association, has been really involved with Maidan. Many of Ukraine's well-known musicians have been spending most of their time on the square these last few weeks, and I think Dmytro has barely left at all. He'd like to invite you to come by on Friday night and give you a 'behind the barricades tour,' you know, more than you would see just walking through."

That Friday night, my mother-in-law was staying with the kids, and Natalya and I had tickets to see *Eugene Onegin* at the National Opera. With music by Tchaikovsky and a story based on Pushkin, it was difficult to think of any entertainment more Russian than watching *Eugene Onegin*. After the opera, Natalya returned home, and I walked downhill toward Maidan until I caught sight of Ihnat.

Ihnat helped me find Dmytro, who was standing with several other young men. All wore homemade armor, much of which looked like haphazard plastic sheeting duct-taped together for a last-minute roller derby match. Dmytro smiled broadly and wrapped me in a bear hug. "Come on," he boomed. "There's a lot to see. We're fighting for our country. I bet you've never seen anything like it."

Walking over to Kyiv's city hall, Dmytro beamed with pride, talking about the city-within-a-city on Maidan. "You know, Maidan is the only part of Kyiv with effective snow removal. We're all volunteers, and we're more effective than normal city services. Trash removal, food delivery—all volunteer. We cannot give Yanukovych an excuse to wipe us out, such as keeping too much trash piled up." But it was clearly more than that. Showing that the protesters could deliver basic services themselves was not just a point of pride but one way to show a Ukraine that worked, even if on a very small scale.

"No drinking is permitted on Maidan, Chris. Can you believe it? Strictly enforced by the SDF."

This part was difficult to believe. Generally, in any group of three men out in public in Kyiv, at least one would be drinking, but more normally all three. Alcohol was a way of life. But inside the makeshift walls, life and priorities indeed seemed different.

The facade of city hall bore just a few signs of the fight that had raged there several nights before when Berkut attempted to storm the building—mostly paintball splatters and some broken windows. Inside, the building was heavy with the smell of cooked cabbage from a free food station on the first floor. From the top of the stairs directly ahead, the rambunctious folk songs of a group of sturdy, mustached older men in traditional Ukrainian outfits echoed through the hall. The building had become a potent symbol of Euromaidan after protesters had successfully held off riot police a few nights before. As we walked up the stairs, Dmytro recalled that night: "You know, it was the Lviv paintball guys who really deserve the credit. Those jokers spend most of their weekends running around in the forest shooting rubber bullets at each other just for fun. They practiced defending this building for days ahead of time. When the moment came, they were brilliant. That was the hour they had been waiting for, and for a very long time."

In the large, second-floor hall, hundreds of protesters slept while others watched the news on a large projection screen. In the front of the cavernous room, three intellectual-looking middle-aged men were chatting with passersby at an impressive desk labeled "City Self Government." The longest line was at the registration desk where new arrivals could volunteer for jobs within the Euromaidan area. At another desk, two lawyers offered free legal help. A large clear fiberglass box for cash donations sat on a nearby desk, nearly full. "Don't put any money in the box," joked Dmytro. "Someone would take a picture and say that the US was funding Euromaidan. They'd kill for that kind of propaganda."

Dmytro looked proudly around the operation. "Self-organization. All of it. . . . We will prove that we are serious and can organize. Let's go."

Dmytro led us out of city hall back toward the center of the protest camp. At that point, city hall was still a Maidan outpost outside the growing protest area. Several SDF looked at us as we exited the gap in the barricades, but they asked no questions. "Just 'face control,'" said Ihnat. "We don't look like titushky or provocateurs."

Dmytro snickered. "One funny thing that we see a lot are titushky from the anti-Maidan who slip into Euromaidan food stations. They sneak in, and keep getting more helpings. They smile like they've really gotten away with something, which is funny because we know exactly who they are. We tell them to bring their friends, perhaps they'll learn something about us. They still think that they are very sneaky and clever."

Yellow and blue light rained down from the large electric signboard over the square displaying waving Ukrainian and EU flags. Dmytro led us to a large military-style tent. "The Afghan war veterans gave us the tent, and the space on the square," he commented, lifting the flap and leading us in. About ten young men inside the roomy tent were installing warehouse-style shelving units with small tablet PCs lined up on each shelf. "This is the IT community's contribution. The equipment is all donated. This is where my production company is making our contribution too. We'll be up and live later tonight, and everyone here on the square will be able to come in, use social media, and let the world know why they are here and what they are doing. Kids need to let their parents know that they are OK. And we need the world to know what we're fighting for and what this all means."

He looked over the work of the young techies. "Now the tech community will have a place to sleep on Maidan. It's our own little nest where we can invite our brothers-in-arms. We hacked the big screen over the square, and that showed folks that we tech people could be fun and useful. In a day or two, we'll have free wi-fi throughout the square. We all give what we can to the effort." He introduced me to a few of the young guys, who all seemed more interested in getting the tablets networked than chatting with some random foreigner.

Emerging from the tech nest into the cold night, we turned toward the "Afghantsi" tent—the domain of the aging, but unquestionably tough, Afghan war veterans. At the tent door, a leathery older man in tobacco-scented fatigues crisply introduced himself: "Volodymyir, Tent Two commandant. State your business." Dmytro introduced me as a diplomat, and Volodymyir, Tent Two commandant, somewhat sheepishly apologized for the small amount of mess inside of the very tidy tent. Dmytro asked him about the struggle on the square on Tuesday. "It was intense," said Volodymyir. "But there was no fear. We have a saying in our business that you can only die once."

Though a young rock music producer, Dmytro clearly reveled in their company. "Just look at their faces," he beamed. "With them on our side, could we really lose?" We all sat and drank hot tea out of little glass cups in metal holders. The Afghantsi and the young tech kids didn't seem to have much in common outwardly. But somehow on the square, they were brothers, sharing tents, real estate on the granite paving stones, and wi-fi. The Afghantsi made the tech kids feel tough, the tech kids made the Afghantsi feel smart and modern. It was just one of a million small alliances on the square, contributing to building the community that was Euromaidan.

Afterward, Dmytro led us over to the Instytutska Street barricade, where on Tuesday night hundreds of Berkut used their riot shields to push onto the square. At the barricade, a front line of SDF in hard hats stood, gazes fixed outward from the square toward the lines of riot police several hundred feet away. Like the barricades, the SDF looked haphazardly arranged in height, age, and stature. Under their orange helmets, their clothes and "equipment" varied from soccer knee pads to sticks to heavy patched coats to balaclavas completely covering a few faces. But all of the volunteer defenders of the square looked determined and ready. At exactly 11:00 p.m., another equally diverse and homespun group in hard hats marched up, keeping time with their heavy boot steps. The SDF guarding Instytutska then turned on command to leave the barricade. Only then did I recognize that this was a changing of the guard, with a rough precision designed to instill confidence in the SDF's ability as defenders. Ihnat and Dmytro left me for a few minutes to tend to some issues in the tech tent.

I wasn't going to be able to talk with those standing watch, so I approached some of the other men who were there to support the SDF. "This group will be there until 2:00 in the morning," a tall man with silver hair said to me. "Three-hour shifts. If it keeps getting colder, we may go down to two-hour shifts even though the guys argue they can take it. They want to show that they are tough, but we need to keep them healthy and ready."

I introduced myself, and the silver-haired man peppered me with questions about running a small business in the United States. "So I own a few auto repair shops in central Ukraine. I spend most of my time trying to look unprofitable to ward off the racketeers and crooked tax guys. It's not too hard—lots of the time, with all the bribes I pay, my business really is unprofitable. So what's the business licensing process like in America?" One of his friends, a shorter bald man came over to listen. "At how many points do American businessmen need to pay bribes for imports? I'd be happy just to have a single point at which to pay one bribe—that would be fine. It's the different levels of bribes that really kill you. You pay off one guy, but somehow don't realize that you later need to pay off his boss too, and you hadn't budgeted for that."

"You see why we're here," his friend sighed. "Younger people have their reasons, older people have theirs. For us, we just can't make a living under this system. We need a change. I just feel like we can't live like this anymore."

The silver-haired man nodded, then spoke directly to me. "There is something you can do. Get your government to sanction Yanukovych—sanction him and his dirty lieutenants hard. Money is the beginning and end of what these guys care about. They need foreign places to hide their money, and foreign locations to take their girlfriends and mistresses. Tough Western sanctions would get their attention, and only the US has the balls to make the first move. It could save all of us on the square. I could beg if that would help."

Dmytro returned, and we said our goodbyes to the two men. "There's somewhere else I'd like to take you," said Dmytro. "I told you that the artistic community is all in for Maidan. There's a few more folks I'd like you to meet."

We left Maidan via the neighborhood uphill from the square. Next to the Soviet-era apartment blocks were a few older, pre-revolutionary apartment buildings. We entered one and rang the bell of an apartment. A thin, lanky man with a dark beard and deep eyes who looked like he was on his fourth cup of coffee this hour opened the door. "Chris, meet Viktor," said Dmytro.

Viktor was a filmmaker who produced music videos for many of Ukraine's top bands. He was a middle-aged rock bassist whose half dozen or so friends were spread throughout the apartment, chatting. "We've been shooting a lot of video on the square," he said casually. "We've got a project going called 'Babylon 13.' It's really important to us." He continued in Russian. "What's happening here and now, all around us, is unique. It can be part of Ukraine's contribution to world culture if the world stops long enough to notice it.

That's where we come in, with good images, good stories." We sat down in the kitchen, the traditional conversation perch in this part of the world. "You know, we in Ukraine have really given nothing to world culture but obscene corruption. Now we're working to change that. Our cameras can be the world's eyes regarding what's really going on in Maidan—the birth of a new country. Come on, let's go upstairs."

Upstairs was a well-apportioned renovated attic—a winding, long, thin corridor along the side of the building, angling along the lines of the building's outer walls and with the steep angle of the roof cutting into the head space. Along the walls were tables with dozens of computers, mostly new iMacs, at which a handful of young people were absorbed in editing videos. We stopped at one workstation. "Chris," said Viktor. "I'd like you to meet the chief technology officer of Euromaidan."

A college kid, thin as a rail with an intense stare, stood up and shook my hand. "Welcome to our playground," he laughed. "Pull up a chair."

"So, how do you get a great title like chief technology officer of Euromaidan?" I asked. He looked at me quizzically. "I volunteered down at city hall, like everyone else," he answered. "SDF, garbage crew, chief technology officer—we all come in through the same door." He opened up his web browser and pulled up Facebook. "Social media is a big part of the lifeblood of Maidan. That's how we all know about events, threats, calls for action—anything. We used to maintain some of our own websites to get information around, but the constant denial of service attacks from Russia were killing us. So I switched us over to bigger websites like Facebook and Twitter. Hackers can drag down my little site pretty quickly, but not Facebook." He scrolled through some of the recent postings on Euromaidan's social media profiles, most of which were patriotic and covered with Ukrainian flags. "Morale is important," he noted solemnly.

"But the information flow is not just one way," he said, pulling up a "City Band" map on the popular "Yandex" website. "Tuesday night was a big test for us. We could see that Berkut and the other Yanu bandit forces were on the move." He pointed at the screen. "We have cameras here, here, and here. We have other folks who watch around the edges. All information feeds into this map, where we track Maidanivtsi movements, Berkut and interior ministry, paid pro-government demonstrators, and others. It was really valuable to have all of this in place once the assault that we were all expecting finally came. It was a powerful tool." We continued chatting until Viktor remembered that we were distracting someone with an important job.

Walking out of the attic, we passed an imposing display case with books and a large collection of Japanese anime female figurines. In front of the case was a thigh-high mortar cannon. Viktor saw me looking at it.

"Don't worry," he said dismissively with a wave of his long arm. "That's just in case things get really bad."

6

MAIDAN'S POETICS VERSUS
STEEL SHIELDS AND BLACK HELMETS

By mid-December 2013, the Ukrainian state and a growing segment of Ukrainian society were at loggerheads. Conflicting approaches to politics and society were embodied in two centers of power that were facing off on the streets of Kyiv. One was the internationally recognized government of President Viktor Yanukovych, democratically elected in 2010, well-organized and self-confident, thoroughly corrupt, and only slowly becoming aware of just how serious was the challenge confronting it. The other was Euromaidan, a rising mass movement, loosely organized and still evolving, centered in Kyiv but with supporters throughout the country; a movement gaining consciousness of its growing strength, but with competing goals being championed by the loose collective of those claiming its leadership.

In Moscow, Putin and his associates closely watched the drama unfold on the streets of Kyiv and elsewhere throughout Ukraine, a country they viewed as within their rightful sphere of influence and control. They pumped out a steady stream of poisonous propaganda on Euromaidan to the Russian public through their captive domestic mass media. While this propaganda fulfilled the goal of grooming Russian TV audiences to view any anticorruption social movement—especially those that might have appeal in Russia itself—as disguised tools of Western spies and modern-day Nazis, the role of producer and consumer of this type of vitriol was always strangely ambiguous. Did the Kremlin simply want its own citizens to believe this outrageous spin, or was it really that paranoid itself? It seemed that Moscow's sticks and carrots had brought Yanukovych back into the fold, but the question of whether he would stay there and the uncertainty as to the outcome of the contretemps in Kyiv likely troubled Kremlin leaders. They had won important battles, but they needed to ensure that they had won the war.

On December 13, Ukrainian Deputy Prime Minister Boyko left for Moscow to pre-negotiate the outcomes of Yanukovych's upcoming trip. At home, his government was moving to bolster its position. Additional trains from southern and eastern Ukraine to Kyiv were added to the normal railroad schedule, presumably to transport fresh pro-government demonstrators to the anti-Maidan rally. The head of the Dnipropetrovsk Party of Regions posted on his official website that he was sending 10,000 people to the anti-event. Ministry of Defense staff complained to the press that army field kitchens were being diverted to feed the anti-Maidan's anti-protesters, offending the military's idea of its own apolitical role. In sum, there was no de-escalation on the horizon.

I was assigned the 6:00 a.m. Saturday task force shift, the same day that Diplomatic Security notified me it was time to begin the byzantine process of renewing my security clearance. Susan Stewart, head of our Embassy's medical unit, emailed all Embassy staff: "You are not alone during this Euromaidan situation in feeling stressed. Studies show that more and more people are feeling the effects of overload. Many of us are experiencing feelings of stress, anxiety, depression, and burnout. Our personal and work lives have gotten busier and more hectic, and we all feel pressed for time. That can make us feel overwhelmed and out of control. But life doesn't have to feel that way." Perhaps it didn't have to feel that way, but it did.

"How about this year's Christmas cards?" I asked Natalya that Saturday afternoon at home after my shift ended.

I couldn't say that Christmas cards were uppermost on my mind. While Andrew and Elena may have had visions of sugarplums dancing in their heads as Christmas approached, my head was filled with update emails and urban campfire smoke.

"Well, there's a Christmas tree down on Maidan to take some pictures with," I responded jokingly. By now pictures of the "revolution tree," three stories of Ukrainian flags and protest banners, had spread across Ukraine. In the past, we took the kids to Maidan and Khreshchatyk regularly. Before Euromaidan, Khreshchatyk Street was closed to traffic on weekends, and our kids roller bladed and rode their scooters along the side of Maidan. They knew the area well but hadn't been there since things had gotten dicey.

Half an hour later, Andrew was strapped into his booster and Elena into her car seat, and we were driving toward Maidan. Getting out of the car, Andrew noticed the smell of campfires. I told him that people on the square were burning wood for heat. "Do they get to make s'mores?" he asked.

We entered the square through one of the gaps in the barricades, which seemed to grow like mythical beanstalks. Elena just looked around, fascinated, as if she had just entered the world's biggest snow fort. Ours were not the only kids on Maidan that day; parents pushed babies in strollers, and a few youngsters played ball. The crowd was diverse and positive. There was no menace or feeling of danger despite the security personnel in the distance. We walked up to the impressive Instytutska barricades. Against the backdrop of the makeshift wood, tire, ice, and barbed wire barricades, we took a picture we still treasure of Andrew standing guard protectively over little Elena. We also took several pictures next to the "revolution tree" and admired the Maidan street art. We talked about the fighting a few nights before while standing on the ground where it happened.

"So, what will happen to these people?" Andrew asked, standing surrounded by crowds of protesters, young and old, some singing and some silent, some there for the first time and some who hadn't left for weeks. "We just don't know yet," I said, honestly. No one did.

By now Maidan attracted some distinguished sympathizers, including Senator John McCain (R-AZ) and Senator Christopher S. Murphy (D-CT). A few days before their arrival, Elizabeth asked me to serve as Senator Murphy's control officer. This meant that I would arrange his schedule, liaise with his staff before his arrival, and accompany him to respond to any requests, changes, or problems. Senator McCain arrived in Kyiv on Saturday, December 14, and Senator Murphy was slated to follow on Sunday morning. That Saturday morning Yanukovych's Party of Regions held a large rally, marching 100,000 people from their camp in Mariinsky Park to European Square, the doorstep of Maidan. From the anti-Maidan stage, Prime Minister Azarov played the gay card, stating that his government's signature on the Association Agreement would have meant legalizing gay marriage in Ukraine. While Maidan banned alcohol, anti-Maidan clearly did not. Intoxicated and unhappy anti-Maidanivtsi imparted an edgy feel to the gathering, as if possibilities for sudden violence lurked within every interaction. The close proximity of the two camps put everyone on guard. Maidan and anti-Maidan began a battle of loudspeakers, each trying to drown out the other.

Embassy observers noted increasing numbers of titushky armed with identical nightsticks. Were these now standard issue for the thug brigade? We also received reports that three Russian government planes had landed in Kyiv, one possibly from the presidential fleet at the main commercial airport with two more at the cargo airport. Another report claimed that Interior Ministry personnel were being withdrawn from their posts guarding nuclear power plants around the country to come to Kyiv. As evening fell, the anti-Maidan camp dissolved as many returned to sleep in the trains that brought them to town or to bed down in local dormitories. Meanwhile, Euromaidan was just getting started. Ukraine's most popular rock band, Okean Elzy (Elza's ocean), featuring iconic rebel Svyatoslav Vakarchuk as lead vocalist, took the main stage for a free concert. By the end of the night, the anti-Maidan's new stage on European Square was disassembled without explanation.

At some point during the day, news that the collapsed red basalt Lenin had vanished left everyone at the Embassy puzzled. How do several tons of carved red basalt just disappear? Meanwhile, the prosecutor's office had finished its investigation and chosen a trio of fall guys for the November 30 attack on demonstrators: Kyiv mayor Oleksandr Popov, deputy secretary of the National Security Council Volodymyr Sivkovych, and Kyiv police chief Valeriy Koriak. The inclusion of Mayor Popov indicated Yanukovych was willing to sacrifice one of his own to try to put this behind him. After Senator McCain's full day of meetings on Saturday with the foreign minister, opposition and religious leaders, and even a rock star, it was time to call it a night. Everyone knew that the following day was the wild card main event—the Maidan visit, with the US senators scheduled to speak from the big stage.

On Sunday morning, I went to Boryspil Airport, about eighteen miles east of Kyiv, to meet Senator Murphy and his lead staffer, Jessica Elledge. Eager to go from the moment they exited the plane, on the car ride back into town both bombarded me with questions about the course of events in recent weeks.

By now the anti-Maidan camp at European Square, overflowing the previous day, was a ghost town. The remaining anti-Maidanivtsi had withdrawn to Mariinsky Park. On Maidan proper, a new newspaper, *The Voice of Maidan*, was distributed to all those entering between the barricades. Checking my BlackBerry, I learned that Dmytro Shymkiv, the general manager of Microsoft Ukraine, whom I knew through our struggles to legalize the Ukrainian government's software, had been living on Maidan for the last week. Dmytro was a heavyweight in Ukraine's IT sphere and an all-round impressive guy. If his presence was any indication, Maidan's students and artists were being joined by executives.

Senator Murphy joined up with McCain's delegation, and the two senators—one a Democrat, the other a Republican—met with several high-ranking Ukrainian government officials. Then, it was time to go to Maidan. Normally, the Embassy would have asked for a large police presence to ensure the safety of our important visitors. But there was no way that the protesters would allow police onto Maidan. Our Embassy Regional Security Office (RSO) team had adapted to this brave new world—this parallel Ukrainian ministate in effect—negotiating with the various Maidan Self-Defense Force (SDF) heads regarding access and security issues on Maidan. The SDF even agreed to wear certain T-shirts so that our security team would recognize them easily.

We arrived at the north end of the Maidan protest city in a generic white GM Embassy van. John McCain and Chris Murphy got out first through the awkward side doors. The rest of us quickly jumped out behind them. The van could go no farther into the protest city, but there were still another hundred yards or so to the imposing Maidan stage. The Maidan SDF was ready, locking arms to form human walls on both sides of a clear path they created for our group. The faces of the interlocking SDF were serious under their hand-painted helmets. In the freezing weather, many wore balaclavas covering their faces, their clothes a jumble of camouflage, bicycle knee pads, and haphazardly layered coats. But they certainly seemed to have the respect of the throng of silent onlookers behind them. Given the sheer number of people on the square as the senators made their way through the crowd, the solemn silence of the square—the scene of frequent rock concerts, prayers, and rousing speeches—made it seem unreal. As always, the Maidan air was thick with campfire smoke and the smell of boiling cabbage as our group approached the stage.

A few minutes later, we led the senators up a flight of stairs at the back of the massive stage. Senator McCain took the microphone. It was only then that I could see the full crowd in front of the stage. There were at least several hundred thousand people, maybe many more.

"We are here together speaking for the American people in solidarity with you. . . . America is with you. I am with you," boomed his voice from the loudspeaker system, followed quickly by a Ukrainian translation. The crowd listened intently, interrupting his speech several times with loud cheers and pro-US slogans. After Senator Murphy spoke, our group exited the back of the stage and threaded through the barricades and the SDF gauntlet to the waiting embassy van. Everyone trundled inside quickly. It was bitterly cold.

"John," said Senator Murphy, turning to McCain, "You've been in this part of the world a lot, doing this for such a long time, I'm sure that this is all old hat to you. But for me, that was something really incredible." "No," responded McCain thoughtfully. "I don't think I have ever seen anything like that before."

As McCain, Murphy, and their staffs flew out on Monday morning, December 16, Maidan kept teaching us new words. On social media, a fourth *viche* was announced for the next day on Maidan. The *viche* was a large-scale extreme exercise in direct democracy dating back to medieval times in Slavic lands. Essentially an outdoor town hall–style meeting, it was a venue where leaders could make direct appeals to citizens who then could approve or reject their speeches by mass acclamation. In the context of Maidan, *viches* were a way to get a sense of the "street" and to gain collective approval for various demands that the organizers were making of the government. At the Embassy, it was hard to judge how important these *viches* really were. Three of them had already taken place, including one just the previous day, and they didn't seem to have had any major impact. Were they just another stratagem to increase turnout on the square, or were they a real and legitimate decisionmaking mechanism? The next *viche* was set for the day of Yanukovych's upcoming trip to Moscow— clearly not a coincidence.

Eric Johnson, our public affairs officer, who was turning into our Embassy's secret poet laureate and reporter, continued his beat on the Maidan. After his walk through the protest camp that morning, he sent the Task Force an impressionist word painting that is worth quoting at length:

Even before I enter the Citadel's inner walls, a crowd of 150 people listening intently to a talk at Maidan's Open University catches my eye. The speaker is talking about how to develop Ukraine's economy without its current pervasive corruption and how Ukrainian embassies around the world might be able to help. Wish him luck and move on. . . . And just as in revolutionary Petrograd where Rosta windows appeared in all the post offices to inform the people of what was going on, the Citadel has its own "wall newspapers" pasted up on billboards, bus stops, and various other flat surfaces which now serve as information kiosks where the many voices of Maidan compete to be heard. Stickers are pasted next to children's drawings ("Let the sun of Europe shine on Ukraine") and pithy slogans ("Ukrainian government no longer represents Ukrainians") hang side by side with long hand-scrawled rants. My favorite wall is near Berehynia—an anti-GOU comix series which tells the story of official corruption and the rule of lawlessness in Ukraine. . . . The Citadel's defenses continue to mutate. The European Wall is down to just one controlled access point. Some of its Defenders have even customized their shields by painting St. George's crosses on them or slogans like "Odesa is with the people!" In anticipation that the invading Berkut horde will cut power as well as cell phone and internet connectivity before their next attack, the Cossacks guarding city hall wall have brought in Cossack war drums to sound the alarm and rally their forces. . . . And although there is a small group gathered around the Euro-piano in front of city hall singing old songs and another in front of an oil drum fire listening to an accordion player play a jig, tonight's mood seems more somber and subdued than it was over the weekend. Everyone seems to be waiting for what tomorrow might bring—the fourth *viche*, Yanu's meeting with Tsar Putin and the possible sale of Ukraine.

There was no letup in the onrushing stream of events. Maidan protesters fanned out to various Central Election Commission offices to protest reported falsification of the previous day's parliamentary by-elections results in five districts. On a lighter note, a flash mob of over a thousand appeared on Maidan spelling out "66 Kolya, Ciao!" hoping that Prime Minister Azarov, on his sixty-sixth birthday (Kolya is the informal version of Mykola, his first name), might be leaving the scene. Russian journalist Dmitriy Kiselev claimed that the United States was interfering in Ukrainian affairs by delivering $17 million to Batkivshchyna via the diplomatic pouch. At the Embassy, we wondered how a foreign political party would even receive a diplomatic pouch shipment. Come on, doesn't someone need to have diplomatic status to get a diplomatic pouch shipment? But such outlandish claims needn't make any sense to influence their target audience.

On Tuesday, December 17, President Yanukovych flew to Moscow on the private plane of Donetsk steel magnate Rinat Akhmetov for his Kremlin appointment. It was time to formalize the oral agreements reached during his meeting with Putin in Sochi.

In the ornate splendor of a Kremlin hall, Yanukovych and Putin signed twelve documents, including the overarching "Ukrainian-Russian Action Plan." Most of these were agreements to boost economic and industrial cooperation, such as settling outstanding trade cases, resuming joint aircraft production and other industrial cooperation, constructing a bridge across the Kerch Strait to connect Crimea with Russia, jointly celebrating the two-hundredth birthday of Ukrainian nationalist poet Taras Shevchenko, regulating border control and the fight against drugs, and jointly responding to emergency situations. But no one believed that these public documents were the most important outcomes of the trip. The most important outcomes might well be oral understandings that only two people in the world, Putin and Yanukovych, fully understood. That made life difficult for the average Ukrainian bureaucrat trying to read the tea leaves. Fortunately, clarity came swiftly.

At a surprise press briefing after the meeting, the real headline came out: Russia would deliver a huge financial bailout and gas discount. Russia agreed to provide Ukraine $15 billion in financing from its sovereign wealth fund, the first $3 billion of which would be handed to Ukraine through a Eurobond purchase within days. Also, Ukraine's gas price would drop from a staggeringly punitive rate of over $400 per bcm (billion cubic meters) to a manageable $268. Given the sorry state of Ukraine's economy and government budget, this cut the Yanukovych government the kind of financial slack they needed to keep the current corrupt, inefficient system lurching forward. One could imagine a collective sigh of relief at the Ukrainian Ministry of Finance.

After the deal, the Ukrainian government's mood seemed outwardly triumphant. Prime Minister Azarov announced, "Today I can firmly state that we have reached a turning point. . . . Nothing right now threatens the stability of the financial and economic situation in Ukraine." Flush with the promise of forthcoming Russian cash, Azarov promised to increase welfare payments by 22 percent for low-income families, raise government subsistence support for children, and boost the minimum wage by 18 percent. Party of Regions parliamentarian Volodymyr Makiyenko saw the deal as boding very well for the electoral future of his party: "Now we can pass a budget which addresses social issues, and with this budget we will enter the New Year wonderfully looking towards the—sorry to mention it—election campaign season."

From the Maidan main stage, opposition politicians questioned how much of Ukraine's sovereignty Yanukovych had signed over in exchange for Russia's concessions. The Ukrainian Democratic Alliance for Reforms's (UDAR's) Klitschko suggested that Yanukovych might be using Ukraine's state firms as collateral for the loans, while Svoboda's Tyahnybok said that only the presence of protesters on the Maidan prevented Yanukovych from committing Ukraine to join the Customs Union that very day. But with only around 20,000 assembling for the fourth *viche*, Kyiv's protesters still seemed to be in a state of shock. Many wondered whether it was too late, whether Ukraine had already been sold. A group of young women from Maidan brought a pumpkin to the Russian Embassy in Kyiv to pass on to President Putin. According to Ukrainian tradition, a woman gives a pumpkin to a suitor to reject his marriage proposal.

The next day, my colleague Eric Andersen invited me to a meeting with a good contact from the Finance Ministry. I gladly accepted. Meeting Eric's friend, a sharply dressed young man, that afternoon at a small downtown café, I wondered whether he always looked so depressed. We tried to be positive. Eric said, "Well, I guess this deal with Russia gives you guys some breathing room."

The young man laughed bitterly. "You cannot really call this deal a great victory. At the ministry we were told that the first tranche would be five billion, but now it is three. We had already run our budgets figuring that we would get five. And I'm assuming that three is all that we will get out of the promised fifteen."

That was surprising, so Eric asked why. "Everything in this deal is written to maximize Russian pressure on Ukraine. First, the 5 percent interest is really more like 7 because it doesn't include commission rates. So it's pretty close to what we could have gotten on the commercial market anyway." He took a long sip of coffee. "But unlike if we had gotten financing on the commercial market, Russia can basically demand back all of their money at any time. With our government permanently on the edge of the fiscal abyss, don't you think maybe that this would give them some little bit of leverage over our every major decision?"

He glumly continued. "The gas prices are renegotiated quarterly, and the future bond interest rate is not set and can be manipulated. I've already said it, but everything is calibrated to put maximum pressure on us." "Were there any other agreements made in Moscow that concern you?" I asked. He took another long, rough sip from his delicate-looking white coffee cup. "In Stalinist politics, you only find out what secret protocols exist when they are published after fifty years. Come on, unless your CIA is doing a really bang-up job, none of us around this table knows what was agreed to or not agreed to in Sochi or Moscow. The secrecy and unpredictability are killing us, since no one can plan for anything. Don't forget that we all thought that we were signing the Association Agreement until the moment that presidential order came out. My minister thought we were signing, and that's what Deputy Prime Minister Arbuzov thought too. There's a layer of crazy, unpredictable politics working at the presidential level that even those right around Yanukovych have no access to. In my job, I make budget plans and projections. In this environment, really, what is the point?"

That ended the conversation. We all just sipped the espresso-style coffee, served as black as Ukraine's budget abyss.

That same day, we and many other foreign diplomats in Kyiv received an extraordinary open letter, signed by twenty-three current and former Ukrainian diplomats—two former foreign ministers, many more ambassadors, and others. The pathos and wounded personal and national pride expressed in this letter, a letter that broke ranks with the foreign ministry leadership, was unlike anything I had ever read from diplomats.

One feels proud or hurt for one's country when one is in diplomatic service. The Vilnius Summit became a foreign policy disaster. Each of us at different times and in different positions did everything possible to have Ukraine finally cross the foreign policy Rubicon on the way to united Europe. Instead of this, the nighttime beating of the peaceful Maidan became a bloody Rubicon inside the state. Instead of a peaceful, independent, and predictable Ukraine, the world saw savages with military insignia; instead of a proud sovereign state which is able to protect its national interests, a beggar with an outstretched arm; instead of European integration reforms, cheap populism. . . . It is with great sympathy that we imagine how difficult it is for our colleagues to look into the eyes of European partners. . . . We appeal to all our colleagues in Ukraine and abroad to remember that Ukrainian diplomats don't trade their country and their own people. We always were, are, and will remain with Ukrainians, wherever they are—on Maidan in Kyiv or any corner of the world. Sooner or later we will reach our goal to which we devoted many years of our lives—the creation of a wealthy, prosperous, stable European Ukraine.

After spending tens of thousands of hours preparing the Association Agreement, it was easy to imagine disillusionment inside Ukraine's Foreign Affairs Ministry. But it was still remarkable to see it expressed in black and white on paper in such stark terms. The next day the Foreign Ministry released a statement, mirroring Putin's language, demanding that "foreigners [meaning Westerners] stop interfering with the internal affairs of Ukraine." But while "Western interference" was theoretical and based mostly on dark conspiracy theory, tangible Russian interference was apparently still welcome as long as it supported the right side.

As they had agreed, Presidents Putin and Yanukovych held separate news conferences in Moscow and Kyiv on Thursday, December 19, to answer questions on their summit two days earlier. Putin addressed 1,300 Russian and foreign journalists at Moscow's World Trade Center. Interviewed by a handful of friendly journalists in Kyiv, Yanukovych held his first live broadcast press conference since the start of the political crisis. While the two events were some five hundred miles apart and held at different times, they seemed quite in sync, a kind of long-distance duet:

Putin: "Today we can see that Ukraine is experiencing serious economic, social and political problems. . . . If we really say that Ukraine is a brotherly nation and a brotherly country, then we should act the way close family members do and support the Ukrainian people in this difficult situation."

Yanukovych: "The [Russian] money will be used to increase pensions, salaries, and social benefits; it will create the conditions for improving people's lives. The social part is key, and social payments will not be less than in previous years. We will watch this matter very closely, as it is of fundamental importance for us."

Putin: "Let me say again that this decision is not about the interests of Ukraine's current government, but is about the interests of Ukraine's people."

Yanukovych: "We expect to construct with Russia two new blocks of the Khmelnytskyi Nuclear Power Plant. . . . We will have a lot of joint projects in shipbuilding, aircraft construction, power engineering, transport engineering."

Putin: "At one point, Ukraine took American fuel and used it at Ukrainian nuclear power stations. All the rods got deformed. You see what happens? These are serious things."

Yanukovych: (referring to the United States and EU) "It is important that our internal problems are not interfered with by any country. They mustn't think that they can boss us around as they like, either on the Maidan or not on the Maidan. . . . I am categorically against the fact that someone comes to our country and tries to teach us how to live here. . . . We have to learn to negotiate and defend together our own national interests. And running around looking for some kind of master who already has interests here in Ukraine—we don't need that. We do not need to humiliate ourselves. . . . We do not need to go out with an outstretched hand."

Putin: "We are not against [Ukraine's] association [with the EU], but are simply saying that we will have to protect our own economy because we have a free trade zone with Ukraine, and we will not be able to leave those doors wide open in the present situation if Ukraine opens its doors wide to the European Union. We will have no choice but to close our doors."

Yanukovych: "As concerns the Eurasian Union, we filed a written bid in Astana in August this year to consider Ukraine's participation in the Eurasian Union as an observer."

Putin: "If Ukraine adopts EU commercial standards, they won't be able to sell us anything at all. Do you see? So, Ukraine will immediately become—and this is just by definition, you don't need to think about it too hard, just read the documents—an agricultural appendage [to the EU]."

Yanukovych: "[Euromaidan protests represent] an unconstitutional attempt to seize power. This is not the first time this has happened to our government. I went through this already [during the Orange Revolution] and I strongly opposed it. I am categorically against, categorically against, attempts to initiate this kind of process."

Putin: "No one was trying to strangle anyone here."

With such a score that was written in harmony for a duet, could there be any doubt as to the identity of the chief lyricist?

———————

Meanwhile, after three weeks of crisis operations, we at US Embassy Kyiv were sleep deprived, overstimulated, overcaffeinated, and jumpy. For me and my family it was time for a break. Unlike those sleeping in freezing tents on the square or wearing black Interior Ministry helmets, we had that luxury. Of course, given the situation, it felt bizarre, and more than a little like going AWOL, to hop on a plane and head to Dubai. After the past few weeks, I could barely imagine stepping away from the information fire hose and removing myself emotionally from what was going on. However, it was far from AWOL. Elizabeth, in her wisdom, forbade me from even thinking about canceling our trip. We all needed a break, even if Natalya and I refused to admit it. I wondered if the whole situation would be over by the time we returned.

The contrast between Kyiv and Dubai could not have been greater. Dubai was incredible—warm and new, opulent and odd. We wondered what our first "Muslim Christmas" would be like. Given the preponderance of foreigners, we found that Dubai celebrates Christmas with gusto. There were no shortages of Santa Claus sightings in the United Arab Emirates as we wandered through some of the most over-the-top shopping malls I've ever seen.

On the escalator in one of those malls, I caught sight of a familiar Ukrainian face. In Andrew's small class of twelve kids at Kyiv International School, there was one other father who occasionally showed up at school events generally dominated by moms or nannies. While the State Department paid for our kids' international school tuition, the Ukrainians who sent their kids to the school were able to pay the high tuition themselves. This dad owned a distinctive, high-end theme restaurant close to Kyiv's stadium. I recognized him right away—deep tan, light hair, the confident gait of a successful entrepreneur.

After exchanging pleasantries, we sat down for a cup of Starbucks coffee in the huge mall atrium while the boys, off the leash of parental supervision, ran up and down the long escalators. I asked him about his business. "Well, not a lot of profits these days, but that's all right," he sighed. "Some things you just have to do. Most of the food we make now goes straight to the Maidan. We don't make any money from that."

"Really?" I asked, a bit surprised at this revelation. "So, how did you get involved with the Maidanivtsi?" "You know, Chris, it goes back to the Orange Revolution," he remembered, suddenly a bit nostalgic. "I never gave much thought to my country. I guess you could say that as a young man I was a Soviet person, and Ukraine never meant much to me. Then I had some friends who were going out onto the square back in 2004. I didn't really get it or understand what it was all about. It was there on the square that I heard our national anthem and actually listened to it for the first time. I saw guys my age, old women, and kids working together to bring firewood to the square to keep each other warm. I really can't explain it. It just felt like I was part of something bigger for the first time. I got swept up in it. Of course, in the end, we just got used by our politicians, and life didn't actually get any better. I think a lot of people just gave up entirely on our political process after that and gave up on caring in general. But I'll keep sending food as long as there is hope. And there really is hope now. I feel a bit more like my younger self when I support the Maidan. And you know, they must win. For real this time. They *must*."

After the boys had exhausted themselves running up the massive down escalators, Andrew crashed down on my lap, panting. His schoolmate's father and I finished our coffee and parted with a handshake. After a few more days in the Arabian sun, Natalya, Andrew, Elena, and I boarded our discount Hungarian airline "Wizz Air" turboprop plane to return to the hope and the struggle taking place on and around the frozen granite paving stones of the Maidan.

Events in Ukraine hadn't taken a vacation. While we were gone, EU officials stated that they were previously prepared to facilitate a $20 billion loan if Yanukovych had signed in Vilnius. Prime Minister Azarov denied that this money was ever on the table. Vice Prime Minister Yuriy Boyko suggested to the press that Yanukovych was willing to hand control over Ukraine's gas pipeline system to a 50-50 percent Russian-Ukraine consortium on "brotherly" terms, which would help Russia meet another of its longtime goals—increasing control over the infrastructure that delivered its natural gas to Europe. Meanwhile, Russia's $3 billion purchase of Ukrainian Eurobonds went through in Ireland, and Ukraine's Cabinet of Ministers released an odd and mathematically adventurous document to justify the government's actions by claiming that Ukraine would have lost $36.9 billion in 2014 had it signed the Association Agreement. A fifth and then a sixth *viche* were held on Maidan. The numbers of those camped out there started to fall due to the freezing weather, dejection following the Russia deal, and the start of the holiday season. The sixth *viche* had the lowest attendance of any to that point. Still, the Maidan's creative spirit was still in evidence. Some enterprising Maidanivtsi had painted the oil drums and pipes making up some of the barricades like wrapped presents and candy canes to give the ramshackle fortifications a holiday feel.

Away from the square, life was getting increasingly dangerous for those supporting Euromaidan. Tetyana Chornovol, an investigative journalist who was active on Maidan, had spent Western Christmas eve (December 24) staking out the private residences of Minister of Internal Affairs Vitaliy Zakharchenko and Prosecutor General Viktor Pshonka. At about 1:30 a.m., a group of men in a black Porsche Cayenne began aggressively chasing her car and ran her off the road. The men pulled her from her car and viciously beat her before traffic police found her and took her to a local hospital for the first of three surgeries for her serious injuries. Images of her blackened, broken face, with her nose fractured in five to seven places, and a video of the car chase from her dashcam rapidly made the rounds on the internet, causing a massive uproar and calls for accountability. She was not the only victim. Dmytro Pylypets, a Euromaidan activist in Kharkiv, survived being stabbed twelve times by unknown assailants. One Kyiv Automaidan activist was shot and injured while attackers burned his car. This was one of three strikingly similar attacks on Automaidan in three cities over two days. On Christmas Day, demonstrators outside the US Embassy held photos of Chornovol's bloody face and signs demanding sanctions against Yanukovych and his cabinet.

When Chornovol was well enough, Ambassador Pyatt and a group of other Western ambassadors went to visit her in the hospital. She was already less bloodied, but some of her fingernails had been torn off and she was clearly still in quite a bit of pain. "I'm fine, they only tortured me for a little while, I'll make it," this remarkably courageous woman told the group.

When one of the ambassadors said that she should be certain not to drive alone at night anymore, she responded, "Why? You don't like the way I drive?" Everybody laughed, and Chornovol, too, laughed at her own joke, causing her swollen lips to crack again and start to bleed. She picked up a nearby cloth to dab away the blood. "The success of the protests, that is the main thing," she said. "I just want to get back to work."

As did I. I returned to work on December 30, spending the morning catching up on the events of the past ten days. When I had left for Dubai, I wondered if the crisis would be over in ten days; now, as the New Year approached, the situation only seemed to be getting more violent and unpredictable.

Even the fight to get the Ukrainian government to legalize its software took on unusual dimensions through the Maidan prism. It was primarily a fight between Microsoft—led in Ukraine by Dmitry Shymkiv, who was back from extended leave spent sleeping in tents on the square—and the Ukrainian government as represented by Mykola Kovinya, head of the State Intellectual Property Service of Ukraine. So it was Maidan against the government again.

Shymkiv emailed me: "Mr. Kovinya continues to play his game. He refused to sign the agreement proposed. . . . Kovinya still keeps me and our Public Sector lead on his 'blocked' list, so we cannot even dial in." The context was clear—here was another Yanukovych administration official who could not be trusted. However, Kovinya himself emailed me: "Chris, I have extended myself greatly to offer Microsoft something which should work. I could get in real trouble and they are still asking for things I cannot deliver. Please help."

The end of Ukraine's fiscal year, which was the deadline for a deal, was just hours away. I worked the phones trying to restart the dialogue between the two tired, mistrustful sides, passing messages and proposals between them. As the clock counted down toward midnight, they reached a compromise on a $60 million package to legalize the pirated software that the Ukrainian government had long been using and replace it with licensed versions. Plenty of questions remained regarding how the deal would be implemented and whether it would fall apart. At least on this one issue, though, our Embassy had helped broker a compromise between one reformer (who happened to represent an American company) and the government. Was it also possible to work things out on a much larger scale between the two warring camps or was a showdown inevitable? Our ambassador and Political Section were working hard to encourage a compromise. Software legalization was tough enough, but finding the way out of Ukraine's political crisis would be infinitely tougher.

In the officially atheist Soviet Union, New Year's Eve became the biggest holiday of the year, and its importance in countries of the former USSR still eclipses that in much of the rest of the world. New Year's Eve is when Santa (called Ded Moroz, or Father Frost) comes, and when families gather around the tree. A huge street party with live music from the Maidan stage and fireworks boomed across downtown Kyiv. The hundred thousand or so attendees attempted to break the world's record for the largest group singing a national anthem. As always, Maidan was creative and changing. While Russian television continued to claim that Maidan protesters were anti-Russian nationalists, the Maidanivtsi had set up a prayer shrine with candles lit for the Russian victims of two recent suicide bombings in Volgograd, Russia. There was only sympathy, not animosity. On other parts of the square, vendors had added a new popular item to their Maidan T-shirts and refrigerator magnets—Yanukovych and Azarov dart boards.

Following tradition, at the stroke of midnight Yanukovych addressed the country on television from the ancient Pecherska Lavra monastery's main cathedral.

It is a difficult time, probably the most difficult year in the history of independent Ukraine. It was a year of achievements and challenges, frustrations and new hopes. In the long run, 2013 became a year of progress for us. Through Maidans and national panel discussions, political arguments and sincere dialogue, we are moving the way of mutual understanding and national consolidation. This path is extremely challenging but we must go through it jointly, side by side.

Natalya and I stayed home and greeted the New Year of 2014 with the kids.

Kyiv and the Maidan protest world slowly returned to life on New Year's Day. The Ukrainian government would be officially closed for the next eight days until after Orthodox Christmas, and this was traditionally the slowest time of the year for business in the city. Around 6:00 p.m., a large nationalist procession of perhaps ten thousand—mostly Svoboda and others carrying red-and-black flags—made its way through the protest camp and past St. Michael's and St. Sophia's cathedrals. Unlike some earlier marches that seemed to have been staged for Russian propaganda purposes, this one seemed real. The emotions seemed genuine, and the date was the 105th anniversary of the birth of WWII-era Organization of Ukrainian Nationalists leader Stepan Bandera. At one point near the square, the procession encountered a sole pro–Red Army protester with a banner. Eric Johnson witnessed the rightists grab the sign and tear it up. Both sides looked ready to fight, one man versus thousands. Ghosts of World War II always haunted Ukraine, ready to materialize at any moment.

As Eric watched, Maidan SDF intervened and surrounded the group, making sure that the lone pro–Red Army guy could leave unharmed. "No beat-ing!" they yelled as the man filtered back into the crowd. Among the Maidan SDF defending the pro–Red Army protester, there were plenty of Svoboda and other nationalist volunteers. But they followed different instructions on the square and had different goals. They were not there to fight the Second World War again. Their concerns were contemporary. What kind of country would Ukraine become? Could Ukraine triumph over the corrupt political culture that had taken such deep root? Such questions could not be answered through street fights over how to interpret seventy-year-old crimes. The men of the Maidan SDF's Second Sotnya had hung a huge Mahatma Gandhi sign at European Gate reading, "At first they will try to ignore you, then they will laugh at you, then they will fight against you, but then victory will be yours." The ethos of nonviolence still defined the square at that point.

Meanwhile, a nationwide campaign against activists escalated. Euromaidan activists in the eastern steel town of Kryvyi Rih were targeted: one was beaten, another had his car tires slashed, and a third had his car windows broken. A Euromaidan activist was kidnapped from a railway station in the northwest city of Dubno and held for two days and nights in an abandoned cellar without water or food. He was released after people in a passing car heard his cries for help. His burned passport and notebook were found in a garbage pile near the building. He told police that he received threats a few days earlier warning him to stop taking part in Euromaidan activities. Back on Maidan, unknown ar-sonists escaped after they were discovered trying to set fire to the Trade Unions Building. The Ukrainian traffic police, or DAI, started making visits to Auto-maidan activists' homes to deliver court summonses for illegal behavior on the roads, and Automaidan returned the favor by conducting rallies outside DAI headquarters. Following the pro-Bandera march on New Year's Day, a Svoboda parliamentarian and lawyer were summoned for a police interview and then beaten by unknown assailants as they departed the station. The Maidan SDF announced that they were reorganizing themselves into twenty-five "sotnyas," or groups of one hundred—the approximate size of a military company.

The crowds on Maidan were smaller after the holiday. Many observers, such as Vijai Maheshwari of the Daily Beast, wrote that Russia's largesse had put the protests on the path to oblivion. He quoted one local hairdresser as saying that there was no continuing crisis for protesters to respond to following the Russia deal: "There's no reason for them to be there any longer. It's like hanging around at a party after all the girls have left." Open Maidan University had left the square, leaving passersby to speculate on whether they would return after the holidays.

For those activists remaining on the square, creativity helped to dilute the monotony of days stretching into weeks. On the Instytutska barricades, a painting riffing off of the Angry Birds cell phone game depicted round protester birds, dressed in traditional Ukrainian clothes, flying at black-clad Berkut birds. Within days, a Ukrainian software firm offered a free "Angry Ukrainians" game through the Google app store, letting players launch little blue and yellow birds to knock over helmeted security officers, statues of Lenin, and other targets. In a guerrilla marketing effort, protesters created fake cigarette packets reading on the outside: "Isn't it bad enough that Yanukovych is your President, but you have to smoke too?" Maidan SDF often personalized their orange helmets with traditional folk or holiday designs during their downtime. A popular spot on the square was a small stage with three judges' chairs beside a mannequin of President Yanukovych in a cage—the traditional place for an accused defendant in a Soviet courtroom. Anyone could sit in the chairs, and friends could snap pictures of themselves "judging" Yanukovych.

On Orthodox Christmas Eve, January 6, Orthodox and Greek Catholic priests, as well as a rabbi, an imam, and a Protestant minister, conducted services from the Maidan stage. The diversity of the night was further enhanced by the performance of a group of Crimean Tatar drummers. Around the same time as the religious services were taking place, unknown assailants assaulted Euromaidan activist Ihor Mashkevych in a Dnipropetrovsk restaurant. He suffered a concussion and required seventeen stitches. Mashkevych's offense had been to collect donations and supplies in Dnipropetrovsk for Maidan organizers in Kyiv. Although we did not personally know these people who risked themselves for the protest movement, whenever we read about these attacks, it felt like a punch to the gut. The Embassy constantly advocated for peace and reconciliation through reform. Such brutal assaults reminded us that we were getting further from our goals, not closer.

On that Orthodox Christmas Day, the struggle battered the religious realm. The Ukrainian Orthodox Church had two main branches, the "Moscow Patriarchy" headed by Patriarch Kirill in Moscow, and the "Kyiv Patriarchy" headed by Patriarch Filaret in Kyiv. In a Christmas Day television interview from Moscow, Patriarch Kirill of the Russian Orthodox Church (and the

Ukrainian Orthodox Church's Moscow Patriarchate) warned that the Maidan movement could potentially split Ukrainian society and threaten the spiritual unity of Russians and Ukrainians. Patriarch Kirill had long advocated the concept of "Russkiy Mir" (Russian world), as a spiritual bond between Eastern Orthodox believers in different countries. Putin himself, who on multiple occasions had employed religion for his own geopolitical goals, also began using the term when speaking about the need for his government to intervene on behalf of Russian speakers in other countries. In an interview the same day, Patriarch Filaret of the Ukrainian Orthodox Church-Kyiv Patriarchate called Kirill's statement "untrue," asserting that Kirill's Russkiy Mir concept was not about "spiritual unity" but rather about establishing "an empire in a nice package." The dividing line between Moscow and Kyiv couldn't have been clearer.

On Wednesday, January 8, the Ukrainian government was officially back at work. Viktor Medvedchuk, leader of Ukraine's pro-Russian faction with close personal ties to Putin, posted on his Facebook page an accusation that Hromadske.tv was "a US government initiative . . . organized by the CIA to support the protests and a coup in Ukraine. . . . Their task is to destroy and wreak havoc!" In reality, Hromadske.tv was an internet television station registered as an NGO started in June 2013 by a group of Ukrainian journalists. It was true that the station received a small US Embassy grant, and this was long publicly acknowledged by both the Embassy and the station. Such grants were intended to promote press freedom, not tell anyone what to say. The grant was no secret, but it was enough to expose the station to the false accusation that it was doing the US government's bidding. Big lies are built on small truths. Also, they began broadcasting shortly before Yanukovych's November 30 attack on student protesters. During the crisis, Hromadske became well known for its live feeds from the protest zone and for going to great lengths to fact check rumors and accusations made on both sides of the conflict. It was reliable, real-time journalism, and many observers at our Embassy watched it often. Medvedchuk's "Ukrainian Choice" party didn't limit its mud-slinging campaign to Hromadske. On the way to work, I saw a new bus stop light board campaign with little male stick figures joined by hearts and little female stick figures holding hands. "Association with the EU—It's a Gay Marriage," read the top of the poster. A group of Ukrainian LGBT organizations immediately issued a press release denouncing the campaign and urging the LGBT community not to participate in a "paid protest" rally that anti-Maidan groups were attempting to bring to the Maidan to paint the Maidan movement as pro-gay.

The next day, Ukraine's state energy firm Naftogaz and Russia's Gazprom signed an agreement confirming Putin's offer to Yanukovych in Moscow to slash Ukraine's gas prices. If used wisely, this might have helped Ukraine begin to narrow its gaping state budget deficit. Instead, the Ukrainian Cabinet of Ministers immediately announced that they would further subsidize the already heavily subsidized price of consumer gas across Ukraine in a transparent play for popularity during the ongoing crisis. Instead of helping to balance Ukraine's budget, the lower gas prices would replenish the financial slop trough for the corrupt oligarchs who profited by diverting subsidized, cheap gas, supposedly intended for consumers, into more profitable channels. It would also take Ukraine even farther away from fulfilling the demands of the International Monetary Fund, which had pressed Ukraine to raise gas prices closer to their actual cost as a means of making the Ukrainian government solvent. As a bonus to Russia, Ukrainian minister of energy and coal industry Eduard Stavytskyi announced that Ukraine would no longer seek to purchase "reverse flow" gas from Slovakia, meaning that Russia would be Ukraine's sole supplier. It was an ideal outcome for those wanting to boost Yanukovych's popularity vis-à-vis Maidan while simultaneously drawing him further into Russia's orbit. That same morning, Prime Minister Azarov announced that his government should begin new negotiations with the EU on signing the Association Agreement and the Deep and Comprehensive Free Trade Agreement while "balancing" this move through promoting increased trade with Commonwealth of Independent States (CIS) countries and "cooperation" with Russia. But this attempt to appear equidistant between Brussels and Moscow no longer fooled anyone. Meanwhile, Embassy observers reported that the crowds on Maidan continued to dwindle. It seemed that the protests were petering out. But then, contrary to expectations, Maidan was soon back in the headlines.

Though neither the EU nor Batkivshchyna, her own political party, were having any success convincing Yanukovych to parole Yuliya Tymoshenko from prison, Yanukovych had released her former minister of internal affairs, Yuriy Lutsenko, in April 2013. Lutsenko had recently become quite active on Maidan. He was involved in protests on the evening of Friday, January 10, when a group of nationalists confronted Berkut stationed in buses outside of Kyiv's Sviatoshynska police station. After Lutsenko attempted to mediate, protesters began throwing rocks at the Berkut buses. The remaining riot police then ran out of their buses and beat Lutsenko unconscious. Peacemaking often doesn't pay.

That clash grabbed headlines, but smaller, less dramatic, confrontations also continued regularly. Eric Johnson messaged the Task Force on Saturday morning, January 11:

> About 100 paid Party of Regions or Medvedchuk protesters— "concerned citizens"—showed up with a bunch of identical posters ("Revolutionary HQ—Go Home") and brand new Ukrainian flags and tried to make it past the far gate on the TSUM [high-end Kyiv department store] barricade. The SDF reacted in force by putting up a human wall to prevent anti-Maidan from mixing with Maidan—an explosive combo. An argument ensued as to who were the real Ukrainians. Then the SDF started singing the national anthem (reminded me of Estonia's singing revolution for a moment there). There are a couple of pro-Russian and pro-GOU [government of Ukraine] TV cameras here. And there are a bunch of titushky or undercover cop types (not much difference) hanging around the edges. No uniformed police in sight. Eventually, the anti-Maidan protesters backed off, and the rain helped thin their numbers. Meanwhile, life on the Maidan goes on—although the Cossacks of the 4th Sotnya (the inner wall) are on full alert.

On Saturday, the fake LGBT-Euromaidan provocation rally organized secretly by Viktor Medvedchuk's pro-Russian Ukraine's Choice party, which the real LGBT community had anxiously predicted, actually took place.

John Bush reported from the scene: "My wife and I were downtown this morning and stopped by Besarabskyi Market for the faux Pride march. It was heavily stage-managed, with roughly equal numbers of marchers and reporters/ photogs—about thirty people in each group. . . . The event looked exactly like a gay pride parade as imagined by a Soviet commissar. . . . There was an utter lack of fabulousness."

Later in the week, real LGBT activists went to Medvedchuk's Ukraine's Choice office to present Medvedchuk a tongue-in-cheek "Certificate of Appreciation" for his and his organization's "contribution" to developing the LGBT movement in Ukraine. Satire, too, was a weapon employed in the ongoing struggle, but unlike batons, it left no bloody marks or cracked heads.

While our eyes were focused largely on Maidan in Kyiv, other Euromaidan events were popping up in cities throughout Ukraine, not only in places one would expect like the western city of Lviv, but also in those that one wouldn't, such as Yanukovych's eastern hometown of Donetsk. The Maidanivtsi turned out to be master organizers. The idea of creating a coordinating body to give regional Maidans a sense of inclusion and purpose had been percolating for some time in the activist community. Late in the week, we heard that the first All Ukraine Maidan meeting would convene over the weekend in Kharkiv, which seemed a surprising, audacious choice. Not only had recent knife attacks, car burnings, and spurious police prosecutions for unrelated crimes shown that the city was not safe for Euromaidan activists, but it was a town run by the unsavory duo of Dobkin and Kernes. Ukrainian investigative journalist Bohdan Butkevych described Kharkiv Region governor Mykhailo Dobkin and Kharkiv mayor Hennadiy Kernes at that time as "two figures known for their Ukrainophobia, eccentricity, criminal record, and personal loyalty to Viktor Yanukovych." Some of Dobkin's recent greatest hits included offering to make Kharkiv the new capital of an anti-Maidan Ukraine (Kharkiv had been the administrative center of Soviet Ukraine from 1919 to 1934), tweeting that the notorious Molotov-Ribbentrop Pact of 1939 should be annulled to give western Ukraine back to Poland, and laughing at photos of a badly beaten Svoboda parliamentarian. No less offensive, Kernes had recently publicly called a female parliamentarian who resigned from the Party of Regions "a whore." Kharkiv seemed an improbable venue for an All-Ukraine Maidan meeting. Nevertheless, Kharkiv's undaunted Euromaidan protesters had attracted sympathy through their perseverance and sense of humor. At a rally in late December, for example, they held a tongue-in-cheek ceremony to unofficially change the name of Kharkiv's Lenin Street to Lennon Street. On New Year's Eve, Kharkiv Euromaidan activists gave police and their city council members copies of the Ukrainian constitution, EU symbols, and chocolates, "so they would smile more often."

Given the likelihood of trouble and the need to know the ground truth once the inevitable mutual accusations started flying, the Embassy assigned two officers, Tim Piergalski and Tuck Evans, to travel to Kharkiv for the weekend to serve as invited observers. They were not to participate in any way in Euromaidan's meetings, but if things got out of control and we needed to urge the Ukrainian government to call off the dogs, we could use their observations as the basis for our reaction. So off Tim and Tuck went to Kharkiv.

The next morning, Tim sent his first email:

> Approximately 1,500 Party of Regions protesters gathering this morning at site of regular Maidan protests (no Maidan protesters present— "All Ukraine Maidan" plenary session starts this afternoon). Stage set up with audio equipment, etc. Old Soviet music. Five or so professionally printed banners repeated over and over: "Yanukovych is our President," "Youth for Yanukovych" (old women holding it), "We are against fascism," "No to Euromaidan, Yes to Stability," etc. Mood slightly more festive than anti-Maidan rallies at Mariinsky Park, but very contrived feel remains. Some police presence, but normal officers, not VV [Interior Ministry] or Berkut. No titushky visible.

The cars carrying the Euromaidan delegates and observers were blocked for a tense half hour before the pro-Yanukovych protesters allowed them to pass. Tim and Tuck continued to share via email what they saw that afternoon and into the next day:

Tuck, 1:45 p.m.: "Representatives (100 and counting) of the All Ukrainian Maidan Forum are arriving at the snap-designated meeting site—the Ukrainian Orthodox Church (Kyiv Patriarchy) St. Ioanna Bohoslova located on the outskirts of Kharkiv . . . [Euromaidan's] central figures are here. Also, there appears to be a Crimean Tatar delegation. . . . But after a quick gathering, we are told to exit to a 'new location, TBD.' So we're all getting back into cars. No police. No titushky. Some television cameras."

Tim, 2:40 p.m.: "Kharkiv Euromaidan's wandering spirit quest continues at Kharkiv's autocephalous church, gathering for spiritual songs in a side chapel. A few delegates were hit with eggs while standing outside. Some people who may be undercover cops (too old to be titushky) following the group around— Democratic Alliance reps apprehended one and turned him over to the police station. Service interrupted as the organizer shouted that titushky were interfering with Self-Defense Forces outside. Audio equipment being set up as plenary session begins. Unclear what is happening outside. Those in the small, crowded plenary room/chapel appear calm."

Tim, 3:53 p.m.: "Opening plenary session concluded, about to split into small working groups in different venues, and we are going to KHRG [Kharkiv Human Rights Protection Group, a local NGO] office. . . . Emphasized that Maidan is not a revolution or a coup."

Tuck, 5:05 p.m.: "A cold, windy night in the center of Kharkiv. At 4:45 the pro-Regions rally next to the Shevchenko statue continues (started at 10:00 a.m.). About 1,000 cold protesters in front of the stage, some fairly jovial. . . . Emcee (always in Russian) talks in boilerplate, 'We support this decision (doesn't say what decision) because we support a free and strong Ukraine.' Music acts sing a mix of US and Russian pop tunes (Katy Perry's 'Firework')."

Tuck, 6:44 p.m.: "Regions rally was still going strong. . . . Highlights include an energetic 1970s pop collage performance that sparks honest titushky dancing when the generic male singer and his female backups blast Village People's 'YMCA' ('You can have a good meal, you can do whatever you feel'). People almost know the dance although most hand gestures are murky after the 'Y.' Ironically followed by Abba's 'Money, Money, Money.' A nervous moment as a parade of 400 opposition protesters, UPA [World War II–era Ukrainian Insurgent Army] flag in the vanguard (but Svoboda, UDAR, and Batkivshchyna represented) march past the demonstration on the other side of the street. They are accompanied by a police escort of about 30, including five riot police bringing up the rear."

Tuck, Sunday (next day), 9:19 a.m.: "Embassy team in Kharkiv is fine. . . . One of the working groups that met at a bookstore at around 5:00 p.m. (Embassy team was at another location—Kharkiv Human Rights Group) were attacked by thugs while meeting in the bookstore. Broken glass door. Gas used. Some of the volunteer guards were roughed up, one beaten severely (photo available on Maidan forum coordinator's Facebook page)."

Tim, Sunday, 9:57 a.m.: "About 15 titushky across the street from registration point today, same number of police between protesters and titushky to keep order. A few Gryfon battalion police [special police] in reserve off to the side. Everyone calm. Some delegates had registration badges ripped off their necks during the bookstore scrum yesterday; therefore all re-registered today to prevent impostors from entering session. As forum group walks to meeting point, police form column on side. Titushky also following on other side of the street. . . . Still many proposals from the crowd to amend what was decided in groups yesterday. Seems to be too many differing views to obtain consensus."

Tim, 1:31 p.m.: "Forum concluded at 12:50 with national anthem. Another to be planned. A few radical voices began to visibly annoy majority, who coalesced against them. . . . Rallying on minor square as anti-Maidan is still in the usual Maidan spot. . . . Same Ukrainian Telekom truck that disrupted opposition rally last night by blasting noise over protest speakers. Truck full of titushky, surrounded by protesters and police. Protesters chanting for police to remove masks. Press all over it."

Tim, 1:50 p.m.: "Regions' march passing right in front of Maidan rally as police in full riot gear surround Ukrainian Telekom truck on one side with normal cops on other side. Guy on top of truck setting up speakers, pointing them at Maidan rally. Maidan serenading the passing Regions column with national anthem. Chanting *hanba* [shame] at approaching titushky (same group that has been following Maidan all day). Truck just started blasting music (from the Orange Revolution, strangely) completely drowning out protesters."

Tim, 2:03 p.m.: "Music from Ukrainian Telekom truck very effective—I was two meters from the opposition speaker and couldn't hear what he was saying. Brief scuffle when truck carrying bigger sound system showed up. Fireworks. Self Defense Force surrounded opposition truck, then police provided extra security, drawing thanks from protesters. The escalating sound system war is absurd. . . . Unidentified speaker is inside truck, now fully surrounded by police in full riot gear (minus shields)."

Tim, 2:26 p.m.: "New opposition sound system puts them on equal footing. Speaker and music blasting. Emcee says: 'Hey-ho, if you're not jumping, you're titushky!'"

And for one brief moment, the struggle for the future of Ukraine became a tense but oddly joyous dance-off.

On Sunday back in Kyiv, there was yet another *veche* on the Maidan. The crowd listened respectfully to opposition leaders and other speakers, but the real fan favorites were Automaidan. When Dmytro Bulatov, an Automaidan founder and leader, took the stage, the crowd roared. Maidan was generating its own heroes, figures who were unknown one month before. Bulatov left the stage to caravan with several hundred fellow Automaidan drivers once again to Mezhyhirya, the symbol of the Yanukovych regime's venality. As they reached the area around Mezhyhirya, rows of buses and police cars blocked them from delivering a "people's summons" to Yanukovych's estate. They eventually put the "summons" on a police bus and returned to Kyiv. Back on the square, the firebrand speech of chocolatier and former economy minister in Yanukovych's government Petro Poroshenko was riling up the crowd.

Amid all this excitement, it was time for me to visit Maksim Maksimov at the CIS Institute again and check on how the Russia deal was progressing. As things were swinging in Russia's direction, Maksimov was in a great mood—chatty, with a bit of swagger. He looked like a man who had just gotten a big Christmas bonus check and saw his career on an upswing. He was the cat who just ate the canary and desperately wanted me to see the crushed feathers dangling victoriously out of the corner of his mouth. While taking out her pen to make notes of the conversation, Valentyna looked uncomfortable to be back at the CIS Institute.

"As you know, Russia worked hard to prevent Ukraine from signing the Association Agreement," Maksimov started casually. "The Europeans put very tough conditions on Ukraine, and Yanukovych understood that the EU would support Yulia Tymoshenko's candidacy for his job. That really tipped things in our favor. Anyway, did you really expect him to accept that? Do you guys know the man at all?"

I let that gibe pass unanswered. I had come to listen, not to duel. I asked him about the implementation of the December 17 Putin-Yanukovych agreements and whether it would bring Ukraine out of its financial morass.

"Let's get real here," he warmed to the task. "The two main parts of the December Moscow agreements, the $15 billion loan and the gas discount, are just payments to secure Russia's geopolitical goals. Regarding the gas discount, the average Ukrainian will get nothing, of course. This is a payment to Ukraine's oligarchs for their loyalty to Russia and for agreeing to change Ukraine's foreign political course. We all know that the price may spike upward again if Ukraine decides to change its integration direction toward the EU."

"And the loan?" I asked.

"The loan gives Russia good publicity and helps to control the Ukrainian government. It is a double win. The bond's terms definitely contain strong loan repayment terms which guarantee Ukraine's future good behavior. We can get that cash back at any time, you know, if they upset us."

"But there were other provisions as well," I pointed out. "Like resolving some of the Russia-Ukraine trade disputes and building some new infrastructure."

"As to Russia's opening of its own borders to Ukrainian goods, this depends purely on Russia's good will. It can't be done quickly, and it won't be done at all for sensitive goods from vulnerable industries. . . . And the Crimea Kerch bridge . . . this is an absolutely useless project, and no one on either side needs it. But what it really means is huge corruption opportunities, and its supporters know this. That's the main driving force behind it."

What he was saying tallied with what my colleagues and I believed. But why in the world was he admitting it? It was like that cliché moment at the end of an action film when the bad guy, after tying the good guy to a ticking time bomb, turns to his victim and with a smirk on his face spells out the details of his entire brilliant plan. As I listened to Maksimov, I was beginning to wonder if this also happens in real life.

"But all of this cash coming in from Russia will help buoy Ukraine's economy in certain ways," I interjected.

"Well, Ukraine will soon start its presidential campaign," Maksimov sighed, leaning back in his chair, like a self-important professor resigned to the monotony of tutoring a rather dense student. "Its situation is difficult and won't improve in the short or middle term since much of the money from Russian loans and other commercial borrowing will be blown just to secure Yanukovych's election victory. That's kind of obvious."

"And you don't think that the Euromaidan folks will have any influence over how this all plays out?" I asked. As if it was business as usual amid the country's largest crisis in a decade, he hadn't mentioned the turmoil facing the country even once during our conversation. "Maidan doesn't have any influence on Ukraine's relations with Russia anymore," he pronounced magisterially:

It just weakens the position of opposition leaders who clearly don't control it. I think that only Yanukovych benefits from it now, as allowing Maidan to continue shows that he adheres to democratic principles by allowing peaceful gatherings. It also helps him keep his base supporters in eastern Ukraine riled up by proving that the narrative about the laziness of western Ukrainians is true. It's exactly what those in eastern Ukraine already believe—the east feeds the west, and "They are protesting while we are working." It's a strong narrative for Yanukovych's core supporters, and Maidan actually helps reinforce it. He's winning, you know. There's no denying it.

"Speaking of folks from the east, I'm sure that you've seen this so-called 'Tsaryov list,'" I asked, referring to the list published by Party of Regions parliamentarian Oleh Tsaryov of people he wanted expelled from Ukraine for "promoting color revolution." Proving that the list was propagandistic fiction, it even included the Embassy's Brian Fink who, I knew for a fact, had nothing to do with Euromaidan. Neither did the rest of us. So I asked, "This list included someone from our Embassy who certainly has nothing to do with anything Tsaryov would like to pin on him. Why Brian Fink? It doesn't make any sense."

Maksimov indulged me by raising his eyebrows. "The Tsaryov list initially contained thirty-four names, ten of which were Georgians and Americans. Ukrainian intelligence already has its own lists, and wants to declare about 240 people persona non grata—mostly Maidan activists who are from NGOs which have received grants from your esteemed nation."

The conversation trailed off. I wasn't sure where to go from there. Our Embassy's Public Affairs Section looked for the brightest young Ukrainians to give grants and enroll in training programs. I had met a few of them, and they were generally idealists with a strong desire to work hard to improve their own communities. I also knew that our US government programs were what we said they were. Our media transparency programs were about media transparency, and our anticorruption programs were about anticorruption. The thought that these young folks would be painted as spies, revolutionaries, or agents of foreign influence just for attending a class or filling out a grant application was chilling. It meant the demonization of some of Ukraine's brightest hopes for its own future. Sure, they could leave Ukraine and make their lives somewhere else, but it was Ukraine that would suffer for their loss. I felt a bit nauseous.

Maksimov perked up again. "By the way, we'll have a celebration later this month for the 360th anniversary of the Pereyaslav Council," Maksimov mentioned. Historians differ greatly on what actually happened at Pereyaslav on January 8, 1654, but the Russian version of events, which Maksimov wanted everyone to accept, centered on an arrangement whereby the Ukrainian Cossack Hetman Bohdan Khmelnytsky pledged allegiance to the Russian czar in exchange for protection from groups loyal to the Polish-Lithuanian Commonwealth.

"We'll have a meeting of Slavic nations right here," Maksimov continued. "You interested? Expect some drunk Cossacks and plenty of vodka. . . . It'll be a good time." It was an invitation to play the token foreign enemy imperialist at the party. He seemed to like having one around for entertainment. It was a role I was willing to play only if I was getting something in return. This time, it seemed the only reward on offer was humiliation.

On Monday, January 13, the number of people on Maidan began to rise again following the end of the holidays and the January 10 clash, which left Yuriy Lutsenko in intensive care. The Interior Ministry's Valeriy Mazan told the press that police were justified in carrying weapons during that incident and "had every right to use firearms" against the protesters when they slashed the tires of a police bus, although the truth was that they hadn't. The mention of a possible police escalation from batons to guns sent ripples across the Maidan. At an opposition party briefing for foreign diplomats that Monday, all three opposition party representatives stressed that it was increasingly difficult for them to prevent protesters from using violent tactics. Iryna Herashchenko of UDAR made the point quite clearly: "The Yanukovych people have not given any ground, and protesters keep seeing their friends arrested and beaten without obtaining any result. . . . They feel that we in the opposition parties are too soft." Svoboda head Tyahnybok later added that many protesters increasingly believed that the opposition's strict line against any use of violence was playing into the government's hands. On both sides, gradual escalation while blaming the other side continued to be the order of the day. On Wednesday, January 15, sightings of Berkut bus movements led to credible rumors of a new imminent government attempt to clear the Maidan. A local journalist posted on his Facebook page that an attack on the square was imminent: "Lights will be turned off. Special ALFA police units will be involved from inside of Maidan; Berkut from outside of Maidan. Their first task—to occupy city hall and neutralize opposition forces there. Small groups of police will start attacking from the subway entrances (especially Teatralna station). They will use trucks to block streets." In the end, he was wrong and that night was quiet. But everyone's personal nightmares were still quite alive.

Meanwhile, I continued to work on several other projects unrelated to the ongoing unrest. Ihnat, Dmytro, and I still continued planning for our pro—

intellectual property rights concert, convinced that the crisis would be over sometime soon, and we could return to our day jobs. Ihnat and Dmytro were working to book StereoPlaza, Kyiv's largest indoor rock music venue, for the show. Dmytro was working to land some of Ukraine's biggest music acts for the event. We tentatively set the date for March 6. That was still eight weeks off. Surely the crisis would be settled by then, we thought. After all, we humans consider worst-case scenarios, not expect them.

7

RULES OF DICTATORSHIP, FIRES OF RESISTANCE

January 16, Thursday. Kyiv's attention suddenly turned to the Verkhovna Rada—Ukraine's parliament. The Rada was typically a slow and deliberative body. But without warning, the Ukrainian press scrambled to understand a whole clutch of new laws flying out of the building like fireworks from a burning warehouse. First came a law simplifying procedures to strip parliamentarians—presumably opposition parliamentarians—of their immunity in order to allow their prosecution. Then a law allowing courts to issue default *in absentia* verdicts without the defendants present. Then a law, like one recently passed in Russia, requiring any civil society group with funding from international donors to register as a foreign agent.

But the news soon got much worse. After the 2014 budget was passed according to normal parliamentary procedure, the body then abandoned normal rules and rammed through a stack of controversial laws in about twenty minutes by hand votes. Under this unusual procedure, the parliamentary speaker could count votes by hand if the electronic voting system failed. It had not failed. But still, the speaker suddenly began declaring that laws were passed—supposedly counting all necessary 226 votes for passage of each bill in just a few seconds. Then the next hugely controversial bill passed in seconds, and so on. If a legislator took a bathroom break, they might have missed the whole drama. The laws had not been approved by the relevant committees or even read by most legislators. By 3:00 p.m., the newspaper *Ukrayinska Pravda* (*Ukraine's Truth*) was labeling the event, "the 20 minutes that destroyed Ukrainian democracy." Twenty minutes was actually charitable—most bills were passed in three seconds or less while many parliamentarians were out of the legislative chamber.

The details of what would come to be called the Black Thursday Laws, or the Dictatorship Laws, surfaced over the following hours. They comprised a comprehensive package of criminal punishments aimed at protesters; a legal cannon targeting Maidan. Drivers in groups of more than five cars would lose their licenses and vehicles. Installation of tents, stages, or sound systems without police permission would get offenders fifteen days in jail. Reporting news without registering with the government as a reporter would earn a heavy fine and the confiscation of cameras or other equipment. Participation in a peaceful gathering while wearing a helmet, such as the orange ones worn by Maidan Self-Defense Force (SDF), or a uniform was punishable by ten days in jail. Provision of unrestricted internet access to the public, as my friend Dmytro was doing from the IT tent on the square, could get you a $6,800 fine. Slander was returned to the criminal code with a sentence of two years, while the spreading of "extremist materials" would get you three years. "Group violations of public order" were now punishable by a three-year sentence, and churches were banned from participating in anything the government deemed as extremist activity. Gathering information on Berkut officials, judges, or other law enforcement officials could garner a three-year term. The government also granted itself the power to ban selected individuals from accessing the internet. The list of punishments went on and on. In a gloating interview on Hromadske.tv, parliamentarian Tsaryov, the same man who put one of my Embassy colleagues on his list of people who should be expelled from Ukraine for crimes that existed only in his fantasies, announced, "I'm liking the country better and better!"

In Washington, State Department spokesperson Jen Psaki issued our obligatory rebuke: "The United States expresses its deep concern that the Ukrainian Rada pushed through several controversial measures today without adhering to proper procedures. Some of these measures will restrict the right to peacefully protest and exercise the freedom of speech, constrain independent media, and inhibit the operation of NGOs. If Ukraine truly aspires to a European future, it must defend and advance universal democratic principles and values that underpin a Europe whole, free, and at peace, and not allow them to be systematically dismantled." The EU, the Organization for Security and Co-operation in Europe (OSCE), the Council of Europe, and many other countries, organizations, and international NGOs issued their own statements against the laws.

As they often did, the Maidanivtsi took to the web, posting pictures of people on the square wearing metal cooking colanders and pots on their heads to protest the new law's antihelmet provisions. An old Churchill quote that "the fascists of the future will be called antifascists" became one of their internet memes. But despite the humor and memes, the mood was darkening. The Rada had adopted the legal infrastructure for a repressive regime of a kind that Ukraine had not experienced since the Soviet days, something like Lukashenko's Belarus. The realization was sinking in that the protesters really "couldn't go home again." The failure of the protests wouldn't mean a return to the same old same old corruption and stagnation. The Dictatorship Laws showed it would now mean something much worse. Yanukovych signed the laws railroaded through the Rada by his party as soon as they hit his desk. He signed other decrees dismissing his chief of staff, Serhiy Lyovochkin, and the commander of Ukraine's ground forces. All signs pointed to his enthusiastic desire to start implementing the Dictatorship Laws. Over the next few days, protesters continued probing the limits of the new laws. About one hundred assembled outside the Lukianivska police station close to my apartment wearing makeshift helmets, mostly colanders and kitchen pots, asking to be arrested as an act of civil disobedience. Another protester submitted an official request with the traffic police for himself and a group of friends to travel together in six cars for a weekend trip to the sauna. Meanwhile, Party of Regions (PoR) stalwart Oleksandr Yefremov referred to the Maidan as a fifth column, stating that he would prove that it was all just a Western "special operation"—mirroring the talking points of Kremlin press secretary Peskov. Despite our efforts, the center of gravity continued to drift away from peaceful political compromise and reconciliation. At the Embassy, we continued to hope that a violent confrontation was avoidable. But the situation was actually on the cusp of a sharp turn for the worse.

Baiting the opposition and Maidan over social media, pro-Russian Ukraine's Choice leader Viktor Medvedchuk posted, "What does the opposition do each time it is unhappy with something? Call a *viche*!" Many protesters actually agreed with his insinuation that past *viches* hadn't accomplished much. But in the aftermath of the Dictatorship Laws, another *viche* was announced on the Maidan for Sunday. The protest leaders needed to take the temperature of the square.

January 19, Black Sunday, the day began slowly on Maidan, with a relatively small crowd of about twenty thousand growing slowly larger as more trickled in. Police were not out in great numbers, but they were positioned prominently with video cameras focused on the entry points to the square. The government's message was clear—under the new law, "group violations of public order" could carry a three-year prison sentence. And now, Mr. or Ms. Protester, you are on tape. We have evidence and can come after you anytime we like.

Helmets and masks, now illegal, were more prominent on Maidan than before, though mostly colanders and pots with string holding them on under the chin. They were now a symbol of defiance. When the speeches began, the square was packed with over fifty thousand people as more filtered in. From the main stage, opposition leaders called for an immediate presidential election, the creation of a "People's Rada," and a new constitution. When the crowd heckled the opposition, demanding that the "Big Three" opposition figures stop bickering and choose one person to lead them, Batkivshchyna leader Arseniy Yatsenyuk retorted that there was one leader, the Ukrainian people. Then, in the haphazard organic decisionmaking of Maidan's unfiltered democracy, the protesters made a historic misstep.

As the event wrapped up, several Automaidan leaders called for a march to the Rada to demand that lawmakers overturn the Black Thursday laws. Marching from Maidan to the Rada would mean marching up Hrushevskoho Street into the government quarter past the Cabinet of Ministers. Several police checkpoints and many hundreds of Berkut and Interior Ministry personnel guarded the fortified street. Suddenly a clash seemed likely, and neither the political opposition leadership nor the foreign diplomatic community were in any position to stop the momentum. Opposition contacts later told us that they tried to intervene to no avail. Our Embassy observers Marine Corps attaché Michael Skaggs and Marine staff sergeant Shane Parlow sent the Task Force updates on what they saw:

Shane, 4:02 p.m.: "There are ten thousand people taking over the barricade at Euro/Hrushevskoho." And a few moments later: "Clarification. The police checkpoint. Or it was."

Michael, 4:06 p.m.: "Flares thrown at police. Smoke canisters fired. Hrushevskogo and Euro plaza."

Jennifer Babic, Regional Security Office (RSO), 4:21 p.m.: "All: Police and protesters are clashing on the Maidan. Please avoid the area. For those that live close to Maidan, please remain indoors. RSO will update as we receive information."

Maidan organizers took to the internet, calling the clashes a provocation and asking Maidanivtsi to stay away from them. Embassy observers saw "regular-looking Maidan people" fade away, being replaced by those wearing far right symbols, including those of Pravyi Sektor and football "ultras." Euromaidan leaders had struggled successfully since November 30 to avoid the searing clashes that would allow the far right and the Ukrainian government to raise the level of violence to the bloody conflagration they both seemed to crave. Now that dreaded moment had arrived:

Michael, 4:50 p.m.: "A lot of gas. Protesters firing fireworks at police."

Shane, 5:17 p.m.: "Fire started on bus nearest stadium. It is combusting and people are moving back. Crowd yells various chants of 'bandits out.' A CS-like gas [chlorbenzylidene malonotrile; not as strong as US military riot grenades] has gone off and lightly saturated area. Protesters ripping bricks and throwing at VV [Interior Ministry troops]. Lots of momentum. . . . It just fell. . . . Thousands rushing barricade."

Shane, 5:33 p.m.: "Increasing amount of GoU [Ukrainian government] riot grenades being thrown. People are getting injured from it. Many people are condemning the people who throw bricks at VV, stating they should be peaceful. Someone just sustained a face injury. GoU grenade blew up in his face. GoU IS USING GAS, firsthand."

Michael, 5:39 p.m.: "Seems gas is getting stronger too."

On the Maidan stage, Yatsenyuk called for protesters to stay peaceful to avoid giving the government an excuse to clear the square. "Political change requires patience," he implored. Svoboda's Tyahnybok told the crowd that true success could only come through peaceful means, and that it was Maidan's enemies who wanted to create an emotional and violent reaction in the streets to provide an excuse to crack down and keep Ukraine under their control.

After the Ukrainian government cited the need to set up an artificial Christmas tree and small ice rink on Maidan as the official reason for the violent beating of protesters on November 30, 2013, protesters transformed the tree's metal shell into their own "Revolution Tree"—a symbol of the uprising.

Banners hanging from the Globus pedestrian bridge marked one edge of the protest city. The concrete stairs on the upper left of this photo later became the venue for the first protester deaths by automatic gunfire in February 2014.

Maidan protest zone, December 16, 2013.

Senator John McCain takes a picture of the crowds on Maidan from the Ukraina Hotel. He earlier commented to Senator Chris Murphy that he had never seen anything like it.

Following a meeting in Kyiv at a time of high tension, Senator John McCain consoles Ukrainian pop singer and protest leader Ruslana Lyzhychko.

Youth street entertainment
in the Maidan protest
encampment.

Interior Ministry troops, many of whom were young
conscripts, guard Kyiv's government quarter.

Ramshackle barricades and other fortifications,
such as this one on Institutska Street, grew and
were periodically destroyed by government forces
(and subsequently rebuilt) during the course of the
Euromaidan protests.

In one of many internet memes widely circulated in the
Ukrainian protest community in December 2013 following
President Yanukovych's return from a summit meeting with
Russian President Putin, Yanukovych is imagined telling Putin,
"Congratulations on your excellent purchase, I thank you."

In this widely circulated internet propaganda map attributed to
the "People's Militia of Donbas," the Russian ambition for its
"Novorossiya" zone included a huge swath of Ukrainian territory.
While this map includes eight Ukrainian regions (in red) as
Novorossiya, only a portion of two of the territories, Donetsk
and Lugansk, were actually destabilized and brought outside
Ukraine's control.

After months of peaceful protests, the passage of the Dictatorship Laws led to violent clashes on Hryshevskoho Street near the Cabinet of Ministers on January 19, 2014.

A protester argues with a group of Ukrainian Interior Ministry troops across a military truck used as a government barricade on January 19, 2014.

On December 11, 2013, U.S. Undersecretary of State Victoria Nuland and Ambassador Geoffrey Pyatt break bread with government security forces on the Maidan after an evening of struggle. While photos of the undersecretary giving cookies to protesters were quickly used for propaganda value in Russia, those reports did not note that she had quite similar interactions with security forces loyal to President Yanukovych.

Russian forces in uniforms without insignia began an invasion of Crimea in late February 2014. These photos of the so-called "little green men" were taken outside a Ukrainian military base near Perevalne on March 4–5, 2014.

The Donetsk Airport, a modern and beautiful steel and glass facility named after famed composer Sergei Prokofiev, was reduced to rubble by fighting between Ukrainian and Russian proxy forces in early 2014.

A residential building damaged by artillery in Pervomaisk, Luhansk Oblast.

A Ukrainian tank destroyed in the village near the farmhouse Stepanivka.

A cemetery for the recent war dead from eastern Ukraine in Lviv.

Shane, 5:51 p.m.: "Things have calmed (comparatively), and protesters have created a human wall with linked hands, back to VV across entrance to Dynamo and to the street. No more riot grenades. The press stationed on the pedestal directly in front of the projector screen got hit by at least two riot grenades from GoU. Protesters seem to have homemade flashbangs [stun grenades] made from 1 L bottles."

By the end of the night, three of the twenty-four journalists at Hrushev-skoho would be hospitalized with concussions and one with a broken arm.

Michael, 6:17 p.m.: "Dozens of grenades fired at once. At least one person down seriously and carried away. Sotnyas reorganizing and preparing for assault."

Shane, 6:23 p.m.: "Water cannon being used to push away those who get too close at base of projector. Riot grenades go off at least three per minute, injuries on both sides. VV [Interior Ministry] building up, about 1,500 now. VV fragged one of their own guys. Gas grenades getting stronger."

Assistant Secretary Toria Nuland (from Washington), 6:41 p.m.: "You guys calling for calm, nonviolence on all sides?"

Shane, 6:51 p.m.: "GoU [government of Ukraine] water cannon used to disperse personnel on and near vehicles. Many gas and riot grenades. Berkut joining ranks."

Bruce Donahue, Embassy Kyiv deputy chief of mission, 6:53 p.m. (to A/S Nuland): "Yes, we're working on an Embassy statement urging nonviolence."

Media reported that Ukrainian Democratic Alliance for Reforms (UDAR) leader Klitschko was on the way to Mezhyhirya for emergency talks with Yanukovych.

Shane, 7:30 p.m.: "It appears the sides are at a stalemate. The protesters will get all motivated, do a battle cry, and rush the line near the charred bus, throwing rocks, homemade flashbangs, and Molotovs. GoU responds with five to six riot/CS grenades (although they sometimes throw them at the press and not the rock throwers). Neither side is gaining/losing ground, and events seem to repeat themselves every five minutes. Protesters are trying to pull charred bus away to expose GoU lines. There are at least ten cars parked here too . . . not the best time to leave them overnight at the stadium. Charred bus remains the primary battleground. Some Berkut are seen at front of their line. They are getting hit with rocks, each about 2–3 lbs. and at a rate of 100 to 250 per minute. GoU riot grenades are now the big 'crowd pleasers.' It looks like some of the VV/Berkut are throwing rocks back, and also dud grenades."

On Espreso TV, Automaidan leaders claimed that none of their people were still on Hryshevskoho and that those currently fighting police were provocateurs and 'Kernes's titushky.' The Interior Ministry announced that it would investigate the incident under Article 294, signaling that anyone involved could get up to fifteen years in prison. On the Maidan stage, a concert by a Polish folk rock band was stopped due to the sound of explosions, and an organizer took to the stage to reiterate that Maidan leadership did not approve of anyone clashing with the Interior Ministry on Hrushevskoho:

Michael, 8:21 p.m.: "VV formed a group to protect charred bus. Molotov cocktail hit them. About six on fire."

Shane, 8:41 p.m.: "Back and forth fireworks, rocks, and Molotovs. Second water cannon arrived. First one may have been damaged by Molotov."

Images of the violent clash, including buses on fire, Molotov cocktails flying through the air, and aggressive-looking young men in face masks wielding batons and Ukrainian flags, instantly circulated through the Russian press and social media as evidence of the vicious, fascistic nature of the Ukrainian protest movement. With research based on postings on the Russian social media site Vkontakte, *Ukrayinska Pravda* reported that the violent fringe drove the fighting on Hrushevskoho that night, especially the right-wing group Pravyi Sektor. While only one city block away from Hrushevskoho, Maidan seemed a world away. The concert restarted amid a surprising calm:

Sasha Kasanof, Embassy Kyiv's Political Chief, 9:45 p.m.: "Colleagues: Given the evolving situation and potential for more headline news overnight, we will staff a system of shifts through tomorrow morning, as follows...."

Shane, 10:04 p.m.: "Protesters got the green paddy wagon truck from the barricade to catch fire. They finally got [the fire started] from the tires. The crowd gets frightened easily and there was a wave of 250 in hysteria running from the area, then returning. A heavily injured protester was just carried out of here. That fire is quite large." A few minutes later: "Bus also caught fire. The fire keeps people back so the GoU is saving on gas grenades. That fire is super black and has secondary explosions . . . four buses on fire now. More riot grenades being tossed over buses."

Patrick Self (Embassy Air Force attaché and newly arrived observer), 11:37 p.m.: "Protesters are digging up the pavement stones for more ammo. Chanting continues. Stun grenades are now airbursting over the crowd." Media outlets reported that government troops began using rubber bullets, often specifically targeting journalists.

Patrick, 1:02 a.m. (January 20, Monday): "New development. Government just threw two Molotovs into the crowd of protesters."

Overnight, the lines between the protesters and government stabilized. According to the press, protesters suffered over one hundred injuries, and more than sixty Ukrainian government security personnel were hospitalized. The spin began immediately on all sides. Deputy PoR head Mykhailo Chechetov told journalists that the violence was planned by the United States and was intended to bring Ukraine into NATO—a sick joke to all at the Embassy who had been trying desperately to discourage violence. Boris Yeghiazaryan, a well-known artist and Maidan activist, posted on Facebook that the fight on Hrushevskoho Street was planned by the Yanukovych government as a provocation. At the Embassy, the fuzzy facts seemed to point to a miscalculation by Automaidan that was seized upon by far-right activists and others on both sides who thought that a descent into violence was in their interest. The US Embassy was on the polar opposite side of the equation. I realized that the month-and-a-half-long golden age of bringing my children onto the square and casually listening to Open Maidan University lectures was over. The Hrushevskoho clashes were just beginning, and a corner that the US government hoped to avoid had been turned. The only bright spot was that Yanukovych had told Klitschko that he would enter negotiations with the opposition. We could continue to press for a peaceful outcome; like before, like always. But the omens were dark.

On Monday morning, January 20, demonstrators and security forces continued their "gift exchange" every few minutes: flashbang grenades from the police, Molotov cocktails and stones from the protesters. Photos of protesters stripped naked in the freezing cold by police on the street began making the rounds on social media. The nauseating Russian propaganda line that the West was financing unrest in Ukraine continued. Russian Parliamentary Committee chairman Leonid Slutskiy said that "through various NGOs [Western countries] fund provocations that translate into street riots and pogroms, which are not consistent with civilized European ideas, but which they have so insistently urged in Ukraine." Skirmishes on Hrushevskoho continued throughout the afternoon. After Yanukovych announced that day that he would not be in the group negotiating with the opposition on the crisis, the big three opposition leaders announced that they wouldn't attend either.

In yet another move harking back to medieval Kyiv, about ten protesters on Hrushevskoho began piecing together a six-foot-tall wooden trebuchet, basically an oversized catapult, presumably to throw more stones and Molotov cocktails from behind their lines.

Staff sergeant Shane Parlow, back on observation duty, wrote, "The barricade on the side entrance to Dynamo is being reinforced, and they are building what looks like a siege ladder. They are building it to get access to top of dynamo arches. Definitely getting medieval here. . . . Crowd growing, between seven and ten thousand now. Elevated fire bombers have run out of ammo and take about seven minutes to re-arm. Trebuchet being troubleshot for more power. They did get the plans from the internet." The internet trebuchet broke, but the fighting continued. By evening, the crippled trebuchet was converted to a massive rubber band slingshot. All of this engineering school drama unfolded reality TV–style on several live internet feeds.

It seemed like the entire Embassy spent the night of January 20–21 awake. I had the 2:00 a.m. shift in the Task Force, and reports were coming in from all directions. Lieutenant Colonel Michael Skaggs and Staff Sergeant Samuel Jerome from the Defense Attaché Office and Liz Zentos and Greg Pfleger from the Political Section were all walking around the protest zone trying to separate fact from fiction.

Around 2:50 a.m., Berkut forces stormed the protester barricades on Hrushevskoho, destroying the protesters' trebuchet and driving them back from the charred bus skeletons that they had been using for cover. Our observers then saw the government forces voluntarily move back to their previous positions after disassembling much of the protesters' barricade. There were multiple reports of large groups of titushky amassing downtown, possibly those brought into Kyiv from various smaller towns on a so-called "titushky safari."

Tuck Evans from Public Affairs wrote in: "The link attached is a live feed of an activist driving around Kyiv and identifying what appears to be roving groups of 50 to 200 titushky. Reports continue of titushky beating up people who walk by or smashing cars of suspected activists."

Ambassador Pyatt wrote at 3:30 a.m.: "Thanks. Please keep feeding desk and Rubin and Melia information since DC is awake and working this. I'm also getting calls."

Greg Pfleger wrote in: "Large group of titushky coming through Shev-chenko park, going down Volodymyrska. Nearing Bolshogo Hmelskogo now. Estimated 100."

Liz Zentos reported: "Continued tweets about location of titushky. Re-ports that a group was in the Silpo [grocery store] in Podil [a region of Kyiv], then hid in a school. Some reportedly in vegan café off Striletska. Reports that some have been 'caught' and are being beaten up by protesters. . . . Klitschko says tonight's events are a provocation so Yanu can declare martial law." Klit-schko, who said that he would once again meet with President Yanukovych, reiterated the pledge of opposition parliamentarians that security personnel that "joined the side of the people" would be given amnesty. Not that he actu-ally had that power, at least for the moment.

January 21, Tuesday, 5:00 a.m.: A disturbing development—two Euro-maidan activists, Ihor Lutsenko (unrelated to former Minister of Internal Af-fairs Yuriy Lutsenko) and Yuriy Verbytskyi were kidnapped from the hospital where Lutsenko had carried the injured Verbytskyi. At 7:00 a.m., the fighting on Hrushevskoho stopped briefly as orthodox priests stepped out between the two sides to conduct a religious service and pray for peace. A few hours later, someone sent an Orwellian text message to all mobile phones in the vicinity of Hrushevskoho: "Dear subscriber, you are registered as a member of the riots." Automaidan activists apprehended a group of ten titushky and took them to the Trade Unions Building off Maidan for questioning, which they broadcast live online. The captured titushky said they had been paid up to $30 to come to Kyiv and "smash cars, block roads, cause disorder, and start fights."

Sports rivalries were also politicized as the Kyiv Dynamo "Ultras" (mean-ing soccer "super fans") offered to pay for the damage to cars caused by Do-netsk Shakhtar Ultras who had come to the capital to work as titushky. On their VKontakte web page, Kyiv Dynamo Ultras leaders stated that they were against both "pro-Russian and anti-Russian policies," but they decided to take to the streets to defend Kyiv against titushky from other cities bent on wreaking havoc. Two days later, the Donetsk Shakhtar Ultras called on their members not to work as titushky and to discourage others from doing so. Part of their beef came down to, of course, soccer. The new Dictatorship Laws re-quired identification when buying soccer tickets, a requirement they detested. By the end of the week, the Ultra fan websites of "Dnepr" in Dnipropetrovsk, "FC Zorya" in Luhansk, "Tavria" in Crimea, "Chernomorets" in Odesa, and

"Metalist" in Kharkiv all called on their fans not to work as titushky. Rock star Slava Vakarchuk of Okean Elzy, Ukraine's most popular band, announced that he would join Kyiv's anti-titushky patrols. Soccer fans and rock stars united.

January 22, Wednesday morning: A modicum of calm returned.

Leonid Hmelevsky from the Defense Attaché Office wrote in: "On Maidan, a very small crowd—perhaps a couple hundred at the stage and a couple of thousand total visible. Stage is inactive, except for a periodic rendition of the national anthem (no Ruslana). Maidan and Hrushevskoho are in a 'quiet' stand-off. . . . I used the quotation marks as the most active component on the protester side currently is the Battle-Euro-Babushkas [European Combat Grannies] Drum Team, who generate a great volume of sound nonstop. Troops (MOI [Interior Ministry] and Berkut) calm."

During the day, mothers of Interior Ministry officers circulated a Facebook message calling on other Interior Ministry family members to come to Maidan at 6:00 p.m. to ask their children to "stop executing criminal orders." The big three opposition leaders announced a new negotiating framework with the Ukrainian government, demanding that the Yanukovych administration: (1) withdraw Berkut and other special forces from central Kyiv; (2) recognize that the Dictatorship Laws were illegitimate; (3) return Ukraine to the 2004 Constitution, thereby reducing the powers of the president and protecting free and fair elections; (4) dismiss Prime Minister Azarov and the current government; and (5) conduct early presidential and parliamentary elections.

That evening, Ihor Lutsenko resurfaced. His still unknown attackers dumped him with a bag over his head into a forest outside of Kyiv. Lutsenko wrote on his Facebook page, "I should note the high professionalism of the kidnappers—they were real experts." Convinced he was going to die, his kidnappers made him kneel and pray in the woods after half a day in captivity. It turned out to be a mock execution, and he survived with a concussion. Yuriy Verbytskyi, the friend he had brought to the hospital, was still missing. As the evening progressed, skirmishes restarted on Hrushevskoho Street; protesters threw Molotov cocktails, and security forces responded with stun grenades and rubber bullets. In the no-man's-land between the two sides, Embassy observers saw two brave figures who remained there for much of the night—an orthodox priest in black robes holding a cross and the mother of an Interior Ministry soldier holding a sign reading: "You are ALL my children." Fighting continued through the night. At approximately 8:20 a.m., two to three hundred Berkut riot police charged forward and dismantled the protesters' barricades on Hrushevskoho Street. Protesters advanced a few minutes later and Berkut calmly retreated to their original positions.

That morning of January 22 brought word of the first protester casualties, posted on social media. Serhiy Nihoyan, a Ukrainian of Armenian descent in his early twenties, died in the hospital from injuries sustained when he fell from the colonnade of the Dynamo stadium during confrontations with police. Graphic video of Berkut beating protesters on that precipice during the night quickly circulated. Another two protesters reportedly died from gunshot wounds, though our Embassy observers did not see any indication that live ammunition was used during the night. Later that morning, Ukraine's General Prosecutor's Office confirmed the deaths of two men from gunshot wounds in the vicinity of Hrushevskoho Street while continuing to deny that any government forces in the area had firearms.

In the morning, protesters began rebuilding their barricades on Hrushevskoho. In the early afternoon, government troops again descended to destroy the ramshackle fortifications.

Michael Willis of the Defense Attaché Office wrote in: "Crowd at/retreating thru Maidan gate. Panic. VV [Interior Ministry] and Berkut forces conducted attack. Swept crowd down Hrushevskoho and around Dnipro hotel. The SDF rallied 20 meters from gate and held. Lots of chaos here." Once again, government forces cleared the barricade, but within hours, protesters had retaken the area. Then government troops cleared protesters from the area again, the latest movement of the undulating tides.

Michael Willis wrote in at 1:10 p.m.: "At least two more males carried into Maidan with bleeding head injuries. Appeared unresponsive." Then, after a few minutes: "Maidan awoken. Square filled with onlookers facing Hrushevskoho, standing room only around stage and east side. Column of armed protesters forming on Instytutska Street headed to Euro square gate, approximately 200 fighters."

Leonid Hmelevsky wrote in: "Maidan stage NOT attempting to de-escalate. Fifteenth Sotnya marched to Hrushevskoho. I anticipate more clashes."

Shortly thereafter, an Interior Ministry armored personnel carrier arrived at the square to smash barricades. Both local press and our Embassy observers confirmed that Berkut specifically targeted journalists, throwing flash grenades into areas cordoned off for journalists even though there was no protester activity in the vicinity. Journalists were targeted as enemies.

Overnight, State Department deputy spokesperson Marie Harf criticized both the actions of the Ukrainian government and right-wing protester groups like Pravyi Sektor, who sought to crank up the violence in Kyiv. However, she once again declined to answer any questions about what sanctions the United States might levy. Since the start of Euromaidan, the protesters, civil society groups, international NGOs, and others pressured the US government to take some action against culpable Ukrainian government officials in reaction to violence on the streets of Kyiv. Then on the morning of January 22, there was the first such movement—visa sanctions. The Embassy announced, "In response to actions taken against protesters on the Maidan in November and December of last year, the US Embassy has revoked the visas of several Ukrainians who were linked to the violence. Because visa records are confidential under US law, we cannot comment on individual cases." The Embassy did not "name and shame" those losing their visas, but at a minimum we could put the thought into the heads of Ukrainian government officials before they ordered violence that they could lose something they value. It was a small step in the right direction.

Around noon, January 22, the Embassy's Regional Security Office (RSO) was notified that there would be a massive demonstration at the Embassy that day. The protest was called the Kyiv Dwellers for a Cleaner City, presumably because they wanted to sweep protesters from Maidan. The group wanted to bring between two and five thousand people to the US Embassy in the largest demonstration our mission had ever seen. These were not friendly protesters asking the United States for sanctions against Yanukovych; rather, they believed that Maidan was a CIA conspiracy designed to destroy Ukraine. RSO quickly received permission from Deputy Chief of Mission (DCM) Bruce Donahue to shut down the Embassy early, but we were all instructed to remain accessible by cell phone or BlackBerry. Natalya and I agreed that it was a good afternoon to work from home.

Like us, most other American and Ukrainian staff evacuated from the Embassy, but RSO and the Marines went into overdrive. Ambassador Pyatt, always on the job, was one of the handful other than security officials still in the building. At 4:00 p.m., the Marines were "reacted"; stationed in strategic areas around the Embassy compound, geared up in tactical vests ready to stand their ground. No one knew what to expect. Our regional security officer and her deputy, Jennifer Babic, were supervising the defense of the mission. RSO deployed several Ukrainian members of their team by the Beresteiska Metro station, the point at which they expected most "Clean Citizens" to arrive. Around 4:30 p.m., they called in. "People are starting to show up," a team member told Jennifer. "A lot of people." "OK," said Jennifer. "How many, approximately?" "Oh, there are thousands of people here. Thousands. They just keep coming."

This was it. No doubt the mission was about to come under siege. RSO sent an email: "Avoid Embassy—no one in or out. At least 700–1,000 demonstrators are surrounding the Embassy. If you are working at your desk, close your blinds. No one can enter or leave the Embassy. The parking garage is locked and closed."

Dave Howard and Joseph Rozenstein from the Management Section quickly ran around the mission with Jennifer to pull down the shades, remove potted plants from window sills, and turn out the lights. If anyone outside had a gun—by no means a groundless fear—they shouldn't know where people were inside the compound. Jennifer ran up to the ambassador's office on the fourth floor. The exterior window of his large office probably made him closer to where the protesters would be than anyone else in the building.

"Sir," Jennifer began, out of breath, "I know you want to stay here and work, and I know you probably want to watch this demonstration. But I need you to turn your lights off and I need you to pull all your shades down. Please." "Okay, I understand, Jennifer," he said. "How about if I just have my desk lamp on, you know, and pull all the shades?" "That's fine, but you cannot go to the window and you cannot leave your office," Jennifer responded. "You have to stay right here, and please don't go anywhere because I need to keep track of you but I can't sit up here in your office with you. I have to be downstairs with my Marines in case, God forbid, something happens." "Okay, no problem," Ambassador Pyatt agreed.

Leaving his office, Jennifer saw Ambassador Pyatt's office manager, Marsha Phillipak-Chambers, looking shaken. "My god," Marsha asked. "Are we going to be OK?" "We're gonna just watch what happens for now. Just keep your windows down, keep your lights off, and just stay here. I'll keep you updated as things play out. Close the front office door, don't let anyone in unless it's me, and we'll go from there," Jennifer instructed.

Rushing back to the RSO suite, at first it was hard for Jennifer to make out on the monitors what was going on outside. In Kyiv, January streets were already completely dark by 4:30 p.m. Individuals weren't visible, but Jennifer could see a dark mass flowing out of the woods closest to the metro station. It just kept advancing. Typically, protesters would assemble in the relatively small open area across from the Embassy's consular entrance. But this time thick columns circled the embassy on all sides. They outnumbered those inside the compound by a factor of about a hundred to one. What next? Would they attempt to scale the wall and come inside?

Fortunately, they did not. Instead, for the next two hours, the roughly 2,500 persons stood outside in the dark in the cold snow, holding signs, chanting, and sometimes singing. Then around 7 o'clock, they departed as if on cue, filing back through the woods toward the metro station. This time it was a peaceful demonstration. The RSO, Jennifer, and all of us at the Embassy wondered what would come next. For the titushky who took part in the rally (only one portion of the participants), the denouement came the next day. According to local press, a group of titushky near the Universytet metro station surrounded the car of the organizer of the rally to demand payment for their services. When no cash was forthcoming, they burned the car.

Meanwhile, the Ukrainian Ministry of Finance reported that they were expecting another 2 billion in Russian cash to arrive in the next few weeks in the form of a second Eurobond issue in Ireland. The Russian side, however, said nothing about more money for Ukraine. Press, pundits, and diplomats like us all suspected that there was a concrete "ask" the Russians would demand from Yanukovych before releasing the next tranche. We also suspected that Moscow wanted the Maidan situation "solved" before the Sochi Olympics so as not to distract from Russia's showpiece event. As Vadim Karasev, a Ukrainian think-tanker, wrote, "Putin will not lend for the revolution, he will lend for stability." The next 2 billion Russian dollars seemed unlikely to make it into Ukraine's coffers as long as the Maidanivtsi were still on the square.

Recently, I had been making the rounds trying to find out where the Russia deal stood—an urgent task given the likelihood that new Russian money might well be tied to Ukrainian government actions on Maidan. I spoke with everyone I knew who might have any insight, including contacts at the Ministry of Economic Development and Trade, the Ukrainian president's Think Tank, the Commonwealth of Independent States (CIS) Institute, and the Institute for

Economic Research and Consulting. The fighting on Hrushevskoho cast a dark shadow over the city. Ukraine's situation was highly unstable, and the Russian government was slow-rolling implementation of the deal. This made sense from Moscow's perspective as it provided Russia with maximum leverage. "My institute has not been asked to research any aspect of the Russia deal," I was told at the Economic Ministry's research arm. "I doubt that anyone with any real economic expertise was in on the details. All the calculations were purely political." The Ministry's Department of Cooperation with CIS countries confirmed that none of the trade provisions had been enacted. The Russians were waiting . . . but for what, exactly? Meanwhile, the Kremlin signaled that it might give Ukraine some of its financing in the form of transferring International Monetary Fund (IMF) Special Drawing Rights (SDR). If so, this would be a clear message to Ukraine: "The IMF refuses to unlock funds for you after years of negotiation with them, but we, Russia, can unlock IMF funds for you at will." Quite clever. The meetings were over, and I drafted a cable to Washington with the incomplete information I had gleaned in Kyiv.

Since the Hrushevskoho battles began, a new smell, the noxious pungency of burning rubber tires rather than the warm campfire smoke of wood fires, permeated the Maidan. On January 22, the Ukrainian government officially lifted a ban on using fire hoses in freezing weather to control civil unrest. Independent Russian TV channel, Dozhd, the first channel in Russia to air footage of Russia's own nascent protest movement in 2011, aired footage of a shattered first aid station on Hrushevskoho Street, which had been destroyed by Berkut. At the World Economic Forum in Davos, organizers abruptly dropped Ukrainian Prime Minister Azarov from the list of speakers, then banned him from the event entirely even though he had already arrived in town.

In a grim press conference, Kyiv police announced that they had found two bodies bearing signs of torture, such as having their heads wrapped in tape, in the Boryspil district forest where the activist Ihor Lutsenko had previously been released by his kidnappers. Within hours, his family identified the body of Yuriy Verbytskyi, the man kidnapped from a hospital at the same time as Lutsenko. Police stated that they were opening up a case into Verbytskyi's torture and murder.

From the Maidan stage, the "Big Three" opposition leaders stated that they made no progress during their meeting with Yanukovych earlier in the day. They promised that they would be back on the front line the next day if police shot protesters again. Claiming that the government wanted to declare a state of emergency in order to bring more armored vehicles into Kyiv, Svoboda's Tyahnybok told the crowd that "there can be no retreat." Batkivshchyna's Yatsenyuk said that Yanukovych could be open to repealing the Dictatorship Laws when PM Azarov returned from Switzerland. "There is only one choice left, to stop the bloodshed," Yatsenyuk said. "If I get a bullet in my head, so be it." Klitschko said that while Yanukovych might be willing to repeal the January 16 laws, he was not open to early presidential elections. "I am willing to come under fire to defend the interests of my people," he concluded, again offering to head to the front lines at Hrushevskoho.

Construction of new barricades along Khreshchatyk Street continued throughout the night of January 22–23 while the Defense Attaché Office's (DAO's) Michael Skaggs reported the first use of nonlethal metal ammunition by security forces: "Confirm use of shot, 4–5 oz. Pic enclosed. I've seen a few hit. Painful, no penetration. Indiscriminate fire through smoke."

After the Russian Embassy requested more information about missing Russian journalist Andrey Kiselev of Lenta.ru, Ukraine's Interior Ministry stated that he was detained with an "aggressive group of men . . . armed with bats and chasing buses carrying members of the Berkut special police task force." From the Maidan stage, organizers asked for all fighting to stop until 8:00 p.m., when opposition leaders would return from another round of talks with Yanukovych. Speakers from the Maidan stage accused the Berkut of taping nails and other shrapnel to flash grenades to make those nonlethal weapons deadly.

On January 23, Thursday morning, Automaidan reported that fifteen of their activists had been kidnapped overnight. Later in the morning, the disappearance of Dmytro Bulatov, a leader of Automaidan, hit social media. Bulatov was an executive and a competitive wakeboarder who became a local activist for improved infrastructure after his son got stuck in an open storm drain on his bike. Word of his disappearance hit Maidan hard. He was one of their own who had already become something of an icon.

Meanwhile, Moscow kept up the drumbeat of false accusations and insinuations. Russian presidential spokesman Dmitriy Peskov stated that Russians "regret and resent when it becomes obvious that there is external intervention in the internal processes taking place in Kyiv." Ukrainian parliamentarian Tsaryov riffed on the same theme, telling the Russian press that militants stormed the Hrushevskoho barricades only after meeting with our Ambassador Pyatt and the UK's Ambassador Smith. "Over a million dollars were put into a special account one day before the latest crisis started," he lied without even fake evidence. Party of Regions (PoR) parliamentarian Yevhen Balytskyi, inventively slandering both the West and the protesters in a single sentence, added a new twist to the fantastical plot of a foreign conspiracy by stating, "We're not excluding that one of the dead protesters may have been killed by a sniper or professional mercenary from NATO countries brought in on orders from the radical wing of the opposition."

Perhaps Balytskyi was an aficionado of science fiction. If so, I suppose that he also couldn't with 100 percent certainty exclude the possibility that extraterrestrials or time travelers from the future were responsible for the violence. Of course, most people knew why such fantasies would be spun and why many would believe them. Casting the participants in the protest movement as tools of Western intelligence was intended to put Yanukovych back on the right side of the moral equation in the minds of his supporters and justify any violent actions the Ukrainian government might take. Painting the West, and especially the United States, as a serial malevolent meddler is often an effective ploy and rings true for many in that part of the world. We all understood this, but it still stings to hear lies told about you.

Then, another explosion hit social media—video and pictures of police taunting and humiliating a young male protester, stripped naked in the subzero weather on the street outside of a bus. The video, shot by *Ukrayinska Pravda* newspaper, showed the naked man being slapped and kicked while officers posed for pictures with him. "That one's going to go viral quick," Elizabeth wrote to our section. She was right. Patriarch Filaret of the Ukrainian Orthodox Church's Kyiv Patriarchy was watching. A few days later, he told Channel 5 in an interview, "That naked man in the snow raised his head proudly. This inspired me. This is the Ukrainian nation. Even naked, we are dignified and cannot be conquered. In this man I see Ukraine, and she will not be beaten."

Major events were unfolding outside of Kyiv. Lviv media reported that up to 2,000 protesters occupied the office of the Yanukovych appointee Governor Oleh Salo while he was traveling to Kyiv. The protesters told the press they want to "take power into their own hands." Following the lead of those in Lviv, approximately 1,000 protesters in Rivne stormed their local Regional State Administration building, which also housed the Rivne headquarters of the Party of Regions. They began negotiations with Oleksiy Hubanov, acting head of the Regional State Administration while the governor was vacationing abroad. By early afternoon, protesters also occupied government headquarters in four other regional capitals in western Ukraine: Ivano-Frankivsk, Khmelnytskyi, Lutsk (Volyn region), Ternopil, and Zhytomyr. These regions all had governors appointed by President Yanukovych, highly unpopular in western Ukraine. Lviv governor Oleh Salo was forced to resign in the middle of the street on camera, though he later retracted his resignation saying that he was pressured by "radical extremists." In western Ukraine, there were a few broken windows but no real violence. By the end of the day, after protesters seized the Cherkasy regional administration building, protesters controlled the main government administrative buildings in seven of Ukraine's twenty-seven districts.

By the end of the night, the unofficial truce expired but nonetheless still loosely held. Staff Sergeant Shane Parlow wrote in from Hrushevskoho: "Anxiety steadily increasing, a few civil arguments broke out: 'What are we doing?' 'Waiting.' 'Do you really want to wait forever?'. . . Positions are readying for combat, staging Molotovs and picking up their weapons of opportunity. There have been a few bullhorns sounding, getting the crowd wound up." But compared to the previous several nights, the relative calm was noticeable.

On Maidan, the crowd waited for the big three opposition leaders to return from another all-day session with Yanukovych. UDAR leader Klitschko, Svoboda leader Tyahnybok, and Batkivshchyna leader Yatsenyuk appeared on the Maidan stage around midnight, calling for peaceful patience. They stated that during the lengthy negotiation they were only able to address one of the protesters' demands—the release of Maidan activists without any further criminal charges. They begged the crowd for more time to address other demands from Maidan. After Klitschko urged protesters to wait until Saturday so the leaders could continue negotiating, some hecklers yelled that he was a traitor and a provocateur. After almost being whistled down, Tyahnybok called for a vote on whether to continue talks with the government. The crowd's answer—no. For now, Maidan gave the opposition leaders no mandate to keep talking with Yanukovych on their behalf.

January 24, Friday morning: We awoke to news that the radical group Spilna Sprava had seized the Ministry of Agriculture building on Khreshchatyk. Spilna Sprava (loosely translated as common cause) was a radical group founded in 2010 by lawyer Oleksandr Danylyuk to fight corruption within the Yanukovych government. While the group supported free and fair elections and clean government, it also had no compunctions about using violence and radical methods to achieve these goals. While Spilna Sprava's politics were center-left as opposed to Pravyi Sektor's hard right views, their parallel extreme tactics put the two groups together in the category of the Maidan movement's radical fringe. Mainstream Euromaidan leaders castigated and criticized both groups for their actions which they saw as dangerous and counterproductive.

Yanukovych finally dismissed Chief of Staff Lvyochkin, replacing him with Yanukovych confidant First Vice Prime Minister Andriy Klyuyev.

Patrick Self from DAO, back on observation duty:

We had the opportunity to speak with the volunteers working in the main medical point (*medpunkt*) on Hrushevskoho, which occupies a library close to the main action. The *medpunkt* was running 24 hours a day and staffed on eight-hour shifts by a total of three medic "brigades" comprised of approximately fifteen doctors/medics each, all volunteers. . . . When asked about recent injuries, the staff indicated their suspicions that the government forces were starting to use nonstandard crowd control measures. For example, based on the wounds of some of their patients, the doctors assessed that the government was firing nonstandard ammunition—basically high-velocity rounds with extra powder. Even though they were still plastic slugs, the rounds traveled fast enough to cause fatal injuries. Additionally, the medics claimed that the government was also firing 12 mm shot rounds (plastic) that would explode into approximately thirty pieces of shrapnel upon firing. One medic claimed that the government was also employing standard hunting rifles instead of riot control weapons. This same medic also claimed to have witnessed a jury-rigged stun grenade with nails and other metal shrapnel attached to it. Secondly, a patient was admitted apparently suffering from psychotropic gas, quite different from the tear gas normally used. The medical staff was friendly to us as Americans, but quite security conscious as well, asking to see proof of diplomatic accreditation. They were all volunteers, and feared reprisals from the government, especially in light of the dismantling of a *medpunkt* a couple of days ago. As we were departing, several staff members made personal and emotional appeals to us for material assistance, in one case even to the point of tears.

More news flowed in from the provinces. In Rivne, police and district administration officials announced that they were joining the protesters as they left the administration building. Euromaidan protesters now occupied the district administrative buildings in six regions and had attempted to occupy six more. Three other provinces saw major protest movements (Kyiv included, of course). Altogether there was major protest action in fifteen of Ukraine's twenty-seven province districts—more than half. The balance of power between the Ukrainian government and that part of Ukrainian society embodied by the Euromaidan movement was visibly shifting.

We knew that Ukraine was now attracting international attention, but it was still surreal when Ukraine became a regular topic in the White House press briefing given how ignored the country was prior to the unrest. Statements from White House and State Department spokespersons underlined what we were trying to do in the field—promote a dialogue leading to peaceful resolution. Contrary to Kremlin propaganda, there were not different public and private faces to the US government's position on Ukraine. They were identical. I saw it every day.

We read the White House press briefing exchange between White House press secretary Jay Carney and journalists:

Journalist: The situation in Ukraine seems to have really deteriorated over the past couple of days. I'm wondering what the US thinks of this dynamic right now between the government there and the protesters.

Jay Carney: Well, you're correct in your assessment and we condemn the violence taking place in Kyiv and continue to urge all sides to immediately deescalate the situation and refrain from violence. We welcome the news that President Yanukovych is meeting directly with opposition leaders. Political dialogue to address the legitimate concerns of the Ukrainian people is the necessary first step towards resolving this crisis. Next, we need to see concrete steps taken by the government.

Journalist: And then just trying to get on this point, should he resign? Should President Yanukovych resign?

Jay Carney: Again, it's not for the United States to make that determination. What we are calling for is an end to the violence. We made clear our view that it is incumbent upon the Ukrainian government to, in a nonviolent way, respond to the legitimate aspirations and grievances of the Ukrainian people.

Those working these issues at the Embassy knew this at a gut level because it was the policy we were pursuing on the ground. The United States was chastising Yanukovych for his behavior against protesters, not pushing him off a ledge. His hard-line behavior was ultimately bad for him, bad for us, and bad for Ukraine. A compromise in which everyone, including Yanukovych, got some of what they wanted was still the goal. Yanukovych was the elected leader of Ukraine, and it was his responsibility to lead Ukraine out of the quagmire he created through his own actions. But his public statements, which were all over the map, were not helping. On January 24, he promised to "amend" the January 16 laws and dismiss all officials responsible for the November 30 violence on Maidan, but he also claimed that Maidan was being manipulated by armed foreigners and that he would use "all lawful means" to take care of it. He always wanted to have it both ways, but the time for hedging bets was running out whether he realized it or not.

Staff Sergeant Shane Parlow, on observation duty that day, encapsulated the stark difference between the feeling on Maidan and that a block away on Hrushevskoho. It was like crossing from West Berlin to East Berlin in the days when the Berlin Wall still stood, crossing from light into darkness:

> It is quite demoralizing to make the walk from Maidan to Hrush. It is like walking into a new universe. Maidan is well lit, well fed, warm, full of entertainment and recreation. Rounding the now dormant Dnipro Hotel you notice all light is being sucked into the black hole of tire-fires. I assume it is similar to crossing the river Styx, but in this scenario Kharon is paid in air sacs from your lungs as black smoke fills the air. Maidan is a 4-star hotel compared to how life is on Hrushevskoho. The war drumming started at 1745, with no violent intentions noticed, just a re-motivating of the troops.

Late that Friday night, January 24, there was disturbing news from a Kyiv neighborhood far from Maidan. Witnesses heard gunshots in the Holosiivskyi district and saw two unidentified men flee. A twenty-seven-year-old policeman lay dead, shot in the head. In Cherkasy, an early morning bombing close to a police station shattered windows but caused no injuries. Meanwhile, Maidan organizers denied police allegations that Maidan SDF assaulted and detained three police officers on the square, stabbing one.

On January 25, Saturday did not feel like a weekend at the Embassy. Everyone not at work was glued to their BlackBerry. Local protesters stormed another regional administration building, this time in Vinnytsya. A protester, Roman Senyk, died in the hospital as a result of injuries sustained from a gunshot suffered on Hrushevskoho Street three days earlier. The Interior Ministry insisted on their right to use force to retrieve two of their troops who, they claimed, were being held illegally on Maidan. Maidan organizers repeatedly denied they were holding him. Minister of Internal Affairs Vitaliy Zakharchenko, a figure loathed by the Maidanivtsi, told press that "our attempts to peacefully resolve the conflict without resorting to military confrontation are of no effect." Then, we received news that certain protesters were seizing the Ministry of Energy building in downtown Kyiv.

Oleh Voloshyn, former spokesperson for the Ukrainian Foreign Ministry, sent me and other diplomats and journalists an ominous message:

> Dear friends, we are a step away from civil war. The government, pushed and manipulated by Putin, has lost its last elements of common sense and is preparing a violent attack on the protesters that would only start a military conflict since people are not going to succumb to the Moscow-sponsored kleptocratic dictatorship. There's a huge despair in the passive position of the EU. It is Europe's slow and bureaucracy-filled way of dealing with the recent crisis that should be blamed for current violence. I hope you can use public channels to join those who are calling on the West to impose urgent financial sanctions against Klyuyev as a regime coordinator today. He plays on the Russian side hoping to win. He should be shown the immediate high price of his gambling. Please support us or we will all have to forget about peace in Europe since this conflict will sooner or later drag you all into turmoil. With best wishes, Oleh Voloshyn.

At around 8:00 p.m. on Saturday night, the big three opposition figures emerged from a fresh round of meetings with the presidential administration. According to the presidential website, Yanukovych had offered significant concessions, including dismissing the Azarov government and making Yatsenyuk the new prime minister with Klitschko as his deputy. Also on offer would be a public debate between Yanukovych and Klitschko, amnesty for protesters, a working group on possible constitutional changes and amendments to the January 16 laws, and the gradual removal of protester and police forces from the city center. On the surface, it sounded like the kind of compromise that the United States had been hoping for, but there was an insurmountable obstacle.

The big three were set to take the Maidan stage at 10:30 p.m. Then, from Yatsenyuk's official Twitter account, problems: "No deal @ua_yanukovych, we're finishing what we started. The people decide our leaders, not you." When the "Big Three" took the stage, they pledged to continue talks, but made it clear they would not accept Yanukovych's deal. They said that they would continue to fight for repeal, not amendment, of the Dictatorship Laws. Their logic seemed clear and compelling. If they had accepted the proposal, Maidan would have perceived that they had sold out the cause they had championed in exchange for top government posts for Yatsenyuk and Klitschko. Maidan perceived the Big Three as relatively conventional politicians, and they worked with these opposition leaders but never trusted them completely. So no deal, but at least the talks would continue.

For many hours, Embassy observers noted the gathering of protesters at Ukrayinskyi Dim (Ukraine house), which was the five-story convention center at the intersection of Hrushevskoho Street and Khreshchatyk. US Vice President Joe Biden had given a speech there in 2009 that, five years later, was even more apropos in the Euromaidan era:

"Near the end of his life, one of the authors of America's freedom, Thomas Jefferson . . . wrote a letter to his old friend and political foe, John Adams. [In the letter, he said,] 'The generation which commences a revolution rarely completes it.' In any true democracy, freedom is the beginning, not the end. . . . And here in Ukraine, yours is a revolution still in progress whose promise remains to be fulfilled."

Vice President Biden, channeling Thomas Jefferson, could not have known at the time just how prescient his words would turn out to be five years later.

9:30 p.m., Shane Parlow, observing from a distance, wrote: "The real estate moguls at Ukrayinskyi Dim (750 people) are taking a card right out of the game 'Kapitalist' (Russian Monopoly) and enacting the resistances' right of eminent domain. Ukrayinskyi Dim is believed to be housing titushky and VV [Interior Ministry]. We can see people from the rear of the building on some of the upper floors. They are wearing dark uniforms. Protesters have successfully blocked all entrances to the building."

10:30 p.m.: "Ukrayinskyi Dim is under siege; assess it to be the next flash point (or one of many)."

By midnight, live internet video feeds showed protesters flooding into the building. Ambassador Pyatt responded immediately with a pithy two word email: "Not good." This did not bode well for the de-escalation we sought. As usual, Ambassador Pyatt was up most of the night, working the phones. At 2:16 a.m., he emailed Task Force: "Just spoke to Minister of Internal Affairs Zakharchenko who called to warn of the possibility of security force action at 'Ukraine House' where militia is besieged by several hundred (maybe a few thousand) demonstrators. I counseled strongly against forceful action. Noted this would close the door for the further negotiations that Klitschko and Yatsenyuk have offered. Working with opposition on the scene to deescalate, but Minister says he will not accept the 'walk of shame' by his men that the opposition is seeking. Insisted that Klitschko and Poroshenko are behind 'the radicals.' 'I cannot be blamed for using force if necessary to rescue my men.' Not good. Got confirmation via text that Klitschko will go to the site to mediate. Received message from Ruslana earlier that it's beyond her control."

But Ambassador Pyatt, supported by the overnight shift in the Embassy control room, and those of us at home on our phones, was not going to stop. This was it—this was the moment that justifies the countless hours of observations downtown, forging contacts on all sides, and showing up for work in the morning on no sleep. It was a moment when knowing what was going on and why gave us the chance for an intervention that could save lives in the name of the American people. That's what happened. Throughout the night, a trickle of Interior Ministry troops left the building. By 5:00 a.m. on Sunday, January 26, reports on social media indicated that all government forces had peacefully left the building without a major confrontation. The crisis was nowhere near over. But no blood was spilled that night. The Embassy's work meant something.

The ambassador wrote in again to Washington and the Task Force before dawn on Sunday: "Just called by Interior Minister Zakharchenko, following up our last conversation around 2 a.m. His first purpose was to express appreciation for our help in assisting to de-escalate the situation and counseling against violence at the Ukrainian House. . . . I reiterated our rejection of violence on either side and urged an early resumption of the dialogue between Yanu and opposition. . . . Crisis averted last night but it will happen again and again, quite possibly today when there are large numbers back on the Maidan. The bitterly cold temperatures today are something of a blessing if they help keep the crowds down. . . . In terms of roles, we need to find a European to start carrying some of this firefighting burden. And quickly." Ambassador Pyatt quickly reached out to Euromaidan supporter and former Minister of Internal Affairs Lutsenko to emphasize the need for the protesters to hand Ukrayinskyi Dim back to the government to de-escalate the crisis.

That Sunday morning some grim news circulated across Maidan. The body of a protester, hands bound and bearing signs of torture, was found in the Obolonskyi district of Kyiv. This seemed surreal. I knew the district from taking my kids there to enjoy the large indoor waterpark inside the Dream Town shopping mall. Sunday morning, Channel 5 displayed images of live Kalashnikov rounds on the roof of the recently stormed Ukrayinskyi Dim, implying that government troops fired similar rounds from that position. However, our Embassy observers doubted this was true as they hadn't observed any live fire. A funeral for slain Belarusian protester Mykhaylo Zhyznevskyi began on St. Michael's Square with thousands attending. The crowds on Maidan swelled to approximately twenty thousand.

Regional protests, most of which had previously occurred in western Ukraine, now broke out in the east, in Yanukovych's political heartland. In Zaporizhzhya, just north of Crimea, about six thousand Euromaidan protesters stormed the regional administration building that was surrounded by riot police. By nightfall, the police violently dispersed the Zaporizhzhya protesters. Throughout the night there were unsettling reports that the injured were disappearing from the town's hospitals. Around the country, suddenly every titushky had a bat. In Yanukovych's hometown of Donetsk, a pro-PoR rally protectively encircled the regional administration building while titushky attacked protesters with these newly standardized bats. In Kharkiv, as Governor Dobkin released photos of himself posing with Interior Ministry troops, local Euromaidan SDF supported a Maidan rally against another group of titushky with bats. In Dnipropetrovsk, men armed with bats followed several thousand protesters marching to that region's regional administration building. In Kirovograd, protesters used snow to blockade authorities inside their own regional administration building. Word came of protest actions in Kremenchuk. Then Poltava. Then Odesa. Then word of police violently beating back protesters in Vinnytsya and Dnipropetrovsk. In the midst of the news from the provinces, Elizabeth forwarded me a message from DCM Bruce Donahue. "We need to do some more travel and find out what's going on out there," Bruce wrote. "You'll be on tap for some observation outside of Kyiv," Elizabeth informed me. I mentally packed my travel bags.

That night, Euromaidan SDF led a group of foreign ambassadors, including Ambassador Pyatt, on a tour of the square and the Trade Unions Building to show that, contrary to claims by both the Ukrainian and Russian governments, there were no stockpiled weapons. By the end of the night, radicals from Spilna Sprava, the group that recently seized the Ministry of Agriculture, also invaded the Ministry of Justice building. As Klitschko unsuccessfully attempted to coax them to leave, the group fortified the building's entrance with bags of snow and used water to create a slippery, icy approach to the front door. According to DAO's Leonid Hmelevsky, acting as the Embassy's observer,

> They are not leaving anytime soon, and have been busy. . . . We also overheard a Belarusian journalist speaking about the [Justice Ministry] takeover. . . . He confirmed that the Justice Ministry was occupied by SpS [Spilna Sprava]; he claimed that the building was not defended, except for a couple of guards and several older women on duty (*cher-hova*) who locked the safes and left after the attack started. He further claimed that SpS invited them to return to work in the morning, although somewhat in jest. He did say that the 'official' SpS position is that the occupied ministries should continue to work under the deputy of the appointed minister. Lastly, he stated that neither SpS nor Pravyi Sektor recognize the main opposition parties and view their representatives as guests of the Maidan.

January 27, Monday morning, at 2:30 a.m., Minister of Justice Olena Lukash went on TV to demand that the group vacate her ministry or President Yanukovych would call off negotiations and declare a state of emergency. But by morning, DAO's Michael Skaggs reported that they were still there: "MOJ still occupied. Four SpS outside. They are masked and armed, protected by a table with three items: two [orthodox religious] icons and the Constitution of Ukraine. The barricade blocking the street is manned by about six sentries. The Khreshchatyk metro entrance next door is still open and being used." Meanwhile at the Ministry of Agriculture, midlevel employees began bringing documents to their new "building managers" to expose some of the ministry leaderships' corrupt operations. Spilna Sprava immediately began posting the documents on the internet.

In the morning, although Justice Minister Lukash appeared ready to make good on her threat to request a state of emergency, a Ministry of Foreign Affairs spokesman denied that any such moves were afoot. Lukash told journalists that the building's occupiers had sprayed water throughout the building, which then froze, making the office "a veritable ice rink." Prime Minister Azarov called an emergency cabinet meeting, highlighting the increasing disarray inside the government. A journalist interviewing Spilna Sprava leader Oleksandr Danylyuk asked how many ministries his group planned to take over. "All of them," he responded. Danylyuk had a bad reputation within the protest movement as a loose cannon going back several years. Euromaidan leadership denounced Spilna Sprava's seizure of the Agriculture, Energy, and Justice ministries as provocations and publicly distanced themselves from Danylyuk.

As usual, Ambassador Pyatt had back-to-back meetings all day Monday. Klyuyev, as the new presidential chief of staff, told the ambassador that negotiations with the opposition were "almost complete" and that Yanukovych was supposedly "ready to compromise on all key issues." But this was in jeopardy, he said, because of Spilna Sprava's recent building grab. Ambassador Pyatt made clear that the "Big Three" opposition leaders and Euromaidan leaders, too, disavowed these actions and had tried unsuccessfully to stop them. Continuing political dialogue was critical to resolving the current crisis, Pyatt told all his Ukrainian government contacts. A state of emergency or use of force would close the political space needed for such negotiations. Conflict and bloodshed would isolate Ukraine and impede EU integration. The United States strongly opposed such a course, but it appears that "others" were pushing Yanukovych in that direction, intentionally increasing tensions. The ambassador reiterated US commitment to nonviolence and political dialogue and stated that the United States would condemn extremism on all sides. Implementing Pyatt's pledge, State Department spokesperson Jen Psaki condemned the new Spilna Sprava seizure of government buildings in Ukraine.

For those wanting to move Ukraine irrevocably into Russia's orbit, pushing Yanukovych toward open, gratuitous violence made a certain grim sense. If Yanukovych committed a bloody atrocity, he would be ostracized by the EU, and Brussels would stop all moves toward an Association Agreement with his government. If the bridge to Europe was burned, a pariah Ukraine would have only Russia to rely on for financing, trade, and international political support. A serious crackdown in Kyiv would also serve as a potent warning to Russia's own dissidents and nascent protest movement.

In the Russian media, violent images from the Hrushevskoho Street clashes provided a perfect backdrop for renewed vilification of the Ukrainian protest movement. On Rossiya One TV's *Vesti Nedeli* (*Weekly News*) program, antigovernment protesters were referred to as criminals, militants, and most importantly, Nazi sympathizers. "Hatred stokes this revolution," the correspondent intoned. "Unlike the West, Moscow is not interfering" in Ukrainian affairs, the presenter continued, predicting that Ukraine would disintegrate if the current movement succeeds. Suggesting that Ukraine would lose Crimea, he said, "Once everything is over, Ukraine's current revolutionaries will only be able to have seaside holidays abroad. The Kyiv-Simferopol air service will be an international one. The highway to Odesa will be blocked by a border post." On NTV's *Itogovaya Programma* (*Conclusion Show*) in Russia, Ukrainian Communist politician Oleksandr Holub claimed that the United States was paying protesters in Kyiv.

Our observers were back in the protest zone that Monday morning. The battles on Hrushevskoho were largely over.

Staff Sergeant Samuel Jerome wrote in at 7:10 a.m.: "On Hrushevskoho, about one thousand present to include two hundred 'Mothers of the World.' Still chipping ice away and peaceful. On the south side of Maidan, an 'ammunition identification board' is up for all to see what the GOU [government of Ukraine] has used against protesters thus far, pics attached. Based on what we have seen fired and have seen laying around Hrushevskoho, this board is well done and mostly accurate. The board displays cartridges and their respective projectiles. The live 7.62 round in the top center is supposedly from the roof of Ukrayinskyi Dim. The grenade at the bottom is a stun grenade with nuts taped on, and a metal cup on the bottom. The man with the beard admitted that he had constructed the enhanced grenade as a display example. Other than this grenade, the metal 'gold' nonlethal slug, and the live 7.62 round, our observers have seen all of this ordinance."

Meanwhile, the Yanukovych administration was burnishing its authoritarian credentials and beefing up its paramilitary forces. Local press reported that the Cabinet of Ministers decided to expand the riot police, both Berkut and Griffon, to 30,000 strong—a sixfold increase. The Cabinet was also reportedly developing a draft directive on limiting internet access, including the creation of a special commission empowered to block or shut down Ukrainian websites.

According to press reports, UN secretary general Ban Ki-moon called President Yanukovych that Monday morning to urge a "meaningful, sustained and inclusive dialogue by all parties in order to find a solution to the crisis and prevent further bloodshed." They agreed that former Dutch ambassador to Ukraine and current UN special envoy to the Middle East Robert Serry would come to Ukraine to attempt to help mediate. Vice President Biden also had a long phone call with Yanukovych, expressing support for ongoing negotiations, warning against declaring a state of emergency, and urging Yanukovych to pull back riot police to de-escalate tensions. The press also reported that Yanukovych and opposition leaders would continue negotiations that night. Foreign Minister Kozhara briefed the diplomatic corps, acknowledging that the Cabinet had considered calling a state of emergency, but ultimately decided against it. Copying Euromaidan's recent tour through the Trade Unions Building to show that there were no stockpiled weapons, the Ministry of Interior offered a tour for ambassadors of the government lines at Hrushevskoho. Ambassador Pyatt declined.

One person whom I definitely wanted to see again was Volodymyr Lanovyi. In our first meeting, he was the only person I had met who had accurately predicted dramatic upheaval in Ukraine. At the time, I thought he was being apocalyptic and hadn't believed him. Now that he had been proven right, I was very curious to hear what else he had to say. *Ekonomichna Pravda* had just published an interview with him under the headline, "The Government Has Destroyed the Country," in which he described Russia's plans to create a common trade bloc with Ukraine for grain and military items export as an attempt to establish control over the nation.

He discussed this topic when we met in another local café on Monday, January 27. Toward the end of a long and interesting conversation, he raised the subject of titushky, the thuggish young men now omnipresent in Kyiv.

"You know, I'm quite interested in the titushky phenomenon," he began. "I first saw them when I was observing the presidential elections in 2004—the deeply flawed, falsified elections which led to the Orange Revolution. Anyway, while I was out observing, I noticed groups of young, muscular men who were intimidating voters. They also seemed actively involved in fraudulent voting from what I could gather. I was intrigued. Who were these people? So I started to look into it."

Lanovyi looked like he was putting on his invisible social science professor hat. "I started talking to them. One here, one there, until I began to see some patterns. The most important pattern was that they were young people who had some sort of brush with the law. Many of them admitted that police had told them they could get their sentences reduced or scrapped if they agreed to cooperate with the police in the future. So it appeared obvious that the titushky chain of command ran up through police organizations."

"This is all very similar to how criminal organizations work here in Ukraine, using loosely affiliated young men to fill out their ranks when they need extra muscle," Lanovyi continued. "That isn't a coincidence, of course. We have a president who is a former criminal, and when he came onto the national political scene, he just brought in tactics and methods that he found useful in the past."

He paused and looked at me to see if I understood his point. "So foreigners like yourself think that it is something strange or amazing to see police and criminals working the street together in Kyiv right now. But with a head of state with a strong background in the criminal world, it is all actually pretty natural." He paused again. "So, that's where we are right now."

After our meeting, I referred back to what Tuck Evans had written a few days before regarding the titushky he observed in Kharkiv:

> One general observation is that it was the same loose "team" of titushky attacking the Euromaidan Forum in Kharkiv throughout the weekend. ... As far as I could tell from my discussions with the titushky, these are local Kharkiv guys who fit the boxer/wrestler/thug profile we've heard before. ... In some cases there appears to be direct interaction/assistance [between police and titushky]. The video attached seems to be clear evidence. It captures the tail end of a titushky attack on the Forum demonstration at Kharkiv's Yaroslav Mudryi monument. A titushky, immobilized by the Maidan Forum members, covers his face and goes to ground until police units surround him, then let him run off (news reports say he "showed them a document"). A police commander locates the knife the suspect dropped, taps it with his foot, and then lets a second titushky put it in his coat and run off.

Tuck's report meshed with Lanovyi's minilecture to me. Law and disorder were working together hand in glove.

I continued my listening sessions at that same small café, meeting both Svitlana Zaitseva from the Economics Ministry and Oleh Voloshyn, the former Yanukovych administration adviser who was now writing impassioned emails against the government. Both seemed glum and depressed by recent events. "The Rubicon has been crossed," said Voloshyn. "When a government basically declares war on its own people, where do you go from there?" For her part, Zaitseva calmly told me over coffee, "It's not easy to keep up your enthusiasm to work for a government that beats people in the street." I knew she'd be much more comfortable discussing the intricacies of trade policy than what was going on in the streets. But in addition to being a trade expert, she was also a mother and a citizen, and the subject was impossible to avoid.

Some time after midnight, Minister of Justice Olena Lukash spoke to the press following another round of negotiations between Yanukovych and the opposition. Both sides agreed to repeal the January 16 laws at the parliamentary session the next day, but Lukash left the door open to the possibility of readopting some of these same laws later. She reported that opposition leader Yatsenyuk had rejected the prime ministership. Amnesty could only be offered to protesters if they left occupied buildings and roads, she stated, noting that "negotiations will continue." By morning, Spilna Sprava agreed to vacate the Ministry of Justice building, but not the other buildings it occupied. Probably not coincidentally, the pregnant wife of the group's leader, Oleksandr Danylyuk, was detained at Kyiv's international airport after police allegedly found drugs in a pack of Orbit chewing gum in her bag. Danylyuk immediately took to social media to accuse the police of hostage taking.

January 28, Tuesday morning, the eyes of Kyiv turned toward the Rada with an expectation of fresh drama. The Rada building was surrounded by a thick cordon of Berkut riot police, and the tense session did not disappoint. First, in a tectonic shift, Prime Minister Azarov offered his resignation. (Incidentally, this was a few hours before *Ukrayinska Pravda* published an exposé on his wife's impressive assets in Austria.) The prime minister's resignation automatically triggered the dismissal of the entire cabinet. Then, throwing shade at the short-circuited parliamentary procedure used to pass the Dictatorship Laws, a group of parliamentarians associated with Donetsk oligarch Rinat Akhmetov announced that they would only vote through proper protocol—

no more funny business. The Rada then voted to repeal nine of the twelve Dictatorship Laws, sending the action forward for the president's signature. Shortly thereafter, PoR parliamentarians took to social media saying that they were getting threatening text messages during the voting from a Belarusian number. One parliamentarian posted a picture of a text message reading, "You will burn in hell, and in your sleep the heroes who were murdered on the criminal orders of your godfather [Yanukovych] will visit you." No one knew whom the threatening messages were from, but they seemed to visibly tick off Yanukovych's supporters in the hall. They immediately voted to reinstate four of the repealed laws, then recessed to write a few more pieces of legislation to vote on later that day.

Revealing the sorry state of relations between government security forces and society, *Ukrayinska Pravda* that day published a how-to guide entitled "Guard the Hospital: How to Protect the Injured from Police." My heart sank when I read that. Meanwhile, from the Maidan stage, Klitschko was loudly applauded when he called on the Ukrainian government to release any infor-mation on missing Automaidan activist and leader Dmytro Bulatov. In the early evening, protesters on Maidan received a mysterious group text message in English stating, "You made a lot mistakes [*sic*]. Urgently go to the US Em-bassy." Even if the grammar was deficient, the message was clear. The United States was supposedly the puppet master manipulating the Maidanivtsi—the Russian propaganda worldview in action.

We soon heard that Yanukovych had accepted the resignation of Azarov and the cabinet. While traveling in Brussels, President Putin commented on the shakeup, reminding journalists that he committed to loan Ukraine money based on an oral agreement with Azarov, and Azarov made certain unspeci-fied commitments in return. Again, the issue of secret agreements made with Putin behind closed doors rose to the surface. While this seemed to call into question whether the Russian government would stick to its plan to keep loaning Ukraine billions, Putin affirmed that Russia still planned to hand over the money. He could play the good cop. But in Moscow, Deputy Prime Minister Igor Shuvalov, playing the bad cop, contradictorily said that there was no agreement yet on another tranche of funding for Kyiv. Ukrainian pundits opined that Russia would delay the next $2 billion bond purchase so that the Kremlin could use this as leverage to ensure that Yanukovych would appoint a new government with figures "familiar" to Moscow, giving them direct lines into multiple levels of the Ukrainian power apparatus.

When the funding would arrive was not an academic question. Ukraine would owe $1 billion in foreign debt repayments in the next four weeks and $5 billion by the end of July. Ukraine also owed Russia about $1 billion per month for gas, and Russia's Gazprom was demanding payment in full of $2.7 billion in Ukraine's gas debt by the end of the week. This was compounded by the fact that Ukraine's state budget was wildly unrealistic, built on inflated growth and revenue projections. So holding back their $2 billion disbursement could give Russia a very powerful tool for influencing Yanukovych's actions. Meanwhile, our Political Section heard rumors from within the Ukrainian government that Russia might be preparing new coercive trade measures against Ukraine, such as creating artificial problems with customs clearance for Ukrainian products at Russia's border to further ramp up the pressure.

Staff Sergeant Samuel Jerome, on observation duty, sent the Task Force a photo, with his own sardonic comment, of a new Bentley with Kyiv plates that had crashed into a barricade in the government district: "Just because you're rich doesn't mean a barricade will get out of the way for you. This happened at the MoJ [Ministry of Justice] barricade. He had to have driven on the sidewalk to get around the top rope cordon and didn't notice they iced the street. Oops!" Despite Ukraine's generally low income level compared to neighbors like Poland, streets in the government quarter were always crowded with Bentleys, Porsche Cayennes, and Audi A8s. The photo encapsulated the current state of affairs in Ukraine. Right there in immutable pixels was a rolling slice of corrupt luxury smashed into a barricade of protesters' ice bags. Late that same afternoon, two unscheduled trains from Donetsk and Simferopol arrived in Kyiv holding recruitees assigned to participate in anti-Maidan demonstrations in Mariinsky Park. Several of them told Channel 5 journalists that they expected 400 hryvnia (about $47) for their participation.

While Russian propaganda wallowed in a mud bath of lies about the United States manipulating Euromaidan, Washington continued promoting a peaceful resolution of the crisis. Vice President Biden called Yanukovych again, this time to congratulate him on the repeal of the January 16 laws. According to the official readout, Biden encouraged Yanukovych to continue working with the opposition to find a peaceful resolution of the crisis. For the moment, the pace of events seemed to be slowing down, but not stopping. After reports of gunfire within the Ministry of Agriculture, currently occupied by Spilna Sprava, the Task Force saw a Twitter post saying that Svoboda was attempting to remove that group from the building. A standoff ensued, leading to a fight and a few injuries before Svoboda succeeded in ejecting Spilna Sprava. Later in the day, the group was also expelled from the Ministry of Agriculture. Many of the hated Dictatorship Laws were already off the books, and the political opposition seemed to be securing promises of more real concessions from Yanukovych. Many of my colleagues and I took a deep breath. Is this how it ends? Did the fires of Hrushevskoho finally lead to the flexibility on both sides needed to end this crisis? A possible solution seemed within sight. How were we to know we were in the eye of the storm?

US President Barack Obama mentioned Ukraine in his State of the Union address to Congress and the nation on Tuesday, January 28, 2014: "In Ukraine, we stand for the principle that all people have the right to express themselves freely and peacefully, and have a say in their country's future." It was just one sentence, but it set the right tone. It was something we could cite in the course of our business in Kyiv to show that the top levels of the US government did care.

January 29, Wednesday afternoon, Elizabeth forwarded me a message from a well-informed contact in the international banking sector. "I'm hearing from various good sources that trade restrictions are reappearing on the border with Russia. Despite what Putin said yesterday, they are trying to send not too subtle messages that Russian interests need to be taken into account in the formulation of a new government in Kyiv." Soon, truckers reported that something was indeed going on at the border—all certificates of origin needed "forensic document inspection," which could take ten to fifteen days, and customs authorities required full prepayment of customs duties immediately at the border without the usual preferential rates for Ukraine. As intended, this meant that nothing moved, and perishables would soon rot. Meanwhile in Moscow's Duma, legislators again used the term associated with anti-Semitic riots to accuse the West of orchestrating "pogroms" in Ukraine.

Then came another email from Elizabeth with the subject line, "This is getting ugly." A few days before, during Spilna Sprava's seizure of buildings, Ambassador Pyatt had asked the Political Section to reach out to that group to find out whether they really had occupied the Justice Ministry or whether it was actually someone else. This was a vital piece of information to know quickly for the ambassador. The occupation of the Justice Ministry threatened the peace and compromise we were fighting for, and we needed to know if we had any leverage to get it to stop. Tim Piergalski sent a message to Spilna Sprava contacts asking whether the news was true.

Tim's text was not just intercepted, it was altered and falsified. In a Russian language translation of the message, now leaked to the press, one sentence was changed from a factual question about whether the buildings were actually occupied, to a request: "Make sure that the building is well protected (are the barricades strong enough)?" By falsifying just a few key words, whoever was responsible for altering the message had converted it from a simple question by our Embassy to find out the ground truth in a rapidly changing environment into a supposed directive from the conspiratorial Americans whom Russian media accused of masterminding Euromaidan. Tim's altered and falsified email became the foundation on which an edifice of defamatory accusations was constructed. Articles that expanded on the "revelation" included additional outlandish assertions, including the preposterous assertion that the United States was providing Batkivshchyna and the rightist Svoboda party with $20 million per week in support and direct payment to militants. We all knew Tim well, both professionally and socially. A nice young guy with a short beard who was just beginning his career at State, it was almost comical to imagine Tim as the spearhead of a US-backed "color revolution." Like the earlier accusations against Luke Schtele while he was managing TechCamp, Brian Fink at USAID, and J. P. Gresh in the Defense Attaché Office, these new allegations were absurd if you knew the personalities and jobs of the people involved and understood the issues they were actually engaged in. Of course, the target audiences for these monstrous fabrications had no such knowledge. Thus, it was far too easy for the virus of these dark conspiracy theories to find hosts. Demolition is far easier than construction. Lies are far easier to tell than to eradicate.

Like most of my colleagues at the Embassy, I was far too busy to fixate on these personal accusations and the shameless innuendos directed at our mission. I was interested in finding out what knowledgeable people in town thought about the likely impact of Azarov's resignation on the Russia deal. I made the rounds of the Economic Ministry, Ukrainian customs, and various think tanks.

As usual, Dr. Burakovsky turned out to be uniquely well informed and perceptive. I asked him about the seemingly contradictory messages coming from President Putin who said that previous arrangements with Ukraine would stand regardless of the new government, and Russian Deputy Prime Minister Shuvalov who said that all bets were off if Yanukovych installed a pro-Western government. "These messages are two sides of the same coin, really," Burakovsky offered, sipping hot tea in his office. "Putin has gone out of his way to be more appealing in the months before the Olympic Games in Sochi. His words in Brussels were the ones more likely to get picked up in the West, and this was his message meant for Western consumption. Mr. Shuvalov's message was quite clear and threatening and meant for us here in Kyiv. And you've seen what's happening at the border. And why wouldn't Russia employ some trade pressure? It's been very effective in the past, after all."

At the point when our conversation was winding down, Dr. Burakovsky took a softer tone. "Can I bring up another matter?" he asked. "I have a colleague, Artur Kovalchuk, who is in jail right now. He was returning from Maidan on January 20 with two friends, and they ran into a group of about fifteen titushky. The titushky beat them up pretty bad, and they broke Artur's nose. Afterward, Artur and his friends called the police to report the incident, and amazingly, the Berkut arrested them for participation and organization of mass disturbances and attacks on police at Hrushevskoho Street, despite the fact that the fight didn't happen anywhere near that area. That crime carries a four- to fifteen-year penalty. I just wanted to ask you, as a favor, if someone from the Embassy could attend his hearing tomorrow just to show some international interest in the case. I would really appreciate it." He seemed to have a real and personal concern for his colleague. I agreed to ask the Political Section to send someone knowledgeable about the judicial process, which they did. Kovalchuk was given house arrest pending trial.

In addition to everything else, I needed to focus on progress in the intellectual property rights sphere, specifically whether the Ukrainian government's deal with Microsoft for software legalization was progressing. The answer from Kovinya and others was clear. They would stick to the plan, but there might not be any payments to Microsoft until April—three months away. I didn't understand the delay. On my way out, a young staffer whom I had met before stopped me. "You know why we can't do anything until April? Because we don't have the cash, even if our government gets the two billion dollars from Russia this week. That money is already spent, basically. But in April, there will be big deals on military infrastructure in Crimea, and of course, the Russians will pay for this. It will be a big sale. We'll have money then." Could the Russians be planning to use their leverage from the current crisis to solidify their position in Crimea? I couldn't know if this was true, but it certainly was interesting. I returned to the Embassy to write up a long day of meetings.

That night, in a conversation broadcast on Russian television, Putin told Russian Prime Minister Medvedev that it was "reasonable" to wait until after the formation of a government in Kyiv before providing any additional financial support. Good cop and bad cop were reunited.

Meanwhile, in Kyiv the Rada again became the center of action. Rival PoR and opposition protester amnesty bills were making their way to the floor, but the two sides remained deadlocked. Just when it appeared that the PoR might allow a vote on the opposition's amnesty bill, President Yanukovych made a surprise appearance to "consult" with his party's parliamentarians. Social media reports claimed that Yanukovych threatened to dissolve the parliament if his party allowed a vote on the opposition's amnesty bill. Much screaming, mostly from Yanukovych himself, could be heard through the doors while he "caucused" with his MPs in the Rada's basement. At 10:35 p.m., the Rada passed the president's version of the law, granting amnesty to the protesters only after the fighting on Hrushevskoho fully ceased and the fighters departed. After the Rada session was adjourned and the national anthem played, opposition MPs taunted PoR MPs by chanting "Raby!" ("Slaves!"). Activist Oleksandr Aronets, who was filming the Rada session, claimed that certain PoR parliamentarians were pushing voting buttons for others in violation of procedure. But most importantly, the harsh provisions of the new amnesty law seemed unlikely to convince any protesters to leave Hrushevskoho, to say nothing of Maidan. The bill brought the crisis no nearer to resolution.

January 30, Thursday morning, social media noted that another protester gravely wounded during the fighting on Hrushevskoho Street had died in the hospital. Kyiv's police released the names of two police officers who were killed on Hrushevskoho. Then, an unusual press release from Yanukovych's office announced that the president was taking sick leave due to an acute respiratory illness and high fever. He had not yet signed the law passed two days earlier repealing the Dictatorship Laws, and now he was dropping out of sight. His office released a statement regarding the death of Interior Ministry Captain Dmytro Donets, who died of a heart attack in the line of duty. It claimed that the Ukrainian government had met all its responsibilities to try to resolve the crisis, including the passage of an amnesty bill, and that it was the political opposition that continued to aggravate the situation. During a meeting between foreign ambassadors and Justice Minister Lukash, Ambassador Pyatt publicly welcomed the amnesty bill in comments widely reported in the Ukrainian press. He also discussed the right to peaceful protest, the urgent need for an accelerated political process to resolve the crisis, and the need to prosecute those responsible for violence and "disappearing people." Meanwhile, in Dnipropetrovsk, Ukrainian intelligence detained two members of the "Svoboda" party, stating that they were preparing an attack on unspecified nuclear facilities. In a country already permanently scarred by the Chernobyl meltdown, that was a terrifying prospect.

The Kremlin was not merely passively observing events. Russia continued to gradually ratchet up the trade pressure on Ukraine, this time on the pretext that Ukrainian pigs and chickens posed a danger to Russian consumers. Rosselkhoznadzor, the Russian Federal Service for Veterinary and Phytosanitary Surveillance, announced that they were stopping Ukrainian pork imports due to "detection of African swine fever in the Lugansk region." A few days later, Russia banned chicken from one of Ukraine's largest farms.

While the Kremlin was engaged in phytosanitary warfare, defending Russia's borders against an invasion by dead Ukrainian hogs and chickens, the United States launched a serious effort to get Ukraine's opposition to take a step back from their maximalist positions and accept a negotiated outcome now that Yanukovych had offered some concessions. Vice President Biden and Ambassador Pyatt had consistently delivered the call for peaceful de-escalation to the Ukrainian government. Now Secretary of State Kerry delivered that same message in a call to opposition figures, inviting them to a meeting on the margins of the upcoming Munich Security Summit. Speaking to Poroshenko, Klitschko, Tyahnybok, Lutsenko, and singer/civic leader Ruslana, Kerry said that he was encouraged by the repeal of the worst of the Dictatorship Laws and noted that the US government strongly urged President Yanukovych to sign the legislation to formalize the scrapping of those repressive measures. Negotiations were the only viable way forward, he emphasized, and the United States supported peaceful dialogue and was willing to work with the United Nations and the European Union to make this happen. He encouraged the opposition to continue to renounce violence and end the takeover of government buildings. The US message to Yanukovych and the opposition was fundamentally the same: renounce violence, listen to each other, and compromise.

Poroshenko noted that the protesters had also made concessions, such as handing the Ministry of Justice and Agriculture buildings back to the government. He said that all buildings would be handed back if the Ukrainian government guaranteed the security of peaceful protesters, approved constitutional changes, and released protest-related prisoners. Klitschko stated that he and the other leaders were doing their best to keep the situation under control, but it would be difficult to ask protesters to return home if they did not see concrete results. Tyahnybok accused the Yanukovych administration of "taking innocent protestors hostage" through arrests on spurious charges to use them as bargaining chips. Lutsenko joked, "Everybody who thought Yanukovych had balls of steel now knows that it is Putin's hands of steel that are holding his balls." Ruslana emphasized that Yanukovych's actions were making it impossible to keep the protest peaceful. While praising their commitment and determination to achieve change through peaceful protest, Secretary Kerry ended the call by asking the opposition to remain united and "reasonable" in order to bring the crisis to a close.

A bit of what initially sounded like good news quickly turned out to be horrifying. Yuriy Stets, a Batkivshchyna MP, tweeted that Dmytro Bulatov, the Automaidan leader missing since January 22, was alive: "Found Bulatov. He's alive. That's all for now. More details later." Then, came word from our Political Section: "Bulatov is en route to Borys Hospital. He was badly beaten. One ear was cut off. He does not remember anything that happened to him. He was left outside of Kyiv and was forced to go door to door asking for assistance." It sounded pretty bad, and soon a horrifying photo of Bulatov's mangled face appeared on the internet. Channel 5 reported, "Dmytro Bulatov is severely beaten and tortured by people with Russian accents—bruises, they cut off a piece of his ear, he was crucified [reportedly, his hands were literally punctured]. All the time he was in a dark room, blindfolded. He was close to Kyiv. After this torture, they abandoned him in the woods. He managed to get to Vyshenky village and called his friends." After visiting Bulatov in the hospital, Poroshenko told Hromadske TV, "Dmytro Bulatov was thrown from a car in the same woods where Igor Lutsenko (another Euromaidan activist) was found. It seems like the same people, the same methods. The people that tortured Dmytro asked him about Euromaidan activists and who finances

Maidan. They said that they know Euromaidan is supported and financed by Americans."

The fact that Bulatov's torturers, who hung him by his wrists, seemed to actually believe that the United States financed and directed Maidan was disturbing. Those unfortunate enough to end up in their grasp said that they were professionals, likely working for some security or intelligence apparatus. Yet they believed things about US involvement in the Maidan that were simply untrue. Had they really bought into their own propaganda? Shouldn't professionals know better? Or were they trying to extract false statements about US involvement through torture, either for use in future propaganda efforts or to impress their bosses/sponsors? There were more questions than answers, and all those questions seemed to lead down dark roads.

Ambassador Pyatt issued a new statement:

America's goal is to see Ukraine put back on the road to political and economic health with a strong focus over the long term on building institutional ties to Europe. It's very important that the efforts on both sides to build communications and to foster reconciliation between the political opposition, the major opposition leaders, and the government continue, and we will do everything we can from outside to support that process, encouraging political dialogue and discouraging violence and extremism. I would note in particular my government's ongoing concern . . . about attacks on journalists and apparently politically motivated disappearances and attacks on civil society and human rights groups.

Ambassador Pyatt's statesman-like expression of American support for a peaceful resolution of the crisis in Ukraine was not matched by comments from Kremlin leaders. Russian Deputy Prime Minister Dmitry Rogozin used Twitter to ridicule Secretary Kerry's upcoming meeting in Munich with Ukrainian opposition leaders: "In Munich, the US Secretary of State will discuss the situation in Ukraine with Klitschko the boxer and Ruslana the singer. What a circus. They still need to bring Verka Serduchka to the negotiations. His/her opinions should be heard by the White House and taken into account." Verka Serduchka was the stage name of a male Ukrainian comedian whose persona as a flirtatious, pop music–singing, middle-aged woman was famous throughout the region and popularized on Eurovision.

As part of the Embassy's increasing efforts to get diplomats out of Kyiv, John Bush traveled to Ternopil, a medium-sized regional capital in western Ukraine. He reported that, "the level of popular mobilization even in isolated areas is impressive. We were also struck by the degree to which locals are consciously modeling Kyiv, to the extent of forming a triumvirate executive model, with reps from the 'Big Three' opposition parties, much as in Ivano-Frankivsk. (This is especially significant, given that UDAR has no members on the district council.) They also have a Maidan yalynka [Christmas tree] built around the flagpole. Pro-tip: Buffalo grass samogon [moonshine] is delicious, and effective against cold weather."

Tim Piergalski wrote from Donetsk in the east:

I got the full set of Ukrainian government talking points from the Donetsk mayor, with an emphasis on foreign states not interfering in Ukraine's affairs. Protesters are foreign funded and imported from western Ukraine, we want stability, etc. . . . No protests or security posture. Looks calm, orderly (apart from guard at mayor's office with two black eyes), streets plowed. No sign of city shutting down for "weather emergency"—but wow, it's cold. . . . Contacts say local police generally cooperative, not hostile to protests, but all changed when titushky started showing up on January 19. Titushky attack with impunity, police do nothing. Many commented that titushky not really from Donetsk, but from small towns nearby where there is no chance to find work. . . . Journalists under threat, lots of intimidation that never gets investigated. NGOs comment that local government generally helpful, but stated specifically that local government here is a lot better than in Kharkiv. The population is generally too afraid to go against the government—not physical fear, but fear of losing job, etc. Opposition incredibly weak—local opposition leaders unknown to public, shut out by media. Two opposition leaders arrested in past year.

January 31, Friday: Late in the day, Yanukovych signed into law measures repealing many of the Dictatorship Laws while enacting his party's version of the amnesty bill. Just hours later, the Interior Ministry announced that because all those they had arrested during the crisis were not "peaceful protesters," they would not be covered by the amnesty. A tweet claiming to identify by name a man seen working with Ukrainian riot police as a Russian sniper from Rostov-on-Don was retweeted thousands of times. In an interview with *Gazprom* magazine, the publication of Russia's giant natural gas enterprise, partly owned by the Russian state, Russian presidential adviser Sergey Glazyev again called for action against protesters in Kyiv: "Either [Yanukovych] defends Ukrainian statehood and quashes the rebellion provoked by financial and outside forces or he risks losing power, mounting chaos, and an internal conflict from which no exit can be seen." According to news reports, Yanukovych was considering another low-key trip to Moscow within the coming week. On Ukrainian TV, former PoR parliamentarian Inna Bohoslovska claimed that Yanukovych had nearly declared a state of emergency three days before, but that a well-timed phone call from US Vice President Biden played a key role in dissuading him.

Social media lit up as police attempted to arrest freshly beaten and disfigured Dmytro Bulatov at his hospital and spirit him out of intensive care. Klitschko and many others went to Bulatov's hospital room, and Klitschko told Hromadske TV that he saw ten policemen on the first floor of the clinic and another fifteen in the ICU where doctors treated the gravely injured Bulatov. Klitschko left ten of his own party members at the hospital to guard Bulatov and said the Batkivshchyna party would also send guards to watch over him.

February 1, Saturday morning: Unknown assailants burned a car belonging to a local employee of the Canadian Embassy. Elizabeth, writing to DCM Bruce Donahue, expressed everyone's fears:

> Bruce—on Monday, could we talk about the effects these kinds of acts are having on our LES [Ukrainian staff]? My impression is that most are fully stressed out because of the semi-state of terror now created. Some ACC [American Chamber of Commerce] company heads alluded to this on Thursday night, and I have heard more anecdotal evidence since about the growing state of fear in many organizations. I am not sure what the Embassy can do, but I do think we need to acknowledge how bad it has gotten and find out what our staff needs. As long as police, titushky and the MOI [Interior Ministry] remain unchecked, and the PGO [the General Prosecutor's Office] and Justice Ministry refuse to investigate violence against activists, any employees associated with Maidan or other so-called foreign agents will be fair game. As the graffiti outside Lukianivska metro says, "We know where

your families live." And given the history of violence and intimidation in this region, everyone understands that shorthand.

Bruce wrote back quickly, affirming that this needed to be addressed.

Our reporting on life in the protest city continued. That cold morning Assistant Army Attaché J. P. Gresh wrote to the Task Force. After describing a calm scene on Maidan, he related his conversations with government forces in the area: "A bit on the life of VV [Interior Ministry] recruits: I talked to 'John' at Hrushevskoho who led me inside the barricade (I needed to show ID) and escorted me around. He is a former Colonel in the VV as of 2010. He said that those kids in the VV are all conscripts and are serving their one year of service as mandated. Some are cadets. However this is the last year of conscript service, and in December of this year, the last conscript will leave service. They are moving to an all-volunteer force. As expected, they hardly get paid anything, and pay was low in 2009 as well even for Colonels (around 70 dollars per month). According to John, it was previously understood to whom they would take an oath: the people. But he isn't sure how it is now, and he said that 'those kids don't understand anything at the moment.' VV conscripts only serve for one year."

A little later, J. P. wrote from Ukrayinskyi Dim: "[It] is a hive of activity. . . . Inside the main atrium, there is an info-center, clothing bank, and small chapel. Automaidan and the 'commandant' of the building occupy the two upper tiers on left and right of entrance. Looks like the Open University is trying to get set back up in here. . . . Overall, the mood was energetic and tense. . . . On Maidan, the mood has picked up a bit and there are about a thousand present in all. Songs definitely better here with 'Myla Moya, Vstavai' and 'Lenta za Lentoyu.' Lots of vendors! You can even get a burning bus/Molotov cocktail refrigerator magnet!"

Meanwhile, across town, Oleg Tatarov, deputy chief of the Interior Ministry's Main Investigative Directorate, announced at a press conference that his organization was investigating the Bulatov kidnapping and torture as a crime committed by protester and opposition forces in order to "influence the public mood" and "cause a negative reaction in society." He was actually suggesting that protesters were just slicing themselves up for propaganda value. As proof, he cited the fact that Bulatov's friends and family were not cooperating with the Interior Ministry investigation. This was no surprise. Given what was happening in Ukraine, why would Bulatov's friends and family work closely with these types of officials? The Interior Ministry's statement was nauseating. By now, Bulatov's case was attracting substantial international attention. German Foreign Minister Frank-Walter Steinmeier offered Bulatov medical care in Germany. Likely in an attempt to deflect international pressure over Bulatov's torture, the Interior Ministry accused protesters, and particularly Svoboda, of torturing a police officer in the basement of the occupied Kyiv City Hall building. Svoboda quickly issued a public denial.

Another troubling development rattled Kyiv as a new pro-Yanukovych extremist group named Red Sektor claimed responsibility for burning Automaidan cars. Similarly, Kharkiv governor Mykhailo Dobkin helped create the new extremist "Ukrainian Front" group to rid Ukraine of its supposed "fascist occupiers," that is, Euromaidan. Mirroring the language of Russian propaganda, Ukraine's Communist Party joined PoR parliamentarians Tsaryov and Kolesnychenko in calling for a "federated" Ukraine, the practical implications of which would be to eject a number of Ukraine's eastern regions into an increasingly distant orbit from Kyiv, their motion more and more warped by Moscow's gravitational pull.

The Kremlin was strongly pushing for a "federated" Ukraine broken into several semiautonomous federal districts—all of which would hold a veto over any major national-level decisions. If that were to happen, certain districts with which Russia had strong connections, such as Crimea and the Donbas (Donetsk and Lugansk), would be able to block decisions, such as the signing of an Association Agreement with the European Union, giving Moscow a de facto veto on all major Ukrainian decisions. No wonder the Kremlin, which since Putin's ascent relentlessly centralized its own authority over the vast Russian Federation, favored federalization in Ukraine, a country whose population was less than one-third, and its territory less than 4 percent, of its own.

Secretary of State Kerry met with Ukrainian opposition leaders at the Munich Security Conference, stating afterward that the United States and the European Union "stand with the people of Ukraine" in their fight for the right to choose their own alliances. Elsewhere at the conference, Ukraine's Foreign Minister Leonid Kozhara and Vitali Klitschko clashed at a discussion panel. At one point, Klitschko confronted Kozhara by pulling out pictures of government forces beating protesters. Kozhara lamely denied that Automaidan's

Bulatov was tortured, explaining that he was merely scratched on one of his cheeks (despite photos showing that he was missing much of one ear). He accused Klitschko of siding with people "who wear some logos and emblems that look like Nazi-style emblems."

In Ukraine itself, an increasingly bitter and personally targeted campaign against protesters intensified. For example, Oleksandra Dvoretska, a human rights activist and founder of the NGO "Action" in Crimea, found a poster with her picture attached to her apartment building in Simferopol with the following ominous text: "Your neighbor, Oleksandra Dvoretska, is a betrayer of Crimea and supports the criminal Maidan. On her conscience is the blood of murdered people. She works for an NGO that is financed by American intelligence. She was trained as extremist in the US." Two unknown men kidnapped Nataliya Matskiv, a Euromaidan supporter in the western Ukrainian city of Kalush, near her house. They tied her hands behind her back, forced her inside a car, and spray painted her face black. They then threw her out of the car in a local park, yelling, "This is a warning for you!"

February 2, Sunday morning: Eric Johnson emailed the Task Force from his walk past the Maidan stage: "Emcee welcomed all to the 'info meeting' at 12:35 and thanked folks for showing up despite the cold weather. Would say over 5K here in front of the Maidan main stage right now as the crowd continues to grow. Other groups of people continue moving toward Hrushevskoho. Emcee compared Ukraine today to Stalin's USSR in 1939 where people just disappear. Starts reading the names of some of the missing. Asks for help in finding their whereabouts. . . . The crowd has hit the 20K mark as more continue to come (I had to wait and squeeze my way in at the Cossack Redoubt gate). Crowd is now filling the overflow up Instytutska Street where I am now. Ukrainians got courage. Prayers continue at 1:15."

That same day, Bulatov was flown from Kyiv to Riga, Latvia, for medical treatment.

Meanwhile, Russian media coverage of Ukraine became ever more shrill and abusive. The previous line that Euromaidan and other protesters were fascists, directly tied historically to the German SS, was continued and intensified. Now withering criticism of Yanukovych for "softness" toward the protesters was added. On Rossiya One and State TV, commentators called Yanukovych a "traitor" and accused him of capitulation for offering government posts to the opposition on January 25. According to the Russian press, he was refusing to do "what was necessary" to defend the country.

February 3, Monday morning: Spilna Sprava head Danylyuk announced that he had fled to London, accusing elements on Maidan of being a "fifth column" working to "suppress the revolution." Unpopular with other protesters for not being a team player and despised by the Ukrainian government for his group's seizure of government buildings, he seemed to have run out of friends. President Yanukovych returned to work from sick leave. The Ukrainian hryvnia, normally trading at about 8.2 per dollar, was finally really starting to slip, reaching 8.74 per dollar, then 8.85, then over 9, then 9.4 for a short time on Wednesday. In January, the National Bank of Ukraine had spent between US $1 and $1.5 billion the country could ill afford to support the hryvnia. Now it seemed that the massive expenditure was wasted. By the end of the week, Fitch, one of the big three credit rating agencies, downgraded Ukraine's credit rating from B– to CCC.

These developments backdropped our preparations for a particularly busy week at the Embassy—Assistant Secretary Toria Nuland was returning for another working visit. Her team planned to concentrate on bridge loans or other desperately needed financial help for Ukraine. Her schedule included meetings with Yanukovych, opposition leaders, and the oligarchs who frequently pulled the strings in Ukraine. My colleague Eric Andersen was designated her control officer, always a heavy burden. In the Economics Section, we all volunteered to share some of the workload. For example, I would attend her meeting with billionaire oligarch Victor Pinchuk to take notes. We all expected the visit to come during a relatively low activity protest season in the run-up to the 2014 Sochi Winter Olympics (February 7–23). The Kremlin would likely pressure Yanukovych to keep things calm and quiet during the games if they hadn't convinced him to crack down before the games started. Yanukovych adviser Hanna Herman stated publicly that Yanukovych would not make any decisions about "constitutional issues" until after his visit to Russia on February 7. Vice President Biden spoke again with Yanukovych, and as far as we could tell, he seemed to have a calming influence on Ukraine's weakening strongman.

February 5, Wednesday morning: More provocations. Oleh Tsaryov, the inflammatory PoR member of parliament from Donetsk, claimed in the Russian media that US soldiers had "landed in Lviv." Then, Ukrainian Communist leader Petro Symonenko stated, "Nuland, the deputy secretary of state admitted—and dear journalists please tell this to all the people of Ukraine—that since 1991 these [NGO] organizations, as I am convinced, for their subversive activity against the people of Ukraine have received five billion dollars." Symonenko stretched the truth so far out of shape that it was unrecognizable. Five billion dollars was the total amount of *all* US aid to Ukraine since its independence, zero dollars of which were earmarked for "subversive activity." Adding to the anxiety level, a new message was circulated from RSO: "A crowd of protesters is congregating near the Consular CAC (compound access control, or what most people would just call a gate). They appear to have a large amount of produce, which may be thrown at Embassy personnel or vehicles. All employees should avoid this area until further notice. . . . RSO will provide updates as the protest develops. Thank you."

Following the economic news in Ukraine, we were accustomed to bad, depressing stories. But one headline looked surprisingly positive: "Ukraine Posts $2 Billion in Surplus of Balance of Payments in 2013, Central Bank Says." Was there some hope then? Several hours later a new headline popped up: "Government Accidentally Confuses Its Balance of Payment Shortfall with Surplus." No, nothing had changed in Ukraine after all.

While the slow-motion crisis dragged on, religious leaders continued to speak out. Patriarch Filaret of the Ukrainian Orthodox Church's Kyiv Patriarchy repeatedly offered words of support for protesters and sometimes physical asylum. His fellow ecclesiastic, Archbishop Andrey Tkachev of the Ukrainian Orthodox Church's Moscow Patriarchate, offered the following "Christian" prayer at the end of his service (as reported with a full recording in *Korrespondent*):

I pray that God sends to the hearts of the people [protesting in Ukraine] misfortune and that God sends them sickness at home and abroad, that they devour each other, let the serpent eat the serpent. I will not worry for them. They are terrible enemies of our future and of today. I have no compassion for them, I will not pray for them. The Ukrainian people are breaking apart and going crazy and can expect only a bitter pill. They occupy all of Kyiv, howling in their incomprehensible language. I don't know what to call Kyiv today, just a poor and miserable city.

His imprecations shattered like ice dropped on the paving stones of Maidan.

"Think this guy is available for weddings?" Elizabeth quipped as we were all reading the media reports.

Outside the Embassy, protesters piled up banana boxes into barricades with a banner reading, "Ukraine Is No Banana Republic!" Borotba, the group that organized the protest, immediately put up a video accusing the United States of, among other things, funding titushky through intelligence channels. This was one of the strangest and most nonsensical accusations I had yet heard. Meanwhile, Radio Svoboda reported that in Kryvyi Rih in eastern Ukraine, local titushky were renamed the Kryvyi Rih "Guard" and incorporated into the police force as a special division.

Into this far from auspicious environment, Assistant Secretary Nuland arrived by commercial airliner from Prague on February 6, 2014. In Brussels, European Commissioner for Enlargement and European Neighborhood Policy Stefan Fule told the European Parliament that the EU "stands ready to assist all sides" and that the EU "will be ready to extend our assistance, based on a genuine commitment to political and economic reforms, in cooperation with the IMF and other international actors." Meanwhile, Yanukovych dismissed several of his top regional security chiefs, including those in Lviv and Volyn—both areas in the west where his government had effectively lost control in recent weeks. Protest activity remained comparatively quiet.

After a meeting with Nuland, Czech Minister of Foreign Affairs Lubomir Zaoralek told the Czech press that if Yanukovych used force against protesters it would spoil his relationship with the West permanently. From the Kremlin's perspective that was very likely precisely the point. In a fresh interview with Russia's *Kommersant* newspaper, Putin adviser Sergey Glazyev stated that the Ukrainian government was making a mistake by delaying a military solution to the crisis, and that if the Maidan would not disperse itself then violent suppression of the protesters was "inevitable." All of this reminded me and many of my colleagues of a chilling reference in a recent article by Edward Lucas of the *Economist*. Lucas wrote, "But there was one more element to the [Putin-Yanukovych] deal which I could confirm with only one source, and did not reveal. It was that Putin wanted Yanukovych to 'dip his hands in blood.' Only by forcing an irreversible breach with Europe and America could the Kremlin be sure that its Ukrainian satrap would behave."

In the same interview, Glazyev also made the absurd claim that the United States was spending $20 million per week on financing and arming the Ukrainian opposition, and that "there is information that the militants are being trained and armed on the territory of the US Embassy." Somehow I hadn't bumped into any of them in the cafeteria line just yet. Maybe they had room service. How could such a thing happen, even theoretically? Was there a set of al Qaida training camp–style monkey bars in the basement I missed? Perhaps an armory next to the ping-pong table in the back garage? The accusations were so incredibly stupid that it was hard not to laugh. But that didn't mean that plenty of people didn't believe Glazyev when he seemed to speak authoritatively about his "information."

To get a better feel for what was going on around the country, the Embassy was sending staff members to the far corners of Ukraine, but I had thus far avoided making any arrangements to travel outside Kyiv because I felt uncomfortable leaving Natalya and the kids in Kyiv amid the current uncertainty. But then my number came up. "Chris, you should go somewhere interesting, where something's happening," Elizabeth suggested. "John's just been out west, and Chris Greller was just in Donetsk."

"Crimea?" I suggested. I had been there a few times, and felt I had a bit of a feel for the lay of the land. Also, the Crimean parliament had issued some stridently anti-Maidan statements, while the Crimean Tatars, a Turkic people who suffered deportation and cruel repression under the Soviet system, seemed all in for Euromaidan.

"I was thinking the same thing," Elizabeth responded. "It seems important. Pick one other region out in that direction as well, and get Valentyna to start making appointments. You should take Valentyna and Drew," she added. Drew Bury was a junior officer who worked in the General Services Office on motor pool and other issues. Since his "cone," or his eventual career path, was economic affairs, he was spending a few months with us to acquire some experience in his specialty. He also had the greatest mustache at the Embassy, dark and suggestive of a fun kind of old-timey villain. His mustache had even acquired its own nickname, Fluffy. I contacted Valentyna and Drew, and we started planning. Looking at the map, we decided to go to Zaporizhzhya, in southeast Ukraine, adjacent to Crimea, after first visiting the Crimean capital of Simferopol. We could get there by train, and we knew that recent protest activity there had been forcibly crushed.

Between upcoming travel, the Nuland visit, and keeping on top of new developments—15,000 Euromaidan protesters were marching on the Rada—our section of the Embassy was buzzing with activity. Then, just minutes before Ambassador Pyatt headed into Nuland's meeting with Yanukovych, during which he would have to surrender his communications devices, he forwarded an ominous tweet alluding to a leaked telephone conversation between himself and Nuland. "What's this about?" he demanded, just before going silent for the lengthy meeting.

An email from Eric Johnson followed, but the ambassador would not see it for another four and a half hours: "A YouTube video appears to be an intercepted phone conversation between you and A/S Nuland talking about Klitschko's possible position in the new Cabinet. They have added lots of 'illustrative' material. From the time reference points, it sounds like this conversation goes back to Yanu's first offer to have Yats as PM and Klitschko as DPM." Everything in our section came to a halt, and we all gathered around a single computer to listen.

The recording started somewhere after the beginning of the call. The voices certainly sounded like our ambassador and Assistant Secretary Nuland. As the video was first circulated on the internet by Dmitriy Loskutov, a Russian government official serving as an aide to Deputy Prime Minister Rogozin, there wasn't much doubt where the "kompromat" was from. And the timing, released precisely as Toria Nuland began her meeting with the president of Ukraine, couldn't be coincidental. We listened:

Pyatt: I think we're in play. The Klitschko piece is obviously the complicated electron here. Especially the announcement of him as deputy prime minister and you've seen some of my notes on the troubles in the marriage right now so we're trying to get a read really fast on where he is on this stuff. But I think your argument to him, which you'll need to make, I think that's the next phone call you want to set up, is exactly the one you made to Yats [Yatseniuk]. And I'm glad you sort of put him on the spot on where he fits in this scenario. And I'm very glad that he said what he said in response.

Nuland: Good. . . . don't think Klitch should go into the government. I don't think it's necessary, I don't think it's a good idea.

Pyatt: Yeah. I guess . . . in terms of him not going into the government, just let him stay out and do his political homework and stuff. I'm just thinking in terms of sort of the process moving ahead we want to keep the moderate democrats together. The problem is going to be Tyahnybok and his guys and I'm sure that's part of what Yanukovych is calculating on all this.

Nuland: I think Yats is the guy who's got the economic experience, the governing experience. He's the . . . what he needs is Klitch and Tyahnybok on the outside. He needs to be talking to them four times a week, you know. I just think Klitch going in. . . . He's going to be at that level working for Yatseniuk, it's just not going to work."

Wow, this was clearly intended to be dynamite exploding in our faces. The negative implication was obvious—it sounded like there were two US government officials talking about who they would "choose" to lead Ukraine as if it was their decision. But sitting around that computer, we had all heard and participated in so many of these types of conversations about which direction we would like to see things go in Ukraine, only later to see events proceed in an entirely different direction. It was something like playing at being Tom Brady or Peyton Manning in your living room or in a sports bar before the kick-off of the Super Bowl. From what I had seen, the US government had no illusions that we could pick the winners and losers in Ukrainian politics. But it was important for the United States to figure out what we believed would be the best for Ukraine, including the configuration of an ideal government for national political reconciliation. That didn't mean that we were going to get it, but we would work toward it. We could give our advice when asked, but first, we needed to get our own thoughts together. That's what I heard when listening to the leaked recording. However, I immediately grasped from the recording that the leakers released it because it would make us sound like interfering imperialists:

Nuland: OK . . . one more wrinkle for you Geoff. I can't remember if I told you this, or if I only told Washington this, that when I talked to [UN undersecretary for political affairs] Jeff Feltman this morning, he had a new name for the UN guy Robert Serry. Did I write you that this morning?

Pyatt: Yeah I saw that.

Nuland: OK. He's now gotten both Serry and Ban Ki-moon to agree that Serry could come in Monday or Tuesday. So that would be great, I think, to help glue this thing and to have the UN help glue it and, you know, fuck the EU.

We all looked at each other with nervous smiles. That was certainly the sound bite which would be remembered. She had put into three words something that we had all felt in Ukraine—a continuing frustration with the ineffectiveness of the EU in this situation. My personal frustration went back to being told that "the sales job is over" on the Association Agreement a few months before Yanukovych made his fateful U-turn. That frustration was not born of any dislike for the EU. Quite the opposite. We all valued the promise of peace and stability the EU stood for and just thought that it needed to be a more effective advocate for its own interests in Ukraine. We understood Toria's sentiment, which was expressed in private and now leaked by a foreign intelligence agency in an effort to undermine Nuland's diplomacy in Kyiv. A short time later, State Department spokesperson Jen Psaki called the tape a "new low in Russian tradecraft."

Eric Andersen was with Toria, and we knew he would be the one to tell her about the intelligence operation/leak. When he returned to the Economic Section in the middle of the day, he looked a little shell shocked. We all gathered round.

"How did she take it?" asked Chris Greller.

"Just fine . . . I think telling her was harder on me than her," he said.

"And the 'Fuck the EU' part?" I asked. "Did you get to use the F-word in front of the assistant secretary?"

"Yup," Eric said. "She said, 'They got me saying 'Fuck the EU'? Awesome!' If someone was trying to get under her skin, they don't really seem to know her very well."

Indeed, far from being deterred, Nuland and Ambassador Pyatt chose to return fire by Twitter. Nuland assembled the three opposition leaders who were the subjects of the leaked call as a damage control measure, and Eric snapped a candid photo of Nuland, Pyatt, and the Big Three sharing a gut-busting laugh as they listened to the call together. Yatsenyuk, for one, was doubled over in a guffaw. The ambassador tweeted out the photo with the caption: "Enjoying Dima's tweet here in Kyiv."

Toria Nuland met Viktor Pinchuk for an early dinner at his penthouse office. From my seat at the table as note taker, Eric's description seemed spot on. She moved past talking about the tape release in the first few minutes of the conversation, casting it as a nasty but ultimately insignificant annoyance, and moved on to the real business of the day—discussing how best to move Ukraine toward political reconciliation and European integration. Pinchuk described the great difficulties inherent in convincing Yanukovych to compromise, but said that US pressure had been effective in stopping Yanukovych from ordering a brutal crackdown. As the owner of London-based EastOne Group Investing and the massive InterPipe steel conglomerate, Pinchuk had attracted friends like the Clintons through his charitable work. The food, from pumpkin soup to scallops, was sumptuous, as were the panoramic floor-to-ceiling views of the city visible past some of the sculptures from Pinchuk's amazing art collection.

In Moscow, Kremlin spokesman Dmitry Peskov confirmed that Putin and Yanukovych would meet the following day on the margins of the Sochi Olympic Games opening. Yanukovych would leave Ukraine that night. Rumor had it that he was seeking Putin's blessing to name Andriy Klyuyev as Ukraine's new prime minister. Putin adviser Glazyev was also at his old games again. In 1994, when Ukraine returned the Soviet nuclear weapons on its territory to the Russian Federation and joined the Non-Proliferation Treaty, it signed the Budapest Memorandum under which Russia, the United States, and the United Kingdom gave Ukraine assurances that they would protect its sovereignty and borders against the threat or use of force or economic pressure. Now, Glazyev threatened that Russia may "intervene [in Ukraine] under the terms of the 1994 Budapest Memorandum" because of alleged (and fictional) US interference. Meanwhile in Kyiv, Maidan protesters from the Democratic Alliance NGO presented the Russian Embassy with two gold-painted toilet bowls to protest "President Putin's interference in Ukraine's internal affairs."

February 7, Friday afternoon: After a press conference at the Embassy, Toria Nuland was "wheels up" from Kyiv. Planning for our Crimea-Zaporizhzhya trip was going well. Valentyna arranged meetings with regional government leaders, opposition figures, journalists, and others. I also urged Valentyna to make appointments with those we don't typically agree with or meet. We were particularly looking forward to a meeting with Russian nationalist party leaders in Crimea. The travel orders emerged from our bureaucratic machine, and we were almost set.

Meanwhile, the protest areas were still remarkably quiet compared to a few weeks before. The DAO's Patrick Self wrote in from observation duty: "All quiet at Hrushevskoho. About 150 VV [Interior Ministry troops] on the front lines in a relaxed posture. Same goes for the protester side. Relaxed mood, about one hundred milling around. The SDF guards tell me that the VV held a morale-boosting music concert today around 1,500–1,600 hours, complete with singers and dancing girls (in camouflage). During the concert the VV had grown to more than 1,000–2,000 in numbers. SDF never felt threatened, however. In fact, they said the concert sucked. That's all from Hrushevskoho. Still smells like burnt rubber here."

Then, the Turkish media reported that a Ukrainian man claiming to have a bomb was trying to hijack a plane to travel to Sochi. Other passengers calmed him down and searched his bags, and the highly intoxicated man in fact had no bomb. But in the hyper–security conscious atmosphere of the Sochi Olympics, it was one of those fraught, high-tension moments when everyone at our mission wondered whether this was the preplanned provocation that would suddenly burn down the house we were standing in. Actually, it was just some drunken idiot. We all hoped for a quiet weekend, but our dedicated Defense Attaché Office observers would still be making their rounds on the square.

February 8, Saturday morning, kicked off with Medvedchuk's "Citizens for a Clean Kyiv" attempting to take down some Maidan barricades for their "Clean the Maidan Day." Maidan SDF, including many prominent female members, responded quickly, leading to a tense standoff that turned musical. An SDF trumpeter appeared, playing the national anthem, and on the Maidan the Sotnyas started singing along. Press arrived to film the melodious stand-off. A Batkivshchyna loudspeaker truck showed up, and after leading the protesters in some chants, they switched to music to calm down rising tensions on the street. The hugely popular band Okean Elzy then took the Maidan stage, and the Maidan SDF began waving their sticks and shields like cell phones or lighters at any other rock concert. Some Soviet tunes emanated from the Clean Citizens, but they were outnumbered two to one and overpowered by the wattage from the main stage.

Eric Johnson wrote in from the scene:

> Now more Okean Elzy. . . . Loudspeaker called again on the pro-Russian provocateurs to take their money and go home. Anti-Maidan groups appear to be from Kharkiv and from outside of Kyiv—students bused in courtesy of Dobkin and Kernes. Maidan moms are talking to them. Most don't even know why they are here. They are definitely not "Citizens of Kyiv." The standoff continues. . . . Life goes on with a few hundred listening to church service at Main Stage. SDF on alert, but not overly so. Coffee truck baristas keep pouring espressos and the

street vendors keep vending. New gear for sale includes a T-shirt of one of the first protest posters back from 2011 of a grandmother and her cat with the slogan: "My grandson voted for the [Party of Regions] so I left my house to my cat." But the new Euromaidan playing cards are my favorite: Yats is the King of Hearts (no points for guessing the Queen), Klitschko is the King of Diamonds, Mr. T is the King of Spades, and of course Yanu is the King of CLUBS. . . . Ah, Maidan. Where else in the world can you walk among hundreds of men armed with bats, rebar, and sticks wearing camo and balaclavas and yet feel perfectly safe?

Yanukovych arrived back in Kyiv that Saturday after the press published pictures fueling speculation that he was in the doghouse with the Russians. He was seated by himself in the back row of a VIP box at the Sochi Olympics, away from the other former Soviet leaders sitting next to Putin. While pundits in Kyiv had expected that he and Putin would discuss the release of the next tranche of Russia's $15 billion in pledged loans for Ukraine, his spokesman said that Putin and Yanukovych, "had a conversation at the stadium. . . . There was no official bilateral meeting." Maybe Putin asked how he liked his seat out in Greenland?

February 9, Sunday: The "death by a thousand cuts" tactics used on protesters continued. The Interior Ministry announced a criminal investigation against the NGO Chesno, or "Honest," which was most famous for investigating corruption in President Yanukovych's inner circle, for alleged illegal fund-raising and money laundering. Singer and Maidan leader Ruslana spoke on Maidan about recent death threats against her. She said that she started getting these threats after she spoke out in favor of sanctions against Ukrainian government officials, and she played phone messages for the crowd that threatened she would either be shot or given the "Bulatov treatment." The road from Zhytomyr to Kyiv was blocked by police, likely to prevent vehicles from entering the city for the *viche* scheduled for that afternoon. It was time for me to pack and play with the kids a bit. Tomorrow, I would be in Crimea. And within weeks, Crimea and the rest of Ukraine would be forever changed.

8

"WHO BENEFITS FROM WHIPPING UP HYSTERIA IN OUR QUIET LITTLE CRIMEA?"

Clutching a small travel bag, I took a taxi that Monday morning, February 10, to Kyiv Boryspil for the quick hour-and-a-half jump to Simferopol. I bumped into Drew at the airport security line. Valentyna, who hated to fly, was already southbound on a train. Prior to takeoff, I again reviewed the excellent schedule she had put together. A comprehensive series of meetings was in place: government was covered through slots with the Simferopol mayor and the Crimean Ministry of Economic Development and Trade, Crimean Tatar issues through a meeting at the Majlis (the Crimean Tatar's traditional representative body) and Crimean Tatar–run ATR television. Also on the schedule were meetings with independent journalists, ruling Party of Regions local officials, and even a local Euromaidan activist. We would also try to see some representatives of different voting groups. The quick trip was designed to give us a broad view of the current state of affairs in Crimea and the neighboring region of Zaporizhzhya.

Crimea was unique and beautiful as I remembered from my first visit in 1995. As a Floridian, I'm used to the water but easily impressed by mountains. With a warm climate and a rugged, rocky charm, Crimea always struck me as a kind of Sovietized version of Hawaii. My first visit there was during my college days in Moscow, traveling with seven fellow international students to a literary conference on the great Russian writer Alexander Pushkin. Only one of us, a bright young woman from Japan, the only non-American in our group, knew enough Russian to get much from the event. But it was also an excuse for us all to get out of Moscow and stay a week in the old Soviet writers' union house in Yalta. We took in the incredible local sights, including the gravity-defying "Swallow's Nest" castle perched precariously on a cliff over the sea, and the regal Livadia Palace where Churchill, Stalin, and Roosevelt hammered out the shape of the post-WWII order. But my strongest memory was stopping with my classmates among the ice cream vendors along the Yalta embankment to watch a small group of protesters scale the local clock tower to move the hands back from Kyiv time to Moscow time. The flag they then hung on the tower wasn't Russian, but Soviet. This was just months after the Soviet Union had imploded.

Much had changed since then. During my more recent visits, there was no contradiction between Crimea's existence as a majority ethnic Russian territory and its status as an integral part of Ukraine. Crimea always had the superficial air of a sleepy, shaggy post-Soviet resort hub comprising equal parts of vodka, sunscreen, and rust. It had arrived there via a strange and circuitous historical route worth summarizing briefly as background to what we observed during our final short visit before history took one more unexpected turn.

In 1783, Catherine the Great incorporated Crimea, then a part of the Ottoman Empire, into the Russian Empire. Russians became increasingly conscious of Crimea during the Crimean War (1854–1856) through the stories of Tolstoy and others who described the heroic military sacrifice of Russian troops in battles there. Crimea became a symbol of Russian battlefield glory against the West. Some sixty years later during the Russian Civil War, Crimea was one of the last bastions of the pro-Tsarist White Russian forces until they were defeated by the Bolsheviks. Crimea became part of the Russian Soviet Federative Socialist Republic in 1921. During the Second World War, Crimea was occupied by Nazi forces. In May 1944, after the Red Army reconquered Crimea, Stalin began a massive, brutal, forced deportation of Crimean Tatars, a Muslim minority resident in the peninsula for centuries, to Central Asia on trumped up charges of their collaborating with the Nazis. This sordid example of "ethnic cleansing" and collective punishment forever changed the demographic composition of the peninsula. In 1954, the year after Stalin's death, Nikita Khrushchev, the emerging new Soviet leader, moved Crimea from the

Russian Republic to Soviet Ukraine. For Khrushchev, this was like moving a ruble from his right pocket to his left. Given the centralized nature of the Soviet Union, it didn't make much difference. The decree transferring Crimea to the Ukrainian Soviet Socialist Republic cited the "integral character of the [Crimean] economy, the territorial proximity and the close economic and cultural ties between the Crimea Province and the Ukrainian SSR."

Geographically, Crimea is connected by land only to Ukraine, not Russia, through the narrow Isthmus of Perekop, only five to seven kilometers wide, as well as by several bridges. Only after the dissolution of the USSR in 1991 and the proclamation of Ukrainian independence did the Soviet decree have any real impact.

For centuries the Crimean port city of Sevastopol hosted Tsarist Russian, then Soviet, naval forces. After the USSR was dissolved, ownership of the Soviet Black Sea Fleet stationed in Sevastopol became a matter of contention and negotiation between Russia and Ukraine. For years as they tried to sort through the issue, the fleet continued to fly the flag of the Soviet Navy—an entity that no longer existed. In 1997, Russia and Ukraine finally signed a treaty dividing the fleet, the naval base, and various armaments. Russia leased certain naval facilities in Sevastopol from Ukraine for twenty years, until 2017. Over the years, various Ukrainian politicians, most prominently Ukrainian President Yushchenko in 2009, threatened not to renew the lease. But the following year, under freshly elected President Yanukovych, Russia and Ukraine signed a treaty that exchanged a lease extension until 2042, and possibly beyond, in exchange for discounted natural gas from Russia. The final result was that Russia's hold on its naval facilities in Sevastopol was not weakened despite Ukraine's independence. The Ukrainians were willing to rent, only the price was in question.

By 2012, Yanukovych's Party of Regions was unquestionably Crimea's dominant political force as support for openly pro-Russian political parties in Crimea had precipitously declined after their disastrously unproductive terms in local office in the 1990s. After strong showings by communist candidates in 1998 and 2002, by 2006 Yanukovych's bloc of candidates won four times as many seats in Crimea's parliament as the next best performing party. In 2010, Yanukovych's PoR won 48 out of 50 Crimean regional parliamentary seats. While locals grumbled about the Party of Regions importing Yanukovych cronies from Donetsk into Crimea, there was no significant organized opposition there posing any real threat to Yanukovych's party.

In Kyiv, we read news reports that Crimea's parliament, especially parliamentary speaker Volodymyr Kostyantynov, used escalating rhetoric, including calls for "fraternal Russian help" in case of a change of power in Kyiv. Kostyantynov made frequent trips to Moscow, where he made similar comments. On January 24, the presidium of the Crimean Supreme Council called on Yanukovych to issue a state of emergency, and on February 5, they passed a resolution calling for Crimea to claim broad autonomy if the central government issued major changes in "fundamental law," whatever that meant. Consistent with the WWII legacy that still exerted great influence in Crimea, this bill concluded, "On behalf of the people of Crimea who elected us, we are saying that we will not give Crimea to extremists and neo-Nazis who are looking to seize power in Ukraine by dividing the country! The people of Crimea will never engage in illegitimate elections, will never recognize their results, and will not live in a fascist Ukraine!" The threat to declare broad "autonomy" led to allegations of separatism and an investigation by the SBU, Ukraine's intelligence service. We had also seen reports of paramilitary "self-defense" groups associated with Russian nationalist parties emerging in the Crimean countryside with opaque leadership structures. But at the same time the Crimean parliament was hyperventilating, we had also seen media reports of small Euromaidan protests in Simferopol as well as support for European integration from the Crimean Tatars Majlis, which represented 10 to 15 percent of the population. In order to sort out these contradictory developments, it was time to get a firsthand look.

After landing in Simferopol, Drew and I took a taxi down the winding mountain road to the city itself. We arrived at the clean and comfortable "Ukraine" hotel in Simferopol, where Valentyna met us with a fax and a frown. It was from the Crimean Ministry of Economic Development and Trade. While thanking us for our interest in meeting, the letter closed with the line, "According to the Vienna Convention on Diplomatic Relations of April 18, 1961, such meetings are handled exclusively through the Ministry of Foreign Affairs of Ukraine." This was a kiss-off and a lie. As US diplomats, we met with local government officials constantly, just as Ukrainian diplomats in the United States met regularly with local American officials. The practice was never in violation of the Vienna Convention. But their disingenuous excuse revealed that officials of the Crimean autonomous government were deferring completely to Kyiv. Their excuse for rejecting us was that they were totally loyal to their capital and relied on their superiors in Kyiv to deal with foreigners.

"That's not all," Valentyna added. "I got another call, and Mayor Ageyev is not going to meet with us either." Unlike the Economic Ministry meeting, we already had an agreed time and place for the Simferopol mayor meeting. Someone had decided that we shouldn't meet, and also decided to wait until we were on the ground to let us know. There was no point in taking this personally. We knew it was just a small-minded slap to Uncle Sam's face.

"Not a problem," I told our little team. "We have plenty of other meetings. It's their loss. Let's wash up and get to work."

We each had our own roles in this three-person team. Valentyna was constantly working her cell phone, confirming and rescheduling meetings and translating during them when necessary. Drew took meticulous notes for the post-trip reports, and asked questions on his subjects of interest. I led most of the meetings on our side. I tried to ask open-ended questions and let our interlocutors talk about what was important to them. I did have a few questions to ask everyone, but other than those, I didn't assume that I always knew the right questions to ask. It seemed better to let those who lived in Crimea direct our conversations about local affairs.

In half an hour, we were strolling down a quiet, tree-lined street in Simferopol. At the corner stood an ornate, pastel blue-green building with arched second-story windows and Tatar and Ukrainian flags flying out front. This was the Crimean Tatar Majlis, or parliament, the seat of the representatives of the Crimean Tatar people. Their stated goal was to advance the Muslim Crimean Tatar people's interests with the local and national governments, for the purposes of the "elimination of the consequences of the genocide, committed by the Soviet state against Crimean Tatars, [and the] restoration of the national and political rights of the Crimean Tatar people and implementation of its right to free national self-determination in its national territory." We had a meeting scheduled with Refat Chubarov, Majlis chairman.

Upon entering through the heavy wooden front doors, a young man introduced himself and led us to a conference room upstairs. Chubarov, Vice Chairman Aslan Omer Kirimli, and Majlis foreign affairs head Ali Khamzin greeted us cordially. "Tea?" asked Chubarov. Within moments, a young woman whisked in cups of steaming, fragrant tea.

"You've come at an important time," Chubarov said. He explained that the Majlis and nearly all Crimean Tatars supported reformist efforts in Kyiv, including Euromaidan. "European integration is vital for the future of Ukraine, and thus, it's vital for us," he said. "We want economic opportunity like anyone else.

But you understand, we don't draw attention to our positions. We are the minority people here in our own land. We don't want to create unnecessary friction."

I explained the US Embassy's position that the protests in Kyiv should be resolved peacefully through negotiation, and discussed the various false accusations that the United States was somehow behind the Euromaidan movement. "Do the Crimean Tatar people believe that any foreign forces are influencing the course of events here?"

Chubarov did not hesitate. "We think seriously about the threat of Russian intervention or even invasion after the Sochi Olympics." That was stronger than I had expected. "But taking Crimea would not be as easy as Abkhazia. Please understand that we've been pushed off this land too many times before. It will not happen again."

I was shocked and I don't shock easily. Was he merely intending to get our attention, or was he actually predicting the first use of force to grab territory in Europe since World War II? "Do you really think that such a move could be possible here in the twenty-first century?" I asked.

"All necessary preconditions exist for Russian intervention. The Crimean parliament has asked for Russian support, and our Crimean local officials travel to Moscow constantly without any involvement from the Ministry of Foreign Affairs in Kyiv. You should watch closely how local paramilitary organizations are being created. God forbid, all it would take would be a provocation in which two or three Russian families would be killed, and a swift Russian intervention would be assured. You know, Russian marines from Murmansk were moved into the Russian base in Sevastopol recently. This could just be part of their Olympic security plan, but history has taught us to be a bit paranoid."

Indeed it had. We spoke for a while about the relationship that the Majlis had with the Party of Regions and with Crimean local officials. But every time we veered too far into discussing standard Ukrainian politics, he wanted to ensure that we understood that the Majlis felt threatened. "People know that we support European integration even if we are quiet about it. They seek to discredit us. Several months ago, a crazy video started circulating on the internet with supposed 'proof' that one of our top officials was somehow involved with Tryzub, a right-wing Ukrainian nationalist group. This was, of course, all nonsense. I went to the local Security Service of Ukraine office to ask for some help with the video and the threats which started pouring in. This kind of affair can get people killed, sadly. They didn't offer to help us at all."

"What do you make of the reports that Russian nationalist groups are forming paramilitaries in rural and outlying areas here in Crimea?" Drew asked.

"Well, it's true," he responded. "And it's threatening. They claim that this is to guard against those fascists from outside, from Kyiv. But Kyiv is a long way away. I do know that these 'self-defense' units in villages are emphasizing recruitment of gun owners. No one knows how this will play out."

We finished our tea. "Please, stay in touch with us," Chubarov intoned seriously as we shook hands and left. The Majlis folks were on edge for good reason. In Chubarov's own words, history taught them to be paranoid. But during exceptional times, paranoia and prescience are hard to parse.

A short taxi ride from the city center took us to an aging brownstone office building. After passing through a dingy lobby, we wandered the narrow halls for a few minutes before finding the offices of the Center for Journalistic Investigation and its Press Information Center. The Center was a bastion of independent media in Crimea that provided training programs for journalists from across Ukraine and neighboring countries. They also produced print publications and even a television show on current events in Ukraine. Our appointment was with Valentyna Samar, an independent journalist who reported on Crimea.

Ms. Samar, with a short-cropped blond bob and wearing a light jacket, projected the professionalism of a long-time observer of local events. We made our standard introductions at her desk next to the small studio where her group produced TV and radio programming.

"Given the events in Kyiv," I asked. "How is the Party of Regions doing here? Is their support still solid?"

"Absolutely solid," she answered. "There is no change here. It has been quite easy to demonize the protesters, through newspapers and even videos shown in public places like buses. Regarding Maidan, and just in general, slogans about fascists are quite popular here. Most people don't actually analyze them very deeply. Everyone loves to believe that they have the chance to fight the Great Patriotic War all over again."

"How about the pro-Russian parties?" I asked. "Aren't they having a bit of a renaissance after being dormant for so long?"

She said: "Well, suddenly the pro-Russian parties have new sources of income, so they are rising from the grave. This is a bit of a mystery, though we think we know where the money trail begins. But these parties only get into the parliament now with Party of Regions backing, so they are quite polite. This relationship has only gotten closer now that they both perceive a common enemy—the Maidan protesters."

"But the rhetoric of the Crimean parliament has gotten so strident," I said. "Isn't it a threat to Yanukovych when they say things that sound like separatism?"

She leaned back in her chair: "The Party of Regions and Yanukovych co-operate with pro-Russian parties in Crimea because they are very useful. They can be controlled, and for him, they are a helpful counterpoint to nationalist groups in western Ukraine. But Yanukovych is not stupid. To talk about separatism means discussing Yanukovych losing something that is his, and he won't stand for that. He needed to shut that down, and he did through the Security Service of Ukraine investigation. That sucked the momentum out of that particular initiative. Crimean separatism born here, among our own people, is effectively dead."

"How does the Russian Federation influence the situation here?" I asked. "It's really not too hard. For example, our parliamentary speaker, Volodymyr Kostyantynov, is about 1 billion hryvnia in debt through the companies he owns," she added. (This was about $120 million dollars.) "Details are sketchy, but much of this debt is effective leverage in Russia's hands. No wonder he travels to Moscow so much, saying things that make them so happy. Corruption is key in this regard. Corruption means everyone has a price, and that our politicians can be influenced or controlled."

"But controlled for what purpose? What is the end game?" I asked.

"Our situation in Crimea is dangerous," she noted gravely. "Several factors could lead to Russian intervention in Crimea, including the presence of the Russian naval base and the presence of so many Russian military retirees of a certain mindset. The ease of engineering social conflicts between the Russian and Crimean Tatar populations as a pretext for intervention, and again, the high level of corruption among Crimean politicians, which leaves them vulnerable to foreign manipulation, makes such intervention possible."

"But what do you mean by intervention?" asked Drew. "Would getting the Crimean parliament to mouth Moscow's propaganda line be enough, or are you talking about an actual Abkhazia-type direct intervention?"

"It all depends, and I can't pretend to know the future," she answered. "A lot depends on how things progress in Kyiv. Of course, we are all glued to our TV screens. It is an incredible drama."

We thanked her, wished her the best, and left her small offices and studio. With our government meetings unexpectedly canceled, it was time for dinner and an early bedtime at the "Ukraine" hotel.

The next morning we took a taxi down a dirt road leading out of town. Far from the city center, we stopped at a modern-looking, flat-faced gray office building and climbed to the second floor offices of ATR television, the Crimean Tatar channel. Since 2006, they had broadcast news and cultural programs, mostly in Russian but also in Tatar. Our appointment was with Liliya Budjurova, a political talk show host and correspondent who, like Valentyna Samar, was someone who knew recent events in Crimea well. The ATR staff led us on a brief tour of their meticulously clean and well-appointed studios and offices.

I started by asking her how locals perceived events in Kyiv.

"There are some really nasty anti-Maidan videos played on trolleys and buses, just to raise the political temperature here. Money for this comes out of the regional budget for 'social public awareness,' so it is sponsored by our local government."

"Are they effective?" I asked.

"Oh, very, I'd say," she answered. "Lots of folks here are quite eager to go out and fight the 'fascists.' People here support the Party of Regions, despite the corruption and everything else."

"So, there's no sympathy for Euromaidan here?" I asked. "We read that there were a few Euromaidan rallies in Simferopol."

Budjurova waved her hand dismissively. "When our extremely small Euromaidan meets here, they are treated like freaks to ridicule. In that way, they are useful to local authorities. We Crimean Tatars generally support European integration, but at this point have no desire to get out on the street and protest. Here in Crimea, it would be counterproductive."

"So, would you say that the political temperature is now rising here?" I followed up.

"You know, everything is generally quiet," she replied. "But our authorities, especially in the parliament, are working to inflame tensions and passions. Who benefits from whipping up hysteria in our quiet little Crimea? The only answer that makes any sense is Moscow. What are they preparing for?"

"I don't know," I stated honestly. "Do you have any ideas?"

"We cannot exclude an Abkhazia scenario here," she said.

"The chances of a Russian invasion of Crimea are very low, maybe around

5 percent," she offered. "But the chances could rise up very rapidly if there is major instability or the formation of a pro-Western government in Kyiv. Also, it could increase if our own Crimean parliament gets mischievous again."

"How about the reappearance of pro-Russian parties and the creation of new militias?" I asked.

Her expression hardened. "Short of wholesale intervention, Russia can always use pro-Russian parties here as a kind of 'fifth column' to be utilized in the future. They are a tool for their use at will," she said.

So here was another group of well-informed and worried Crimean Tatars. The image forming in our minds was coming into sharper focus.

After the Crimean local government cancellations, I was worried that our meeting schedule was a bit unbalanced. Meeting with Crimean Tatar groups and independent journalists was vital, but they were the people most likely to agree with the US interpretation of events in Kyiv. So I was greatly looking forward to meeting Sergei Shuvainikov, a deputy in the Crimean parliament and a leader of the Russian Unity party whose stated goal was to defend the rights of Russian speakers in Crimea. Moscow was trumpeting its propaganda line that Russian speakers in Crimea and eastern Ukraine felt deeply under threat after events in Kyiv. I wanted to see how alarmed or threatened Mr. Shuvainikov claimed to be.

We met in our hotel lobby for coffee. Shuvainikov, broad-shouldered and stout with a business jacket over his casual sweater, shook my hand and immediately gave me a few copies of his own in-house newspaper. Over the large red masthead reading, "Russian Front—Sergei Shuvainikov," was the slogan, "It's time to be Russian!" A quick, polite glance at the four-page paper revealed a lead article entitled, "Fascism Will Not Pass!" There was also a photo of a man burning an EU flag, and accusations that a new academic work on the history of the Crimean Tatars published in St. Petersburg was false and promoted Russophobia. I was looking for a contrary viewpoint, and Valentyna had found the right guy.

We introduced ourselves and ordered coffee and tea. "Thanks so much for meeting with us," I opened before introducing our small group. "So, what are your party's priorities right now? What are your plans for the near future?"

"Well, I'm going to Kyiv quite soon to request more money for Russian language resources in our schools here in Crimea. The Ukrainian budget is being pushed through right now, so this is an important time for budget requests.

We don't want them to forget about Russian language education, especially in the early grades."

His plans were surprisingly calm, healthy, and normal. It sounded like what advocacy should be—trying to get the best deal for your constituents through the normal rules of the game. Despite the hysterical pronouncements in the parliament and his own newspaper, he was not in crisis mode. His language was dispassionate. He continued talking about his work to promote Russian in local schools.

"So, how do you interpret events in Kyiv right now?" I asked.

"It's a real tragedy, a real shame," he said. "These people on Maidan are fanatics who are trying to pull us away from our natural brotherly relationship with Russia."

This brought me to what I really wanted to ask about. "And what type of role would you like Russia to have here in Crimea? How active should they be?"

He took another long sip of tea. "We want Putin to be more active here in Crimea, certainly," he added. "But what would be most useful to us would be the Russian government's moral support. Their words of encouragement for Russian communities abroad help tremendously. We do want a less passive Russia in Crimea. But at the end of the day, we can take care of ourselves."

"Is that why yours and other pro-Russian parties have been creating militia groups?" I asked, a bit provocatively.

"Yes, we created a small paramilitary group, about seven hundred men, to defend Crimea against fascists," he calmly noted. "This is to defend law and order under Ukraine's legitimately elected president. As you know, given events in this country, these are uncertain times. We can make our own army if we need to, with or without any Russian support."

This was much less dispassionate. There was now an edge to his voice. I hadn't raised the question of Russian support for these militia groups—he had, in order to deny it. But unlike on Maidan, it was unlikely that these were unpaid volunteers—someone was funding these new armed groups. In our next appointment with Andriy Krisko, head of the Crimean office of the Committee of Voters of Ukraine (CVU), an election watchdog NGO, we soon learned more about them. He was unsettled by the new paramilitaries.

CVU personnel spent their days buried in the mind-numbing minutiae of voter rolls and candidate registration requirements, attempting to expose and fight those trying to warp the system for corrupt purposes. This should be a nonpartisan activity supported by all political parties, but Ukraine being Ukraine, CVU naturally tended to butt heads most often with the biggest cheater—Yanukovych's Party of Regions.

"My friends, ordinary people in Crimea," Krisko began, "were not too concerned at first about the new voluntary units as they were supposed to patrol with the police, but now they are acting independently. Our parliamentary speaker Kostyantynov went to Moscow to speak with people about these units, but why are people so interested in this topic in Moscow?" The question just hung in the air.

He continued, "Many recent moves, such as statements from the parliament's presidium and the recent Party of Regions meeting, are likely being conducted to prepare for a greater Russian role in Crimea. If the Russians start giving stronger signals of a willingness to intervene, many sectors of the population will begin voicing even stronger encouragement for them."

"Is that because of the backlash against Euromaidan?" I asked.

Krisko replied, "It's funny—whole movements are created to fight Euromaidan, although they barely exist here. The initial negative campaign against Euromaidan, you know, that they are fascists and that sort of thing, was quite successful."

Krisko's face broadcast a quiet concern. Our hour-long appointment passed quickly. Now it was time to talk to the people who barely existed, the scorned object of those who railed about the supposed danger of fascism rearing its head in Ukraine.

Our last meeting in Simferopol was with Andriy Shchekun, a Euromaidan Crimea activist. We met him for lunch at an open-air café in the middle of town. A tall, solid man with a firm handshake and a broad grin, Shchekun was in a good mood.

"I came here to Simferopol in college to study," he mentioned. "Then I got married and stayed. It's a great place for kids, a great place for anyone, really. But a bit backward in some ways. As far as corruption, municipal services, and democratic development, we've still got a long way to go."

"So, did your activism start with Euromaidan?" I asked.

"No," he laughed. "I've been an activist here for a really long time. Different issues at different times, but all about reform and improving our community. All the police know me. I've actually got a good relationship with them. They tell me the boundaries, and I make sure that my guys stay within them. We're trying to improve Crimea, not to get anyone sent to jail or destroy property. I want to show people here that we can have a useful role in reforming things for the better."

"You say 'your guys.' Are you a big group?" I asked, knowing from other conversations that they weren't.

"We're pretty small, actually," he admitted. "I had a hard time convincing my like-minded friends to stay here in Crimea and not go to Kyiv to the big protests. They feel that protesting here is a useless gesture. Why waste time when it seems that nothing will ever change in Crimea? My answer is that this is our community. Why go somewhere else to try to improve that place for other people? Let's tackle our own corruption. Let's start in Crimea, in Simferopol, on the very streets where we live."

The shashlik, or kabob, arrived and we all started to eat.

"Do you get the feeling that outside forces are influencing what's going on here in Crimea?" I asked.

"Look, I really don't buy into that," he interjected. "I don't really look at our situation globally, I look at it locally. Who cares what they think in Brussels or Moscow? I just want to concentrate on my town, my kids' school, whether our local officials are on the take, and where our trash goes. I support European integration because it will help with all of those kinds of things in the long term. But the starting point is here, at home. I don't spend too much time right now reading the international page of the newspaper, you understand."

We finished our meal. I appreciated that Andriy was a friendly guy, but given the small size of his group and his intensely local focus, I didn't expect to hear from him again. It was time to catch the train out of Simferopol. The train station was just a long series of white arches leading to a large white clock tower topped with a spire holding a red star aloft. Valentyna, Drew, and I sat down in our train compartment, which was a posh upgrade compared to my student days in Russia when I rode in the cheap seats.

"So," Drew mused. "How alarmist are we going to be about all of this when we get back to Kyiv?"

"There's a lot of concerned people here," said Valentyna. "It has changed a lot in the last few months. But the whole country has."

"We'll just report everything as we heard it," I said. "We'll be as alarmist as we can without predicting invasion or something crazy like that."

As the train clacked north out of Crimea we reflected on our visit. Why would Russia do something flagrant and dangerous in Crimea when they had such a good track record of getting Yanukovych to do whatever they wanted? It would be like stealing a car when you already had a spare key and could use it anytime you wanted. With Yanukovych in power and Russia holding the upper hand, Crimea seemed likely to stay sleepy. But this logic rested on the seemingly reasonable assumption that Yanukovych would remain in power in the near term. Few people guessed just how shaky his grip had actually become behind the scenes. While we were talking our train passed silently from Crimea to the Kherson region of Ukraine. Within a month that trip could only be made across a dangerous and unrecognized "international border." We had no idea that we would be the last American officials in Crimea before the invasion.

We arrived well after midnight in Zaporizhzhya, taking a taxi from the train station to the blocky modernist yellow and white Reikartz hotel on the edge of the city. Zaporizhzhya was part of Yanukovych's political heartland, and PoR support was still quite strong there, though maybe a bit tattered by recent events. Zaporizhzhya was one of the most polluted regions of the old Soviet Union and retained that dubious distinction in independent Ukraine. We read in the press that a fledgling Euromaidan movement was broken up there a few weeks earlier. Protests in places like Zaporizhzhya must have been much more disconcerting to Yanukovych than similar protests in western Ukraine where he might expect them. Tomorrow, we would ask around about what happened on January 26.

I fell asleep immediately after setting my alarm for an early morning breakfast meeting at the hotel with Roman Pyatyhorets of the local Committee of Voters of Ukraine, a recent Euromaidan activist. We would also meet with local journalist and protester Bohdan Vasylenko, as well as Valeriy Zotov, editor-in-chief of *Pravda*. These appointments were intended to give us some background before meeting Zaporizhzhya governor Oleksandr Peklushenko, a Yanukovych confidant. Unlike our local government engagements in Crimea, that meeting remained on our schedule.

We held separate discussions with Pyatyhorets and Vasylenko in cafés and with Zotov on the lawn outside his office. From these individual conversations, we wove together the story of the last month in Zaporizhzhya in the words of these three men. The snowballing crisis eventually exploded locally on January 26:

Pyatyhorets: "There was really no opposition to speak of here in Zaporizhzhya, especially if you are talking about the established political opposition parties in Kyiv. But we've always had a number of good NGOs here. Back in 2013, a group of reform-minded NGOs started a new anticorruption initiative under the slogan, 'Stop Kickbacks.' We started sending letters to the local prosecutors' office about violations of government procurement regulations. We even got them to start a few investigations. Procurement was our priority as it is the main way that corrupt officials get public money into their own pockets. Anyway, this was a popular initiative, and we started to get some public support. When Euromaidan started in Kyiv, we saw our goals and theirs as basically the same. So we transformed ourselves into the Zaporizhzhya Euromaidan, with NGO people playing the roles that political opposition people might have taken in other regions. It was all pretty organic. Because we already had some credibility and a grassroots following, we quickly became the largest Euromaidan movement in southeast Ukraine. The movement kept growing until the big attack on January 26."

Vasylenko: "Two months of protests had passed, and we didn't have any real results. Many of us wanted a more visible approach, so we decided to protest directly in front of the regional administration building and beat drums and light campfires. That's how things got started on the twenty-sixth, which will now always be known as our 'bloody Maidan.' Several days before that, a number of strange guys started joining our protest. You know, guys with face masks who spoke like real Russians. Our protest group had grown, but it was still small enough that we pretty much knew everyone. But not these guys. Who were they? Isn't it obvious? The government claims that the protesters are fascists. So if the fascists aren't here, they must create them. These were provocateurs placed among our own people who were there to cause violence. We've seen this as the template for cracking down on protests throughout the country. Some of the face mask guys started throwing rocks at police and administrative buildings. They would start some kind of scuffle with the cops, then fade back into the crowd. We didn't see them after that. I guess their job was done and they called it a day. Maybe they knew what was coming. Anyway, there were some fights and some injuries, so our people with a medical background set up a makeshift clinic inside of the theater off the main square. At about 9:30 at night, the police surrounded us with a wall of shields and started throwing stun and gas grenades at us. But the most dangerous beatings were the ones given by the titushky working with the police. The police beatings stopped after a few hours, but the titushky were out looking for people to beat up until about 7:00 the next morning."

Pyatyhorets: "Anyway, we have video of police giving money to paid semi-criminal enforcers to participate in the anti-Maidan. These titushky were told not to worry about causing any sort of injury to Euromaidan protesters, and they were given 200 to 300 hryvnia [About $25 to $37 dollars] per day for this kind of work."

Vasylenko: "One girl I know was severely beaten in the theater. I know that the police took this one other kid and exploded a flash grenade right in his face. His hearing is really damaged. It'll take both of them quite some time to recover. Police came right into hospitals and arrested injured protesters that night, dragging them out of their hospital beds."

Zotov: "Police and titushky attacked two pro-government TV journalists, one of which was a regional TV journalist. They even went after off-duty journalists who they recognized in the area."

Vasylenko: "I saw some titushky rob two small photo stores near the theater lobby, taking money and cameras. I remember one journalist from state media—this would be kind of funny if it wasn't so sad—who was attacked by a few titushky. He tried to explain to them, 'Hey guys, I'm from state media, you know, from the government, so we're on the same side.' They didn't listen to him at all, and beat him and smashed his camera. It was open season on journalists, regardless of which side they were on."

Zotov: "I received some information that various police units were told that they needed to deliver at least fifty beatings that night in order to receive their 'administrative awards.' Whether this bonus was cash or some kind of medal or commendation, I don't know."

Vasylenko: "I don't know how it works in other places, but in Zaporizhzhya, the titushky follow local government instructions after they've been filtered through the local criminal authorities. This was really interesting to see on January 26, when our own governor Peklushenko began to question what the titushky were doing. Maybe he has a conscience. He stood in front of a crowd of titushky early that night and asked them to cool down a bit. The titushky were really confused because, after all, they were stirring things up based on instructions from the local government. They didn't know if Peklushenko was just telling them to back off to look like a good guy for public consumption or if he really meant it. The governor yelled out for a local criminal boss who was standing close by, a genuine mafia man, and asked him in front of the crowd to tell his boys to back off. He obliged, and the titushky listened immediately. That was their chain of command. Now you tell me, is this kind of government normal?"

Zotov: "When the government calls one thousand thugs out onto a town's main square, it's not simply corruption anymore. It's some kind of active state promotion of criminality. In other countries, police may occasionally get information from criminal informants, but here they give the crooks bats and instructions."

Our interlocutors explained how January 26 was a watershed for both the local protest movement and the regional government:

Pyatyhorets: "After breaking up the protest, police put sixteen protest leaders under house arrest under charges that could carry fifteen years in prison. Many others fled Zaporizhzhya. So it was after this, our 'bloody Maidan,' when opposition political types from outside of Zaporizhzhya came in to lead our Euromaidan. Some of us who were there from the beginning resented it, but our ranks were so depleted by the arrests and those who skipped town that there wasn't much we could do about it. Anyway, I guess we have more similarities than differences so we accepted it."

Vasylenko: "You know, for about one week after our 'bloody Maidan,' there were hordes of titushky inside the regional administration building. I guess they were there for added security. But it was an amazing scene—there was our governor, our city and regional councils, and all of our other local officials surrounded by and mixed in with all of these drunk, smoking, bored criminal muscle men. It was a picture I will never forget. It's hard to still believe in our local government with that image in mind."

Pyatyhorets: "Most of our current local leaders have criminal backgrounds, and if we were operating under European standards, these histories would disqualify them from government. So, needless to say, those guys are committed to a pro-Russian path. This predisposition is reinforced by some direct financing from Russia to pro-Russian groups. Russian citizens who speak excellent English and drive expensive cars come to visit our region regularly now. They provide funding for our pro-Russian groups. I have a video of one such transaction which took place in the open in a local restaurant. After a grant agreement was signed, a bag with $200,000 in cash was handed over. But they are really wasting this money! A few weeks later, I saw the pathetic protest march that was purchased.

There were only fifty to one hundred people! I actually know the guy who leads this group personally, so I yelled out to him that he should be able to do much better with $200,000. He seemed shocked that I knew the actual amount."

After learning about the violence a few weeks ago on the square outside of Zaporizhzhya's regional administration building, it was surreal to walk across that same square, now quiet and orderly, with my colleagues. We silently filed into the gray and brown marble Soviet brutalist building, showing our passports to a woman seated inside the door. We made our way upstairs to a large, wood-paneled waiting room outside the governor's office. "Please wait a moment," his receptionist requested in polite Russian.

A moment turned into a half hour. Men in suits with serious expressions, knowing we were seated there but not acknowledging us, rushed in and out of the large door that led to the great man's office. In and out. And in. Somehow, it was clear that our presence was driving up everyone's stress level considerably.

"Please, you are welcome to enter," the young woman announced after the long wait.

About ten local officials sat around the table, including the town's mayor and various local economic officials. Governor Peklushenko stood and offered each of us a cold handshake. A stout man pushing sixty, Peklushenko seemed at once both focused on us and distracted. We sat in the center of a large conference table, I directly across from Peklushenko.

"I hear that you are from the US Embassy's economics section," he projected louder than necessary. "Let me tell you why Zaporizhzhya is an excellent place to invest," he continued, his face starting to redden. "Did you know that Zaporizhzhya is the home of Motor Sich, famous around the world for the manufacture of aircraft engines?! Let me tell you a bit about our iron mines!" As he continued to speak, citing economic statistics about the region, his reddening became more obvious, and at times, his hands began to shake. "We are a major source of nuclear and hydroelectric power, making us ideal for industry!" Veins on his temples popped out and slowly receded before being replaced by new bulging veins on his forehead. "Zaporizhzhya is Ukraine's FOURTH LARGEST STEEL MAKER, AND IS QUITE IMPORTANT FOR UKRAINE'S OVERALL ECONOMY!"

I stopped taking notes. His team was mostly looking down at their shoes or gazing into their empty yellow notepads. I looked into his eyes, and Peklushenko was on the verge of tears. There was a surreal disconnect between his flat memorized investment sales pitch and his mannerisms, which resembled that crew member from the movie "Alien" just before an extraterrestrial clawed its way out of his stomach. He screamed a monologue for about thirty minutes. Finally, he stopped long enough for me to ask a question, which I knew had to be innocuous. Otherwise, his head just might explode.

"Thank you so much, Governor for your introduction to Zaporizhzhya's economy," I said, trying to strike a calming tone. "If I may ask, what are the sectors that American investors should look most closely at in Zaporizhzhya?"

He looked at me suspiciously. "All of them, ALL OF THEM! Did you know that we have a FIRST RATE TRANSPORTATION INFRASTRUC-TURE!" He was then off to the races for another twenty minutes, visibly sweating and shaking.

Finally there was another break, and fifty minutes into our one hour meeting, I had to find a way to get to the point in the most innocent way I could think of. "Governor Peklushenko," I asked as calmly as I could. "Do you foresee the recent events in Kyiv affecting Zaporizhzhya?"

Now his suspicion narrowed into a white-hot beam of hate. "That would depend on the plans of your State Department and your American CIA, about which I know nothing," he said, suddenly quieter and razor sharp. "You have not let me in on your plan for my region."

Wow. I don't think they taught me about this scenario back in training at the Foreign Service Institute. "Sir," I started cautiously, "It is not in the interests of the United States to interfere in the internal affairs of Ukraine or Zaporizhzhya. Such matters are for the people of Ukraine and your region to decide. The kind of rude interference you seem to suspect us of is not only completely against the principles that we operate under, but also would not help our own long-term interests. We have no desire to be seen in this light. It is not what we do."

He stared at me, for about thirty seconds, before speaking. "Your words are sweet, but they go down with a bitter aftertaste," he responded. He sat silent for a few more moments. "You know, I actually have a great deal of respect for the United States. Yours is a great country, mostly because you are not afraid to use force against your own people when you need to; you know, when it becomes necessary to keep your country under control."

He was baiting us, of course, and I had to reply without further fueling his paranoia.

"Our country has a long history of supporting peaceful protest at home," I said calmly. "It's required by our constitution. We haven't been perfect at this, and we've made a lot of mistakes through the years. But it is our ability to find compromise between different groups, not an ability to oppress them, which had made us great. When we made mistakes and slipped into oppression, it always made us weaker as Americans."

"Yes," he scoffed. "Have you seen our western Ukrainians? Sleepy, dazed . . . we go to work every day in the industrial heartland to prop up their lazy, poetic existence . . . we toil in the factories so that they can sit around and read Shevchenko and throw Molotov cocktails at us . . . what kind of compromise can you really suggest?"

"That's really up to your government," I responded. "I only suggest that compromise is better than conflict."

He suddenly stood up as if freed from the invisible cage that had been confining him. "Let me tell you about our president, Viktor Fedorovych Yanukovych. Viktor Fedorovych is an incredible man, a truly incredible man. A remarkable, irreplaceable human being, I tell you. Two meters of solid beauty, solid beauty."

He started to walk around the table, arms waving wildly as he talked.

"I went to see him in 2005. This was after the Orange Revolution, and everyone considered him a defeated man, a nobody. But not me. I always had the greatest respect for him. He suggested that we play chess. He had plenty of time at that point. I won the first two games. Then, he turned around and beat me ten times in a row. Ten times! Yanukovych, our president, plays the long game. You would make a serious mistake to underestimate the brilliance of our beloved president."

He continued for the next hour, regaling us with stories of Yanukovych rallying skittish Party of Regions parliamentarians in Kyiv and Peklushenko's own trips to Mezhyhirya. Peklushenko never returned to his seat for the rest of the meeting, pacing the room while talking. Our hour-long meeting had run over two, with our group speaking for less than sixty seconds total. Then, with a handshake and finally a smile, we left, walking back outside of the regional administration building onto Zaporizhzhya's 'bloody Maidan' Square. I felt like I had just been a minor character in a scene from one of Gogol's satiric stories.

"That was the single most bizarre meeting I've ever had," I said to Drew and

Valentyna, still not sure I understood what had just happened. "His personal stress cauldron overfloweth."

"Well, that 'two meters of beauty' comment was kind of on the verge of erotic," joked Drew. "It's an exaggeration, anyway. Yanukovych is 1.9 meters of beauty at most, on a good day in elevator shoes."

"Let's just get out of here," added Valentyna, who had obviously not enjoyed the spectacle.

As we walked away, it seemed clear that Governor Peklushenko initially thought that we were going to try to plant a sharpened American flagpole in his chest, or at least try to eat his face. Considering our small group—a young guy with a mustache in his late twenties, a kindly intellectual Ukrainian grandmother, and myself, a balding white guy in his late thirties—I didn't think we looked all that threatening. And as far as the propaganda narrative that the United States was fostering revolution in Ukraine, paying Maidan protesters, trying to boot out the Party of Regions, and the like. . . . one would think that Governor Peklushenko, from his high post, would be a producer and distributor of such propaganda, not a consumer. Wouldn't he know better? Maybe his own intelligence officials had informed him better? The answer seemed to be a decisive no. Our meeting was not for public consumption; there was no reason for him to put on a show. He seemed to really believe that the three of us embodied a nefarious meddling black hand manipulating Ukraine's destiny. Of course, he had no evidence as there was none, but he didn't need any. It was just an article of faith; a belief that this was how "great powers" operate. If one had the power to meddle and manipulate others, why wouldn't they?

His performance seemed outrageous and even comical that day, but he was clearly more acutely aware of the dangers he faced personally than we were. A year later, on March 12, 2015, Peklushenko would be found dead in his home in a suburb outside of Zaporizhzhya with a gunshot to the neck. Authorities said suicide, but few believed it. I'll remember him as a conflicted figure—a superfan of the monumentally corrupt Viktor Yanukovych who actually told his brutal titushky to back off when he witnessed the human carnage. That didn't make him a hero, but maybe that made him better than some. But his apparent belief that the United States was the source of the very real threats facing him was tragically misplaced.

We had one more meeting that day with a PoR city councilwoman and pro-government journalist who told us that the local anti-Maidan was only pro-

Yanukovych, not pro-Russian (as those in our morning meeting had claimed), that Zaporizhzhya's Euromaidan protesters had provoked police, and that the Euromaidan protesters did not represent local values. We listened. She smiled and was very polite, but after Governor Peklushenko's hundred-decibel performance, her words barely registered. We were tired, and maybe a bit deafened. We shook hands and left with our notes for dinner and sleep. We woke up at around 5:30 a.m. on Wednesday to get to Zaporizhzhya airport. We boarded an "Air Motor Sich" Antonov AN-24, which, as I learned on Wikipedia while waiting to take off, was last produced in 1978. This one didn't look even that new. With dainty fringed homemade curtains over the windows and shag carpets, it looked like someone took their grandmother's kitchen and made it into a plane. I closed my eyes. I told myself that if the plane had survived this long, it would likely live one more day.

Shortly after grandma's kitchen landed back in Kyiv, police in Zaporizhzhya found the charred body of local Automaidan leader Serhiy Senenko in a burned-out car on a rural road between two small villages outside the city. According to local media, his body was burned so badly that his wife could only identify him by his wedding ring. The initial police report stated that the car caught fire because of a gunshot that had pierced the gas tank. But within days, the Zaporizhzhya police announced their amazing working theory—the death was a suicide related to Senenko's personal debts, and that Senenko had shot his own gas tank then jumped voluntarily into the flaming vehicle to escape his worldly troubles. Shortly thereafter, an obscure radical anti-Maidan group calling itself "Ghosts of Sevastopol" claimed that they had committed the murder. The working theory of the Zaporizhzhya police might have come from a Grade-B Hollywood action movie, but credibility didn't even seem to be a goal.

The three days I spent in Crimea and Zaporizhzhya were a comparatively quiet interlude in Kyiv, although not without events worth noting. After a court refused to release four Afghan War veteran protesters, a large group of "Afghantsi" Afghan war veterans surrounded the courthouse in Kyiv's Podil district. Anti-Maidan activists collected the required 100,000 signatures on the White House's "We the People" website to get an official response to their petition that the United States "take part in the elimination of radical terrorist groups using methods of US intelligence agencies that dispersed demonstrators of 'Occupy Wall Street,' and also 'end the secret financing organized by the US Embassy [in Kyiv] . . . of radical groups.'" In Brussels, European Commission president Jose Manuel Barroso came out against imposing sanctions on the Ukrainian government. Disturbingly, in the central Ukrainian town of Kremenchuk, a thirty-four-year-old judge who had recently sentenced two protesters to house arrest was shot and killed at his home. In Odesa, arsonists burned the home of a former police officer who had helped the protest movement. The Russian Embassy's Political Counselor claimed during a public debate that Ukraine was moving inevitably toward "federalization"—the Kremlin's desired outcome. An unknown assailant splattered opposition leader Arseniy Yatsenyuk's head with green dye after he visited Yuliya Tymoshenko at a Kharkiv hospital.

Meanwhile, Moscow continued its dishonest smear attacks against Euromaidan and the United States. Russian Foreign Minister Sergei Lavrov was back out on the stump, railing against Euromaidan in a new editorial and sanctimoniously telling journalists, "Disorder and street violence in any country of the EU is understood as exactly what it is: a threat to social order and to the democratic structure. The Russian side has never tried to sow any doubt on this position, it hasn't allowed its representatives to hand out cookies to protesters who are without any morals."

In his topsy-turvy world, the ideals that actually drove the protesters to Maidan, such as fighting corruption and outrage at the autocratic Dictatorship Laws, were ignored and replaced with cheap excuses to stand around to get cookies from Toria Nuland. Would a younger Sergei Lavrov, less burdened by his current responsibilities and not beholden to Vladimir Putin, actually have espoused such beliefs if he had spent a week on Maidan talking to the actual people there? Or was idealism so alien to his nature that the very notion would be absurd? Except for those precious seconds when I was lying in bed on the verge of falling asleep, the crisis situation didn't allow time to ponder such questions about the hearts of others.

February 14, Friday afternoon, brought a Valentine's Day protest. From the Embassy's Regional Security Office: "Protesters are lighting flares and burning photos on the sidewalk in front of the Consular gates. Please avoid this area. All pedestrian and vehicle traffic must exit through the main gates until further notice. Thank you." The same day, to lighten the mood, our Public Affairs Section distributed a Valentine's Day video with various Embassy colleagues reciting in Russian and Ukrainian why they love Ukraine.

Indeed, there were some hopeful signs on that Friday. Maidan organizers acknowledged that the government had released many arrested protesters and that there was real progress on an amnesty bill. More opposition leaders announced that they were ready to enter a coalition government. The protesters agreed to partially restore traffic on Hrushevskoho Street. In Washington, the State Department spokesman acknowledged and encouraged the progress: "The United States welcomes today's announcement in Ukraine of the release of all those detained in the Euromaidan protests and commends the opposition for their decision to vacate occupied government buildings. We consider this an important step to de-escalate tensions and create space for a peaceful, nonviolent solution to Ukraine's political crisis. . . . We encourage all sides to continue to de-escalate tensions and search for a peaceful, mutually acceptable compromise to the current crisis." Once again, it felt like maybe Yanukovych, the protesters, and we were all heading for a soft landing.

But not every movement of Ukraine's thousand-sided Rubik's Cube inspired such optimism. Yanukovych was still talking tough, saying that his government had the power to "put anyone in their place." Elizabeth sent a grim note to the section: "Further to what [DCM] Bruce [Donahue] has been hearing from Maidan organizations, who fear retreating because of personal safety concerns, I met with a good contact in publishing who has spent a lot of time on the Maidan and knows lots of the organizers. He's hearing more frequently things like 'they won't catch me alive' and said that the silent repressions (staking out homes, threatening kids and families, burning cars and homes) have led most on the Maidan to believe there is no point in negotiating with Yanukovych and company, because the minute the West thinks the political situation is settled and shifts its attention, the security apparatus will roar back with vengeance against any protesters. The SBU has lots of lists."

David, always looking out for his team, wrote to us: "Regional psychiatrist Dr. McDavid is coming through next week. . . . We have all been going through a lot during the recent months of turmoil here. . . . Dr. McDavid's stress session may be useful in this regard, and the availability of his office hours is potentially a valuable resource for you and/or your family members." Most of us felt that we were too busy to spend time evaluating our own emotional state. We needed more meetings, more knowledge, and to send more cables back home. Maybe that next one could make a difference. Reflection and introspection could come later.

February 15, Saturday morning, another small group of Medvedchuk's

"Clean Citizens" approached the barricades and had another standoff with Maidan Self-Defense Force (SDF). Eric Johnson, ever the meticulous observer, wrote in to the Task Force that morning: "The standoff continues at Hrushevskoho but feels somewhat de-escalated with only one line of VV [Interior Ministry troops] facing relatively few SDF. As a lone artist paints a Hrushevskoho landscape from atop one of the burned-out MOI busses, SDF technicians work on their psy-ops sound system aimed across the line—wait, they just got it running again. . . . My contacts in the medical underground (they run the underground hospitals and get injured protesters out of the country through their underground railroad) are gearing up for hundreds of casualties in case the political options fail and there is a second Battle of Hrushevskoho. Overall there is a definite sense of somber unease in the air. The street barricades are still up on the approaches to the back sides of Ukrayinskyi Dim, which remains a hub of activity. The number of Sotnyas continues to grow—I just spotted the 32nd Hutsul Sotnya. The Hutsul Mountain Rifle Regiment of the Polish Army was known for its fierce resistance of the 1939 Nazi invasion of Poland." By the end of the night, protesters had begun to open up and partially dismantle some of their barricades on Hrushevskoho Street in accordance with the de-escalation plan, and they seemed ready to honor promises to hand back city hall the next day. Protesters walking away from city hall would clearly signal a welcome step back from the brink.

February 16, Sunday morning, the action moved back to city hall as anticipated. The Defense Attaché Office's Leo Hmelevsky wrote in at 10:59 a.m.: "Ambassador, some indications that city hall may be handed over. I will ask some questions. Three ambassadorial vehicles on the scene (OSCE [Organization for Security and Co-operation in Europe], Kazakh, and Switzerland)." DCM Donahue was also at city hall: "We just walked thru city hall; will need repair. Guys still sitting in lobby and now have formed out front facing the building with Svoboda flag. People and press walking thru city hall." In a few minutes, the OSCE inspection was finished, and the building was handed back to the Ukrainian government after months under protester occupation. At the same time, Eric Johnson wrote in from Hrushevskoho, which was being peacefully cleared: "A tractor showed up at 11:50 a.m. escorted by Maidan SDF. After a delay at the first barricade, it drove up to the second barricade, where it also stopped. It then moved up to the third barricade and started clearing debris. It drove off at 12:15 after moving debris for twenty minutes. More people have come up to watch the goings on. Some have brought food from home, as well as cigarettes, to give to the SDF." Then, word arrived on social media that protesters had left the regional administration buildings in Poltava, Ivano Frankivsk, Ternopil, and Lviv. The de-escalation was real.

This was a huge victory, and in line with exactly what we at the Embassy had hoped for: peaceful de-escalation based on some sort of compromise. As another *viche* started on Maidan, this brief shining moment was immediately tarnished. Fifty Svoboda-affiliated protesters re-entered city hall, saying that Prosecutor General Pshonka had not lived up to the government's side of the bargain by dropping charges against all protesters. Over 2,000 criminal charges were still outstanding. Minister of Internal Affairs Zakharchenko said that the amnesty law would be "fairly implemented" after protesters left the occupied buildings, but needless to say, there wasn't the requisite trust between the two sides for an easy mutual de-escalation. Eric Johnson again wrote in from the scene that night: "A rambunctious crowd of about 500 stands in front of city hall. A line of SDF, including Cossacks from the 4th Sotnya, have formed a human wall to block access to the building. They are turned facing the crowd and banging on their shields with their sticks to make a ruckus for the benefit of those inside and the press. . . . A rock and roll street band plays in the background. The crowd breaks into spontaneous chants of 'Slava Ukraini' with others answering 'Heroyam Slava.' And now the national anthem. Feels like a wild carnival ride—another Sunday evening in the new Ukraine. If only there weren't so much at stake." A few hours later: "The 'wild carnival ride' mood has been replaced by a 'Speaker's Corner at Hyde Park on a Sunday afternoon' mood. Everyone is standing around in groups engaged in animated discussions about the future of Ukraine." At around 8:00 that night, Prosecutor General Pshonka announced that the amnesty law would be implemented in full the following morning. Maidan SDF who had earlier vacated the building announced that they would continue to surround it and block access until the prosecutor fulfilled his promise.

February 17, Monday morning, while the Embassy was officially closed for Presidents' Day, the email system was still buzzing. The Ukrainian press reported that protesters around the Dynamo stadium found shells and spent live-ammunition magazines—something our own Defense Attaché Office strongly doubted. Overnight, far right groups attempted to retake the recently vacated city hall building but were stopped by Svoboda SDF—an example of the moderate right stepping up to control the far right. Eric Johnson again reported from the scene in the morning: "City hall is back under Ukrainian government control. You can tell because they followed the Interior Ministry's lead and took the handles off their front doors. Guess that's what happens when you are afraid of your own people. . . . The new entrance to city hall is around back and guarded by four nasty Interior Ministry policemen dressed in new, all black uniforms. They told me to get the hell away as there was nothing to see in the courtyard. . . . In front, three city workers are cleaning up the place. Two of them are taking down the flags that had been flying from the twin flag poles. Perhaps in an indication of where their true feelings lie, they then ran the EU flag back up the flagpole. . . . Incidentally, on my walk over, I spotted an SDF Amazon walking hand-in-hand with her much less physically impressive non-SDF boyfriend. Ah, Maidan!"

While some real progress on rapprochement between the two sides was visible for the first time, opposition and PoR parliamentarians couldn't agree on an agenda for the next day's session as politicos sympathetic to Maidan continued to push for constitutional reform that would return Ukraine to its 2004 constitution. If they were successful, this would substantially reduce the power of the presidency. The feared General Prosecutor's Office began the process of closing cases against Maidan activists in accordance with the amnesty law. There were new signs that both sides might at last be close to forming a technocratic coalition government that could unite the country. Back in the Economic Section, we closely tracked rumors, backed up by a statement from Russia's finance minister, that the next part of Russia's "bail bond" program, slated to be either a $2 billion or $3 billion bond purchase in Ireland, would proceed by the end of the week, assuming that Yanukovych announced a new Russia-friendly prime minister and government. But as Ukraine owed Russia billions in gas debts, it was highly likely that the loan money would go straight back to Russia's coffers without filling any of Ukraine's urgent needs. Crimean parliamentary speaker Kostyantynov announced a new trip to Moscow, but that was no shocker—for some reason, he couldn't seem to let two weeks pass without boarding a flight to Moscow. Immersed in the details of what was going on hour-by-hour, it was easy to miss the rapidly approaching storm, the darkness, the massacre.

9

THREE DAYS IN HELL: FEBRUARY 18–20, 2014

February 18, Tuesday. The day started out like many other days of the last few months. David and Elizabeth were busy responding to requests for information from the State Department Operations Center in Washington on the upcoming Russian loan disbursement. The barricades on Maidan and Hrushevskoho remained unchanged; the EU flag inexplicably remained flying over Kyiv City Hall despite the withdrawal of protesters. There were no obvious clues that a spasm of violence could soon crush the positive momentum built up over recent days.

On Tuesday morning, the focus returned to the Rada, where many protesters had pinned their hopes on several bills on constitutional reform and other issues. Protest leaders had promised to march on the Rada if these bills were not considered. Inside, the Rada gridlocked as the opposition attempted to block the podium after the speaker refused to register any opposition bills for discussion. The protesters then made good on their threat to march. Police and protesters clashed outside; flying cobblestones versus rubber bullets and tear gas. Suddenly, rapid-fire media reports bombarded us. Protesters broke through police lines near the parliament, with an estimated 50,000 people blockading the Rada and restarting tire fires on Hrushevskoho. Police injured two women with rubber bullets closer to Maidan. More clashes occurred inside Mariinsky Park, the base camp for anti-Maidan protesters close to the Rada. Government forces used tear gas in multiple locations.

Local media reported sighting snipers on rooftops around Maidan. From the Embassy Regional Security Office: "RSO has received word that a large group of protesters is en route to demonstrate at the Embassy. Please use caution when exiting the compound. RSO will update as more information becomes available." Protesters also showed up at the EU mission, demanding that the Europeans "stop support for extremists." From human resources (HR): "Task Force reactivated effective immediately." Then, the Batkivshchyna party announced on social media that protesters may move inside the parliament, presumably somehow advancing straight through the fortified police lines, to stay until the speaker registered the opposition's bill on returning to the 2004 constitution. Then another message from HR: "Please be advised that the session on how to protect yourself in times of stress, led by our visiting regional psychiatrist, will take place at 15:30 tomorrow in the multipurpose room." Timely.

We stopped our work to watch Kyiv's TV 5 as multiple Maidan Self-Defense Force (SDF) sotnyas marched up the hill toward parliament to reinforce the protesters already on the scene. Then came word from Lypska Street in the government quarter: protesters were storming Party of Regions (PoR) headquarters in a Molotov cocktails versus fire hoses fight. Photos soon showed the PoR building on fire. Ambassador Pyatt sent out a tweet, immediately cited as the US position: "After weekend progress in Kyiv, sorry to see renewed violence. Politics needs to happen in the Rada, not on the street." A distraught Klitschko told the press: "It all depends on Yanukovych now. What counts is not hours, but minutes." Maidan leaders called on social media for all medical volunteers to come immediately to the square; casualties were expected as reports rolled in of Interior Ministry troops attaching bolts and other shrapnel to supposedly nonlethal flash grenades. Our observer, Staff Sergeant Samuel Jerome, could see the escalation firsthand: "Protesters on the same roof as Interior Ministry, shooting fireworks at them. Pellet gun fired from protesters (see photo). Water hose putting out fires of Molotovs on buildings and benches and tires coming in. About 3,000 protesters. Skirmish on roof between eight protesters and Interior Ministry troops." Svoboda seized a new building, the House of Officers, to use as a clinic. Within the Rada, an ambulance was called to help Speaker Rybak "get his blood pressure back under control."

Just before 1:00 p.m., the Defense Attaché Office's (DAO's) Shane Parlow wrote in: "Instytutska erupting. Thousands of protesters pushing in. One bloody Interior Ministry guy escorted by SDF toward Maidan. Not being beaten, possibly to receive aid." As roughly two hundred Berkut retook the fire-damaged PoR headquarters building, Euromaidan released photos of Health Minister Bogatyrova climbing over a barricade to escape the protest zone. I couldn't stop my mind from wandering back to one of my first meetings in Ukraine, when an AIDS activist described to me Bogatyrova and her son's schemes to suck money meant for people with deadly diseases out of the government. There she was, someone who had symbolized the corrupt mess that Ukraine had become, with one of her assistants lending her a hand to climb over a ramshackle wooden and concrete pile in her designer leather shoes.

About five hundred protesters arrived outside our Embassy and immediately set tire fires billowing noxious black smoke. They then threw a bottle of red goo, apparently supposed to be fake blood but looking more like cherry Jello, on the US Embassy sign. They then strung animal organs—hearts and kidneys—over the sign for good measure. They then started scratching up the windows of the consular entrance with keys and breaking off small sticks and twigs in the gate locks in an attempt to cause some damage. Ukrainian police used tear gas to disperse the group. This was different than previous protests at the Embassy. Now the odor of violence and menace was intended to waft into our nostrils.

The Task Force continued pressing our Embassy observers to verify social media claims in which both sides accused the other of using live ammunition. Our observers chimed in: "From your Marine Combat vets on the ground, there have been no indications of live lead rounds fired. That sound would be distinguishable. Only the quieter less-than-lethals heard by us here." But with all the sticks and clubs and modified nonlethal ammunition, there was still plenty of opportunity for maiming and death. Pravyi Sektor called on gun owners to come to the square that afternoon after they accused the Interior Ministry of planning to launch a live ammo assault. Euromaidan protesters in Mariinsky Park, usually the home of anti-Maidaners, stockpiled cobblestones to throw during the next skirmish. *Ukrayinska Pravda* online published pictures of Interior Ministry snipers with long guns on rooftops near the presidential administration on Instytutska Street. Protesters started a new tire fire under the archway next to Kyiv City Hall.

Meanwhile, we were still trying to track the expected $2 billion Russian disbursement to Ukraine, painfully aware of the interplay between these disbursements and the situation on Kyiv's streets. David emailed Assistant Secretary Nuland and the National Security Council: "Russia's release of $2 billion in financing to Ukraine appears linked to an assumption on Moscow's part that President Yanukovych will shortly announce a prime minister candidate to its liking. . . . A well-placed contact told us the funds are already moving." We all knew that another anticompromise prime minister in the Azarov mold would move Ukraine further still from peaceful crisis resolution. Given Moscow's pressure for a violent crackdown, hearing that the Russian money was moving was not a good omen for peaceful conciliation.

As the active skirmishes began, the toll of the morning's clashes became known. Pictures of two dead protesters appeared on the internet, with a third death reported and seven protesters in critical condition. The Ministry of Interior reported that thirty-five police were hospitalized.

I took an Embassy car to a meeting that afternoon with Svitlana Zaytseva at a café near the Ministry of Economic Development. Driving down Lesi Ukrainky Street, the car stopped. Marching toward Maidan was a long column of at least three to four hundred Maidan SDF, many wearing balaclavas over their faces. I saw the flag of the 31st Sotnya, as well as plenty of Svoboda flags. Their faces grimly determined and carrying sticks and shields, they marched down the street two-by-two. Many carried bricks, rocks, or fire extinguishers. After waiting about five minutes for the column to pass, we proceeded.

Then, the email arrived that we all dreaded but expected to see: "FLASH—Berkut Attacks." From DAO's Michael Skaggs: "Berkut attacked down Shevchenko from Liuteranska. Most protesters ran. Now MOI [Interior Ministry] owns that block. 5,000 protesters facing off on Sadova and Instytutska. Water cannon truck driving down Institutska. Crowds running in panic." Then from DAO's Shane Parlow: "1,000 Berkut assaulting Khreshchatyk metro, climbing barricade. They showed a lot of discipline, not beating . . . that many. They let the elderly depart. . . . Hundreds of refugees from the battle of Instytutska are pouring through the single file Horodetsky entrance. There are many music students who evacuated their classrooms. The front line of Berkut assault is at Globus [the entrance to the underground shopping mall on Maidan]. Thousands . . . maybe seven thousand on Maidan. Mood is depressed and eerily quiet when no speakers are on stage. Berkut pounding shields to demotivate. Protesters are throwing rocks from Globus bridge at 2,000+ Berkut, who control October palace. . . . Berkut pushed to end of October palace, and own European Square down to the core barricade. . . . Maidan SDF deployed at least 500 fully geared fighters to the lines, imminent attack is in the air while citizens watch silently. All that is left is Maidan's core on the north and east." The Interior Ministry announced that as protesters had reoccupied Kyiv City Hall, the amnesty was off. SBU head Yakimenko and Minister of Internal Affairs Zakharchenko demanded a complete end of protests by 6:00 p.m. or the government will "be forced to take harsh action."

Then came word from the Embassy's General Services Office: "The whole metro system is shut down. Staff may leave immediately, encourage car-pooling. Official Americans are strongly recommended to keep a low profile this evening." Online press reported that Berkut were storming Ukrainian House. The Interior Ministry announced that a police officer had died en route to the hospital from a gunshot wound to the neck. Rescuers who extinguished the fire at the PoR headquarters announced that they found charred bodies inside. The downward spiral accelerated.

A commentary circulated by the Russian Ministry of Foreign Affairs again blamed Western countries for the violence in Kyiv: "What is happening now directly results from the policy of connivance pursued by Western politicians and European structures which turned a blind eye to the Ukrainian radical forces and their aggressive actions from the start, thus encouraging them to escalate things and be provocative against the legitimate authorities." Ukraine's Foreign Affairs Ministry under Yanukovych seemed to be reading from the same script. Referring to the State Department spokesperson's statement on February 14 that Ukraine should de-escalate tensions and create space for a peaceful, nonviolent solution to Ukraine's political crisis through the formation of a multiparty technocratic government, they stated: "We urge all international partners, among them the United States, to abstain from attempts to put pressure on the composition and the formation of a new Ukrainian government. These issues are exclusively an internal affair of Ukraine." Russia's more direct and seemingly successful attempts to influence Yanukovych's new cabinet and encourage a violent crackdown apparently weren't worth mentioning.

The Embassy's Consular Section issued another warning to US citizens, this time mincing no words: "The US Department of State informs US citizens of the increased risks of travel to Ukraine due to the ongoing political unrest and violent clashes between police and protesters. February 18th has seen a sharp escalation in violence between protesters and police. The Ukrainian Security Services have announced that following today's violence they may take extraordinary measures beginning this evening."

In downtown Kyiv, unbridled escalation reigned. Social media broadcast pictures of two new armored personnel carriers (APC) moving toward downtown. Euromaidan tweeted that Kyiv's fleet of dump trucks were ordered to report downtown at 11:00 p.m. to help haul away its barricades. So far, our DAO observers consistently disputed claims made on both sides that their foes were bringing lethal weapons to the fight. DAO nearly daily reminded the rest of us that photos purporting to show lethal firearms actually just showed pellet guns, and that the recoil of certain weapons was characteristic of nonlethal rounds rather than of live ammunition. That all changed in a single email from Staff Sergeant Samuel Jerome at 6:41 p.m.: "Confirming lethal weapons: Earlier observed about 30–40 VV [Interior Ministry] with loaded AK-47 walking to reinforce Berkut at Globus. This is to confirm the media report." Other signs pointed to a possible imminent showdown. Channel 5, a protester-friendly media outlet, was off the air and suddenly available only on the internet. Also, shutting down the Kyiv metro system not only had the benefit for the Yanukovych government of making transportation more difficult for protesters, but news reports suggested that the government was using the system to position its own troops. Access to Kyiv by road from cities such as Brovary, Odesa, Boryspil, and Zhytomyr was fully or partially blocked, and the Cabinet of Ministers announced that all roads to Kyiv would close at midnight. At around 6:30 p.m., the big three opposition leaders addressed the crowd from the Maidan stage, telling the large gathering to refrain from all acts of violence. Opposition leaders asked to meet with the press and foreign ambassadors at 8:00 p.m., while Foreign Minister Kozhara would hold his own meeting with the same group at 9:00 p.m.

At 8:00 p.m., it began. There were about 20,000 souls on the square. The Ministry of Interior declared an "anti-terrorist" action against the Maidan, and government forces, including Berkut riot police and regular Ministry of Interior troops, converged in overwhelming numbers on the area in and around the main Maidan stage. Opposition leaders, including Yatsenyuk in a bullet-proof jacket, left their briefing with foreign diplomats to head to the square. Within half an hour, fire was devouring a huge swath of the protest city's tents as police used nonlethal grenades and protesters shot fireworks at police in a bitter battle for the heart of Maidan. Ukrainian television urgently begged women and children to leave Maidan as hazy reports of deaths started to trickle in over social media. Several media outlets reported that Maidan SDF Commandant Parubiy had a heart attack. One Plus One Channel reported that about two dozen minibuses arrived at European Square with commandos armed with assault rifles.

Again, Staff Sergeant Shane Parlow reported: "We have confirmed on the ground seeing MoI [Ministry of the Interior] forces with weapons and live ammunition. This is only a reported observation of these weapons being issued, not fired. Still no indication of that. From being in actual war zones, and seeing and hearing the acoustics on Maidan, once a live round is fired down there, you will immediately see it on the faces of thousands. It will be apparent and clear to all. Not to mention that if a round impacts a person, much blood spatter/bone fragments sprayed on the surrounding protesters." The long, sad descent from early observers listening to engaging speakers at Open Maidan University to later observers watching for blood splatter and bone fragments was complete.

World leaders, including Angela Merkel, tried unsuccessfully to reach Yanukovych. Vice President Biden did get through to Yanukovych, asking him to urgently restart talks with the opposition. The next day, we learned that Yanukovych also reached Vladimir Putin that night.

At the Canadian Embassy, not even a full block from Maidan, a protester with a Canadian passport convinced the guards to open the gates as he fled from Interior Ministry troops. About fifty protesters then flooded into the Canadian Embassy lobby and looked unlikely to leave anytime soon. Government troops were prohibited from chasing them onto the grounds of a foreign diplomatic mission, and they did not. The Canadian Embassy, the embassy of a nation with a huge Ukrainian diaspora, was now part of the protest's occupied zone.

The line of flames licked closer and closer to the Maidan stage, the beating heart of the protest kingdom. The words of the Ukrainian national anthem, booming out from the stage as a mournful singer led the crowd in recitation, were especially bittersweet: "Ukraine has not yet perished, nor her glory, nor her freedom/Upon us, Ukrainians, fate shall smile once more." Within the next hour, the Trade Unions Building towering over the square, the long-standing Maidan headquarters building also used as a hospital for the wounded, was ablaze. Hundreds of injured began flooding area hospitals, where police were waiting to arrest them. Across Ukraine, the weekend's fragile progress toward compromise was also going up in flames. In the western Ukrainian city of Ivano Frankivsk, thousands of protesters surrounded the local State Security Bureau offices and police headquarters, forcing local Berkut to remove their masks and leave in a "walk of shame." Local protesters also moved on the Lviv regional administration building and police headquarters, as well as other key buildings.

The political temperature continued to rise in Kyiv. The Political Section's Liz Zentos wrote in after midnight: "Just passed large group (400+) of men, likely titushky, at Velyka Zhytomyrska and the street that goes down to the spusk [Andriyivskyi Uzviz, a popular tourist street]. Armed with MOI [Interior Ministry]-issued shields and metal pipes." On Maidan, protesters set a government APC on fire using Molotov cocktails. Protesters announced that five had died since the beginning of the storming of Maidan; police announced that they had lost four officers. Police cut Maidan's electricity. In Lviv, demonstrators set fire to an Interior Ministry barracks; in Ternopil demonstrators burned a police station and several police cars. In western Ukraine's Rivne, local protesters attacked a Berkut base. Late in the night, protesters in Lviv stormed a military compound and seized its weapons cache.

Ambassador Pyatt wrote back that night to Washington: "For those not watching the live stream, there's a medieval battle underway on the Maidan now that Berkut have broken through the wall of fire that the SDF constructed. Hand-to-hand combat with shields and clubs. Pity the militia who get caught on the wrong side. There will be many casualties. . . . Just finished up with Poroshenko. He says the Trade Union Building is fully engulfed in flames. . . . Wanted us to understand this has now become Ukraine's Tiananmen Square. At least ten more killed tonight already in Berkut firing. I expect hundreds more injured. Titushky gangs are wandering the side streets—my car was caught between a gang of them and pipe-wielding Self-Defense Forces near the Intercon [Intercontinental Hotel] on the way home. Poroshenko says 17,000 still on the Maidan. Was looking for some sign of hope out of the Biden call. Told him there was no reassurance I could offer and described Kozhara's refusal to be pinned down on the extent of the government's plans for tonight. He said, in all seriousness, 'I need to know how to save lives.' "

I arrived home late, grabbed a much delayed dinner, and walked into the living room. The light was off, and Natalya, Andrew, and little Elena were all silently watching a strange glowing orange image on TV. There was no commentary from the silent television set. After my eyes adjusted, I could see what it was—an image of the city burning at night. We were not Ukrainian, but this town was now our home. The fixed single-camera image of orange flames over downtown, presumably from Maidan tents and the Trade Union Building, was eerie. We didn't need to say anything. It was our home now too, and it was burning at its core.

Throughout the night, half a dozen people jumped from various floors of the Trade Union Building to escape the fire that engulfed it floor by floor. That night the Russian Foreign Ministry toughened their language and were characteristically unafraid to cast blame without any evidence other than that which they created themselves: "That which is taking place is a direct result of the conniving politics on the part of those Western politicians and European structures." We at the Embassy were stunned and saddened by the violence, and the continued deterioration meant that so many of our efforts had come to naught. It was hard even to process the Russian government's continuous ridiculous and slanderous accusations that we were the ones causing it. Of what possible benefit would this violence have been to us? We would not benefit in any way from Yanukovych "dipping his hands in blood"—that would likely mean the end of Ukraine's European dream as the EU and Washington would recoil from contact with his government. We could only lose in that scenario, and it was heading that way fast. As the night ended, reports of seven dead police, as many as twenty dead protesters, and hundreds injured continued to roll in.

February 19, Tuesday morning: Kyiv was by now a place of fear. The Maidan protest still survived on the square, but now only in compressed form. Overnight, directly in front of my daughter's kindergarten, camouflaged men with bats, guns, helmets, and masks pulled journalist Vyacheslav Veremiy and one of his colleagues, Oleksiy Lymarenko, from a taxi and shot Veremiy in the chest. Lymarenko and the taxi driver were severely beaten in what appeared to be the targeted assassination of a journalist. A local NGO said that armed men attacked twenty-seven journalists over the last twenty-four hours. That morning, Kyiv's traffic police were brandishing automatic weapons—something I had never seen in the city. With government security infrastructure under siege in western Ukraine, the Svoboda office in Kharkiv in the east and Klitschko's Ukrainian Democratic Alliance for Reforms (UDAR) office in Kryvyi Rih burned overnight. In the northwestern city of Lutsk, PoR and Communist Party of Ukraine offices were also torched, and the local Interior Ministry building was also under attack. The Party of Regions office burned in Komsomolsk; the Transcarpathian Region Administration Building in Uzhhorod was under protester control. The smoldering hulk of the charred Trade Union Building, now the grave of many injured protesters who had taken refuge there, glowered over Maidan.

School was canceled for both of our kids, and RSO sent an urgent message: "Due to violent clashes between security forces and opposition protesters, employees are authorized to take unscheduled leave and remain home. The city center should be avoided and personnel should make contact with their supervisors. If essential personnel live near the Maidan and they cannot get to work safely, they should notify their supervisor. Continue to monitor the local media and check your email to stay aware of the evolving situation. Keep your radio on and charged, and ensure you have provisions of food and water to last you for several days in the event the infrastructure suffers due to the violence."

But I knew that unscheduled leave didn't apply to us. David quickly wrote to us: "Safety first, absolutely. That said, the DCM [deputy chief of mission] would like significant staffing today. There is a lot to be done and many non-econ ways where we may need to pitch in." But there might be economics projects as well—the $2 billion Ukraine bond issue, expected to be purchased by the Russian government imminently, was just listed in Ireland. Kremlin spokesman Peskov commented that the money might be delayed a bit while the situation in Ukraine "regulated." Later in the day, the Russian government officially announced that the bond purchase was postponed until further notice. When the Irish bonds, only listed that morning, were delisted by the end of the day, it seemed that a condition of the funding, which Russia thought would have been met the night before, had not been fulfilled. In short, Maidan still stood. Russian Deputy Prime Minister Rogozin was coming to Kyiv the next day. Prior to his arrival, in an eyebrow-raising statement, the Ukrainian Ministry of Finance admitted that without external funds Ukraine would go bankrupt in 2015. The pause in Russian funding, which we all guessed was tied to Yanukovych's failure to tame Maidan overnight, was serious pressure.

A year earlier, when Ukraine's idiosyncratic World Trade Organization (WTO) maneuvers had some US government officials wondering whether Ukraine might collapse the entire international trade system, I had asked Washington to support a "model WTO" effort to bring economics students from various Ukrainian cities to Kyiv to listen to US and local speakers talk about rational trade policy. At the time, one key motivation behind the effort was to bring additional attention to Ukraine's bizarre WTO filings. We hadn't delayed the event due to the ongoing crisis since we constantly thought that it would be rapidly resolved. But now it was just one week away. The prospect of young students telling police that they were coming to Kyiv at the invitation of the US Embassy and then getting beaten as a result seemed totally possible. David and Elizabeth agreed immediately to my suggestion that we delay the event by a month.

In a move seemingly intended to thwart any last hopes of a grand compromise, the Ukrainian government opened up a case against the country's major opposition politicians for attempting to seize power illegally. In the western city of Khmelnytskyi, State Security Service officers fired on protesters attempting to seize their building, killing one and injuring two more. Protesters seized the Chernivtsi regional administration building without a fight, while other local protesters stormed the Sumy police headquarters. For the first time since the beginning of the crisis, all businesses and shops on and beneath Maidan closed. The road to Boryspil, where Kyiv's international airport was located, was completely blocked. Local hospitals were reportedly full to capacity and not accepting any new wounded. For us at the Embassy, this meant there was no easy way to get out of the country if necessary, and no guarantee of medical treatment if needed.

At about 11:45 a.m., clashes reignited, with grenades and water cannons fired on protesters. Our observers saw approximately three hundred Berkut on the Instytutska side of Maidan trading bricks, Molotov cocktails, grenades, and pellet gun shots with protesters. The exchange was minor compared to the day before, and this was not a serious fresh government attempt to clear the square. In a press statement, the State Security Service announced a broad "Anti-Terrorism Operation" across Ukraine. According to Ukrainian law, such an operation created the possibility of bringing Ukraine's military into the government's struggle with Euromaidan. This worst-case scenario for a bloodbath was getting easier to envision. Ambassador Pyatt immediately messaged Washington, stating that urgent US-Ukraine military-to-military outreach and diplomacy was vital in order to prevent military-on-civilian violence in Ukraine. Anxiety over the possibility of Ukrainian military involvement in the crisis exploded into bug-eyed alarm with another piece of surprise news— Yanukovych unexpectedly dismissed Volodymyr Zamana as chief of the general staff of Ukraine's armed forces. That he suddenly wanted an absolute loyalist in that job sent a distressing signal about his plans for the military—an institution that had assiduously stayed above the fray thus far.

Public Affairs Officer Eric Johnson shared some more of his observations that afternoon: "I swung by my apartment on St. Michael's Street to pick up my bag. My street—two blocks long—has now become a part of Greater Maidan—and not just because of the new impromptu barricades that have popped up all over it. When I was there at 4 p.m., there were over 100 SDF coming off duty or about to go on duty (gearing up or gearing down) preparing for their shifts on the front line down on Maidan. There were also hundreds of activists—mainly women—moving to and from St. Michael's cathedral carrying food, water, and other essentials. Some of them looked like they were freshly arrived in Kyiv. But the most radical transformation I witnessed was among my middle-class neighbors. I saw a couple of people in the process of offering shelter to Maidaners in their apartments. And two of the younger (previously apathetic) men in my building have now enlisted in the SDF. Bloody Tuesday has made more people in Kyiv rise up and take a stand—at least on my street. But on my commute to and from home/hotel/work, I also noticed that the anger against the GOU [government of Ukraine] appears to be spreading beyond my street. Commuters are pissed at the city government that the metro was closed and remains closed. . . . Commuters are pissed that the 16 and 18 trolleybuses no longer go downtown because electricity has been cut off on Maidan. Commuters are also pissed that surface public transportation which is supposed to be free is not (there were various stories on this yesterday). And people are pissed that the DAI [traffic police], now backed up by VV [Interior Ministry], are blocking streets at key intersections downtown. At several checkpoints I saw pedestrians and drivers venting their general anger and frustration at the GOU and on the cops (many of them who are armed) who are now manning the various checkpoints in Old Town. And this morning, the GOU chokehold appears to be even tighter as the GOU attempts to starve the Maidan to death. As it happens, the Party of Regions's strategy of trying to put a lid on everything and clamping down tight may end up having the exact opposite effect as the pressure appears to be building which just means a bigger explosion in the end."

Although the metro system remained closed, Maidan organizers called a large "informational meeting" for 7:00 p.m. Then came more news from the provinces—protesters stormed regional administration buildings in Zhytomyr and Poltava, with the PoR office in Poltava burned. Opposition leaders emerged from a meeting with Yanukovych after 11:00 p.m., announcing that there would be no storming of Maidan while negotiations continued. According to them, the government had halted plans for a final sweep of Maidan and a pending state of emergency to restart negotiations and stabilize the situation. "We received assurances from Yanukovych that there will be no storming of Maidan," Klitschko told the press. "We are talking about a truce. After all, today the main thing is to stop the bloodshed." Several minutes later, Yanukovych's staff confirmed the ceasefire, but the radical Pravyi Sektor group announced that they would not abide by the ceasefire. After midnight, Maidan doctors brought a body, charred beyond recognition, from the ashes of the Trade Union Building to St. Michael's cathedral. In Khmelnytskyi, a twenty-one-year-old man was killed when local protesters again tried to storm the local State Security Service building and its defenders opened fire for the second time that day.

After returning home, I showed my son Andrew an email from his school: "Kyiv International School will be closed tomorrow February 20, 2014. Due to the status of the events in the center of Kyiv, the recommendation from the US Embassy, and the uncertainty of the local transportation systems, KIS has decided not to conduct classes." After reading the message, he smiled. "See— not everything about a revolution is all bad, Dad," he said.

Yanukovych announced that February 20 would be a national day of mourning. It would turn out rather differently, not as a day to mourn yesterday's loss of life, but one on which new atrocities on an unprecedented scale would eclipse all that came before. Swedish Foreign Minister Carl Bildt released a statement calling the February 18 violence in Kyiv "a dark day for Europe." But the worst storm clouds were just rolling in.

February 20, Wednesday: The day started with the new normal—a flurry of emails on who could make it to work, who couldn't, and which roads were closed. DAO's J. P. Gresh wrote to the Task Force early that morning regarding the DAI traffic police: "All DAI promptly moved out north on Volodymyrska and pulled up their checkpoints. It looked like support for a VIP movement, but very strange. I've never seen DAI move so quickly. I should emphasize that the entire portion of Instytutska from Olhynska down was controlled by GOU yesterday evening." Something unusual was in motion. Ukrainian TV reported that there would be no Rada session that day as previously expected. Natalya and I cautiously made our way to work.

As usual, Russia was in the game, though Deputy Prime Minister Rogozin canceled his visit. Russian Prime Minister Medvedev, playing against type as the bad guy, commented to ITAR-TASS that the Ukrainian government should be tough, protect law enforcement officers, and not let anyone "wipe their feet on you, like a rag." The Russian word for rag, *triapka*, also meant "soft guy," or "weakling." It was a personal insult aimed at a Ukrainian president steeped in underworld culture. The unstated message was clear: only when you stop being a "foot rag" can you have Russian respect and the support you desperately need. You didn't finish the job on Maidan, you weakling.

DAO's Lieutenant Colonel Michael Skaggs was the Embassy observer on the square that morning and the only official American in the vicinity. The condensed Maidan and a row of Interior Ministry troops lined up on the steps of the Globus shopping mall exchanged a few rocks and flash grenades. Security forces formed a line to keep the Maidan compressed and hold the part of the square they claimed during the February 18 fighting. Suddenly, at around 9:30 a.m., the security forces packed up their shields and marched up the hill, a coordinated move obviously following orders. Without explanation, the government troops seemed to be abandoning a key piece of ground that some on both sides had died for just two days earlier. As they ascended the hill deeper into the government quarter, Lieutenant Colonel Skaggs noticed something new—the Interior Ministry troops had reflective tape on the back of their helmets. As a combat veteran, he noted, "There's only one reason to put reflective things on the back of your helmet. That's so people behind you can identify you when they're shooting. So that sort of gives me the chills a bit." He started sending rapid fire messages back to the Embassy.

About sixty Interior Ministry troops were led through the Maidan crowd by a priest. From the Maidan stage, an announcer stated that the men voluntarily surrendered and that SDF commanders were on their way to speak with them. Ambassador Pyatt wrote in, concerned: "If there is a security force operation against Maidan as many now fear, it will be justified as a 'rescue' for these sixty poor guys from the police who were 'captured.'" RSO, as always, was justifiably concerned about the safety of Embassy staff: "Due to an increase in violence this morning, all personnel in the vicinity of the downtown area should seek shelter indoors and remain indoors until further notice. If you are home, stay at home."

As always, the Task Force scrambled to keep up with events. Public Affairs's Andrew Paul wrote to the distro list: "Espreso TV shows SDF advancing toward Globus/Instytutska. Not fighting, perhaps police withdrawing?" But why? Michael Skaggs also saw various SDF and others advancing into the space mysteriously vacated by the Interior Ministry. A group of protesters ran up the stairs toward October Palace, an old theater prominently situated on a hilltop overlooking Maidan. When they reached the top of the stairs, the crackle of automatic gunfire echoed across the square as security troops opened fire on the advancing protesters. Skaggs wrote: "That's live fire. And we'd been hearing nothing but blank fire all of the time. . . . But there's a huge difference in the sound and the velocity, it's obvious immediately." From his vantage point, he could see the group turn to run immediately, and security forces shooting them in the back. "They started carrying the bodies down the stairs, most of which had been shot in the back . . . the dead and the wounded are all shot in the back." Though we at the Embassy didn't want to recognize it, a final line had been crossed. There was no coming back to the table after mass murder, no compromise to paper this over. One side would win absolutely. For the other, imprisonment, death, or exile.

The gunmen at the top of the outdoor stairs up to October Palace withdrew, leading to a momentary lull. Recognizing that the Yanukovych government would likely deny what happened or try to blame it on protesters, Skaggs rushed to the crime scene at the top of the stairs. Everywhere, the blood and gore of death was still on the ground. He started taking pictures: here's where a guy went down, that's where the shooters must have been placed. Running over to the shooters' recent location, he photographed shell casings and other evidence of the atrocity, then quietly made his way back to the Maidan. Around this time, Maidan SDF started sending small teams of around ten men up Instytutska, under the Globus Bridge, to find out what was going on and how far back the government troops had withdrawn. They were unaware that they were entering a trap set by sniper teams placed on top of the Cabinet of Ministers and other buildings, snipers who were about to turn Instytutska Street into a funnel of fire.

The Interior Ministry announced that a sniper had fired on twenty or more police in recent hours. That police were shot as well was important to know. A large mass of titushky on Besarabsky Square was shown on live TV. Protesters retook Ukrainian House in the midst of the fluid chaos, and security officials urgently evacuated the Rada. Embassy contacts stated that many PoR parliamentarians had already left Ukraine. That intelligence reinforced recent press reporting that twenty-six of them had departed on former Prime Minister Azarov's son's plane. One parliamentarian who had previously served in the Yanukovych government wrote to Ambassador Pyatt: "Kindly ask you to meet urgently with EU ambassadors and to support MPs [Members of Parliament] who are going to meet in the Parliament today (I hope so) in order to take appropriate measures to stop war. Yanukovych won't stop." Foreign ministers from France, Germany, and Poland were in Kyiv to meet President Yanukovych. In addition to the Rada, the Cabinet of Ministers, and later, the Ministry of Foreign Affairs were evacuated.

Directly after meeting with Russian government officials in Moscow, back in Simferopol Crimean parliamentary speaker Kostyantynov told local press that Crimea could separate from Ukraine. He soon appeared on Russian (not Ukrainian) television, stating: "Crimea should revert to Russia if the situation in Ukraine does not normalize." Press reports indicated that the extremist PoR lawmaker Tsaryov was leaving Kyiv en route to Moscow. The Kremlin's propaganda organ Russia Today sought to amplify the message of Crimean secessionism, reporting that Crimean Cossacks were uniting to "defend the peninsula and were counting on help from the Russian Federation."

Suddenly, on Instytutska Street, snipers began shooting protesters, out in the open with no cover available. When word of the deaths hit the Maidan, Ruslana cried out from the main stage, asking why people were being shot. Other announcers called on medical teams for help and SDF units to protect them. As they proceeded up Instytutska Street, these medical teams came under merciless sniper fire. Sniper rounds killed dozens, including medics.

Lieutenant Colonel Skaggs was an eyewitness to the bloody massacre:

This is a deliberate attempt to lure people up into an ambush area and then simultaneously kill them one by one with scoped rifles. Which you can—these shots were at about 200 meters, I mean, you could make that shot. I mean, you can see the look on people's faces at that range with those sorts of sights. They knew exactly what they were doing, and they were picking which guy they were going to hit next. I mean, I've seen this. You know, oh, how about the guy in the red helmet, yeah sure, let's get him next. It was just like that for hours. And they just keep coming up the hill, completely outraged by what was going on. They just could not pull themselves back from it. They just keep moving up the hill, and stacking up like piles of wood, up there in this kill zone.

Given the reflective tape on the back of the helmets of Ukrainian government troops and other telltale clues, this certainly looked like premeditated murder. For months, Russian government–controlled media had been screaming for a bloody crackdown. Russian President Medvedev had insulted Yanukovych for not cracking heads, calling him a rag that the protesters wiped their feet on. The bloodlust across the border directed against those wantonly labeled as "fascists" was unmistakable. But those who now lay dead or dying on the cobblestones around Maidan were not the cartoon character Nazis of Kremlin propaganda, but ordinary citizens moved to act by their disgust with the criminality of their own government. State-sponsored murderers, taking aim through their sniper scopes, were killing Ukrainians from different walks of life and with a variety of political beliefs, united only by their love of country and their desire to maintain the hard-won independence of their still young democracy by taking a stand on Maidan. Their deaths were the price of Yanukovych attempting to crush a threat to his power and prove his manhood to his Kremlin cronies. He would show that he was no foot rag, no "triapka."

By 10:30 a.m., eight bodies laid along the sidewalk in front of the McDonald's on Maidan, with another eight on Instytutska Street.

Michael Skaggs passed through this area while on his way out of the square: "And then down there on Maidan itself, in front of the hotel by the McDonald's, there's an aid station. Ambulances cycling through. And as ambulances pull up, they open the back door, pull out the stretcher, pour the blood in the gutter, and put the next guy in the stretcher. And the gutter is literally washed in blood—literally a river of blood washing down that gutter all the way down Mykhailivska."

On the Maidan stage, a speaker held up a Russian Interior Ministry shoulder patch and claimed Russian involvement in the day's killings. Snipers also appeared to be targeting news crews, including a US ABC news truck. Ukraine's Presidential Press service stated that opposition leaders now only wanted a fresh ceasefire so that they could arm militants. There were no signs of compromise.

From the Maidan stage, Ruslana, wearing a Canadian hockey helmet, carrying a cross in one hand and shells from lethal ammo in the other, yelled, "Yanu—why have you ordered your police to shoot the Ukrainian people?" While the Rada speaker and many Party of Regions lawmakers were long gone, some former PoR and opposition lawmakers tried to convene an emergency legislative session at 3:00 p.m. Local media reported that the shuttered metro system was shuttling titushky from one hot spot to another. All Kyiv gas stations were closed that afternoon on government orders. Throughout the day, defections from the Party of Regions accumulated, including the head of Kyiv City State Administration Volodymyr Makiyenko. Fourteen PoR lawmakers quit the party, twelve of which said that they would attend the "renegade" parliamentary session that afternoon and were "with the people." Seven independent MPs also announced that they were "with the people." Around Ukraine, citizens continued acts of civil disobedience, such as blocking trains or buses carrying troops or police to Kyiv.

Ukrayinska Pravda reported that titushky and Interior Ministry troops began wearing identical yellow armbands, presumably to identify each other as being on the same side. Embassy observers noted that there were similar ID armbands on Tuesday outside the Rada. The Political Section's Greg Pfleger noted: "I saw red and white striped plastic tape on the arms of titushky dressed similarly to the SDF; presumably to identify 'ours' from 'theirs.'" Each day, titushky thugs seemed more integrated into the government security apparatus. On the other side of the equation, an anonymous protester admitted to using firearms against Berkut in an interview with Ukraine's Channel 5.

Yanukovych interrupted an epic, multi-hour meeting with European foreign ministers to take a phone call from Putin. Minister of Internal Affairs Zakharchenko signed an order authorizing all his forces to carry deadly weapons, while some hospitals began issuing clubs to medical staff to defend themselves against Interior Ministry forces who now routinely entered hospitals to seize wounded protesters—sometimes in the middle of medical procedures. At 3:00 p.m., the rump Rada session opened unusually with legislators singing the Ukrainian national anthem, echoing the ethos of Maidan. Russian mass media began erroneously reporting that the Rada was "captured by protesters." Also, Kremlin spokesman Dmitry Peskov announced that Putin would dispatch a mediator to Ukraine at the request of President Yanukovych—Russian government human rights ombudsman Vladimir Lukin. Meanwhile, Sergey Markov, a bellwether Russian political scientist and deputy chairman of the Russian Public Forum on International Affairs, began publicly goading Yanukovych to further increase the violence: "The coup d'etat is in full swing. . . . After Yanukovych on February 20 was ready to give the order, the opposition again demanded a truce, and during that truce, they start to attack again. Fascists . . . you can't really negotiate with them." The message from such semiofficial figures in Russia was clear—keep the blood flowing until the Maidan was crushed.

As Yanukovych's government fractured and his domestic support withered by the minute as the dead started to outnumber the living on Instytutska Street, a group of Ukrainian diplomats took control of the Ministry's Facebook account and promised to start "telling the truth about the situation in Ukraine." They posted, "At a time when the eyes of the world turn to Ukraine, when on the streets of our cities our brothers and sisters are killed, Ukrainian diplomats cannot turn away. . . . During this standoff, remember that universal European values are unifying for all Ukrainian citizens. Therefore, we are convinced that the signing of the Association Agreement with the EU, the public support of which started with Euromaidan, can unite us all." In another rebellion, billionaire oligarch Kolomoyskyi announced that his gas stations would continue functioning regardless of Kyiv city orders to close, and various internet service providers called on the Ukrainian government to "stop messing with the internet." And the newly defected head of Kyiv's city administration allowed the metro system to restart operations.

At 3:40 p.m., 227 parliamentarians were registered as present in the Rada, representing a quorum. Shortly after 4:00 p.m., a man walking close to October Palace was shot in the head by snipers. A scuffle broke out in the Rada when one Party of Regions parliamentarian tried to leave, which would have brought the number of attendees below quorum. The Ministry of Defense announced on its website that it was ready to defend and protect bases and armories from attack. A fresh US White House statement urged the Ukrainian military not to become involved with the conflict, for Yanukovych to withdraw security forces from downtown Kyiv, and for protesters to remain peaceful. For hours, the Rada continued to debate a return to the 2004 constitution and the dismissal of acting Minister of Internal Affairs Zakharchenko and Prosecutor

General Pshonka. Local press began monitoring regional airports closely—billionaire Rinat Akhmetov departed Donetsk for London; armored vehicles delivered large boxes of cash for shipment out of Kyiv's Zhuliany airport, the capital's secondary airport; and acting Revenue Minister Oleksandr Klymenko was sighted fleeing with a large suitcase. One rumor had it that the families of both Yanukovych and his son had left Donetsk for parts unknown. An unsubstantiated news report claimed that Rada Speaker Volodymyr Rybak and Deputy Rada Speaker Ihor Kaletnyk left via Zhuliany airport with large bags. Embassy contacts said that the number of private jets departing from Zhuliany airport doubled that night. Meanwhile, protesters blocked access to Kyiv's main international airport at Boryspil to prevent parliamentarians from fleeing—an extreme measure meant to protect the razor-thin quorum present in the Rada. Huge lines at ATMs in Kyiv, Donetsk, and Lugansk pointed to fears of a possible bank run. Berkut brutally broke up a protest in the city of Cherkasy.

Ambassador Pyatt decided to make a public statement supporting the lawmakers who were working to forge some sort of path forward. He released a video with a simple message: "Good evening. I'd like to begin tonight by offering my deepest condolences to those who were killed and injured and their family members, who were victims of the violence on Maidan today. The United States is working as hard as we can to support those who are seeking to build a peaceful prosperous future for this country, and to bring an end to the terrible violence that has happened over the past few days. For today, the most important thing that needs to happen is to move politics off the streets and back into Ukraine's democratic institutions. So, for those of you who are elected members of the Rada, if you are not there tonight working to forge a political solution, you are part of the problem. You are not part of the solution!"

Back in Washington, the heavy Ukraine-related workload—drafting reports, analysis papers, and recommendations for high-level calls and other urgent engagements—led the State Department to set up a Ukraine Task Force to mirror the functions of our Task Force in country. Meanwhile, Vice President Biden and Yanukovych had another in their series of calls that night. Even after the day's horrifying events, the United States, contrary to Moscow's crude propaganda, was not considering any policy that would advocate Yanukovych's ouster. He was a democratically elected leader who still commanded the loyalty of much of the country. By any conventional reading of the situation, were Yanukovych to be sidelined or removed from office, a resolution of the crisis would be even more difficult to achieve. The Ukrainian government could fracture, and the political situation become increasingly unpredictable and impossible for anyone to influence. It was not what anyone at the Embassy or back in Washington saw as a solution. A compromise whereby the Yanukovych administration made strategic concessions to protesters on corruption and European integration remained the only solution that made sense. Those suggesting that the US government was trying to push out Yanukovych were simply advancing their own dark theories without foundation in reality or reference to what we were actually doing. Our public and private positions were the same. Asked by CNN's Hala Gorani whether it was the US position that Yanukovych should go, Ambassador Pyatt answered: "No, it's not. Our position is that President Yanukovych needs to lead his country into a new future, and he needs to do so through the vehicle of a new government, changes to the Constitution and the political order."

Finishing its session late in the evening, the Rada approved a statement condemning the use of force that led to so many deaths. The parliament "strongly condemned" the use of force against peaceful citizens, as well as the use of torture and crimes against humanity. The resolution stated that the State Security Service, the Interior Ministry, and other paramilitary agencies should "immediately stop the use of force against citizens of Ukraine." Lastly, the body "outlawed" the previously announced "anti-terrorism operation," which threatened to bring military force to bear against protesters. After the session, another five lawmakers abandoned the Party of Regions. Yatsenyuk told the press that the resolution meant that all police, military, and other security personnel should return to their places of permanent deployment and that any policeman who used a deadly weapon would be following illegal orders. The new laws seemed a definitive break from Yanukovych's hard line, coming from within his own party. The day's extreme violence had not broken Maidan, but it seemed to have broken the Party of Regions.

By the end of the night, protesters had released all police and security forces they detained during the day's confrontation. Channel 5 interviewed several of the young Interior Ministry conscripts who were captured or surrendered and then held at city hall. A reporter asked why they were shooting at protesters:

Young man: "But we were not the ones shooting!"

Reporter: "Then who was shooting?"

Young man: "The guys behind us."

By the end of the grim night, the casualty totals were shocking. The Ministry of Health confirmed that sixty-seven people had been brought to Kyiv's city morgue that day while acknowledging that twenty-two bodies were possibly still in the street. Thirteen police had been killed and 130 had suffered gunshot wounds. Friction continued throughout the night. Protesters seized a bus of Interior Ministry troops on Khreshchatyk Street, allowing the men to leave but keeping the bus as a platform for Ruslana to sing on. PoR and Communist Party offices burned in several provincial cities. Despite the Rada resolution, there were continuing reports of Ukrainian paratroopers and marines moving toward Kyiv. Talking heads on Russian media ramped up their criticism of Yanukovych. They did not fault him for launching a bloody attack on Maidan, but for being weak and ineffectual and not finishing the brutal job he started. Yanukovych also received late night Russian visitors at 1:20 a.m.—Russian Ambassador Mikhail Zurabov and Russia's government-appointed mediator Lukin. We also heard that Russian presidential adviser Vladislav Surkov, who advised Putin on Ukraine, was back in town. According to Russian media, Surkov had been in Ukraine and met Yanukovych in late January as well as on February 14. Unlike Lukin, or even the Russian ambassador, Surkov could speak to Yanukovych authoritatively as a direct conduit to Putin.

Meanwhile, additional new evidence suggested that Yanukovych was planning to use Ukraine's military against his people. In a newspaper interview, newly fired Armed Forces Chief Volodymyr Zamana said, "The reason for my resignation was my disagreement with the involvement of the Armed Forces of Ukraine in a domestic political conflict. Indeed, this will inevitably lead to an escalation of the conflict and war." Then, media reported that Deputy Chief of General Staff Yuriy Dumanskyi had also resigned the previous night, stating in his resignation letter that he disagreed with attempts to use the military in conflicts inside the country.

Following the previous day's massacre, Kyiv had a different feeling, as if a million individual points of no return had been passed. In recent decades, Ukraine had not been a violent place. But bullets just ended dozens of lives in broad daylight on the most famous national commons in the country. That morning, international media reported that Yanukovych had told visiting European foreign ministers he was willing to hold early elections. A few weeks ago, that would have been headline news leading us to speculate whether a grand compromise was at hand. But now, after yesterday's indiscriminate murders, would that really be enough? Driving to work, I found the streets oddly silent. There were no traffic police and few cars. When I arrived at the Embassy and read my email, I got the impression that there seemed to be a deal in the works between the major crisis players.

The all-night negotiations between Yanukovych, the political opposition, the three EU foreign ministers, Russian interlocutors, and others had yielded the outline of a crisis resolution plan. The president's office offered three concessions: an immediate return to the 2004 constitution, the formation of a coalition government within ten days, and the scheduling of early presidential elections in December 2014. This was a major development—the kind of concessions that our Embassy had pushed for these last two months. It was tragic that it hadn't come in time to save the lives lost the previous day. The basic outlines of the agreement, without details, were posted on President Yanukovych's website. Video posted online featured a sharp warning to opposition politicians from Polish Foreign Minister Radosław Sikorsky urging them to accept the draft deal: "If you don't support this you'll have martial law, you'll have the army. You will all be dead." In this tense atmosphere, lawmakers gathered in the Rada to consider a number of bills, including one on returning to the 2004 constitution. When Speaker Volodymyr Rybak tried to call a break until 4:00 p.m., a fist fight broke out on the floor. At St. Michael's Square, a bus with one hundred western Ukrainian police officers, mostly in uniform, arrived to protect Euromaidan. In Crimea, a planned "separatist" session of the parliament wasn't held—PoR lawmakers merely consulted instead. Strangest of all, presidential guards and other government protection units silently began withdrawing from the president's offices at Bankova Street, although their pullback was not part of the truce agreement.

Then, word filtered out through the press that Yanukovych and the big three opposition leaders signed an agreement, as witnessed by the Polish, French, and German foreign ministers and the Russian human rights ombudsman. In addition to the new constitution, early elections, and coalition government, the final agreement also included provisions on the return of stolen government firearms, the government's promise not to initiate a state of emergency, and the investigation of recent acts of violence in Kyiv. However, the agreement was signed by opposition political party leaders without their consulting Maidan leaders. Soon after, Yatsenyuk, Tyahnybok, and Klitschko took the signed document to the Maidan Council, and within hours had achieved agreement with the NGOs and others on the council to support the agreement. But almost immediately, media interviews with individual protesters on Maidan registered strong disagreement on the street with the terms of the agreement—particularly the fact that Yanukovych would be able to stay in power for most of another year. After the killings of the previous days, this was going to be a tough sell to protesters. Nevertheless, the deal was endorsed by Ukraine's president, the major opposition politicians, the leading lights of European foreign policy, the Maidan Council, and possibly even by Russia (whose representative was present but did not sign). In close coordination with the State Department, the White House immediately issued a statement hailing the new agreement. It seemed to have every chance of holding, even if it produced some loud complaints on the square. Yanukovych had secured an agreement backed by the international community, which kept him in office for nearly another year. Presidents Obama and Putin even spoke by phone about how to quickly implement the new compromise.

Throughout the afternoon, news from the Rada buoyed spirits on Maidan. First, the 2004 constitution was reinstated. Then, legislators passed a new, stronger amnesty bill to release arrested protesters. In another major concession, Minister of Internal Affairs Zakharchenko—a bogeyman nearly as detested by protesters as Yanukovych himself—was suspended from his position by law. Finally, through an amendment to another law, Yanukovych's chief nightmare materialized as the Rada ordered former prime minister and "Princess Leia of the Orange Revolution" Yuliya Tymoshenko released (though this was not effective immediately, and another court ruling would be necessary beforehand). Eleven more PoR members of parliament defected from the faction. Later that night, two more bills silently popped up on the Rada's website for possible discussion the next day: Draft Bill 4171 on Impeachment of the President; and Draft Bill 4170, a no confidence motion regarding Prosecutor General Viktor Pshonka.

The Economic Section's Chris Greller wrote in at 5:30 p.m.: "About 25,000 people on the Maidan. Expanded barricades from the Maidan all the way to European Square. European Square is a parking lot with about seventy-five passenger vehicles on it. Crowd cheered when 2004 constitution passed. A funeral is now taking place on the Maidan. No MOI [Interior Ministry], police, or government forces in sight. Barricades also rebuilt on Hrushevskoho and

Instytutska. Approximately 150 protesters donning helmets in those locations, with about 500–750 others in the area near Dynamo stadium; some playing soccer on the street there." DAO's Michael Skaggs noted a new arrival: "At 1830, a new giant catapult arrived on Maidan. Looks professionally made, although I can't imagine who has such a profession. It looks capable of hurling a large object a long way. See photo." The Yanukovych government had taken state-sponsored violence to the level of gunning down dozens with live ammunition, but Maidan was still there. And getting new equipment, apparently.

As night fell, Maidan's fury at details of the deal welled up to the surface. The Maidan stage was normally a tightly run operation, but that night, there was disorder. The big three opposition leaders took to the Maidan main stage to present the deal they had signed with Yanukovych, only to have the crowd jeer them, booing and catcalling. The open caskets of several of the men killed the day before were passed around the crowd overhead, and their corpses were brought to the stage, accompanied with chants that Yanukovych must step down. Sotnya commander Volodymyr Parasyuk, a young man from Lviv in his midtwenties, grabbed the microphone and gave an impassioned speech that captured the mood of the crowd. "Our kinsmen have been shot and our leaders shake hands with this killer. This is shameful. Tomorrow, by 10 o'clock, he has to be gone." Poroshenko and a leader from the rightist Pravyi Sektor also spoke, but it was Parasyuk who was treated as the voice of the common protesters, their homegrown hero. When Yatsenyuk and Tyahnybok left the stage, Klitschko retook the microphone. Responding to Parasyuk, he apologized for shaking Yanukovich's hand following the signing of the agreement. He said that he was willing to explore other ways to remove Yanukovych if that was the will of Maidan. Before leaving, he said that, despite siding with the protesters for three months, this is the first time they chose not to listen to him. A Hromadske TV journalist confronted Klitschko on stage, calling opposition leaders "betrayers of Euromaidan" and accusing them of signing the agreement without approval of the Maidan Council as previously agreed.

Amid the impassioned screams for Yanukovych's resignation, no one on Maidan or in the diplomatic community guessed the truth—that Yanukovych, the man with an internationally praised agreement with barely dry ink relegitimizing his rule for the next nine months, was already on the run and had been shipping his valuables and cash from Kyiv for days.

At 11:35 p.m., the Task Force email list was inundated with multiple press reports that Yanukovych's plane had departed at 10:40 p.m. for Kharkiv. Foreign Minister Kozhara telephoned Assistant Secretary Nuland to state that Yanukovych's motorcade was attacked on his way to the airport. Kharkiv, home to some of Yanukovych's staunchest supporters in Governor Dobkin and Mayor Kernes, had briefly served as the capital of Ukraine in the 1920s. Dobkin was freshly quoted in Russia's *Komsomolskaya Pravda* newspaper stating that he was ready to defend the country from revolutionaries by making Kharkiv the new Ukrainian capital. For good measure, he called titushky "angel-saviors with beautiful faces and inquisitive eyes." While the Party of Regions congress scheduled in Kharkiv on Saturday gave Yanukovych an official excuse to be there, his departure from Kyiv during this extraordinarily sensitive time shocked everyone. The congress, initiated by Yanukovych confidant First Vice Prime Minister Klyuyev, had the stated goal of advancing the Russian-backed notion of "federalism" for Ukraine—something that most Kyiv analysts considered either a plan to give Moscow a veto over all major sovereign Ukrainian decisions or simply a blueprint to break up the country. But even in Kharkiv, thousands of Euromaidan supporters took to the streets to demonstrate as Yanukovych's plane entered the city's air space.

Suddenly, we received an increasing number of media accounts about officials fleeing the country. Fresh media reports claimed that Minister of Internal Affairs Zakharchenko had crossed the border into Belarus; Prosecutor General Pshonka had taken off from Kyiv Zhuliany airport, his destination unknown. The summer home of the godfather of Ukraine's pro-Russia forces, Viktor Medvedchuk, was on fire outside of Kyiv. Once word filtered out that Yanukovych was gone, government security forces melted away from the government quarter. Overnight, Maidan SDF moved into the vacated spaces, entering the Rada, and stated that they were "guarding and protecting" the presidential administration building, the Interior Ministry, and the Cabinet of Ministers. From the Maidan stage, Ruslana claimed that Yanukovych continued his flight from Kharkiv to Sochi in Russia, where the Winter Olympics were winding down. Former minister of internal affairs–turned activist Yuriy Lutsenko claimed that the State Security Service was opening a secession investigation against Kharkiv's Dobkin and Kernes.

February 22, Saturday morning: The Embassy was again working at full capacity sorting through reports from the media and our own observers in an attempt to discern facts, support Ambassador Pyatt's movements around town, and respond to the constant barrage of questions from Washington. Various reports put Yanukovych in the United Arab Emirates or Sochi. But he was definitely not in Kharkiv where he was supposed to be. Kyiv was eerily quiet. Eric Johnson wrote in: "Although the Big Three are now Maidan political roadkill, the Maidan itself is waking up for what may be a big day. A dozen SDF (going on duty) spotted in front of the Radisson on their way to the Maidan. While the SBU [Ukrainian intelligence] looks quiet, there are new SDF outposts at St. Sophia and elsewhere. My street, now fully a part of Maidan, has two SDF roadblocks. St. Michael's is a parking lot for activist buses. Those staying at the monastery are starting to stir with SDF formations moving down the hill to Maidan. Shouts of 'revolyutsiya' from Main Stage. No police anywhere. By signing the agreement with the opposition yesterday, Yanu has shown he's weak—the worst thing a gangster can do."

Displaying uncharacteristic humility, PoR parliamentarians announced before the start of the day's session that they were prepared "to enter into opposition if not offered a place in the new government" and that they would not be "offended" if not offered a place in the new coalition. One member of the Embassy saw a new sight on the road just outside of Kyiv Zhuliany airport—a ten-person Maidan SDF group checking passports, announcing that they were looking for "wanted" members of the "Yanukovych regime" who might be fleeing.

Kyiv's government quarter, which twenty-four hours before had been teeming with security forces assembled from all over Ukraine, was now a ghost town completely under Maidan SDF control. The presidential administration building was deserted. Parliamentary Speaker Rybak and his deputy submitted their resignations. According to Interfax news, President Yanukovych's personal representative to the Rada, Yuriy Myroshnychenko, admitted that he had no idea where Yanukovych was. If this was a strategic move by Yanukovych, it was certainly a very strange one. As all of the crisis management bills approved by the Rada the day before now awaited the president's signature, Yanukovych's immediate intervention was necessary to avoid a resumption of hostilities and more death. But he was gone.

Suddenly, Channel 5 was reporting live from Mezhyhirya, Yanukovych's palatial personal home that had become a symbol of corruption after it was built on prime land purchased through shady privatization deals. Reporters were swarming inside and outside, filming extravagant details, such as a golden loaf of bread by Yanukovych's bedside, custom-minted gold coins featuring Yanukovych's silhouette, and thousands of pages of accounting records dumped into a canal by the house. Probably most astonishing were photos of a luxurious sailing galleon, permanently docked at Mezhyhirya and outfitted for luxury banquets. Now that their master had vanished, we wondered if even his personal guards had left Mezhyhirya. The Interior Ministry website featured a new message, stating that the Ministry "bowed to the sacred memory of the victims of recent violence," ending with the words "Slava Ukraini!" or "Glory to Ukraine!"—the greeting and battle cry of Euromaidan. Overnight the world had turned upside down.

Two events, distinctly at cross purposes, were unfolding simultaneously. In Kyiv, an extraordinary Rada session opened with President Yanukovych "missing in action" and the government quarter controlled by Maidan. Meanwhile, in Kharkiv, where Governor Dobkin and Mayor Kernes had launched a "Ukrainian Front" initiative three weeks earlier to combat Euromaidan influence in eastern and southern Ukraine, nearly thirty-five hundred participants gathered to discuss a broad devolution of power from Kyiv to the provinces. Their objective seemed to be to kick-start the centripetal spin necessary to push the regions away from the center and possibly break up Ukraine.

At 2:00 p.m., I took the helm of the Embassy Task Force. There was plenty to track, and now that Washington had its own Task Force, our colleagues there were also hungry for information. Late-breaking media reports claimed that Yanukovych's resignation was imminent: Yuriy Myroshnychenko, President Yanukovych's Rada representative, stated that President Yanukovych's resignation would soon appear on his website. Parliamentarian Kyrylenko (Batkivshchyna) also claimed on Twitter that Yanukovych was resigning, and Espreso TV reported the story as well. The official website of the Cabinet of Ministers stated that the cabinet was ready to pass power to a new government in accordance with the constitution. A man identifying himself as chief of the Berkut announced at a press conference from within the Rada that the Berkut was now "on the side of the people," and a military representative also stated that Ukraine's armed forces were "on the side of the people" (i.e., on the side of Euromaidan). A decisive shift of power was taking place before our eyes. The political snowfall of recent months was released in an avalanche, and no one outside of the country—not Russia, the EU, or the United States—could credibly claim any control over where things were heading.

Maidan SDF went out on the streets to round up PoR lawmakers and corral them in the Rada to ensure a quorum. When the session started, Rada Speaker Rybak and the deputy speaker were dismissed "based on their resignations." Batkivshchyna's Oleksandr Turchynov was voted in as the new parliamentary speaker after the Party of Regions failed to nominate a candidate. Parliament named Arsen Avakov, a Kharkiv native and former governor who was a member of Batkivshchyna, as the new minister of internal affairs—a key position in the effort to rapidly shore up the security situation and ensure that there would be no new clashes. SDF Commandant Parubiy announced that the SDF would work together with the Interior Ministry in partnership under the new leadership. It was a new day.

Meanwhile, the Kharkiv conference represented an attempt, backed by Yanukovych regime die-hards and prominent Russian politicians, to create an anti-Maidan political base in Ukraine's east even at the expense of Ukraine's continued existence as a country. It was similar to a 2004 conference in Severodonetsk in which then Prime Minister Yanukovych, disgraced after the Orange Revolution, tried to form a new base outside of Kyiv opposed to the Yushchenko government he so despised. That gambit didn't succeed, and was labeled by most as thinly veiled separatism. Russia's state-managed media breathlessly hyped this new Kharkiv conference. A telling sign was that as the live internet feed of the event began, there were no Ukrainian symbols in the hall. Instead, an oversize red star and plenty of "St. George's" ribbons—the orange and black ribbons symbolizing the Soviet Union's victory in World War II—adorned the hall. In addition to the regional leadership from Kharkiv, Donetsk, Luhansk, Dnipropetrovsk, and Crimea (including the separate administrative leadership of Sevastopol), the governors of the Russian regions bordering Ukraine were there to serve as "observers." Other high-level Russian government officials attended too, including top Putin Ukraine adviser Vladislav Surkov, Duma Foreign Relations Committee head Aleksei Pushkov, and chairman of the Foreign Affairs Committee of the Federation Council of Russia Mikhail Margelov. Clearly the Russian government had high hopes for the event. A resolution from the Congress characterized the Rada in Kyiv as "terrorized and illegitimate" and called on local governments in southern and eastern Ukraine to grasp power locally for "protecting the constitutional order." The resolution also called on Russia to help "restore constitutional order" in Ukraine. Both the calls for foreign intervention in Ukraine and for regional administrations to seize power from the center could be grounds for charges of separatism under Ukrainian law. Euromaidan Kharkiv protesters held demonstrations outside while the Donetsk Berkut guarded the proceedings despite national Berkut leadership in Kyiv announcing that they were now on the side of the protesters. After the congress concluded, Governor Dobkin and Mayor Kernes drove away together shortly before Kernes's private jet reportedly took off from Kharkiv airport at 2:10 p.m. Crucially, Yanukovych, who was supposedly in Kharkiv to attend the event, was a no show.

DAO's J. P. Gresh wrote in to the Task Force from Maidan just before 4:00 p.m.: "Would estimate at least 60K on Maidan and growing. People attending memorials to the dead, listening to speakers, talking with friends. Fireworks launched. SDF still organized and attentive. Some people overcome with emotion and on verge of tears. Ruslana commands attention and respect among this crowd—everyone hanging on each one of her words—talking about the immense responsibility that they collectively and individually bear from here on out—the work is just beginning. 'We are a great country' and 'Let's pay respects to the fallen.' Never forget! The heroes don't die! A light rain falls on Maidan."

In Ambassador Pyatt's second call of the day from Foreign Minister Kozhara, Ukraine's top diplomat welcomed the election of opposition party leader Turchynov as Rada Speaker and agreed that his election took place in accordance with constitutional procedures. Kozhara noted that there were some questions over the selection of the new Minister of Internal Affairs, as this was done in the absence of a prime minister—but the first priority of the new government was to reestablish public order and consolidate security forces. Kozhara thankfully noted that this was happening. After defending the regime so stridently for so long, he just seemed relieved that this period of death and national tragedy was hopefully drawing to a close.

Shortly after 4:00 p.m., Yanukovych appeared in a video message denying rumors that he had orally resigned and called events in Kyiv a coup: "I am doing everything possible to prevent bloodshed. I am receiving signals that many people are threatened. I am trying to protect the people, who are being followed at their offices, on the way to school, and I am trying to prevent further bloodshed. They try to scare me and force me to resign. But I do not plan to resign." He stated that his car was fired on in Kyiv, that Speaker Rybak boarded the presidential plane after he was beaten, and that some PoR defectors are intimidated while others are traitors. "What is happening now is what happened in the '30s in Nazi Germany," he stated. Meanwhile, Party of Regions governors in Mykolaiv, Vinnytsia, and Chernihiv resigned.

Embassy RSO issued a new warning: "If the attached/below flyer shows up on your building, call Post One [U.S. Marines protecting the Embassy] immediately. It states that your building has been taken over in the interest of the revolution. Mobile Patrol will immediately be dispatched to your building and you will be relocated to a hotel. RSO highly recommends you have your 'Go Bags' packed, to include your radio charger, so that if we have to move you with short notice, you have supplies/clothes with you. At the end of this notice is a recommended list of supplies to put in your 'Go Bag.'" The flyer was labeled as being from the right-wing group Pravyi Sektor. Within hours, however, that group's representatives said that the flyer was a hoax and not from their group. Provocations were an integral part of the drama still being played out in Ukraine.

For days, the Embassy's worst fear was that Ukraine's military would enter the crisis and that the bloodshed would increase exponentially. Signals from the Yanukovych camp suggested that he wanted to do exactly that. Therefore, a major thrust of US diplomacy at this point was trying to prevent this horrifying outcome. That afternoon, the new Ukrainian Armed Forces chief of staff Yuriy Ilyin released a public statement calming the worst of our worries: "The Armed Forces of Ukraine are true to their constitutional duty and cannot be embroiled in internal political conflict. . . . At the moment I am in complete control of the situation in the Armed Forces of Ukraine."

Newly elected Rada Speaker Turchynov informed the assembled deputies that Yanukovych had told opposition leader Yatsenyuk by phone that he resigned, but then later posted the video claiming that he refused to resign. "The people of Ukraine cannot depend on the mood of the president who removed himself from events and is at an unknown location," he stated. Turchynov asked the Rada to remove President Yanukovych and hold a new presidential election since the president "withdrew from the execution of constitutional powers, threatening the manageability, state, territorial integrity, and sovereignty of Ukraine, and caused massive violations of human rights and freedoms in the circumstances of extreme urgency." Under Article 108 of the Ukrainian constitution, the parliament has the power to find that the president has resigned in fact because he absented himself, cannot be found, and is not fulfilling his duties. Such duties included signing laws within twenty-four hours.

Parliament also has the power to set election dates under Article 85. Many PoR parliamentarians crossed party lines to rid themselves of Yanukovych—328 of Ukraine's 450 legislators voted in favor of the measure. Several abstained, and many were not present, but no parliamentarians voted against the bill removing Yanukovych. None. Of those present, 36 PoR lawmakers voted in favor while 2 abstained; 32 Communist Party members voted in favor while only 1 abstained. This was as close to universal agreement as could be imagined. Afterward, a round of the national anthem broke out among the lawmakers. It was a remarkable demonstration of legislative will at this critical point in the transfer of power, including from those in the president's own party.

In the State Department, we reserve the term *FLASH* for the most important, urgent communications. It means, "Wake up the Secretary in the middle of the night," or "Pull the National Security Advisor out of his meeting with the Chinese Secretary General." From the Task Force, I sent the message: "FLASH: Rada Votes to Remove Yanukovych from Power with New Elections on May 25." The Rada then appointed new defense and intelligence chiefs, as well as a new prosecutor general.

Our Task Force continued to follow the cascade of extraordinary events. The plane carrying Kharkiv's Dobkin and Kernes crossed over into Russian airspace. After all their tough rhetoric at the separatist conference, they had hightailed it out of the country. According to Hromadske TV, recently dismissed Prosecutor General Pshonka and Minister of Tax and Revenue Klymenko were intercepted at the border with Russia in the Donetsk region along with their armed bodyguards. A video showed both men rushing the security checkpoint and knocking over a metal detector in their frantic attempt to escape from the country in which they had held unchecked power only hours before. Then came electrifying news from Kharkiv: Tymoshenko had left her prison hospital and was en route to Kyiv, or more specifically, en route to Maidan.

It was no surprise that the Kremlin's spin doctors contorted the facts to cast the day's events in Ukraine into a threat to Russia. Deputy Chairman of the Russian Public Forum on International Affairs Sergey Markov asserted, "This shows that [World War II–era Ukrainian right-wing leader] Bandera's followers are planning an attack on Russia, so we need to fight the fascists now. The Yanukovych case teaches that by giving in to the Nazis, you doom yourself to deal with them on less favorable terms. This is what the Munich Agreement with Hitler teaches us. In Ukraine, the fascists rush to power while others are on the sidelines." Regarding the Rada decisions, he said, "Neo-fascist mutineers terrorize their opponents, beat them, take their voting cards, and vote for them. For this reason, all of today's decisions are illegal as the Rada is in the hand of terrorists." Russia's Ministry of Foreign Affairs released a readout of Foreign Minister Sergei Lavrov's call with Secretary Kerry, giving the Russian interpretation of recent events in Kyiv: illegal extremist groups refused to hand over their weapons and actually took control of Kyiv with the connivance of opposition leaders who sit in Parliament, all in contravention to the February 21 agreement. The readout failed to mention that Yanukovych had apparently decided to flee, was unreachable, and had basically gone into hiding after reportedly telling some parliamentarians that he was resigning. Contrary to Lavrov's assertion, protesters did not take over the government quarter with guns; they walked in after government forces abandoned it after Yanukovych took flight following a day of mass murder, which he did not want to answer for. Needless to say, this was the crucial piece of the day's puzzle. This was not an arbitrary or fanciful opinion open to varying interpretations. Despite the Kremlin's attempts to spin the truth, it was the objective facts as seen on the ground by our Embassy observers.

While the Kremlin shamelessly labeled events in Kyiv as a coup, our Public Affairs Section was working rapidly with State Department and National Security Council officials on a White House Statement to be issued that evening: "We have consistently advocated a de-escalation of violence, constitutional change, a coalition government, and early elections, and today's developments could move us closer to that goal. . . . We welcome constructive work in the Rada and continue to urge the prompt formation of a broad, technocratic government of national unity."

On her arrival in downtown Kyiv, Tymoshenko laid flowers at a memorial to the fallen on Hrushevskoho Street before heading to the Maidan main stage. Those assembled on the Maidan greeted her politely but guardedly. She embodied a lot of different things in Ukraine. As an undoubted enemy of Yanukovych, she was therefore "with the people," but many Ukrainians also viewed her as simply the other side of the same coin of the old corrupt system that so many had just died to topple. Nevertheless, although looking the worse for wear after her time in prison as she mounted the stage, she remained an energizing orator. "I did not recognize Kyiv with the burnt buildings and barricades. . . . But this is a different Ukraine, it is free. . . . The people who came to Maidan who died here are heroes. . . . I will do my best to punish the guilty, we should have the most severe punishment. . . . This change is not due to politicians, to diplomats, or anyone else—it is only due to your courage. Your work is not over yet. Only you can change this country—you have the power. . . . I will guarantee that no one will betray you. . . . I apologize for all politicians, no matter which party." She, like other politicians of the old order that had been overthrown by this upwelling of "people power," had much to answer for. Popular revolutions emerge from the order they have overthrown and bear the birthmarks of their passage.

The fight was over in Kyiv, but not elsewhere. Serious incidents continued to occur around the country overnight. In Crimea's Kerch, police stood by as three hundred titushky attacked a Euromaidan meeting. In Kharkiv, the scene of so many events during the day, members of the Russian nationalist organization Oplot (bulwark) drove a car into a group of Euromaidan demonstrators before opening fire, injuring many. The head of the Ukrainian State Border Guard Service told the press that Yanukovych's plane was not permitted to leave Donetsk for Russia because it did not have the proper clearance paperwork. According to this news report, when border guards approached Yanukovych's plane to ask for the flight permission paperwork, armed men offered them cash in exchange for allowing the plane to quickly take flight. After the border guards rejected the offer, they saw an armored vehicle pull up to retrieve Yanukovych as he deplaned. It was a solid sighting, but Yanukovych was still missing.

February 23, Sunday morning: Natalya and I put the kids in the car for a drive around the city. While Kyiv normally spends Sunday mornings slowly shaking off its collective hangover, this was a quiet of another kind. First, in a city of traffic cops, there were no police or authorities of any kind visible anywhere. It was as if a large piece of furniture you barely noticed anymore was suddenly gone without explanation. There were few cars on the road. But most notable was the absence of the air of tension that had become a constant companion in recent months. I had attended several Embassy Emergency Action Committee meetings since last November, and one fact of life repeated many times at those meetings was that we should expect civil disorder should the government lose the ability to enforce laws. There would likely be looting, rioting, robbery, and random violence. But in front of our eyes, law enforcement had melted away, yet there was nothing but peace. No shops looted, no chaos. People were out walking dogs and heading to friends' apartments to talk about what they had all just lived through. There was a collective sigh of relief, and on the square there was subdued rejoicing tempered by the gravity of their collective responsibility for what was to come next. But as Maidan's ethos was always self-control, there was no expectation that criminality would be tolerated in any way. Criminality was "theirs," the European path would be "ours." We drove the kids down toward the Maidan, fires still burning, priests addressing the crowd from the main stage. The kids hadn't been on the square for many months, and it was now different—penned in on one side by a burned building. The people there were no longer just idealistic students and patriots. They'd seen murder up close. Most of them had been viewed through sniper scopes while professionals decided which among them would die. But they stayed. And they won.

Standing here with my family back on the square—this might seem the logical place where this narrative should end. I could offer a few parting notes about saying goodbye to irreplaceable friends, remind readers of the Ukrainians' understandable difficulty in getting a fresh new start after so many years of government mismanagement, and provide a few other grace notes. Standing there on the square, the future seemed clear. It was the Ukrainians' responsibility to rebuild their government and improve their society, and we would offer help where we could along with our European allies. But the road ahead turned out to be anything but clear. Instead, it was filled with obstacles, tank traps, ambushes, and other obstructions put into place by Moscow. The Kremlin was infuriated by the collapse of its plans to pull Ukraine away from Europe, the imagined promised land so many Ukrainians wished to join, and was determined to bind it to itself. Though we couldn't see it, a reaction sharply different from the Kremlin's muted response to the Orange Revolution in 2004 was brewing across the border.

After that upheaval in 2004, President Putin expressed dissatisfaction, but Russia wisely moved on. The Orange Revolution, without any overt Russian intervention, soon collapsed under the weight of domestic infighting and corruption. Similarly, when Yanukovych was elected in 2010, although it was clear that he was a much more pro-Russian politician than his predecessor, the United States congratulated Ukraine on a successful election and moved on. Neither in Washington nor in Moscow did gross foreign intervention in Ukraine's internal affairs seem an acceptable option following Ukraine's several past changes of power.

In a press conference on December 19, 2013, well after the start of Euromaidan, President Putin addressed a journalist's question about a possible change of power in Ukraine: "We proceed from the fact that whoever wins this battle and however the situation unfolds in the future, we will still work with Ukraine and cooperate with it in such a way and such format that is the most interesting and acceptable for the Ukrainian people." In his comments the same day on whether Russia would ever pursue a "Georgia scenario" of supporting separatism in Crimea, while Putin complained about the treatment of Russian speakers in former Soviet states, he still concluded, "But it does not at all mean we are going to swing our swords and bring in the troops. That is simply nonsense; there is nothing like this now and never will be."

If only. The transfer of power in Kyiv in February 2014 should have been the last chapter of this particular story. Those in Ukraine's opposition, newly empowered, and the civil society figures who led Euromaidan, should have been free to succeed or fail in their efforts to turn a new page in the history of independent Ukraine, based on the merits of their ideas, their hard work, and luck. But unfortunately, it was not to be. The victory of Euromaidan soon proved to be the prelude to yet another cycle of bitter struggle in Ukraine, but this time imposed from the outside. So our story must continue.

10

THE KREMLIN FOG MACHINE
HITS OVERDRIVE

In Kyiv, the storm had passed. It was time to clean up the debris and move forward. The storm of public protest that had led Yanukovych to abscond with a substantial chunk of Ukraine's state assets was over. Many of his cronies had also fled. The new government that took the abandoned levers of power in the capital faced a daunting series of challenges, both home and abroad. On Monday, February 24, with our kids finally back at school, Natalya, our colleagues, and I came to work at the Embassy to prepare for the arrival of Deputy Secretary of State William J. Burns the next day. Meanwhile, Russia signaled the increasing unlikelihood that it would actively support a Yanukovych comeback as a prominent Russian state TV host announced that the ousted president had "betrayed his people" when he fled Kyiv. The Kremlin certainly hated the new government, but they also detested Yanukovych for not sacrificing himself to prevent their ascendancy. Meanwhile, the reaction of the Russian veterinary service to regime change in Kyiv was distinctly sour. Resorting to a favorite tactic in recent years, it pronounced that the change in power would have a negative impact on Ukraine's "ability to control phytosanitary standards." Apparently these officials believed that some political systems were inherently dirty, and that this political grime might rub off on meat and vegetables from Ukraine. Predictably—and more importantly—Moscow's financial support, of which only $3 billion of the promised $15 billion was actually delivered, was suspended indefinitely. For its part, the Chinese government, never enamored with Yanukovych, quickly announced that they would work with the new Ukrainian government.

While the Russian veterinary services were sowing fears over fake dirt on Ukrainian meat and produce in Kyiv, protesters, journalists, and the merely curious began to pore over documents in government buildings, where they uncovered real dirt about the alarming intentions of the previous administration. Hennadiy Moskal, a Batkivshchyna Party politician and former deputy minister of internal affairs, showed the press special operations plans to violently suppress the Euromaidan demonstrations drawn up by Yanukovych and company with the help of Russian advisers. According to the papers, the snipers on Instytutska Street near Ukraine's government district were special units of Interior Ministry troops led by a colonel and soldiers from a special Omega unit. The documents also revealed that a former first deputy of the Russian Main Intelligence Directorate stayed at the Kyiv Hotel and helped with preparations, his expenses paid by the Ukrainian Security Services. But most importantly, these documents proved that our fears that Yanukovych would have used the military against civilians were not paranoid—they were spot on. The plans existed and had been approved by Yanukovych's newly installed defense chief. Just as the horrible violence of the February 18 street battles was eclipsed by the massacre of scores of victims by sniper bullets on February 20, those sniper murders were on the verge of being eclipsed by a horror even bloodier.

I couldn't help reflecting that normally, when US diplomacy works to avoid nightmarish outcomes, even if we succeed, there is always a doubt that it meant anything. Perhaps even had we not done anything, maybe the worst would not have come to worst. You never know. But in this case, it was clear. All of our work clearly did mean something—from Vice President Biden's calls to Ambassador Pyatt's sleepless nights to the Defense Attaché Office's (DAO's) observation teams to the hundreds of everyday interactions of Embassy personnel with their Ukrainian counterparts. We had done our part to avoid a tragedy of an even greater magnitude. It really did matter, and these documents proved that in stark terms.

That said, it must be absolutely clear that removal of the democratically elected Viktor Yanukovych was *not* a US foreign policy victory because it *never was* a US foreign policy goal. Whether he stayed or left was a matter for the Ukrainian people, and had he followed US advice on seeking and finding a compromise and forging a coalition with protesters and opposition, he likely could have avoided the escalating series of events leading to his flight and revolution. What the United States could take partial credit for was twofold: the weaponry of the regular Ukrainian military was not used against protesters, and the struggle over Ukrayinskyi Dim didn't turn into a bloodbath. These were victories for human decency over those in power who feel that the perpetuation of their power justifies any human sacrifice. I am well aware that US policy is directed, as it must be, to the pursuit of US national interests. While preserving Ukraine's ability to choose a European future was definitely a goal of the United States, at every moment throughout the prolonged crisis this goal was secondary to helping Ukraine avoid the kind of calamity that erases the humanitarian boundaries within which governments should operate. Some of my college and graduate school professors suggested to me that joining the Foreign Service would make me more cynical about our nation. But through this crisis, I actually became less cynical and more proud of how we implement our values overseas. I became proud that I am paid by my government to do the right thing. Armchair pundits who suggest that the United States created chaos in Ukraine in order to pull Ukraine into our geostrategic camp have no understanding of either how the US government operated abroad under the Obama administration or the amount of apathy within the US government toward Ukraine after so many years of disappointment with that country's corruption and inability to get its own act together. Anti-American conspiracy theories about Ukraine, such as those actively spun by foreign propagandists, may be enticing, but they only draw gullible persons ever farther from the truth.

The gulf between truth and falsity was evident from what we witnessed on the streets of Kyiv and what we read in Russian media reports following the change of government. That same day, Monday, February 24, I accompanied Ambassador Pyatt to a meeting at the Cabinet of Ministers. As we drove up Hrushevskoho, the scene of the pitched street fights that radically changed the course of the protests in January in the aftermath of the Dictatorship Laws, cobblestone pillars previously stacked by protesters to throw at police were now converted into impromptu shrines covered in flowers and candle wax, many now with framed photos of fallen protesters. In the space of a few days, a battlefield was transformed into a memorial; the page was turned. At the Embassy, we still wondered if it was really over. On the street, they knew. It was time to mourn the dead and focus on the business of building an independent Ukraine and righting past mistakes. With many barricades still standing, the ambassador and I left the car to walk up the hill to the Cabinet of Ministers. When we reached the building after a brisk walk, Ambassador Pyatt said under his breath, "Oh my God, check out the hybrid security package." Standing in front of the gray, foreboding Soviet-era Cabinet of Ministers building was a line of guards—smartly uniformed Interior Ministry troops and Maidan Self-Defense Forces (SDF) in rag tag body armor, intermixed, standing in front of the building. It is hard to overstate the cognitive dissonance of this scene. Just days before, these two groups were exchanging Molotov cocktails and flash grenades, engaged in mortal combat. Now here they stood, shoulder-to-shoulder, guarding the Cabinet of Ministers building. It was almost too much to comprehend. Who worked this out? Certainly not us. The Ukrainians themselves knew quite well how to compromise and make peace once Yanukovych had bolted and allowed them the opportunity. The actual meeting at CabMin was boring in comparison to the surreal reception.

On the other hand, a statement from the Russian Ministry of Foreign Affairs that morning seemed to have emanated from an alternate reality, expressing "extreme concern" that "militant thugs and militants of ultra-nationalist organizations . . . have not been disarmed . . . and violence continues." It also accused Western governments of duplicity and using the February 21 agreement as "cover to promote the script of a forced change of power in Ukraine." The Russian media went into hyperventilation mode to portray Kyiv as a city teetering on the edge of apocalypse. Rossiya One's television presenters intoned on Tuesday, February 25, that "genuine lawlessness reigns on the streets. . . . Crowds of uncontrolled armed extremists have launched a witch hunt. Searching for supporters of the previous authorities, they are organizing vigilante justice against prisoners, are burning down synagogues and destroying monuments, and coming to meetings of deputies with assault rifles." The actual mood in Kyiv was the exact opposite. After we had become so accustomed to constant tension in the city during recent months, the sudden massive collective sigh of relief was almost palpable. There was absolute peace on the streets. At the Embassy, DAO's observer mission was suspended as superfluous. There was simply no conflict to observe anymore. We started doing our grocery shopping downtown again, and only the continued presence of the barricades stopped us from bringing the kids to rollerblade again on Khreshchatyk after work.

Meanwhile, in Donetsk, in the Donbas region of eastern Ukraine, the press asked Governor Andriy Shishatsky whether he was opposed to Russian influence in his region. "I am sure that in Ukraine we have enough wise people to solve our own problems," he answered, stressing the importance of the unity of the Ukrainian state and the danger of separatism. While noting that the future of the Donbas was tied to Russia, he pleaded for understanding between Russia and the West. The next day, Donetsk mayor Oleksandr Lukyanchenko confirmed that the Rada in Kyiv was the only legitimate body of power in the country. Ukraine's east, left to its own devices, was hesitant but adjusting.

Yanukovych was gone, but his ghost still hovered in the air. The former president's "acting prime minister" Serhiy Arbuzov announced that Yanukovych was on the job, but temporarily on sick leave—in Moscow. In the Russian capital, Russian Prime Minister Medvedev questioned the legitimacy of the new government in Kyiv even as the European Commission recognized Turchynov's status as acting president.

Meanwhile, the Rada continued to pass new legislation, and the new Ukrainian government sent a diplomatic note to all embassies in Kyiv refuting Russian assertions that they were not legitimate or had come to power through a coup. The letter pointed out that Yanukovych had various responsibilities under the February 21 agreement, including signing legislation returning Ukraine to the 2004 constitution. By stating publicly after the agreement was in effect that he would not sign the new laws, and then disappearing, Yanukovych had violated the terms of the agreement, they said. The February 22 Rada decisions removing him from office were a legal and necessary response to his abdication of his responsibilities under the agreement. They also got in one final dig: "Moreover, such a stance by the Russian side is surprising given the fact that Russian envoy V. Lukin, in fact, refused to sign the [February 21] agreement at the time of its signing."

Naturally, Moscow could not let this pass. The official government newspaper *Rossiyskaya Gazeta* countered, and oddly accused the United States of orchestrating Yanukovych's flight: "Yanukovych would certainly have continued fighting if not for the security guarantees offered to him, his family and aides. As shown by the latest events in Ukraine, only Washington—the Gray Cardinal [pulling strings] behind Maidan—could offer such guarantees.... To get Yanukovych off the Ukrainian political scene, the US State Department was ready to offer him any security guarantees. Americans are great experts when it comes to making people vanish."

According to the increasingly bizarre musings of the Kremlin spin doctors, the United States was responsible for everything on both sides of the equation—creating and funding Maidan, murdering protesters, and Yanukovych's flight. They seemed to be preparing their readers for Yanukovych to pop up at any moment in the northern Virginia suburbs under our supposed "security guarantees." By this telling, the United States was basically omnipotent, unbelievably powerful, and immensely evil. Only the perpetually victimized Russian Federation, standing up for its Slavic brothers, could stand in the way of America's morbid machinations.

Reality was just the springboard for these loopy flights of fancy, and developments could be cherry picked for maximum impact. Anything that contradicted their narrative was "fake" and deemed a plant from hostile foreign intelligence. The importance of any small facts that did support their narrative was blown out of all proportion. If the bogus and outrageous story line was not working, just talk louder and run multiple story lines at the same time to see which one sticks. It didn't matter if the various versions contradicted each other. Credibility was not important. The best consumers of this kind of propaganda were those cynical enough to barely believe in anything they hear anyway. Those disenchanted with the idea that the truth is even knowable were perfect. This opened the floodgates to conspiracy thinking, which is easy to exploit. The perception of a world of smoke and mirrors, where the obvious explanation was always wrong and manufactured just to dupe people, would give these propagandists the widest latitude for their operations. Acknowledging any past mistakes, even when the propagandist was clearly wrong in hindsight, was therefore unnecessary and counterproductive. Creating doubt and confusion over the truth wasn't an unintended consequence, it was the goal. This is what we were up against.

Several legislators introduced bills in the Rada designed to stop the rebroadcast of Russian television in Ukraine as a response to the highly distorted message coming from the Russian press on recent events in Kyiv, and in some cases, Russia's open promotion of separatism inside Ukraine. Russian Foreign Minister Lavrov, not previously noted as a champion of civil liberties, responded: "If this decision is made in Ukraine, it would be a serious violation of freedom of speech." I occasionally exchanged emails with some colleagues in our Moscow Embassy, and they wrote to me that morning: "Wow, did you hear Lavrov defending freedom of speech? That's never happened before! His government is always more than happy to disconnect CNN or EuroNews when they don't like the tone of their reporting."

On Tuesday, February 25, nearly everyone in the Political and Economic Sections focused on the arrival of Deputy Secretary Burns. As per State Department custom, the deputy secretary was referred to by the single letter D, and a D visit was a big deal. During my first year and a half in Kyiv, we had almost no visitors. Now there was a steady stream. The visit of Deputy Secretary Burns, a highly respected Foreign Service Officer with the deserved reputation of being both an incredible diplomat and a down-to-earth human being, caused a lot of excitement. Once on the ground, he hosted a town hall meeting and graciously thanked the exhausted Embassy Kyiv staff, Americans and Ukrainians, for their work in recent months. He met Rada speaker and acting President Turchynov, key opposition leaders, and Ukraine's newly appointed security and defense officials. He also met some Party of Regions leaders, looking to give some dejected politicians from Yanukovych's grouping unexpected respect and convince them that they could be productive in the new system. But the emotional center of the visit was Burns's time at St. Michael's monastery where protesters fled from beatings and the wounded were brought from Maidan for first aid.

Tuck Evans wrote the reporting cable from the visit: "Bishop Agapit guided the deputy secretary through St. Michael's church pointing out the hall where student protesters, bloodied and terrified, sought refuge after the November 30 attacks. The deputy secretary joined Bishop Agapit in lighting prayer candles in memory of those hurt and killed. The bishop, noting that the Church still keeps medical supplies inside in case of further need, told the deputy secretary that St. Michael's role has been modest: 'We just offered space and shelter, and it is people who worked miracles in self-organizing and mobilizing.' The bishop also commented that over the February 21–23 weekend, St. Michael's had received the greatest gathering of people in his recollection, 'many, many thousands, more than even Easter.' The bishop expressed to the deputy secretary his thanks to the American people for supporting the people of Ukraine during the crisis.... Inside St. Michael's compound, the deputy secretary placed flowers and lit a candle at the outdoor memorial honoring those killed during the February 18–20 police attacks on the Maidan—many of them felled by lethal sniper fire as they struggled to assist wounded colleagues. The memorial is an impromptu wooden latticework hung with photos of the dead. It is strewn with helmets, shields, car tires, and personal effects of the 'heavenly hundred'—a reference to the Maidan's Self-Defense Force structures of 'sotnyas' or 100-strong centuria. The memorial has been a touchstone for grieving visitors to St. Michael's and the Maidan community."

Meanwhile, Ukraine's top political personalities jostled for positions in the new government. However, Klitschko, Ruslana, and Tyahnybok stated publicly that they would not serve in the next administration. The new Interior Ministry officially placed Yanukovych on Ukraine's wanted persons list. The next day, the General Prosecutor's Office opened a case against Yanukovych and his top staff for mass murder. Maidan SDF agreed to surrender their weapons and stop covering their faces. After new Minister of Internal Affairs Arsen Avakov disbanded the Berkut, the security organization so despised by the Maidanivtsi, the city of Sevastopol, where the Russian government leased naval facilities and had a heavy military presence, immediately offered them jobs in a political jab. Then a Russian parliamentarian quickly introduced legislation also offering the dismissed Ukrainian Berkut officers positions and expedited Russian citizenship. The Ukrainian hryvnia continued to slide, and the currency that was previously pegged at around eight per dollar now fetched around ten per dollar. This would make Ukraine's crushing foreign debt burden even more difficult to pay using their devalued money.

In the midst of these developments, the Russian military commenced a "no-notice alert" surprise exercise for its Western and Central Military Districts, including the Black Sea Fleet. "THAT might lead to questions," wrote Leo Hmelevsky, Naval Attaché, to the rapidly ramping down Kyiv Task Force. Russian Defense Minister Sergey Shoygu quickly claimed that the exercise had nothing to do with events in Ukraine. On short notice, his ministry summoned all Moscow-based Defense Attachés and said that the snap exercise would involve 160,000 troops, 1,200 armored vehicles, 880 tanks, 120 helicopters, 90 aircraft, and parts of the Northern and Baltic Sea naval fleets. Putin was merely flexing his military biceps, they claimed.

In Kyiv, we were all still acclimatizing ourselves to the rapid rollout of the new Ukraine. Our consul general, Henry Hand, noted: "Times really are changing. Just saw a DAI [traffic police] Prius with a Ukrainian flag on roof. Blue, yellow . . . and green?" The new government released its list of new Cabinet Ministers under Prime Minister Yatseniuk, which included a mix of opposition politicians and Maidan leaders. Two figures on the list, new anticorruption chief Tetyana Chornovol and Minister of Youth and Sports Dmytro Bulatov, had suffered beatings or torture at the hands of the former government. Controversially (and certain to raise hackles in Moscow), Pravyi Sektor leader Dmytro Yarosh was listed as deputy national security council head. The new proposed cabinet was presented to the crowds at Maidan—a crucial step to cementing the new coalition government.

Russia's aggressive statements and military exercises were starting to make Washington nervous. Secretary Kerry told reporters, "For a country [Russia] that has spoken out so frequently . . . against foreign intervention in Libya, in Syria, and elsewhere, it would be important for them to heed those warnings as they think about options in the sovereign nation of Ukraine, and I don't think there should be any doubt whatsoever that any kind of military intervention that would violate the sovereign territorial integrity of Ukraine would be a huge, grave mistake." Also in Washington, the National Security Council and State Department were meeting the same day to discuss a possible $1 billion loan guarantee for Ukraine.

Our colleagues at Embassy Moscow were also busy playing the same armchair game as us: "Where in the World is Viktor Yanukovych?" Their press attaché wrote to us: "According to media reporting, Yanukovych stayed last night at the Hotel Ukraine (Radisson) in Moscow across the river from the Embassy last night and stayed on the 11th floor. He moved today to the outskirts of Moscow into an upscale suburb. . . . The Russian media is treating this story as very likely to be true and it has the ring of truth to it. That doesn't mean it is true, but people are starting to chase this story as if it is." The bizarre circumstance of Ukraine's vanished head of state captivated everyone.

As if on cue, disembodied words floated back from the strange netherworld of missing presidents. Yanukovych confirmed that he was indeed alive, in Russia, and still claimed to be the President of Ukraine. His words sounded like he'd spent his days on the lam watching Russian television. Yanukovych wrote,

I, Viktor Fedorovych Yanukovych, appeal to the people of Ukraine. I continue to consider myself the legitimate head of Ukraine, who was elected on the basis of free expression of will of Ukrainian citizens. . . . We can observe a surge of extremism on the streets of many cities of our country. . . . I have to ask the government of the Russian Federation to ensure my personal security from actions of extremists. Unfortunately, everything that is currently happening in the Verkhovna Rada is illegitimate. . . . In this situation I officially declare my determination to fight for implementation of important compromise agreements on settlement of Ukraine's deep political crisis.

Prime minister-designate Yatsenyuk quickly responded that Yanukovych was no longer president but was a mass murder suspect. Back in Kyiv, Borys Tarasyuk, the new deputy prime minister with responsibility for EU integration, announced that the new government would work to sign the EU Association Agreement quickly—within weeks if possible. The Rada confirmed Yatsenyuk as prime minister, and then confirmed the rest of the new cabinet. The new government was official. Yanukovych was finished, and the Kremlin apparently no longer viewed him as a useful asset in the struggle to retain Russian influence in Ukraine. Putin was now relying on raw power, not rhetoric. But he gave Yanukovych one last chance to make his case, though far enough away from the Kremlin to devalue anything the disgraced Ukrainian leader, still unwilling to give up the ghost of his depleted authority, might have to say.

That Friday morning, February 28, Yanukovych was flown out of Moscow to a military airport in Rostov-on-Don, a Russian city close to the Ukrainian border, to deliver a live broadcast news conference at 3:00 p.m. Yanukovych stated that he would "continue the war for Ukraine's future" against those who used terror to force him to flee. Power was seized by "nationalists and profascist" forces representing a minority of Ukrainians, he argued, but the way out was by following the February 21 agreement. He called for a national referendum to resolve "questions facing Ukraine," stating that "representatives of the West, including the United States, are helping the Maidan." Echoing Russia's criticism of him, he apologized for failing to have the "strength to keep stability and prevent lawlessness." He also called developments in Crimea a "completely normal reaction" to "the banditry and coup" in Kyiv. Eric Johnson, who was watching the press event with the Public Affairs Section's Ukrainian staff, noted, "The responses from PAS local staff were: disgust, nausea, and/or hysterical laughter—often, and at different points during the press conference." Eric's press specialist sighed before giving his judgment, "If Putin was using this Yanu appearance as a trial balloon to see whether it made any sense to continue backing him, it seems to me that the balloon totally burst."

The previous evening, Ambassador Pyatt held his first meeting with new Ukrainian Foreign Minister Andriy Deshchytsia. "The past few weeks I've been on the Maidan rather than focused on external events," Deshchytsia began. "You know, revolution looks easy compared to establishing a new government." Deshchytsia explained that his first priority was European integration, and his second priority was stabilizing Ukraine's relations with Russia. Pyatt pressed him on reaching out to Russian Foreign Minister Lavrov, and Deshchytsia replied that he would, especially given the urgency of the situation in Crimea. "Our new government does not plan to declare a state of emergency in Crimea, which would be counterproductive. Our understanding is that the Crimean parliament merely voted for enhanced autonomy, not breaking away. We can engage in a dialogue with them on that basis. We can work with them. Increased autonomy, if that's what they really want, is acceptable and the basis for a good conversation."

While Yanukovych had popped up in Russia and was being shuttled from one place to another, where his presence was evidently not wanted, the search for his ill-gotten money continued in Kyiv. Prime Minister Yatsenyuk accused the Yanukovych government of stripping state coffers bare, saying that $37 billion of Ukrainian credit had simply disappeared under his watch. The US Departments of Justice and Treasury began working with the Swiss, British, and others to watch for transfers of stolen funds. Meanwhile, volunteers worked at Mezhyhirya to carefully remove and preserve thousands of pages of accounting documents hastily thrown into a canal. These soggy documents, and others like them, were crucial to piecing together the financial schemes by which Yanukovych and his cronies accumulated such amazing wealth during his short presidency. The Swiss soon froze the accounts of twenty Ukrainians, including Arbuzov, Azarov, and the Yanukovych family, and launched a money laundering case against Yanukovych.

That Friday afternoon, February 28, Valentyna and I went back to see Maksim Maksimov at the Commonwealth of Independent States (CIS) Institute. It had been a while. He mentioned that a Chinese Communist Party delegation had stopped by his office when they were in Kyiv. I asked him what the Chinese reaction would be to Russia supporting separatism in Ukraine. After all, as China had its own separatism issues with Tibet and Xinjiang, they could not support breakaway regions outright. Maksimov waved off the question, responding, "They said that they would just react in the same manner as to the Russian actions in Georgia. In other words, they won't come out in support of us but they really don't care that much. Certainly not enough to put their relations with Russia on the line over it." He was right on the mark. Despite their fondness for declaiming high principles, foreign policy consistency was not an absolute standard for Chinese leaders when their interests were at stake.

Valentyna and I made small talk with Maksimov on a number of subjects. Then I asked him about the rumor that the next day, March 1, was going to be a big day for pro-Russian demonstrations in eastern and southern Ukraine. Spring was approaching, and we had seen online calls for a so-called Russian spring in many towns in those regions. I asked him what we should expect. Maksimov smiled. "Big stuff! You just watch tomorrow. It's going to be beautiful. Watch the east."

Putin, as usual, was playing the "protect endangered Russian compatriots abroad" card in the hybrid war game unfolding in Ukraine. Apropos of the theme, also on Friday, February 28, we noted a petition posted online by the Kharkiv Human Rights Group on behalf of ethnic Russians living in Ukraine, signed by 36,000 people in a single day. The petition read,

Dear Mr. President of the Russian Federation, Vladimir Putin: We ethnic Russians and Russian-speaking Ukrainian nationals do not need other countries to defend our interests. We are grateful to you for support, however would like to inform you that nobody has ever infringed our rights on Ukrainian territory. We have always lived freely and happily, speaking in the language we are accustomed to. In school we have also learned Ukraine's state language and know it well enough to feel comfortable in a Ukrainian-speaking milieu. With all due respect for your concern, therefore, we would ask you to not raise an internal question for our country which is not a burning issue for us at Russian Federation state level. Not to mention bringing troops in to regulate a conflict which you may see, but which is not visible to us.

Thank you for your understanding. Yours sincerely, Ethnic Russians and Russian-Speaking Nationals of Ukraine.

It was a valiant but vain attempt to devalue Putin's ace card. Meanwhile, in the Donbas region of eastern Ukraine, Putin opened a second front in his hybrid war to punish the insubordinate Ukrainians.

While the eyes of the world were increasingly focused on Crimea, a pro-Russian self-proclaimed "People's Militia" began storming government buildings in Donetsk. At the Donetsk regional administration building, armed men hoisted the Russian flag and one Pavel Gubarev, a thirty-year-old with a history of membership in the neo-Nazi "Russian National Unity" paramilitary, declared himself the "People's Governor." A similar group then stormed the regional administration building in Kharkiv, also raising the Russian flag. Then Mykolaiv. Then Odesa and Dnipropetrovsk. I recalled Maksimov's advice to watch for something beautiful that day—I suppose that for him, this was beautiful.

‖

STEALING SIMFEROPOL

While the new government struggled to shore up Kyiv's fractured authority throughout the country and began to address the multitude of problems inherited from the ousted Yanukovych regime, the government of Vladimir Putin, smarting from Russia's failure to control Ukraine's fate, was unwilling to allow Ukrainians' post-Soviet history to return to its generally peaceful course. The former KGB officer set his sights on two targets—Crimea, which had been part of Russia prior to 1954, and southeastern Ukraine, with its large Russian-speaking population. Unlike Soviet leader Leonid Brezhnev, who deployed uniformed Soviet armed forces to invade Czechoslovakia in 1968 and Afghanistan in 1979, Putin sought to deflect anticipated blowback from the international community by employing a gradually escalating hybrid strategy that combined military force, stealth, deception, denial, and blatant lies—the trademarks of a new Russian strategy toward neighboring states drifting too far from its influence, most particularly Georgia.

By implementing such a strategy, Russia would defile the bedrock principle of stable borders that undergirded peace in Europe after the two great wars. Russia also violated the norms and agreements it has pledged to protect, including the territorial integrity of sovereign states and its specific pledge to defend the territorial integrity of Ukraine after Ukraine returned the nuclear weapons stationed on its soil to Russia in the 1990s.

In late February Greg Pfleger in Political wrote: "I am seeing reporting that [new interior minister Arseni] Avakov just departed for Simferopol with special forces types, that Russian flags are flying over government buildings in Sevastopol and Kerch, and that antitank roadblocks are set up near Sevastopol." Disturbed by this report, I called up some of the people I had met recently in Crimea. None could confirm or refute the media reports, but Andriy Shchekun, the head of Euromaidan Crimea, couldn't contain his happiness and amazement at recent events in Kyiv. "Now the people will finally clean up the corruption and dirt which has accumulated within our democracy through these years," he said, excitedly. "This is our chance to make this place work." With the new minister of internal affairs on his way, the head of Crimea's Council of Ministers Anatoliy Mohylyov told the press that he would enforce resolutions passed in recent days by Kyiv's Rada. In the immediate afterglow of Euromaidan's victory, those in Crimea supportive of recent events in Kyiv were understandably slow to notice the gathering storm clouds on the horizon.

On the Crimean coast in Sevastopol, where Russia leased naval facilities, an extraordinary city council session created an "Executive Body of City Administration" and appointed Russian citizen businessman Alexei Chaly as its head. Meeting participants hoisted Russian flags on both flagpoles near the City State Administration building. At the same time, Russian Foreign Minister Lavrov assured his British counterpart William Hague by phone that Russia was not considering any military intervention in Ukraine. Throughout the Crimean takeover, Lavrov would play his role well, solemnly assuring the international community that what was going on before their eyes wasn't actually happening.

Valentyna had also been trying to contact our acquaintances in Simferopol to ascertain the truth behind the many reports coming out on Crimea. She finally reached independent journalist Valentyna Samar. "Separatists seem to be coming out of every crack in the pavement. Where are they all from? The situation is getting worse and worse. Rumors are that Yanu was allowed to escape from Sevastopol and is already in neutral waters," she told Valentyna. Meanwhile, the Rada adopted a plan for the "defense of Sevastopol" without releasing many details publicly. On the morning of Wednesday, February 26, blogger Sergey Psarev posted video of Russian military trucks in the southern Crimean city of Yalta. "Today at about 1700 hours, two 'Ural' military vehicles with Russian license plates entered in Yalta. At 1:11 and 1:45 [times on the video] you can clearly see the soldiers' machine gun!" He stated that when he asked why the Russian military was in Yalta, a man in civilian clothes shouted at him to put away his camera.

What this meant wasn't immediately clear—a substantial Russian military presence in Sevastopol, including the 810th Russian Naval Infantry Brigade, was legally stationed under an agreement between Ukraine and Russia. These troops could, and often did, move around Crimea after giving local authorities proper notification. But with the Russian government not recognizing the new Ukrainian government, it was unclear whether they would make these notifications through the regular channels. So the lack of a notification could just indicate a breakdown in communication following the change in power, or it could be something darker. But it was clear that the presence of these types of vehicles with armed soldiers in the populated resort town of Yalta was unusual.

That same day, former Ukrainian presidents Leonid Kravchuk, Leonid Kuchma, and Viktor Yushchenko released a joint statement accusing Russia of interfering in Crimea. The statement noted that while Russia is supposed to be a guarantor of Ukraine's independence and territorial integrity, a recent Russian Duma delegation's notion of holding a referendum on Crimea's future within Ukraine represented a threat to the Ukrainian constitution and the nation's territorial integrity. Even while Russia claims that the West is meddling in Ukraine, it is itself actively and directly interfering in Ukraine, especially within Crimea, said the former presidents. In Moscow, Russian Federation Council Speaker Valentina Matviyenko, who is ethnically Ukrainian, dismissed the possibility that Russia could use military force in Ukraine: "Such a scenario is impossible. . . . Russia states and confirms its position that we cannot—we cannot—interfere in the internal affairs of a sovereign state." In front of the regional administration building in Simferopol, Crimean Tatar protesters yelling "Glory to Ukraine" and pro-Russian protesters yelling "Glory to Russia" started a pushing match broadcast live on Ukrainian TV. Amid the tussle outside, the representatives within announced that they would delay any major decisions.

In the early hours of Thursday, February 27, gunmen with grenades and AK-47 assault rifles, wearing "uniforms not bearing any recognizable insignia," entered the Crimean regional administration building, locked the doors from the inside, and raised the Russian flag over the building. Opposition Crimean parliamentarian Serhiy Kunytsyn of Klitschko's UDAR (Ukrainian Democratic Alliance for Reforms) party told journalists by phone that there were 120 attackers, each well trained and precisely aware of their role within the group, carrying enough supplies and weapons to last one month. Acting President Turchynov stated that sightings of Russian troops beyond their assigned areas in Sevastopol would be viewed as evidence of Russian military aggression. In Russia, meanwhile, state media aired breathless reports about supposed lawlessness in Ukraine and the new government's humiliation of opponents and readiness to suppress Russian speakers. Russia's Foreign Ministry issued a new statement that Russia would begin a "strong and uncompromising" defense of its compatriots abroad. *Kommersant-Ukraine* newspaper reported that Russia's Ministry of Economy instructed the Russian Chamber of Commerce to find investors willing to pump a targeted $5 billion into Crimea.

"They are definitely Russian, they also appear to be recently refurbished," reported a member of our Defense Attaché Office (DAO) in a message to the Kyiv Task Force email list regarding fresh photos of armored personnel carriers on rural roads in Crimea. "No such thing as a 'new' BTR-80 [armored personnel carrier], but these are as close as it gets. Through the process of elimination, they could only be from the Russian Black Sea Fleet's 810th Separate Naval Infantry Brigade based in Sevastopol."

The head of Crimea's Council of Ministers, Anatoliy Mohylyov, met with the gunmen occupying the regional government's central offices at 9:00 a.m. He then told his organization's own press service that the gunmen said that they "did not have permission to negotiate," but they would allow Crimean parliamentarians to work in the building while the masked gunmen carried around their automatic weapons. The gunmen let Russian media enter the building but not Ukrainian journalists. Those Russian journalists allowed inside claimed that the men identified themselves as Simferopol Berkut, which seemed doubtful. Back at the Embassy, there were urgent questions to consider with obvious but disturbing implications. From whom was this well-disciplined, well-armed force waiting for permission to speak, and to whom were they reporting? And what business did they want the parliament to take up under their heavily armed gaze? The new Ukrainian government, through spokesmen in Kyiv's Interior Ministry and State Security Service, announced that they were moving quickly to counter threats in Simferopol. Ukraine's Foreign Ministry summoned the Russian chargé d'affaires (as their ambassador had been recalled to Moscow) and presented a diplomatic note: "In accordance with Article 7 of the Treaty of Friendship, Cooperation and Partnership between Ukraine and the Russian Federation, dated May 31, 1997 . . . [we] request for military units of the Black Sea Fleet of the Russian Federation to refrain from movement out of their deployment areas." The note also reminded Russia of its obligations under the 1994 Budapest convention to "respect the independence, sovereignty and the existing borders of Ukraine."

In response to questions from a Russian journalist from Izvestiya, the gunmen demanded that the Crimean parliament vote on secession from Ukraine. It seemed that the parliament's delay of a decision regarding whether to back separatism was not acceptable to the purposefully anonymous commanders of this highly armed group. They claimed to have no authorization to "negotiate," but they were apparently authorized to demand that Crimea's parliamentarians commit treason and break off Crimea from Ukraine.

Within hours, the Crimean parliament passed a law approving a new "autonomy" referendum. By all early indications, Kyiv's new administration was willing to accept enhanced autonomy for local Crimean authorities—if that was truly the goal. After denouncing the "unconstitutional seizure of power in Ukraine" led by "radical nationalists supported by armed gangs," the local parliament's text stated, "Following the fundamental canons of democracy, the leadership of the Crimean parliament believes that the only possible way out of this situation is the application of the principles of direct democracy. We are convinced that only holding a referendum on the improvement of overall Crimean autonomy and the expansion of their powers will allow the residents of the Crimea to determine their future themselves without external pressure and demands." Speaking of external pressure and demands, there was no mention of the fact that the text was passed under the watchful eye of gunmen with automatic weapons. Within hours, legislation was passed setting the date for a referendum on May 25. According to the text of the bill, this referendum was intended to ask voters not about separatism or becoming part of Russia, but simply whether they wanted increased autonomy for Crimea within Ukraine. They also confirmed dismissal of the previous Crimean parliamentary speaker who had delayed discussion of a possible referendum and appointed Russian nationalist politician (and purported organized crime figure) Sergey Aksyonov as the new Crimean prime minister. Aksyonov immediately told reporters he was convinced that the Russian Federation would "extend a helping hand" in Crimea's time of trouble. Later, journalists talked to opposition Crimean parliamentarians who claimed that the vote for a referendum was falsified, as only 40 to 41 parliamentarians were present while 64 votes were registered.

The Crimean Tatar Mejlis voiced an even higher level of alarm in their new statement: "Based on the fact that any attempt to change the status of autonomy threatens inter-ethnic peace and tranquility on the peninsula, as well as the territorial integrity and sovereignty of Ukraine, the Mejlis of the Crimean Tatar people express extreme concern about the situation on the peninsula and appeals to the international community, namely the UN, the Organization for Security and Co-operation in Europe (OSCE), the EU, the European Parliament, the heads of state and government of all guarantors of the territorial integrity of Ukraine, with an appeal to use all legal means to prevent the escalation of tension and change the status of Autonomous Republic of Crimea." Meanwhile, the right-wing group Pravyi Sektor, which was often used as a bogeyman in Crimea to argue that Euromaidan was fundamentally fascist, announced on February 27 that it "decided to refrain from participating in the settlement of the crisis in the Crimea," contradicting an earlier statement that it might send representatives there.

The velocity of Russian military movements continued to increase. The Embassy received reports of two additional Russian ships arriving in the vicinity of Crimea. DAO's Shane Parlow commented: "To add some context on these ships, they are Ropucha I (toad), or Project 775 Large Landing Craft. They are flat-bottomed ships capable of loading and unloading equipment and vehicles at any coastal point. No pier is required, and they can traverse water at extremely shallow depths (it will run aground at 3–4 meters, but the propellers are protected in a shroud and they can drive the nose right onto dry land). The rear and forward sections of the ship open to allow for through and through passage of cargo. They can carry anything from Main Battle Tanks to small UAZs [military utility vehicles]. Normally, they carry BTR-80s [armored personnel carriers] for the Navy's Infantry (Marines), and it can hold 15 BTR-80's and provide billeting for 200 combat troops." At about 1:00 a.m. on the morning of Friday, February 28, approximately 150 uniformed soldiers with helmets and weapons jumped out of four KAMAZ trucks (a Russian automotive name brand) without license plates at the Simferopol airport in Crimea. Ambassador Pyatt wrote in: "Social media all over this. Uniformed navy commandos. A basing agreement violation I believe. Some reports Ukrainian government saying the same. Not subtle or smart." In the waters off Sevastopol, a Russian missile boat blocked ships from Ukraine's border guard in the harbor, and media reported the arrival of eight new military helicopters at the Russian naval base. Later, Ukraine's State Border Service reported that more than ten Russian military helicopters crossed the Ukrainian border while only three had permission to enter. Also that night, Russian forces occupied Crimea's Belbek airfield in Sevastopol, with Russian propaganda organ *LifeNews* tipped off as per usual and present to record the event. By morning, Russian media covered this and other events, claiming (for example, on Russia's NTV) that the action was taken by "representatives of one of the self-defense groups that are now spontaneously springing up, formed by the Russian speakers of the area." While the characterization of these groups as spontaneous reactions to the "fascist takeover" in Kyiv played well in the Russian media space, the groups' weaponry and level of training and organization told a far different and much less spontaneous story. The truth was that Crimea, part of the sovereign country of Ukraine, was experiencing an undeclared foreign military invasion. The local propaganda campaigns which convinced many Crimean locals to support Russian intervention did not change that fact.

As the Ukrainian government began to more directly accuse the Russian military of interfering in Crimea, they asked for consultations with Russia, the United States, and the UK under the 1994 Budapest convention, invoking the convention's Article 6. Under the Budapest convention, all signatories were obligated to defend Ukraine's borders. The evidence that one of the signatories, Russia, was itself violating Ukraine's territorial integrity was becoming increasingly clear. The Rada passed a resolution requesting UN Security Council action on Crimea. Referring to the airport seizures, Minister of Internal Affairs Avakov wrote on Facebook, "I can only describe this as a military invasion and occupation." Oleh Voloshyn, the former Yanukovych official turned Euromaidan supporter, wrote again to the diplomatic community: "After the swift but bloody victory of democratic revolution in Ukraine, my country faces an even greater threat. These minutes, Russian troops in growing numbers occupy Crimea. This intervention includes not only infantry but assault helicopters, APCs [armored personnel carriers], tanks, warships. It's not an exaggeration.

That's the facts on the ground. I don't want to write a lot but it is the greatest military threat to a nation aspiring to be a part of the free world since the Soviet intervention in Czechoslovakia in 1968. Now we will see if the EU, US, and their allies' commitment to basic democratic and international law values and norms is worth a penny."

While the international community contemplated how to respond to Putin's challenge to the international order, Russia's undeclared invasion of Crimea continued to intensify. One of our local staff members wrote, "[Contacts] at the Navy HQ tell us the building of the HQ is blocked by Russian *spetsnaz* [Special Forces]. Ukrainian Navy officers are burning secret documents, and they were ordered (by senior Ukrainian Navy officers) to put their weapons into the stockpiles 'not to provoke.'" Media reported that Black Sea Fleet troops moved on an independent TV station in Evpatoriya on Crimea's western coast. Ukraine's State Border Guard Service announced that approximately thirty Russian marines surrounded its base of operations in Sevastopol, well outside the Russian-leased facilities in the town.

The Russian government quickly rejected Ukraine's request to hold Budapest convention consultations. The Russian Foreign Ministry claimed that the situation in Crimea was the result of "internal political processes within Ukraine," not foreign meddling. They were hewing closely to the same public line as the Russian press, claiming that the heavily armed forces spreading across Crimea with military efficiency were spontaneously spawned indigenous groups wanting to protect Crimea from supposed "fascists" in Kyiv. There was no foreign power intervening in Crimea, by this logic. Moscow likely cared little whether anyone outside Russia believed this lie. If the Russian public did, that sufficed. Of course, even a cursory look at the weaponry and uniforms of the soldiers who seized the Simferopol airport made this argument laughable. Ukrainian media reported on appeals made on VKontakte, Russia's most popular social media website, for men aged 18 to 45 with military experience to go to Crimea, Kyiv, Donetsk, and Kharkiv as "tourists." According to the posting, "The more of us 'Russian tourists' are on the territory of Ukraine, the more reason and official argument there will be for our government to resort to all necessary actions aimed at 'protecting' Russian citizens abroad. The Crimea is now the place where the destiny of all the Russian people and the entire 'Great Rus' is being decided."

Locals in Crimea told *Ukrayinska Pravda* reporters that five large IL-76 transport aircraft landed at a military airfield in Hvardiyske, just north of Sim-feropol, as a convoy of ten Russian armored vehicles moved from Sevastopol to Simferopol. Further reports of smaller groups of heavily armed men "securing" television and radio stations rolled in. Armed men flying the Russian flag com-mandeered police checkpoints on two major roads between Kherson region and Crimea and began inspecting vehicles before they could pass. Meanwhile, the Russian Foreign Ministry continued to claim that the movements of its troops in Crimea were "in full accordance with basic Russian-Ukrainian agreements on the Black Sea Fleet." That agreement required Russia to inform Ukraine of troop movements outside their bases other than regular transport actions, and nothing of the sort seemed to have happened.

Then, around 10:00 p.m. on February 28, media reported that gunmen invaded and took control of Crimean ATR TV channel—the Tatar station. Perhaps I shouldn't have been shocked, since the Crimean media had been in the crosshairs of the Russian military and "separatists" for many days. But I had sat in those offices just two weeks before, I knew the pictures on the walls, the layout of the conference table, and how much their journalists cared about their work and their station. It hit me harder than the others. In the coming hours, armed men also invaded Krymaeroruh, an organization that provided air navi-gation services over the Crimean peninsula. Various reports indicated that the gunmen were either from Russia's Pskov Airborne division or Russian GRU Defense Intelligence. No matter which was true, either variant was ominous. According to the Ukrainian Defense Ministry, Russian naval infantry troops also attempted to infiltrate the Ukrainian naval infantry unit in Feodosia but were initially fought off. Crimean Majlis spokesman Liliya Muslimova posted that Kirov military airfield was captured by soldiers who arrived in sixteen military trucks. The target of these attacks was clearly straight out of the clas-sic Soviet textbook for special operations: military, security, and media. As in the Bolshevik revolution of more than a century ago, take the guns, take the railway crossing, take the newspaper. It was impossible to believe that this had anything to do with "defending Crimea" from "Kyiv's fascists"—they were not attacking any targets with relevance to Euromaidan. This was about Russian forces taking away Ukraine's ability to defend its sovereignty over Crimea in the military, security, and information space.

Russia Today published a fictitious story that "armed men from Kyiv" attempted to attack the Interior Ministry building in Simferopol. Chiming in right on time, the Russian Ministry of Foreign Affairs stated, "On the night of March 1, unidentified gunmen directed from Kyiv undertook an attempt to seize the building of the Ministry of Internal Affairs of the Autonomous Republic of Crimea. People have been injured as a result of this treacherous provocation. . . . This latest [act] confirms the desire of certain political circles in Kyiv to destabilize the situation on the peninsula. . . . We believe it is extremely irresponsible to continue escalating the already tense situation in the Crimea." Then, newly minted Crimean Prime Minister Sergey Aksyonov announced that the autonomy referendum would be moved up from May 25, when it would have aligned with Ukraine's presidential elections, to March 30 in response to the unsubstantiated claims of an attack. He also asked the Russian government for assistance in "guaranteeing peace and calm" in Crimea.

Until this point, the response from the new Ukrainian government to the Russian incursion was restrained, emphasizing calls for international help rather than instructing Ukraine's own military or security personnel in Crimea to resist Russian forces. Their logic was clear—Ukraine would inevitably lose in a straight military conflict with Russia because the hard power balance wasn't even close to equal. Especially in the aftermath of the recent revolution, with Ukraine's military and security establishment still in disarray, it was no match for the muscle the Russian government was quietly introducing into Crimea. Resistance by loyal Ukrainian forces in Crimea would be suicidal, and moreover, it would enable the mendacious Russian media-intelligence complex to reinterpret acts of self-defense by Ukrainian troops as unprovoked Ukrainian attacks on Russian forces that required further Russian retaliation. Also, after the recent sudden change in power in Kyiv, ordering a robust self-defense might have caused unpredictable and dangerous fracturing in Ukraine's security forces. Ukraine's only hope was to keep the fighting at the political level, preferably at the international political level, where the sheer audacity and illegality of Russia's attempt at the first major land grab in Europe since the Second World War should give Ukraine the advantage.

Meanwhile, dramatic events were taking place all over the Crimean peninsula. On Saturday, March 1, multiple news outlets reported that approximately three hundred soldiers and fifteen armored vehicles attacked border guards in the Balaklava suburb of Sevastopol, presenting the Ukrainian border guard with an order from the Russian Ministry of Defense demanding that they capitulate. Then, an Embassy staffer reached the border guards and wrote to the Task Force with their story: "Border guards say they just abandoned Bal-aklava. They took their vessels out into the sea at the same time and now report that three Russian ships are approaching their boats. Border guards called the Russian ships 'missile boats.'" There was nothing pretty or subtle about this. Another division of troops moved on the Ukrainian rocket base in Yevpatoriya. While it was clear that Russian troops without insignias were moving against Ukrainian targets in Crimea for some time already, it was on this Saturday that Russia's Federation Council approved the deployment of a "limited con-tingent of Russian troops in the Crimea for the 'safety' of the Black Sea Fleet and Russians who are there." This action, in response to a request letter from President Putin, was treated by the Ukrainian media as a virtual declaration of war. By evening, the Ukrainian National Security Council called for a military mobilization even though it was clear they would not likely use their military to defend their own territory in Crimea.

Also that day, dozens of men in fatigues charged through the lobby of the aging Simferopol brownstone building where I had met Valentyna Samar several weeks before. They had come to seize her office, the Center for Investi-gative Journalism. Intrepid investigative reporters were no longer welcome or safe in Crimea, and that applied doubly to anyone whose NGO had received Western grant money at any time. Within a few months, Samar would flee her home in Crimea.

No number of Russian government lies could obscure the reality of what was happening in Crimea. An EU diplomat wrote a note to Ambassador Pyatt: "Chubarov, head of the Mejlis [the Crimean Tatar's main organization], informed me some minutes ago that the annexation of Crimea is happening: columns of Russian armored cars are moving in the direction of Simferopol. Administration and TV are already under control of RU military. Tatars are very much afraid that they will be the first victims of the operation." All Kyiv-Simferopol flights were canceled for Saturday, March 1, with Ukrainian International Airlines announcing that this was due to "airspace closure of the Autonomous Republic of Crimea." Someone was also bringing down Crimean telephone and internet service. Ukrainian military expert, blogger, and Euro-maidan activist Dmytro Tymchuk posted on social media: "It's an invasion. Russian paratroops with chevrons removed are capturing military objects. Rus-sian Il-76 are landing at airports. The 36th brigade is under attack. Ukrainian troops are completely demoralized, no resistance. Information coming from many sources on the ground. This is war, or to be precise, a seizure." Meanwhile, Russia's ambassador to the EU Vladimir Chizhov flatly denied to the press that any Russian troops were at Crimea's airports despite the hundreds of photos circulating on the internet. He was just doing his job.

Ambassador Pyatt met briefly with Andriy Deshchytsia. The Ukrainian foreign minister said that all international institutions, including the United Nations (UN), Organization for Security and Co-operation in Europe (OSCE), and CIS, were invited to Kyiv to see how orderly it was, in direct contrast to Russia's disinformation campaign, which cast the city as the seventh circle of neo-fascist hellscape. "They should also come to see that Russian citizens and Russian speakers are not terrified. Because of all of the Russian disinformation, they should come quickly and give us some kind of judgement," he added. "We really want to talk with them [the Russian government]. We started a dialogue today when Medvedev spoke with Yatsenyuk and Duma speaker Sergey Naryshkin spoke with Turchynov. We are also attempting to open a back channel for talks via Ukrainian parliamentarians. There must be a way to work this out." About two hundred demonstrators came to the US Embassy that night, demonstrating peacefully and asking for "help and protection" in order to counter Russian actions.

According to an official readout, President Obama called Putin for an hour-and-a-half to express "deep concern over Russia's clear violation of Ukraine's sovereignty and territorial integrity." Secretary Kerry issued a statement that "the United States condemns the Russian Federation's invasion and occupation of Ukrainian territory." At least rhetorically, the gloves were off. We were calling it an invasion. UN Secretary General Ban Ki-moon also called Putin, urging him to engage the new government in Kyiv as he was "gravely concerned" about events that could "compromise the unity, sovereignty and territorial integrity of [Ukraine]."

All to no avail. Continuing their operations, Russian troops seized another small Crimean airport. In a television interview, influential and hawkish former Putin adviser Andrey N. Illarionov said that the current Russian operation was not only aimed at Crimea, but sought the overthrow of the entire new Ukrainian government. The Ukrainian military, evidently unsure that the Russian military would stop in Crimea, began calling up conscripts to report for duty. Nationalist group Pravyi Sektor said that their VKontakte social media page was hacked, and they had not called on Chechens to attack targets within

Russia as was widely reported in the Russian press. Canada, always strong on Ukrainian issues in deference to their large Ukrainian diaspora, recalled its ambassador in Moscow for "consultations." The Russian press uniformly fell into line, all backing the use of Russian military force in Ukraine.

The next day, Sunday, March 2, began with Russian Black Sea Fleet forces giving Ukrainian marines at Feodosiya at 10:00 a.m. an ultimatum to surrender. Russian media claimed that Ukrainian forces in Crimea were surrendering en masse, not to Russian soldiers who they still denied were present, but to organically spawned Crimean "self-defense forces." The Ukrainian military immediately labeled these claims black propaganda. Calling Russia's invasion troops "self-defense forces" intentionally mirrored the language of Maidan, making it easy to accuse Western governments who supported the rights of Euromaidan in Kyiv of a duplicitous double standard if they criticized the Russian military activity. The clear message was that the West did not care about the principles they espoused, but just used their supposed values as convenient props in their quest for power at the expense of Russia. This narrative fit Russia's self-image as the perpetual victim of various international plots and conniving conspiracies. "The Big Lie" was the subject line of Ambassador Pyatt's first email that Sunday, March 2: "On the bogus Russian narrative of pogroms [organized ethnic massacres], attacks on churches, and threats to Russian speakers, it would be good to push out the Klitschko message of national unity (from a Russian speaker born on a USSR Air Force base in Central Asia). . . . Is RFE amplifying this in Ukraine and Russia? To the extent that Russia seeks to fuel a civil war, we should be pouring water on the flames. . . . PS— Putin did the same thing with Merkel. Country in flames, Russian speakers persecuted, blah blah, blah."

Unwittingly proving Ambassador Pyatt's point, later in the day the Russian media breathlessly quoted border guard reports that more than half a million Ukrainians were fleeing for the Russian border in a "humanitarian catastrophe." However, the official records of the Russian Federal Customs Service (RFCS) belied that claim. For example, the Southern RFCS district continued to process around 2,700 vehicles per day passing into Russia, which closely matched the border station's regular averages. Other Russian customs data from border districts with Ukraine also failed to show the massive outflow that the Russian media claimed. It was a lie. Yet another lie. There were many more to come.

The G8 summit meeting of world leaders was just weeks away in Sochi. Like the recently concluded Winter Olympics, it was planned as a glad-handing symbol of Russia's status as a major world power. With the invasion of Crimea in full swing, however, it was clear that international participation would signal acceptance of Putin's creeping land grab. One by one, the other major powers announced that they were dropping out of the preparatory pre-G8 meetings, signaling that they would likely boycott Sochi. NATO convened an emergency meeting of ambassadors in Brussels on the Crimea situation as Russian forces cut off power to the Ukrainian Navy headquarters in Sevastopol and the Ukrainian flags in Simferopol's central square were replaced by pro-Russian banners. The OSCE in Vienna called a special Preparatory Committee (PrepCom) meeting. With only a few Ukrainian Navy ships remaining in Crimea, Ukraine's Coast Guard vessels withdrew to other parts of the country. Crimean Tatar ATR television continued trying to draw the world's attention even with their studios occupied, broadcasting live feeds from around Crimea of Russian troops surrounding Ukrainian military facilities and security personnel. At a press conference in Simferopol, pro-Moscow Crimean Rada speaker Volodymyr Kostyantynov admitted that he was unaware of any actual physical harm to any Russian speakers in Crimea since the change of power in Kyiv, but he still confirmed plans to hold a referendum on March 30 upon which Crimea would negotiate its relationship with Kyiv. In a huge embarrassment to Kyiv, freshly appointed Ukrainian Navy chief Denis Berezovsky was shown on Russian television swearing allegiance to local Crimean pro-Russian leaders. He was immediately charged with treason. While the Ukrainian Navy flagship *Hetman Sahaydachny* remained loyal to Ukraine, Berezovsky's defection was a massive blow.

In the language of diplomacy, orders for diplomats to deliver an official message to another government still goes by an old French term: a démarche. The State Department sent out a global démarche cable instructing all American ambassadors worldwide to meet with their host government officials at the highest level possible to condemn the invasion of Crimea and ask that those governments publicly support Ukrainian sovereignty. The démarche included a long passage on how to refute erroneous Russian claims regarding Crimea in an effort to unite the international community against the invasion. Meanwhile, the Pentagon suspended all normal U.S.-Russia military engagements.

In Crimea, Russian military pressure under the nominal guise of the just-born "Crimean Army" intensified through fresh threats that the Ukrainian Navy either surrender two ships or face attack. Truckloads of additional Russian troops reportedly arrived in Kerch. Someone I knew well, one of the intellectual property rights contacts who was well connected inside the Ukrainian government, called me that afternoon. "You should be expecting major Russian military moves before Secretary Kerry comes in two days," he said.

As more disturbing news accumulated, I felt that I might have made a huge mistake by not finding a way to get Natalya and the kids to Poland. The dread that had gnawed at my stomach for the last several months got more intense. Assistant Secretary Nuland arrived late that night to have a workday in advance of Secretary Kerry's arrival, but she left early due to a family emergency.

The Ukrainian State Border Guard Service issued a fresh statement on the "systemic attacks carried out by groups of up to one hundred Russian military troops." The blockade of several Ukrainian Border Guard Service buildings continued. Also, according to the state border guards, the "Crimea-Caucasus" ferry line was disgorging a steady stream of Russian military vehicles into Crimea. The Border Guard Service also told the Embassy that their communications and surveillance systems in Crimea were destroyed, and that the Russian military was using cell phone jamming equipment there. Meanwhile, the 10th Ukrainian Saki naval aviation brigade in the Crimean village of Novofedorovka began to transfer its military aircraft and helicopters to Mykolaiv in "mainland" Ukraine after receiving Russian threats.

Secretary Kerry told journalists in Washington that while a US military response was "the last thing anybody wants," all other options were open to respond to Russian actions—including economic sanctions. Kerry called the Crimea invasion an "incredible act of aggression." Russia's status as a G8 member was also under question as its actions put it outside the norms of the international community. Even the Chinese Foreign Ministry, normally oddly copasetic with any and all Russian shenanigans, issued a statement critical of Russian moves, stating that it was China's long-standing position not to interfere in the affairs of other states and that all nations should respect Ukraine's sovereignty and territorial integrity. Meanwhile, Russia's Gazprom hinted that it might massively increase energy prices to Ukraine, which had been lowered under the December Russia-Ukraine deal that Putin struck with Yanukovych. For a Ukrainian economy already teetering on the brink, this could spell disaster. Overnight, the Ukrainian military scrambled jets to respond to two Russian airspace violations.

Increased expectations of economic sanctions against Russia began to bite the Russian economy—the ruble slid by about 3 percent while Russian equities lost about one-tenth of their value. However, President Putin showed no sign of retreating as the Russian Duma registered a new draft law legalizing the annexation of foreign territory if there is no "legitimate functioning government." Under this legal pretext, it seemed even more important for Moscow to continue to insist that the new Ukrainian government was not legitimate and did not properly function regardless of the actual situation. Even though the Russian Duma handed Putin a blank check to use military force in Ukraine, Putin's government continued to pretend that only local forces were active in Crimea. The Russian Duma speaker publicly stated that although force was approved, there was "no need yet" for Russian troops, despite the fact that Crimea was crawling with them.

Marine Staff Sergeant Shane Parlow from DAO, citing his connections among the Ukrainian troops in Crimea, updated the Task Force that night on what he was hearing: "In Sevastopol at the Ukrainian Navy Headquarters, there are 100 Ukrainian Naval Officers and enlisted troops guarding the facility. At approximately 2300 local police arrived, appearing to be providing protection and support for a pro-Russian group. The police then moved in and blocked all entrances, not allowing any personnel movement in or out. Ukrainian Navy states they will fight if their base is breached. No firearms in the hands of the Ukrainian Navy, only sticks and pipes. At approximately 2315, Berkut and other police blocked all roads on the outskirts of Sevastopol, blocking all traffic. Locals assess an attack is imminent. . . . [Separatist military leaders] arrived at the Marine Battalion in Feodosiya via Mi-8 helicopter. They talk through the gate, offering larger salaries among other things. The Marines again swear their allegiance to the Ukrainian flag. . . . Marines in Feodosiya remain ready to fight. They have their BTR-80s staged around their perimeter (each with a 14.5 mm machine gun), mortar tubes, and all members are on high alert and state that they will fight until the end, even though most understand it means the end of their lives. The Ukrainian commanders understand the need for negotiations and continue attempts with local unit Russian commanders."

Father Heorhiy Kovalenko, a spokesman for the Ukrainian Orthodox Church's Moscow Patriarchy (not the Kyiv Patriarchy, which had long supported Euromaidan) made a strong statement against the Russian incursion, decrying Russia's "false excuse" for moving troops into Ukraine as a violation of God's commandment, "do not lie." Foreign aggression means violence, he told parishioners, which is a violation of God's commandments. "Sadly, this is being done by those who consider themselves to be followers of the same faith with us," he said, before concluding that God does not bless those who use violence. The Ukrainian Orthodox Church's Kyiv Patriarchy issued a similarly strong message: "We call on the Russian authorities to come to their senses and stop their aggression against Ukraine and immediately pull out Russian troops from Ukrainian lands. All of the responsibility before God and mankind for the irreparable consequences [of these actions] fully falls on the leadership of Russia. There is no oppression by language, nation, or denomination in our country. Therefore, we witness that all the efforts of Russian propaganda to represent all the events in Ukraine as 'fascist coup d'état' and an 'extremists' victory' absolutely do not correspond to reality." This was quite a contrast to the message from the Orthodox Church's press service in Moscow, which stated on the same day that "the Russian people have the right to be reunited under a single government body" and that "the mission of Russian soldiers is to protect freedom and identity" in Crimea.

Protesters presented a new petition to the Embassy: "We, undersigned representatives of civil society of Ukraine, are deeply concerned with the fact that Russia has begun unprovoked aggression against our country. . . . According to the Budapest Memorandum, the US, UK, and Russia all agreed to protect the sovereignty and territorial integrity of Ukraine . . . we request [the signatories] to take all necessary measures to protect the independence, sovereignty, and territorial integrity of Ukraine. . . . Freedom is a common value of our countries; let's confirm it using real actions and not just words." Just after the protesters departed, Ukrainian media reported that Russian troops seized the office of the Ukrainian president's representative in Simferopol as two large Russian antisubmarine ships arrived in Sevastopol in violation of Russia's lease agreement of the facility.

The new Ukrainian government's plan for addressing the pro-Russian (and likely Russia-sponsored) protests in the east was to deploy new governors, mostly well-connected businessmen, to the area to try to make quick progress on local economic problems and show that the people of eastern Ukraine could trust the new government. Donetsk businessman Serhiy Taruta was given the governorship of Donetsk, and Ihor Kolomoyskyi was dispatched to Dnipropetrovsk. Taruta, a native of Mariupol in eastern Ukraine, had a net worth north of $2.5 billion and held major metallurgical and sports interests. As head of the Industrial Union of Donbas, he had deep roots in the regional economy and understood how the Donbas functioned. Kolomoyskyi's reputation was rougher. Possessing large assets in banking, airlines, and media, Kolomoyskyi had long been accused of using muscle and sharp elbows to get his way in the business world. The appointment of billionaire oligarchs to key governorships seemed at odds with the Maidan's clean slate, clean governance ethos, but it also reflected the new government's recognition that the critical situation in the east demanded people who knew the region, had authority locally, and could bring rapid and noticeable improvements.

Russia's Rossiya 24 channel further increased the virulence of its anti-Maidan propaganda, claiming people were terrorized on Kyiv's streets and that fascists and neo-Nazis were beating the Russian-speaking population in Ukraine. They further claimed that the sniper shootings were a provocation by those on Maidan, arranging the shooting of themselves in a plot orchestrated by foreign embassies in Kyiv—first and foremost, the US Embassy. Through this distorted prism, Yanukovych was supposedly driven out of office by Nazis with guns. Russian churches were under assault. The news was mixed with Second World War stock photos of Nazi atrocities just to be certain that viewers made the appropriately enraging historic connections. At the same time, in a not fictitious act of aggression, Russian soldiers surrounded Ukraine's infantry base in Pryvolne in central Crimea.

Amid the mounting tension surrounding the increasing recognition of Russia's covert invasion, the Rada passed several bills during a closed session on military mobilization and security at key infrastructure points, such as airports and nuclear power plants. They also passed bills requesting a Russian withdrawal from Crimea and asking Western countries, especially signatories to the Budapest Memorandum, to formally observe the situation in Ukraine. Getting international observers into the country to refute claims of lawlessness and persecution of Russian speakers was the best chance for Ukraine to stave off a creeping invasion.

Ambassador Pyatt again met Ukrainian Foreign Minister Deshchytsia that Sunday, March 2. When Deshchytsia asked if Ukraine could request military assistance from the United States and whether the annual Sea Breeze military exercise could be held earlier than planned, Pyatt emphasized that the US response to events in Ukraine was diplomatic, not military. Getting an OSCE or UN observation mission on the ground was key, Pyatt indicated. Our ambassador suggested that Ukraine begin broadcasting more local television shows in Russian and take other steps to assure Russian-speaking populations that they were valued in the new Ukraine. Deshchytsia agreed.

"How were the conversations between Yatseniuk and Medvedev?" asked Ambassador Pyatt.

"Kind of provocative," answered Deshchytsia. "He threatened to deploy additional Russian forces if we continue the 'pogroms.' What are they talking about? Do they actually believe the things they say?" He paused for a while. "What is Putin thinking?" he asked. "Is he crazy?" "He definitely sees the democratic gains made by Maidan as a threat," responded Ambassador Pyatt. "Seeking to reverse what Maidan accomplished starts in Crimea for them. But we certainly don't yet know the endgame. Your policy to avoid provocations and keep things as stable and calm as possible is wise."

Meanwhile, in the east of Ukraine, the "beautiful east" activities that Maksimov had glowingly previewed continued. In Odesa, about three hundred pro-Russian activists attacked the regional administration building. In Donetsk, about fifty pro-Russian demonstrators broke windows trying to enter their regional administration building. In yet more saber rattling, the Russian military began additional snap exercises in its Kaliningrad exclave on the Baltic Sea involving more than 3,500 Baltic Fleet servicemen. Even more distressingly, Ukrainian Ministry of Foreign Affairs spokesman Perebyinis stated that the Russian military was accumulating hardware on the borders of Ukraine's Kharkiv, Luhansk, and Donetsk regions. According to the Ukrainian Defense Ministry, the Russian Black Sea Fleet presented their troops in Crimea with an ultimatum—all Ukrainian troops in Crimea had until 5:00 a.m. the next day to surrender or face being taken by force.

Meanwhile, Russia's information war was unrelenting. Though the Russian government claimed that at least 143,000 refugees had fled from supposed persecution and lawlessness in Ukraine, the UN High Commission on Refugees could find no evidence at all of any significant refugee movement across the Russia-Ukraine border. Meanwhile, Russian television broadcast upbeat reports about how local Crimeans, not Russian military, were asserting control over Ukrainian military units on the peninsula. At the same time, the Ukrainian Defense Ministry published a statement saying that there had been no significant defections among their units in Crimea. Russian television cheered Foreign Minister Lavrov's statements in Geneva criticizing the West, portraying his and other officials' stridently defiant chords as signs of Russia's strength. Valeriya Lutkovska, the Yanukovych-appointed ombudsman of Ukraine, returned from a trip to Crimea and asserted that she had not received a single complaint with regard to the actual violation of the rights of Russian speakers in Crimea. She warned of the dangers of the continuing information war within and about Crimea and urged Ukrainian journalists to work carefully and seek balance to establish credibility in covering events.

Monday morning, March 3, Secretary Kerry announced that he would come to Kyiv the following day. It was an incredibly short time to plan for the visit of a secretary of state, a visit that would be run by David with my wife, Natalya, in charge of logistics. The biggest gift in Secretary Kerry's pocket during his Kyiv visit was a $1 billion loan guarantee for the Ukrainian government, in addition to other technical assistance to get Ukraine back on track toward a much larger inflow of capital from the International Monetary Fund. Kerry visited the new Shrine to Fallen Heroes on Maidan with Ukrainian Orthodox Church Patriarch Filaret and leaders of Ukraine's Muslim, Jewish, and non-Orthodox Christian communities. After a moving ceremony, he held meetings with the new government, Rada leaders, and civil society. He also took time to come by the Embassy for a meet-and-greet, during which he thanked everyone for the long hours over recent months. As he was leaving, he walked up to my son, Andrew, and asked him how he was doing. "You know," he said to Andrew with a smile. "I grew up as a kid of diplomats. I know how it is. Hang in there!" Good advice for all of us.

On the morning of March 4, Putin's Defense Minister Sergey Shoygu ordered an end to the western military district snap military exercise, calling for a return of all Russian troops to their barracks by March 7. While this order appeared to be a de-escalation, Russian troops fired warning shots in the vicinity of the still Ukrainian-controlled Belbek Air Base in Crimea. In a televised address, President Putin took additional potshots at the legitimacy of the new government in Kyiv. Though the entire world was aware of Russian military actions in Crimea, he barefacedly maintained that there was "no need" at present for Russian military action in Ukraine. We learned that Russian government statements, especially from Putin, were only useful for learning the updated version of the Russian propaganda/psychological warfare talking points—not for learning anything useful about the ground truth.

In Geneva on Wednesday, March 5, representatives of the United States, UK, and Ukraine met in Paris for Budapest Memorandum consultations. The other signatory, Russia, was invited but declined to show. All of these countries, including Russia, had guaranteed Ukraine's territorial integrity when it voluntarily gave up nuclear weapons in 1994. The meeting, hosted by Secretary Kerry, concluded with a strong joint statement but no desire to move the conversation beyond diplomatic or economic action as Putin's hybrid war pressed on.

Meanwhile, there were more developments in the mostly one-sided information war. A new telephone call intercept, this time between Estonian Defense Minister Urmas Paet and EU High Representative for Foreign Affairs and Security Policy Catherine Ashton, was strategically leaked onto the internet. In the call, Paet talks about the lack of trust between players in the new Ukrainian coalition government, and then seems to suggest that it was not the Yanukovych government that ordered snipers to fire on protesters, but rather the protesters themselves or some element of the Ukrainian opposition. He repeated a specious claim that he said he heard from a Ukrainian doctor, later identified as Maidan medic Dr. Olha Bohomolets, that the bullets that hit police and protesters were from the same source. Like the intercepted and leaked Pyatt-Nuland "Fuck the EU" call, it was only a fragment of the conversation, released as cut by the leaker. After the recording appeared, Defense Minister Paet immediately said that he was simply repeating rumors he had heard in Kyiv, not asserting fact. Later, Dr. Bohomolets told journalists that she couldn't understand how Paet misinterpreted her words in this way, and that she never suggested or believed that Euromaidan organizers were complicit in their own massacre. But the damage was done, as one of the most outrageous conspiracy theories about the massacre on Maidan now had new legs and was off and running. As we had observers on the Maidan during the opening hours of the massacre, we knew where the firing positions were and that this was a blatant lie; it was dispiriting to hear a pernicious conspiracy theory repeated at the highest levels of European governments. This information operation coincided with the fictitious announcement in Russia that the new government in Kyiv hired three hundred American mercenaries with combat experience from Academi, the firm formerly known as Blackwater, to come to Kyiv. At the Embassy, we could just shake our heads and wonder if anyone believed this stuff. Sadly, the answer was yes.

In a major move in Washington, President Obama that day ordered an asset freeze and travel ban on Russian and Crimean officials involved in the creeping invasion. The same day, more than twenty Jewish community leaders sent an open letter to President Putin rejecting Russian claims that the new government in Ukraine was anti-Semitic or that there was any widespread violence or discrimination against ethnic Jews or Russian speakers.

That afternoon Naval Attaché Leo Hmelevsky was alarmed by word from his naval contacts in Crimea: "The situation at the Ukrainian Naval Forces Headquarters in Sevastopol is critical. The HQ is completely blocked and besieged by an unarmed but hostile mob of demonstrators. A storm/capture of the HQ is highly possible." Following Putin's statement denying direct Russian military involvement in Crimea, there seemed to be a push to "civilianize" these kinds of takeovers, making them appear more like an evil funhouse mirror image of Maidan's takeover of government buildings in Kyiv. Back in Kyiv, the Ministry of Foreign Affairs raised the Ukrainian naval flag in support of the sailors and their family members defending the Ukrainian Navy's Crimean headquarters.

Meanwhile, the Task Force started seeing pictures and reports in the Ukrainian press and social media of a massive convoy, more than forty vehicles, including many buses, streaming through Crimean checkpoints en route to Sevastopol. The vehicles had Russian military license plates identifying them as part of the Southern Military District. Jim Thorn, a consular officer working on the Task Force that day, updated everyone: "Currently the headquarters of the Ukrainian Navy is surrounded by men in black uniforms with no markings (according to our information—possibly Russian Cossacks). Behind them are armed Russian soldiers. . . . Are the thirty buses with armed Russian titushky arriving in Sevastopol preparing a provocation against the headquarters of the Ukrainian Navy?" It wouldn't be surprising—we just received word that the air defense base near Evpatoria was breached by Russian forces. Press stated that "Ukrainian forces refused to freely give up access, but did not fight back."

Russian forces next seized the Ukrainian customs control offices in Kerch. Journalists and amateur observers in Crimea claimed to have spotted the

"Vostok" battalion of the 18th mechanized brigade out of Chechnya, soldiers of 31st Air Assault Airborne Brigade from Ulyanovsk, and elements of the 22nd Brigade from Krasnodar. While the Russian Black Sea Fleet forces were in Crimea under agreement with the Ukrainian government, the presence of any of these other units would represent a clear violation of Russia-Ukraine agreements—though the Russian government continued to refute observable reality in a clear demonstration of implausible deniability. Also that night, about 150 Russian soldiers tried to take control of a Ukrainian surface-to-air anti-aircraft missile regiment around Yalta.

The invasion continued to grind forward. Russian motorcyclists stopped the car of Ukrainian State Border Guard Service Colonel General Mykhailo Koval, the agency's personnel director, slashed his tires, and kidnapped him near the Border Guard's offices in Yalta. Local authorities stated that these bikers merely intended to drive him to the airport and force him to fly out against his will. Sitting in his car outside a café after visiting a besieged Ukrainian naval base, UN Envoy to Ukraine Robert Serry was blockaded by uniformed men without insignia who demanded that he leave Crimea immediately. The men lowered their weapons at the UN envoy, threatening his life. "This is pretty outrageous behavior even by the standards of the Russian invasion of Crimea," wrote Ambassador Pyatt to the Task Force.

Later in the day, the Crimean parliament passed a bill with the stated goal of bringing Crimea "into the Russian Federation with the rights of a subject of the Russian Federation." Given the treasonous language, the bill was clearly unconstitutional. Then, in an epic grab of potentially billions of dollars in assets, the parliament voted to "nationalize" all property of Ukrainian state companies in Crimea. They also decided that the hastily convened upcoming referendum, which local authorities so far had claimed would only address the question of Crimea's increased autonomy within Ukraine, would now have two questions: (1) Should Crimea become part of the Russian Federation? and (2) Should Crimea return to its 1992 constitution under which it had greater autonomy? The second question was merely a fig leaf to cover the fact that the referendum was really about separatism and annexation. It should be emphasized that in the last major parliamentary elections in 2010, pro-Russian parties in Crimea received only 6.8 percent of the vote, and even those parties did not openly support Crimea's separation from Ukraine. Local calls from within Crimea to join with Russia were a relic of the early to mid-1990s. Just days before, the previous parliamentary speaker was unwilling to put treason up for a vote. But with the Russian military sweeping across the peninsula and gunmen in the parliament, everything was suddenly different. Crimea's Deputy Prime Minister Rustam Temirgaliev announced to the press that "the only lawful armed force on the territory of the Crimea is the Russian armed forces." The Russian government still denied the deployment of its armed forces in Crimea outside its basing agreement despite the deputy PM's kind words. The Crimean Tatar Mejlis called for all Crimeans to boycott the referendum whose outcome seemed well known in advance. The next day, Russian and pro-Russian groups would storm parts of the Ukrainian naval headquarters in Sevastopol and beat Ukrainian journalists recording their actions.

At this point, less than two weeks had passed since Yanukovych had absconded from Kyiv and taken refuge in Russia. The swiftness of Putin's hybrid invasion of Crimea suggests that such plans were not hastily cobbled together after Yanukovych had fled. The pieces, including the creation of local militias in recent months by a cabal of Crimean politicians who seemed to spend more time in Moscow than Simferopol, fit together too neatly. Had Yanukovych stayed in power, Russian access to Crimea on favorable terms was guaranteed, and invasion would be redundant. But Kyiv's sudden change in power cleared the way for opportunistic vengeance. Putin's statecraft was steeped in Russian nationalism, wrapped in the robes of Russian Orthodoxy, and aimed at reversing supposed "humiliations" suffered by Russia, including, as Putin saw it, the dissolution of the Soviet Union and the loss of Ukraine, including the Crimean peninsula. Putin, who regularly invoked the injustices supposedly inflicted upon ethnic Russians in the "near abroad"—independent countries that had once been constituent republics of the USSR—as justification for aggressive policies, was following the same script in Crimea as he would soon attempt in the Donbas region of southeastern Ukraine. He likely calculated correctly that the international community, including the major Western powers, would criticize, denounce, and perhaps even sanction him, but would stop far short of any military response to his aggression. To be sure, economic sanctions would sting, but he was prepared to bear them. Sanctions against his inner circle could even have the hidden benefit of forcing well-connected oligarchs to withdraw their assets from overseas back to Russia, giving Putin even more control over them. The sanctions would further feed the official narrative of Russia as a great nation set upon by hostile competitive powers. And the theft of Crimea would be incorporated into a powerful narrative that Putin was the strongman strategist who restored Russia's greatness.

Elizabeth had stopped by my desk. We were all still digesting the latest news that the Crimean autonomy referendum had been moved up for the second time, now to March 16—just twelve days away. What were they in such a hurry to do? Gain increased autonomy within Ukraine, or was the real goal more extreme?

"Would you like to get out to Donetsk?" Elizabeth asked.

I had just been reading about the dueling pro-Ukrainian unity and pro-Russian rallies in the east over the last few days. I knew that Ambassador Pyatt had wanted some of us from the Embassy to join a group of European diplomats heading east to get a better feeling for events on the ground.

"Sure, when?" I asked.

"Tonight," she answered. "Don't you keep your suitcase packed? Get a sat phone, and check in every four hours. Have fun."

12

LOCKING DOWN CRIMEA, PRYING OPEN THE EAST

Greg Pfleger from the Political Section and I were partners for the trip to Donetsk. We headed to Kyiv's Boryspil airport that night to board our Ukraine International Airlines flight. The other passengers seemed jumpy and agitated. A fear of flying, especially among older persons, seemed endemic in that part of the world, and Greg and I joked about it to pass the time in the terminal.

On the plane, just minutes after takeoff, shouts rang out from the back of the plane over the roar of the engine. "Dym idyot! Dym idyot!" someone yelled, then someone else. That was Russian for "Smoke!" Greg and I gave each other knowing looks, as if to say, "God, people really are jumpy here!" Then a terrified cabinet attendant sprinted forward from the back of the plane toward the cockpit. . . . No more knowing looks.

The aft of the plane filled with smoke, which rolled forward past where we were sitting toward the cockpit. The plane felt out of control as it banked sharply to return for an emergency landing at the airport in Kyiv. After a few minutes, which felt much longer, we were back on the ground and had completed a five-minute Kyiv-to-Kyiv flight. We all quickly disembarked and, a bit rattled, sat back down in the terminal. After about forty-five minutes, an airline representative came out.

"Please accept our apologies about the technical problem on this aircraft," he said. "Thanks for your patience. We have solved the issue and are ready to reboard."

"On the same plane?" yelled an older woman in a shawl. "Are you insane? None of us are getting back on that plane!"

The weary-eyed Ukrainian airline worker looked like he expected this reaction. "We have fixed the problem and the plane is safe to fly. Unfortunately, we do not have another aircraft here to take you to Donetsk tonight."

"You get one!" yelled another older woman. "Fly one in from Madagascar! Do what you need to do! No one is getting back on that plane! Do you take us for idiots?" Then an impromptu group of Ukrainian grandmothers from the flight encircled the besieged airline official, berating him from all directions. After a few minutes as the focal point of their ire, the man slunk away. In half an hour, we were on a plane—supposedly a different plane, though who knows—to Donetsk.

With its reputation as a hub of Ukraine's eastern factory heartland, I had expected Donetsk to be gray, Soviet, and bleakly industrial. Actually, I found it to be a pleasant town with plenty of green space, toy stores, and even a good upscale microbrew pub. Under Donetsk native Yanukovych's presidency, money flowed in and the city prospered. The roads were beautifully maintained; the flowers in the traffic medians were tastefully arranged. The stadium for the hometown heroes, footballers Donetsk "Shakhtar," had a state-of-the-art look from the outside. For one last precious moment, it was still an easy place to relax and chat over a decent meal.

In the morning, Greg and I joined British and Spanish diplomats for meetings designed to get a wide range of views regarding the unfolding situation in Donetsk. One important man who suddenly had much more time to chat was the recently fired Party of Regions governor Andriy Shyshatskiy. Pro-Russian protesters had stormed the regional administration building four times in the past two weeks, so life had become pretty difficult and unstable for him. "There were a lot of protesters," he noted. "But we really focused on the ones with the fancy digital radios. Twelve of them. We recognize most of the politically active folks around here, but not those guys. They had special equipment and stood out a bit."

"Do you think that these kinds of protests will keep going?" I asked.

"Well, as long as the Russian money keeps coming, I don't see why they couldn't easily keep up regular rallies with three to five thousand people," he replied. "It's not too hard."

During the meeting Shyshatskiy often seemed lost in thought, reassessing the events of the last month. "You know, it is always the Russian press who asks me if a 'Crimean scenario' is possible in our Donbas, or whether outside agitators could influence our own local sympathizers to the point where they would invite a foreign power to help them break away from Ukraine." He took another long pause. "Coming from foreign media, this disturbs me, because the question itself is built on certain assumptions. I always firmly say no. But the truth is that if the Crimean scenario works well in Crimea, why wouldn't it be implemented in other parts of Ukraine? And why wouldn't we be next in line? A provocation involving some of the Russian tourists could easily be used to justify Russian military action here. The situation is much like that of Crimea. All that is needed is a spark."

We asked him about the use of paid muscle in Donetsk politics. "Yes, our own titushky are having a banner year I would say. I needed some for an event I was going to have a few weeks ago, and there were none available! Can you believe it? They now only accept cash payments, up front. How times change, that they can now be so picky. The pro-Russian groups seem to have them all locked up."

On Tuesday, March 11, Interior Ministry Avakov announced that his ministry had arrested a Russian intelligence officer in Donetsk, and local press reported that the man had explosives that he planned to use in "provocations" around the city. This was ominous—one well-placed bomb could be the official excuse for a full-scale invasion. Yehor Firsov, the lanky, dark-haired leader of the Ukrainian Democratic Alliance for Reforms (UDAR) in Donetsk, was happy to talk about the pro-Russian demonstrators: "We now call those protests 'tourist meetings' since so many Russian 'tourists' seem to show up there. These guys seem inclined to organize violence, but the police don't mess with them at all because no one is certain who is really in power around here these days."

A local political science professor we met agreed with Firsov. "It is mostly Russian citizens, not primarily locals, who have been out in force at recent protests. They came out in our main square with flags bearing slogans such as 'Donbas is Russia.' Around here, no one was ever asking the question of whether Donbas was or wasn't Russia. This is, well, settled business. But here were these young Russian men in black clothes, and no one knew where they came from."

A leader of a local energy firm shared similar sentiments: "The Russian 'tourists' are the most dangerous as they pretend to be local residents. But as our Donetsk demonstrations are not permanent like Maidan in Kyiv, meaning that they flare up and then melt away, it is hard to identify exactly who these people are. But there are a few dead giveaways. I saw the video a week ago of some of these guys burning some banners of our Donetsk 'Shakhtar' football team. They didn't even know what it was—they thought it was some Ukrainian garbage. For anyone from here, that's sacrilege. Everyone loves 'Shakhtar'; it's the pride of our town. This may not mean much for you as an outsider, but for someone from Donetsk, I have to say that it's genetically impossible that these were our guys."

Another local journalist agreed: "Most of these current pro-Russian protest group leaders can be identified as Russian citizens. I've heard them speak and seen them hanging out in their Russian football team shirts. Eight buses with about two hundred Russians arrived downtown for the March 3 protests. We've also seen quite a few demobilized Russian military personnel from Voronezh and Belgorod who are now residing here in Donetsk. As journalists, we can't track down the source of their income. I could make some dark guesses, but really, we just don't know for sure."

"I wouldn't say that there are no locals at the protests, though," said the journalist, correcting himself. "There are some, of course, and this speaks to the effectiveness of the Russian information war here. The Russian TV channels try to smear the entire new government through vilifying the Ukrainian right wing. Of course, Russia has its own right wing, but no one gives them a hard time about it. An absolute majority of people in Donetsk do support a united Ukraine, but many of those same people have also bought into bizarre notions presented to them by the Russian media about Maidan, fascists, threats to Russian speakers, etcetera, etcetera." A prominent local blogger who joined the group late spoke up. "You know, both sides, the Maidan and anti-Maidan, pro-unity and anti-unity, all use the Russian [social networking] websites Odnoklasskini and VKontakte to call their rallies. But the Russian government uses quite active measures on those sites, so that puts the pro-unity folks at a definite disadvantage."

A representative of the Committee of Voters of Ukraine told us that pro-Russian groups were never a big deal in Donetsk before because they were subordinate to the Party of Regions. "But now," he continued. "They have leave to do whatever they want, and they can fall under the influence of minor local leaders with eccentric agendas or actual Russian agents of influence. Many of them are just not from around here. Did you see what happened to Klitschko and Akhmetov on March 8? They were booed, and some people threw rocks at them. Now, say what you want about Klitschko as an opposition leader, but he is first and foremost a champion boxer from eastern Ukraine. Even people who don't agree with him respect him. And Akhmetov employs 300,000 people in Ukraine, most of them here in Donetsk. He is our town's benefactor and kingmaker. No one from Donetsk would have disrespected them like that."

After some scheduling issues, we were finally able to see freshly appointed Governor Taruta. While many of Ukraine's industrial elite had a hard-edged demeanor, Taruta looked like a suave version of Alan Greenspan with better hair. Calm and soft spoken, his bearing contrasted with the chaos outside the regional administration building. His staff was young, mostly Western educated, and in one case, a Canadian citizen. After passing through a line of riot police to enter the regional administration building, we made our way up to Taruta's spacious offices.

"My plan is to protect Ukraine's territorial integrity through improving the quality of life in Donetsk," he explained. "Poverty is the main reason for radicalism, and if we raise the share of small and medium enterprises, we can tackle that. We can get wealth and ownership flowing out to the disenfranchised, and that is the way to give people a stake in stability." It sounded like a practical, well-reasoned plan in the middle of an unhinged chain of events.

One of Taruta's advisers jumped in with a word of warning. "We're likely to get a lot of resistance," he cautioned. "Most of the old holdover mayors are in the pro-Russian camp. Maidan was about transparency, and so are we, and that's very frightening to them and the corruption-friendly way that they do business. They organize buses of folks from their towns to come to the pro-Russia rallies, pay them stipends, and buy everyone lunch. This is mostly because these mayors don't see any good career prospects under the new government due to the deep corruption visible if you scratch the surface. It's a decision based on their personal financial and career interests, not really on any sort of ideology."

Taruta continued: "We'll start with little things to show that we are serious about transparency. I want to invite the local media into our government, right into our offices, in ways that we never have before. I want to increase the effectiveness of our local services through e-governance and other initiatives. I want our constituents to feel that we are responsible to them. We'll do some small symbolic stuff, like having all civil servants wear name badges so that they can be identified and commented on electronically. And we greatly need international support, including US support. I must show this city real positive change in the next six months." His presentation was inspiring, but the ideas spinning out of Taruta's office seemed a long way from the situation on the street.

I turned to one of Taruta's aides who was escorting us out, a slightly portly man in his twenties who looked like he spent a lot of time in front of a computer screen. "It all sounds very promising . . . but the security situation is tough. Do you have the six months you need before locals really feel the benefits of your plan?"

"We simply must succeed," he answered. "We know well that the fate of eastern Ukraine and our whole country depends on it. There's no other choice."

Reviewing everything on the flight back to Kyiv, the puzzle pieces formed a disturbing picture. Was the trouble brewing in the east intended as a distraction during the grab of Crimea, or was it about to become the new headline?

While at home on Sunday, March 9, I saw a media report on my Black-Berry that Andrei Shchekun, the Euromaidan Crimea activist we had met in Simferopol not even one month before, had been kidnapped, his whereabouts unknown. Lots of people were going missing in Crimea, but I had met Andrei, so his disappearance really hit me in the gut. I knew that he had a wife and family and a big friendly smile. For him to be pulled into this kind of violent morass seemed ironic and unfair. He had insisted to me that there was no international dimension to the problems he worked on, that he could care less about any competition between the West and Russia, and that all he wanted was to help clean up his own local government. But he was an ethnic Ukrainian and a Euromaidan supporter, both of which made his Crimean home of the last twenty-three years an increasingly dangerous place to be. His disappearance also provoked a guilty twinge of remorse that accompanied the inevitable question I was forced to ask myself, "He didn't get picked up because he met with me, did he?"

In Crimea, every day brought new reports of attacks on Ukrainian military outposts and journalists. Acting Ukrainian Defense Minister Ihor Tenyukh issued a statement that there were about 18,000 Russian soldiers on the Crimean peninsula. He added, "Moreover, Russia rotates army specialty units within its mechanized battalions. . . . We know every step that takes place in Crimea: how the rotation is happening, where equipment is moving, and what they are doing. For example, Russia has a rotation program in Crimea in which Special Forces from Chechnya are brought in."

Former President Yanukovych held a fifteen-minute press event on March 11, during which he read a prepared statement and took no questions. He defiantly argued from Russia that he was still the legitimate president of Ukraine. He also claimed that the Ukrainian presidential elections planned for May 25 were illegal, that the new government in Kyiv was composed of fascists (of course), and that he would soon return to Ukraine. He barely touched on Crimea and its planned secessionist referendum though it represented open treason in the nation he still claimed to lead. His entire statement was in Russian, not Ukrainian. The same day, the press reported that "uniformed troops without insignia" sighted their weapons on an Organization for Security and Co-operation in Europe (OSCE) observer mission and threatened to open fire if it drove over the border between two Ukrainian regions—Crimea and Kherson.

Meanwhile, reports from our American Citizen Services unit in the Consular Section, such as this one posted on March 12, pointed to gradually increasing pressure on normal folks in Crimea:

> We have a church group of eight US citizens (including three minors and one handicapped) residing in Sevastopol for the past ten years. Until today, they saw no reason to leave the area and reported that the situation was calm as usual, so they were just observing in hopes that they wouldn't need to leave. . . . Then they noticed a significant and very obvious increase of anti-American sentiment among the population. A mere word in English draws too much attention to them. Besides, two of them are African Americans that cannot blend in. There has been no aggression or violence so far. However, the tension grows, and they get unfriendly stares wherever they go. The population is under massive

influence of propaganda from Russian media exclusively having all
Ukrainian TV channels shut down recently, and our missionaries do
not feel safe in Sevastopol any longer.

With Moscow's information war heating up, a new fake email was suddenly
plastered on the internet, supposedly from our own Defense Attaché Office's
(DAO's) J. P. Gresh to a colonel in the Ukraine Armed Forces' General Staff demanding "false flag" operations in Crimea to frame Russia. J. P. was Elizabeth's
husband, and this disgusting falsehood connected to his name was terrifying.
The forged letter read, "Events are moving rapidly in Crimea. Our friends in
Washington expect more decisive actions from your network. I think it's time
to implement the plan we discussed lately. Your job is to cause some problems
to the transport hubs in the southeast in order to frame-up the neighbor. It
will create favorable conditions for Pentagon and the Company to act. Do not
waste time, my friend. Respectfully, Jason P. Gresh, Lieutenant Colonel, US
Army, Assistant Army Attaché." Of course, the implication that the US Em-
bassy/military was ordering attacks on Crimean infrastructure was catnip for
anti-Western conspiracy theorists, as the inventors of the fake letter well knew.
After some Google research, we saw that one of the first distributors of the
bogus letter was a conspiracist blogger from the US southwest who slandered
the parents of children murdered in the Newtown Connecticut massacre to
support a conspiracy theory that the attack was faked as part of a wider plot to
deny Americans their guns. And who on occasion claimed to influence trash
pickup with her mind. Clearly, it was unnecessary to gain the acquiescence of
reliable news organizations to get the planted information out. In the internet
age, any fabulist with a substantial following would suffice.

On Wednesday, March 12, Prime Minister Yatsenyuk held an Oval Office
meeting in Washington with President Obama and gained additional promises
of support from administration and congressional leaders. While reading that
news, I received an update from Valentyna: "While some of the journalists
kidnapped a few days ago with Andriy Shchekun were released, he and his
colleague were not. Nobody knows where they are now." There was nothing to
do other than pray for him. A clash of two groups of demonstrators in Donetsk
on Thursday night left two dead, the first protest-related deaths following the
return of calm to Kyiv. It was a troubling sign that things were deteriorating in
the east. While the Ukrainian press stated that the "street fighters" were bused

in from Russia, the Russian Foreign Affairs Ministry immediately cited the incident as "proof" that "Kyiv authorities are not in control of the situation in the country" and declared that Russia "reserves the right to protect" Russians abroad, whatever that meant.

On that Friday, March 14, Ukraine's Border Guards informed us that they apprehended one of Russia's "green men." Their statement was in imperfect English: "This morning, a border detail patrolling the border area near Chongar settlement apprehended the Russian Federation Armed Forces representative. He turned out to be a native of Chechen-Ingush Soviet Union Republic, a military of unit 27777, Sukharov Ramzan. Kalashnikov rifle and 180 rounds of ammunition for it, Makarov gun, military uniform and body armor were detected in the trunk of the car he was moving by. Circumstances of the incident are being specified now. After filtration measures, the military of Russian Federation Armed Forces will be transferred to other law-enforcement bodies."

A large congressional delegation comprising eight senators headed by Senator John McCain was scheduled to arrive on Saturday, March 15. Several Public Affairs and Regional Security staff from the Embassy had traveled to Donetsk to prepare for the possibility that the delegation would go there. The Embassy personnel were safely on the other side of Donetsk during the previous night's clashes, but they questioned eyewitnesses the next morning. Tuck Evans sent his conclusions to the Task Force:

> Our discussions in Donetsk today suggest that Russian claims of violence instigated against pro-Russian and ethnic Russians are false. The following notes are based on PAS [Public Affairs Section] and RSO [Regional Security Office] teams' discussions with multiple sources (police, local business, taxi drivers, protest participants, and civil society), all of whom witnessed or had observers at Donetsk's Lenin Square last night where Pro-Ukrainian and Pro-Russian groups had a standoff that turned violent. . . . The pro-Ukraine groups at the demonstration were peaceful. . . . Pro-Ukraine group MAY have included some demonstrators from Kyiv or western Ukraine, but the leader of a local Donetsk civil society coordinating NGO commented that many of their partner organizations and members (locals) were at Lenin Square, too. Several sources said the majority of the pro-Ukraine protesters were local Donetsk. . . . Pro-Russian protesters said to be more "mixed." One

source commented they were made up of three elements: (1) Russian "tourists" (ru-titushky) bused into Donetsk several weeks ago, (2) criminal elements brought in from nearby villages (the "typical" titushky scenario), (3) regular pro-Russian/communist/USSR nostalgics from local Donetsk population (the least violent of the three) animated by language and religious fears. Some elements of the pro-Russian groups were extremely aggressive. They threw eggs, fireworks, and eventually rocks at the Pro-Ukrainian protesters. The Pro-Ukrainians did not do this. ABOUT THE ATTACK: The Pro-Ukrainian protesters had filed with authorities for a permit to demonstrate (fixed start and end times). Toward the end of the permitted time, as the Pro-Ukrainian groups were breaking up, the ru-titushky moved in across the divide and started attacking, downing, and beating the Pro-Ukrainian protesters. More disconcerting (and seemingly premeditated) cars pulled up and started distributing metal bars to the ru-titushky, who then launched a more ferocious attack on the Pro-Ukrainian protesters, running them down, etc. Many badly beaten as a result. One commentator noted that the tires of some of the buses that had brought the pro-Ukrainian groups had been slashed to prevent their quick exit, thus better trapping them into beatings by the ru-titushky. The fatalities and most severe beatings appear related to a group who were isolated and retreated to their bus where they suffered an especially savage onslaught from the Russians and pro-Russian elements—rocks through windows etc. CONCLUSION: The Russians are here: solid consensus that there are real, non-Ukrainian (Russian) groups at work here. People repeatedly cited last week's pro-Russian groups burning the Shakhtar football flag as sacrilege to any local. "Nobody from Donetsk would EVER do this," we heard again and again.

Of course, the truth concerned Moscow's propagandists only insofar as the tiniest fragments of it could be taken out of context to support their self-serving narratives and fabrications. Their response to honest reporting was to crank up the volume even higher, knowing that Russia's media-intelligence complex had the biggest megaphone around. One effort among many was a pro-Putin petition signed in Russia by a number of prominent Russian artists and musicians to demonstrate support for the Russian government's policies on Ukraine (and specifically Ukraine's Crimea). Ukrainians ridiculed this petition when it was soon revealed that one of the supposed signatories had been dead for years. While the online version of the petition was quickly changed to remove the error, the old cached electronic version was still making the rounds.

Then, late Friday night, a strange incident in Kharkiv left two dead and five more wounded after what seemed like a staged altercation between unidentified individuals in a blue van with Dnipropetrovsk license plates and a group of pro-Russia protesters led to a gun battle with those inside the city's nationalist Pravyi Sektor office. DAO's J. P. Gresh and Michael Willis were in Kharkiv, and Ambassador Pyatt asked them to go out the next day, look at the scene, talk to witnesses, and get some idea of what happened. J. P. Gresh wrote back: "Consensus seems to be that it was a clear provocation by guys posing as right-wing extremists that started at Ploshcha Svobody and ended up at the Pravyi Sektor office. Some shooting occurred in the back courtyard—windows to Pravyi Sektor office riddled with bullets. Lots of Molotov cocktails. As of last night, the infamous van [used in the initial attack] was still in the courtyard."

On Saturday, March 15, congressional delegation (CODEL) McCain arrived in Kyiv. In addition to McCain, the group included Senators Dick Durbin, Ron Johnson, Jeff Flake, John Barasso, John Hoeven, Chris Murphy, and Sheldon Whitehouse. While the American CODEL was on the ground, dozens of Russian soldiers in helicopters were repelled by Ukrainian forces as they tried to enter a narrow spit of land outside Crimea in the Kherson region to seize a natural gas pumping station. I attended several of the CODEL's events, including the obligatory walk out on Maidan to lay flowers at the memorial to the fallen. Donetsk governor Taruta flew to Kyiv to meet with the delegation as the Embassy couldn't recommend that McCain and the other senators travel to Donetsk given the precarious security situation. Taruta explained his approach to the American senators the same way that I heard him describe it to other Western diplomats earlier.

"The security situation," asked McCain. "Isn't that the real crux of your problems?"

"We'll respond to the security situation gradually by solving the region's economic issues," Taruta replied. "That's the way to deal with this honestly and openly to gain the people's trust."

Taruta impressed as a man doing his best, employing his skills to their maximum effect for his country. Perhaps no one could have foreseen how bad it would get, and that no "normal" plan, nothing reasonable, would have been sufficient.

Sunday, March 16, was the date of Crimea's unconstitutional poll, spearheaded by a Crimean prime minister whose party had only three seats in the parliament. That morning, before the polling had even begun, social media showed telltale signs outside Crimean banks reading: "Dear clients, due to the transition of monetary transactions to being handled in Russian Rubles, the bank will be closed on March 17." No need to actually count the votes—the outcome of the polling was a foregone conclusion.

That morning in Crimea, a Chilean journalist, an UDAR activist, a military prosecutor, and three Greek Catholic priests were reported missing. Outside observers were clearly not welcome. As only approved Russian journalists were able to operate freely in Crimea, it was impossible to get a realistic picture of the situation on the ground. The reports those favored journalists broadcast were uniformly cheery—long lines of voters waiting peacefully to exercise their democratic duty, then emerging and exclaiming proudly that they voted to join Russia and get away from the "fascists." Despite the lack of independent observers, local news and social media sites chronicled various dubious practices, including that deceased citizens were listed on the voter rolls while living Crimean Tatars were not. Crimean Prime Minister Aksyonov predicted 100 percent voter turnout as police reportedly took ballot boxes house-to-house to try to make this forecast come true. By the end of the night, the preordained outcome was officially certified. Crimea's election commission announced that 96.7 percent of voters supported a split from Ukraine. The turnout was quite literally incredible—Euromaidan's Facebook page claimed that 123 percent of Sevastopol's entire 2013 population, including children, voted. The Crimean Rada quickly passed legislation declaring that "the activity of all Ukrainian state organs on Crimean territory ceases, their powers, property, and financial resources pass to the state organs of the Crimean Republic." Thus, Crimea now claimed to be formally "independent" and legally ready to be absorbed by the Russian Federation.

Meanwhile, the EU imposed sanctions against twenty-three Russian and Ukrainian officials involved with the invasion, and President Obama submitted the names of seven more high-level Russian officials to Congress for visa and financial sanctions. In Moscow, President Putin signed a decree recognizing Crimea as an independent state—a move quickly replicated by Venezuela,

North Korea, and the pseudo-state "Abkhazia," which Russia carved away from Georgia by military force in 2008. The newly faux-independent Crimean leadership wasted no time in boarding planes for Moscow the day after the referendum. The Kremlin would move quickly. Delay could only give the West more time to react to the land grab, more time for sanctions, more time for UN resolutions and legal measures in international courts. It was in Moscow's interest to make the seizure a fait accompli expeditiously. French Foreign Minister Laurent Fabius announced that the G8 would suspend Russia's membership. But did the Russian government really care? It was a necessary move but seemed unlikely to make any difference.

On the morning of Tuesday, March 18, President Putin's press office announced that he would deliver a televised live broadcast address on Crimea that afternoon to the Federal Assembly in the Kremlin's St. George Hall. His speech, delivered in the regal white and gold gilded ballroom, was a distillation of all of the themes flogged by the Russian press in recent months. He spoke about the historic connections between Crimea and Russia and the March 16 referendum. He harshly criticized the West for supposed "double standards" for supporting Kosovo's independence and opposing the Crimean invasion. Calling Russia's Soviet-era loss of Crimea an "outrageous historical injustice," he stated that it was only after the fall of the USSR that "Russia realized that it was not simply robbed, it was plundered." Throwing former ally Yanukovych under the bus, he said that he understood Kyiv's protesters who stood against political leaders who "milked the country, fought among themselves for power, assets, and cash flows and did not care much about the ordinary people." However, according to Putin, "these feelings were taken advantage of cynically" by those who "resorted to terror, murder, and riots. . . . Nationalists, neo-Nazis, Russophobes, and anti-Semites executed this coup. They continue to set the tone in Ukraine to this day." He also struck emotional World War II–era chords often and hard, stating that Crimea could not "follow in Bandera's footsteps" by following those who wished to infringe on Russian speakers' rights. The overall narrative was familiar to anyone following Russia's propaganda line on Ukraine, but two of Putin's assertions stuck out: the continued demonstrably false assertion that there was no invasion and that the only Russian troops in Crimea were those allowed under existing Russia-Ukraine treaties, and his assertion that the March 16 poll showed that the Crimean Tatars "also lean toward Russia" despite the fact that the vast majority of that community boycotted the hastily convened election, fearful of what a Russian Crimea would mean for their lives. The years to come would prove their fears were well founded.

Immediately after his speech, Putin signed an annexation agreement with the infant "nation" of Crimea. Perpetual Moscow visitor Volodymyr Kostyan-tynov, Crimean Prime Minister Sergey Aksyonov, and Sevastopol's freshly empowered Alexei Chaly signed for Crimea. The Russian government consid-ered it a done deal. But the practical work of armed occupation continued. The Ukrainian Navy confirmed that a soldier in a topographical mapping unit was killed after masked men in military uniforms without insignia shot him with sniper weapons in Simferopol. After the killing, the Ukrainian military for the first time authorized the use of weapons in Crimea "to protect and preserve the lives of Ukrainian soldiers." Telling their personnel not to fight back was no longer morally tolerable after the murder. Ukrainian press reported that armed men were breaking into the apartments of Ukrainian servicemen's fam-ilies and threatening them. Crimean Deputy Council of Ministers chairman Temirgaliev said that local authorities might "ask" Crimean Tatars to leave land needed for infrastructure development. And a lot of fresh infrastructure would be needed, and for some unknown reason, a lot of it apparently might require Tartar lands.

That night, there was another attack on Ukraine's Naval Headquarters in Sevastopol, this time by unarmed locals, some wearing masks. By morning, Russian soldiers in unmarked uniforms hoisted three Russian flags at the entry gates to the facility. Social media exploded with pictures of dejected Ukrainian naval officers leaving their own headquarters building under the glare of masked, camouflaged gunman, only their eyes visible. Ukraine's naval admi-ral Serhiy Hayduk was taken directly to local prosecutors for some imagined crime. Russian special forces seized the headquarters, as well as several naval vessels that the Ukrainians were unable to move to Odesa. That the conflict had not turned into an actual hot war was a testament both to the restraint of Ukrainian forces and their rational assessment that they would be outgunned in such a conflict. It would not have been a fair fight, just suicide.

In Kyiv, the newly unmasked conflict with Russia meant that there was now no reason to wait to sign the EU Association Agreement—the original reason why Kyiv's protesters took to the streets. Recognizing Ukraine's pre-carious financial and security situation, the EU agreed to drop many tariffs on

Ukrainian imports immediately while Ukraine could wait until November to phase in their own tariff reductions. This would give the Ukrainian market some breathing room, allowing Ukrainian firms to benefit from new sales to the EU before having to open up Ukraine's domestic markets to increased foreign competition. The deal was now on the fast track, set to be signed in just a few days.

Contrary to Russia's rhetoric that Crimea was already "an island" apart from Ukraine, the Crimean peninsula was actually quite economically dependent on the rest of Ukraine. At the time of the Russian invasion, Crimea received 85 to 90 percent of its electricity from Ukraine, with local power plants supplying the remainder. But even these local thermal plants purchased their coal from mainland Ukraine. Moreover, Crimea relied on mainland Ukraine for 80 percent of its water, delivered through the North Crimean Canal, and 90 percent of its food and industrial goods arrived through mainland Ukraine. Breaking this strong and natural economic interdependence would be painful for residents of the Crimean peninsula.

On Tuesday night, March 18, three members of parliament from the rightist Svoboda Party assaulted the head of Ukraine's First National Channel, a public television station, accusing him of treason for broadcasting the Crimea annexation treaty signing from Moscow. Wednesday morning, Prime Minister Yatsenyuk condemned the attack, declaring that it contravened the values of a democratic, European Ukraine. As protesters gathered at Svoboda's offices, it was clear that this incident would be replayed over and over again in the Russian media for propaganda value. Moscow's press had said for months that Ukraine was overrun with rightists who were beating people; now there was finally an incident involving high-level Svoboda figures that reinforced their long-standing narrative. The video would prove very useful across the border. It was an unexpected gift from an unexpected source.

National politics in Ukraine heated up as the presidential election approached in a few months. Chocolate baron, EU integration advocate, former Yanukovych economy minister, and Maidan figure Petro Poroshenko was leading the polls. His confectionery company, Roshen, had factories in both Russia and Ukraine, and his businesses had been under pressure from Russian customs and sanitary officials in recent months. That pressure suddenly ratcheted up on March 20. "At 10:30, a group of unidentified persons seized all production facilities of Roshen in the Lipetsk region [of southwestern Russia]," the head of Roshen Lipetsk's Legal Department told reporters. Factory management was cornered in a conference room while workers were kept outside, unable to begin their shifts. Valentyna and I visited Roshen's modest Kyiv offices and spoke to one of the company's managers. "Under Yanukovych, our politicians were famous for betraying our national interests to Russia. Now the new government is just building up its strength, and Russia is seeing how far economic blackmail will get them with these new people," he said. With economic blunt force and political subtlety, Poroshenko was put on notice that his business interests in Russia were vulnerable.

A flood of high-level Washington officials continued to visit Ukraine. Thursday, March 20, was a 'P' visit. P, Undersecretary for Political Affairs Wendy Sherman, arrived around noon and met acting President Turchynov, who expressed appreciation for US support and requested military aid. As expected, Sherman stated that the United States was looking for other, nonmilitary ways to defuse the crisis. In another meeting, rising young parliamentarians expressed great alarm over the security situation but saw political reform and economic growth as the keys to solving Ukraine's problems. Sherman also met with Petro Poroshenko and toured Maidan before heading to Dnipropetrovsk, where she conferred with civil society activists and Jewish community leaders. Civil society leaders stressed that while their biggest challenge would be fighting corruption, the fear of Russian attack had actually helped to unify their city. Jewish community leaders told Sherman that they were completely supportive of the new government and harshly dismissed the Russian suggestion that they were under threat by "fascists." Their real fear was of Russian military aggression in Dnipropetrovsk. "It's ironic that we are Russian-speaking people who now fear the Russians," one community leader confided to her.

The Russian bear's economic squeeze on Ukraine continued. President Medvedev announced on March 21 that Ukraine owed his nation $16 billion while his government launched further trade actions against Ukraine. The day before, from midnight until approximately 1:00 p.m., Russian customs officials blocked Ukrainian goods from entering the Russian Federation. A high-ranking Ukrainian customs official attributed the action to a Russian Federal Customs Service misinterpretation of an order from Moscow to stop all cargo departing from Russian-controlled Crimea heading to Ukraine's Kherson region. The Russian government appeared focused on keeping Ukrainian assets in Crimea so that they could be grabbed along with the rest of the peninsula.

What stayed could be stolen, what left could not. So the order went out that everything stays.

On March 20, Ukraine's Border Guard officially withdrew its personnel from Crimea "under great pressure." The official announcement attempted to maintain the Border Guard's dignity, stating that "the border guards have done their duty in Crimea. They do not forfeit the state border." It was a bitter pill to swallow, but those left could be murdered. Withdrawal was the only choice.

Patriarch Filaret of the Ukrainian Orthodox Church (Kyiv Patriarchy) had been outspoken throughout the recent months. I thought that his words couldn't get any stronger, but on that day he outdid himself, issuing an eloquent and unequivocal denunciation of the annexation of Crimea:

> The calling of the Church is to testify about the truth. Therefore it is necessary to give a moral evaluation of the annexation, or I should say, Anschluss of the Crimea carried out by the Russian Federation not long ago. On March 18, 2014, Russia's leaders publicly committed three violations of the commandments of God: Do not kill; Do not Tell false witness against your neighbor; Do not covet your neighbor's house . . . (and) anything that is thy neighbor's (Exodus 20:15–17). The consequence of armed aggression of the Russian government against Ukraine has become bloodshed—the murder of the Ukrainian activists by the separatists in Donetsk, the killing of the Crimean Tatar and of the Ukrainian serviceman in the Crimea. Provocateurs, instigated and supported from Russia, sow confusion and call for separatism, and incite civil conflict in the eastern and southern regions of Ukraine. In the Crimea, Ukrainian troops loyal to their oath and their families are subjected to continuous pressure and are intimidated, including using weapons. In occupied Crimea, community activists disappear without a trace. Those who were the occupants' hostages and were released witnessed cruel, inhuman treatment, constant humiliation, death threats, and simulation of execution. The Russian leadership is personally responsible for all this.

The Russian Orthodox Church (ROC) adopted a very different stance. The statement of the Holy Synod of the ROC in Moscow attempted to position the church above the fray: "Having gathered today at a session of the Holy Synod, we once again appeal to Ukraine, so dear to our hearts, and bear witness that the Ukrainian Orthodox Church correspondingly called for and continues to call for peace and for prayer, without identifying with (in contrast with a series of other religious organizations) one or another side of the political conflict." This pious call for peace and prayers in the face of the Kremlin's hybrid aggression likely only sounded convincing to those already wanting to look the other way. The two heads of the Tsarist double-headed eagle, a symbol of Russia, represented the church and the state as two parts of the same organism. Old habits die hard.

Dnipropetrovsk was one of the places in Ukraine's east where concerns about separatism and violence were actually subsiding despite Russia's intentions. In recent weeks, Russian nationalist websites and social media circulated maps of a fictional geographic zone called "Novorossiya," or "New Russia," which not only included recently grabbed Crimea and destabilized Donetsk, but also Dnipropetrovsk, Kharkiv, Odesa, and Zaporizhzhya. Though Dnipropetrovsk was definitely in the crosshairs, businessman and recently appointed governor Kolomoyskyi and his deputy Borys Filatov were succeeding in forging agreements between local government and radical groups on both sides. Public Affairs's Tuck Evans traveled to Dnipropetrovsk to get a flavor of the situation on the ground and wrote, "Several [local] leaders comparing Dnipropetrovsk to Donetsk mentioned that Donetsk is in worse shape because Akhmetov continues to 'play both sides,' whereas the Kolomoyskyi team committed to Maidan from the early days. Filatov's stunt of showing [pro-Maidan] Channel Five in his shopping malls and hoisting the EU flag on his buildings, forcing him to seek shelter from arrest for several weeks in Israel, remains evidence to many that he put skin in the game when others did not. . . . The concerns of civil society now turned to addressing the threat of Russian attack. A headquarters has been established and volunteers are working day and night to plan and equip a group of volunteer national guard. According to one member, over 12,000 signed up. Civil society members also recognized that Kolomoyskyi and Filatov have taken positive steps to regulate the political situation and keep things from spiraling out of control."

Ukrainian social media buzzed with a stirring video of a group of Ukrainian sailors singing their national anthem outside the Ukrainian Naval Academy building in Sevastopol during a Russian Black Sea Fleet ceremony across the street to remove the Ukrainian Navy flag and replace it with their own. However, it was clear that the remaining Ukrainian forces in Crimea were in an in-creasingly desperate situation. Russian forces stormed and seized the Ukrainian ships *Ternopil* and *Khmelnytsky* on March 20. Several days later, Russian forces took control of Ukraine's only submarine, the *Zaporizhzhya*. The Russian me-dia's assertion that local folks who banded together only a few weeks ago were now somehow professionally storming naval vessels with world-class military equipment remained as laughable as ever. Naval attaché Leo Hmelevsky wrote to Ambassador Pyatt on March 21: "Sir, the 5th (Ukrainian) Naval Brigade in Donuzlav/Novozerne (northwest of Sevastopol), which includes several mine countermeasure and amphibious vessels, has so far avoided capture. However, the ships cannot depart the harbor as the exit channel has been blocked by the sunken hull of the decommissioned Russian cruiser *Ochakov*."

Using audaciously twisted logic, Russian Prime Minister Medvedev as-serted that Ukraine owed Russia $16 billion, $11 billion of which he claimed was due to the fact that the Kharkiv Accords, under which Ukraine traded a long-term lease to Navy facilities in Sevastopol in exchange for a discounted rate on natural gas imports, were "subject to denunciation" now that Crimea was incorporated into Russia. Under this specious reasoning, he demanded that the money Russia had paid Ukraine according to the agreement be repaid retroactively. I asked one of my contacts to explain this to me.

"It's pretty amazing," he said. "Imagine that you rented a car, and after paying rent for a few months, you decided to just steal it. Then you send a bill to the rental car company, demanding that they give you back what you paid before. Why? Because the car is yours now, and you never should have paid to rent it because you really should have stolen it earlier. It does take some balls." On that day, the Ukrainian Defense Ministry announced that it had received approximately $1 million in donations from the Ukrainian people the previous day alone, mostly through a new text message donation system.

On Thursday, March 20, Andriy Shchekun, missing since March 9, resur-faced. He was in rough shape. He was released in a "prisoner exchange" and taken for medical treatment in Kherson, close to the Crimean region's border. When he was brought to Kyiv the following Monday for additional medical treatment, Valentyna and I went to visit him in the hospital. We met in the hospital's sunny outdoor courtyard. Limping with his medical robe draped loosely on his gaunt shoulders like he was a huge clothes hanger, he looked the worse for wear. But his broad smile remained intact. "Great to see you again," he offered with a mild cough. "It was wonderful to meet you during those earlier, happier days in Simferopol."

Andrei offered the details of his ordeal to us. He explained that Russian military activity in Crimea ramped up after February 28, and he became involved with the NGO Ukrainian House, which supported Ukrainian language kindergartens in Crimea with funding from the Canadian-Ukrainian diaspora. "I helped organize the large-scale 'Women for Peace' rally in my adopted home town, Bakhchisaray, on March 6," he said proudly. "It was pretty successful. But with everything going on, we wanted to bring a pro-Ukrainian message of peace to Simferopol. We planned to have about 3,000 people out supporting Crimea's status as part of Ukraine." He and another activist, sixty-four-year-old Anatoliy Kovalsky, arrived early on March 9 at the Simferopol train station to pick up Ukrainian flags ordered from Kyiv for the rally.

At the train station, they were roughly grabbed by two young titushky wearing St. George's ribbons who handed them over to local police officers. When they asked the police what this was about and whether they were under arrest, there was no answer. "The titushky said that they wanted to take us with them, but we didn't want to go, of course. We told the police officers that we wanted to stay at the police station, then one of these guys hit me in the jaw so hard that I fell. The police got upset and told them to take us away and not beat us up in the station." So the titushky shoved the two men into a red Volkswagen, blindfolded them, and bound their hands with tape.

"It was only later that I learned where we were brought—it was the military conscription center near the railway station," Andrei said. "They stripped me naked and taped me to a weird piece of furniture. Kind of like a half-circle chair. Then they attached electric wires to me." The actual torturers were not Russian or locals, he said. "The guards called these guys 'spetsy,' or specialists. They spoke in a language I didn't understand, but was probably Chechen or Armenian. More likely Chechen." In the first hour he had two sessions of electroshock and was beaten on the floor when he fell off his chair. He heard someone telling the "spetsy" in Russian that they should beat him in a way less likely to leave obvious marks. "One of them leaned over to me and told me that they had tortured people in Somalia. He said that he would cut out their livers and kidneys and make them eat their own organs. Then he started rubbing his knife on my stomach and chest, cutting me sometimes, asking me again and again where my liver was."

Andrei said that his torturers were interested in three questions: (1) his relationship to Pravyi Sektor and the location of their training bases in Crimea, (2) how Euromaidan Crimea receives money from Euromaidan Kyiv, and (3) how his group planned to disrupt the upcoming referendum. "The answers to those questions are pretty easy—I would tell anyone who just approached me on the street, no torture necessary. I have never had any contact with Pravyi Sektor and I seriously doubt that they have any bases in Crimea. Euromaidan Crimea never spent much money, and what we had was mostly self-funded with occasional help from the Ukrainian diaspora. And we decided some time ago that it would be useless and counterproductive to disrupt the referendum. But the 'spetsy' didn't believe me and kept pushing for 'real answers.' But I gave them the real answers immediately. I don't have much to hide." He wasn't fed for the first three days in captivity.

After the torture, the "spetsy" turned Andrei over to other men whom he called "the guards." "The guards were mostly from the Crimea, Donetsk, and Russia. They called themselves 'The Crimean Army.' They were very aggressive, and it seemed like they had been really sucking in a lot of the recent brainwashing campaign. They believed that stuff, and they were ready to fight to 'liberate' Ukraine from Nazis and start a war with Ukrainian authorities in Crimea."

Andrei was put in a cell with his fellow protester Anatoliy Kovalsky, who was not tortured presumably because of his age. The next day, a new shift of guards began shooting "pneumatic bullets" at Shchekun's legs and hands. Though they created painful wounds, the projectiles fired at his legs didn't penetrate his jeans. One of the small metal pieces did lodge in his hand, though. Three new prisoners arrived that day who the guards said were Ukrainian intelligence officers. "We could hear them being tortured all night. I have no clue if they were really intelligence officers or not. Who knows how they came under suspicion. In the morning, the guards told us that they had switched sides and would work for them now."

The following day, on March 11, Andrei said that more people were brought into his cell. "They brought in the head of our local postal service. Another activist friend of mine, let's just call him Misha, was brought in because he was wearing a Ukrainian flag. Later that day, they brought in the chief of the Simferopol military hospital and put him in our cell. He was with us because he refused to give Russian soldiers the confidential medical records of

Ukrainian soldiers. I heard, though I'm not sure if it's true or just propaganda, that after a few days he did agree to work for 'The Crimean Army.' "

"You never know what will bother you the most during an experience like that," Andrei recalled. "For me, it was that they took the cross off my neck when they captured me, saying that I was not an Orthodox Christian and didn't deserve to wear it. But I am Orthodox, and I'm never without that cross. It was a huge loss, like they ripped off part of my identity. It was only days later when one of the guards gave a cross back to me to wear that I felt that I might survive and that I had a little bit of my humanity back."

The 'spetsy' again tortured Shchekun, this time focusing on the source of his NGO's funding. "At least they didn't strip me that time," he recalled. "But they did use electricity again. I told them that I had got some small grants for local projects from the United States and some European governments, but that this was not a secret and was even on our website. They kept pushing me for some sort of nonexistent 'real story.' " Others were brought in over the coming days. "There was a former Ukrainian paratrooper who struggled when they brought him in and was shot in the legs. A few days later, they cut his ear in a way that reminded me of the photos of Bulatov in Kyiv. There was one guy, an activist, who I only knew as 'Maksym from Odesa.' He admitted to being part of Euromaidan in Kyiv, and they were especially rough on him."

Meanwhile, Crimean Tatar activists organized a prisoner exchange— Ukraine would return Russian servicemen arrested for illegal military activities in Ukraine in exchange for civilian detainees like Andrei. "They took ten of us to Chongar for the exchange," said Andrei, referring to a small village in the Kherson region just across from Crimea. "Then I heard [Crimean Minister of Defense] Valery Kuznetsov talking on his phone, saying that he would hand over four of us now, and maybe more later. I was blindfolded, so it was hard to tell what was happening. When I heard the roar of helicopters leaving the area, I realized that I wasn't one of those four." Andrei's captors took him back to the makeshift torture center in Simferopol.

Sunday, March 16, was Crimean "referendum day." After the polls closed, drunken Berkut came to the cells and began beating the prisoners. "We were very scared," he said. "On the one hand, the Berkut knew that we could be valuable as part of a future prisoner exchange and that they shouldn't kill us. On the other hand, they were drunk and violent and unpredictable, convinced by their own propaganda that we were all fascists and foreign spies. Anything could have happened."

A few days later on Thursday, March 20, it was back to Chongar. This time, Andrei was among those exchanged, leading to his medical treatment in Kherson and then in Kyiv. I asked him whether he thought the torture center in Simferopol where he spent eleven harrowing days was still operating. "Well, they were still bringing new people during the end of my time there. I wouldn't have any reason to think that it isn't."

I reported Andrei's ordeal to Washington, and it was also retold in the local Ukrainian press. But the full implications of a foreign torture base operating in Crimea well before the annexation referendum—and what that would mean for the legitimacy of the referendum—seemed little noticed outside of Ukraine. In early April, I heard about an OSCE special conference on torture, and that the US Mission to the OSCE in Vienna might be looking to bring a speaker. I immediately thought of Andrei. But after I spoke with Andrei, I realized that there were a number of problems. His Ukrainian passport was never returned by his torturers, so he would need to get a new passport from the Ukrainian Foreign Ministry, still in disarray after the revolution, and get an Austrian visa fast. But Andrei was eager to tell his story. For the next few days, I was in frequent correspondence with Andrei, our US-OSCE Vienna Embassy, our own Embassy Kyiv travel office, the Ukrainian Ministry of Foreign Affairs, and the Austrian Embassy in Kyiv. The logistics finally came together nerve-wrackingly close to his flight time. Andrei went to Vienna and told a group of assembled journalists in a side conference room his harrowing story. US Ambassador Daniel B. Baer thanked our Embassy for sending him, letting us know that Andrei "spoke to riveted reporters for twenty minutes." I waited for the breathless news reports to start to show up, exposing the existence of torture facilities in Crimea prior to the referendum. A few online articles appeared to little fanfare. That was it. I was amazed . . . had the world not noticed? Had everyone become so jaded to brutality that we no longer have the ability to be shocked?

On Friday, March 21, four months to the day after the start of the small initial Euromaidan protest, Prime Minister Yatsenyuk signed the EU-Ukraine Association Agreement in Brussels, announcing that the full Deep and Comprehensive Free Trade Agreement (DCFTA), the trade portion of the document, would be implemented only after the presidential elections. As expected, the signing opened up the European market to many Ukrainian products, while holding off the opening of Ukraine's markets to European competition until late in the year.

That day, the new Ukrainian government's anticorruption organs brought charges against former education minister Tabachnyk for skimming money off textbook procurements and improperly privatizing government property. But that paled in comparison to the Interior Ministry's raid on Naftogaz, Ukraine's natural gas giant. Management and key corporate officers were held on site while the Interior Ministry seized key documents. The Ministry announced that more than $4 billion had been pilfered from the company to support a vast kickback scheme with beneficiaries ranging from parliamentarians to local town officials. This was a linchpin of the Yanukovych graft system, and it was coming down. Pictures from the offices of former energy minister Eduard Staviyskyi were a cornucopia of corruption porn, featuring plastic-wrapped stacks of hundred dollar bills totaling about $1.3 million in cash, kilogram-weight solid gold bars, rows of luxury watches, and plastic containers of huge cut diamonds labeled by their carats (two here, five there, eight there). Presumably, these were just the leftover items that he didn't bother to take with him. A few days later, pictures were also released of the offices of Tax Minister Oleksandr Klymenko, featuring a chair allegedly worth $70,000 and a Matrix-style stainless steel conference room. Within a few weeks, anticorruption authorities would accuse fourteen Ukrainian financial institutions of laundering $12 billion on behalf of top Yanukovych administration officials.

On Saturday, March 22, Russian military forces used an armored personnel carrier to break through the gates of Ukraine's Belbek Air Force Base in Crimea. Masked soldiers with automatic weapons, again with no flags or insignias identifying them as Russian, then took control of the base. Air Base Commander Yuliy Mamchur was arrested and taken to a cell within Russia's Black Sea Fleet facilities for the crime of being Ukrainian. Prime Minister Yatsenyuk, just returned from Brussels, told a US congressional delegation led by Senator Kelly Ayotte (R-NH) that an armed cell of Russian agents, "with fake papers like in the movies" was arrested in Odesa. The Russian government reciprocated US sanctions against its officials involved in the Crimea invasion by announcing its own sanctions against a small group of US officials and legislators. Meanwhile, a large-scale buildup of Russian troops on Ukraine's eastern border was making everyone from NATO commander general Philip Breedlove to my music industry friends jumpy. Was it just an idle threat for purposes of intimidation? Preparations for the Russian military to push all the way to Kyiv? Staging to help separatists in Ukraine's east? Only the Russian government and military leadership knew.

While the Russian press continued to propagate its ridiculous claim that Kyiv was a hellish morass of violence, a city where fascists murdered innocent Russian speakers in the streets, Natalya and I started taking the family out again to enjoy the peaceful city. The seasons were changing, spring was in the air, and Kyiv's grass was getting greener. In many ways, the city felt calmer and friendlier than before Maidan. That weekend, the Public Affairs Section sent a camera crew out to conduct street interviews with normal municipal residents, Russian and Ukrainian speakers, to ask about life in the city. They all spoke about how calm the city was. Many invited Russians to come to Kyiv to see it for themselves. The Embassy put the video up on our website quickly to poke at one of the lies being used to justify both the invasion of Crimea and the continued Russian troop buildup on Ukraine's doorstep.

Early Monday morning, March 24, Russian troops stormed and captured one of the last Ukrainian military facilities in Crimea, the marine base in Feodosia. As Naval Attaché Hmelevsky reported to Ambassador Pyatt: "Helicopter gunships were used in the assault. No casualties but a lot of bruises as many of the marines resisted. Initially tensions were very high (handcuffs used), but subsequently a truce was agreed on; half of a day given to finish packing, then marines will be evacuated via Chongar." This led to the final order, given that day by Ukraine's Defense Ministry on instructions from acting President Turchynov, to evacuate all remaining Ukrainian military personnel from Crimea due to threats against the lives of Ukrainian servicemen and their families. Not only would a fight have been a futilely suicidal gesture, but the Russian side seemed to be spoiling for a shooting war that they could use to paint the Ukrainian side as radicals under the control of fascists. Open conflict would have only boosted Russian propaganda, and militarily, the Russian armed forces had an overwhelming firepower advantage no matter how bravely the Ukrainians might have fought. The world looked on.

Later that day, Russian workers, guarded by Russian military, reportedly crossed from Crimea onto a border island in Ukraine's Kherson region and dismantled and stole about $45 million of oil drilling equipment. While this theft was unusual because it involved property outside of Crimea's borders, stealing Ukrainian assets was commonplace by this point. The impact of the "nationalization" of Ukrainian property in Crimea was immense. This grab included five seaports owned by the Ukrainian government and thirteen state-owned defense industry production facilities. Military-industrial complex assets, port infrastructure, and rail infrastructure were all seized regardless of whether they were owned by the Ukrainian government or private individuals. And this did not even count the over $11 billion of Ukrainian Ministry of Defense property taken in Crimea. When the Ukrainian minesweeper *Cherkassy* was taken on the night of March 25 after its lengthy defiance of Russian threats to attack the vessel, the last Ukrainian naval ship in Crimea was also stolen.

The propaganda warriors also continued their own offensive. On Wednesday, March 26, Russia's ITAR-TASS announced that the Ukrainian government was dispatching new American mercenaries from a private military company, veterans of Afghanistan and Iraq, to eastern Ukraine. This was a lie cut from whole cloth, but rumors of the Ukrainian government sending violent foreigners with guns to eastern Ukrainians' hometowns were likely to get attention whether true or not. Recalling the leaked Pyatt-Nuland and Paet-Ashton calls, a leaked recording of Yulia Tymoshenko appeared on the web, with her seeming to say that all Russians should be killed with nuclear weapons. Tymoshenko stated that the recording was doctored, but the damage was done. By this telling, the new Ukrainian government headed by a prime minister from the party Tymoshenko led was murderously, genocidally anti-Russian, and anything that Russia might do to Ukraine was justifiable self-defense.

On Thursday, March 27, the International Monetary Fund announced a working-level agreement with Ukraine to provide between $14 billion and $18 billion under a standby agreement. It would be enough to keep the new government afloat. The same day, the US Congress passed the legislation necessary to implement the $1 billion US loan guarantee that Secretary Kerry offered during his recent trip to Kyiv. But it became clear on April 1 that this money could evaporate as soon as it arrived in Kyiv as Russia's Gazprom announced that it would raise gas prices to Ukraine from $268.50 per BCM to a budget-busting $385.50 during the second quarter of the year, in addition to the past due payment amount of $1.7 billion. The new government was exploring whether it could make "reverse flow" gas purchases from Slovakia to reduce its dependency on Russia, but whether they could pull that off was still an open question.

On that morning, our Embassy's "Ukraine Crisis Situation Report #251" opened with the following sentence: "Russian military control over Crimea is essentially complete, and de facto authorities began nationalizing Crimean businesses and cultural artifacts." Indeed, that day Russian Migration Service representative in Sevastopol Victoria Gachko announced that all Ukrainian citizens without special registration from the local Crimean authorities would be required to leave Crimea before April 19. They were now foreigners in their own homes. On the spurious pretext of protecting ethnic Russians from a nonexistent threat to their cultural identity, the Kremlin had forcibly annexed Crimea. Now it was going one step further and trying to erase any vestige of Ukrainian cultural identity from Crimea—exactly what it disingenuously accused Kyiv of doing to Russian speakers.

Meanwhile, in Kyiv the right-wing Pravyi Sektor was making trouble, unintentionally providing more great pictures for Russian television. Pravyi Sektor members held a demonstration at the Rada, breaking windows in the course of demanding the dismissal of Minister of Internal Affairs Avakov after their own activist Oleksandr Muzychko was killed in a shootout with police in the western Ukrainian city of Rivne. Within days, the Interior Ministry and Maidan Self-Defense Forces would surround Pravyi Sektor headquarters to ensure that the troublesome group was disarmed. At a press conference from his new home base in Russia, former President Yanukovych called for referendums "to determine the status of each region within Ukraine." Contrary to his preposterous claim that this would stabilize the country, it seemed obvious to all that his proposal was a surefire formula to break up Ukraine. He characterized unrest in eastern Ukraine as a natural reaction to "an armed coup by the opposition and terrorist groups with the support of Western countries."

On Sunday March 30, Russian Foreign Minister Lavrov claimed that the Russian government had "evidence" that the right-wing party Pravyi Sektor was behind the February 20 sniper shootings on Maidan. He stated that his government had shared "ample evidence" of this with other countries, though of course, the US government had seen nothing from Russia on this topic. As the new government in Kyiv was actively investigating the sniper massacre, Lavrov's statement seemed simply to be an attempt to muddy the waters and preemptively weaken the impact of the forthcoming Ukrainian report on the killings. The next day Lavrov stated, again with no evidence, that the United States agreed to the "federalization" of Ukraine. This was equally untrue.

One day later, a large assembly of Crimean Tatars gathered in Bakhchisaray, their historic capital in Crimea, to vote for "ethnic and territorial autonomy" from Russian government control. To emphasize the Kremlin's confidence in Russia's secure control over Crimea, Russian Prime Minister Medvedev flew there on Monday, March 31. While Medvedev was on the ground, President Putin signed a decree increasing salaries and pensions in Crimea, giving Medvedev some good news to deliver. Meanwhile, unlike the phantom Ukrainians that Russia claimed were fleeing across its border, the displaced Ukrainians fleeing Crimea to Kyiv were becoming an actual humanitarian issue. The UN High Commission for Refugees estimated that about 5,000 people (not counting the over 3,000 Ukrainian military personnel forced to leave Crimea), mostly Ukrainians and Crimean Tatars, fled Crimea since the Russian invasion. Public Affairs Officer Eric Johnson wrote to Ambassador Pyatt: "Ambassador—On an informal basis, some Embassy staff have started helping internally displaced Crimeans who have arrived in Kyiv. With your approval, we would like to see about doing a more formal assistance program for them—perhaps to include an Embassy 'drive' to collect whatever they might need. Please let me know if this sounds OK to you and we will pursue. Thanks."

On Tuesday, April 1, the State Security Service of Ukraine (SBU) announced that it had detained "O. Bahtiyarova," a leader of the radical pro-Russian group Eurasian Youth Union, for attempting to organize paid demonstrators to attack the Ukrainian Rada to film the violent display for Russian television. Several days later, the SBU announced that it had arrested two Russian agents in Lviv, equipped with guns and explosives, who planned to kidnap a Ukrainian presidential candidate. And the next day, they arrested fifteen individuals planning an armed takeover of the regional administration in Lugansk. In retaliation and consistent with the Russian strategy of "mirroring" the accusations against them, dozens of Ukrainians were then arrested in Russia under charges that they were planning terrorist attacks.

A potential reason why Russia appeared to be trying to get out ahead of the story with regard to the Maidan sniper investigation came out on April 3. SBU chief Valentyn Nalyvaichenko told a news conference that while the actual shooting on Maidan was conducted by forces responsible to President Yanukovych, there was reason to believe that employees of the Russian Federal Security Service (FSB), the modern successor to the KGB, participated in planning and implementing measures against protesters in Kyiv. He also stated that Russian transport planes had brought weapons and 5,100 kilograms of explosives to be used in the operation to Kyiv. Russia's FSB immediately refuted the statements, stating through their PR office that they "do not comment on baseless allegations." But one would have needed to be either living in a cave or deaf in February not to have heard the clearly articulated fire-breathing demands from Russian media and government officials for a bloody crackdown on Maidan. Nalyvaichenko's revelations were no surprise. Neither were Moscow's denials. But by this time, Putin's theft of Crimea was complete.

13

SHOCKWAVES OF TERROR IN DONBAS

Over the weekend of April 5–6, the rumbling in the east grew louder. In Donetsk, about 2,000 separatists attacked police with grenades and, in a topsy turvy echo of Euromaidan, they seized the regional administration building where I had recently met Governor Taruta. Outside, they hoisted the Russian flag. One separatist told the media that the group demanded an extraordinary session of the Donetsk regional council to discuss a referendum on joining the Russian Federation, Crimea style. In Lugansk, another crowd of several thousand attacked the Security Service of Ukraine (SBU) headquarters building to free fifteen previously arrested separatists and seize weapons, injuring two people in the process. In Kharkiv, competing pro-Ukrainian and pro-Russia demonstrations for the most part avoided fresh direct confrontation. Ambassador Pyatt messaged the Kyiv Task Force: "Bad situation all around. Below is one of multiple tweets speculating about violence in Donetsk. Lots of reports referencing radio messages from Russia being intercepted. Donetsk groups calling for Russian assistance. Talk of a special session assembly tonight on separation." US Embassy Moscow's press office wrote to us that day: "[Russian TV station] Rossiya 24 is in full swing right now talking with their reporters in all of the [eastern Ukrainian] cities now and hearing that demonstrators in all of these cities somehow spontaneously decided to seize government buildings. This time they said they plan to hold them. Follows a whole day of propaganda highlighting the failed state of Ukraine and a long and emotional letter reading from the famous Russian filmmaker Nikita Mikhalkov lamenting the seizure of power by the Nazis in Kyiv and how this poses a threat to Russians and their culture. Also, they are highlighting the Gazprom-Ukraine government dispute. Big lie machine in full gear here."

Suddenly, fresh events in the east made the March 1 "Russian Spring" seem like a mere dress rehearsal for the main event. While the Russian-backed protests in eastern Ukraine failed to gain traction at that time, now huge Russian military forces sat just on the other side of the border, likely facilitating the flow of weapons, personnel, and material to mixed local and imported radicals in Ukraine's east. This time, it would be different. As our Public Affairs Officer Eric Johnson wrote: "As Yogi Berra said, this feels like 'deja-vu all over again' except this time it is Putin's peeps who brought the tires, baseball bats, and babushki."

Some incidents would almost be humorous if their implications had not been so serious. In Kharkiv on Monday, April 7, a group of "local residents" stormed the city's Opera House, believing it to be the mayor's office, and demanded the mayor's resignation. Of course, any actual resident of Kharkiv would know which building was the town's major classical concert venue and which was the mayor's office.

In another lighter moment, as separatists demanded a referendum on Donetsk joining Russia, a group of local residents declared that they would have another referendum the same day to ask whether Donetsk should join the UK. Donetsk is a town with an interesting history, and there was a reason why these jokesters chose the UK. It was initially founded in 1869 by Welsh industrialist John Hughes, whose statue stands in the city center. To mock the separatists and their slogans, such as "Glory to Russia!" and "Donetsk is a Russian City!" the group posted slogans such as "Donetsk is a British city! God Save the Queen!" It was a clever parody, but parodies alone weren't going to beat the well-funded guys with guns who didn't seem to have much of a sense of humor.

Russian television also provided some unintentional mirth, as reported by US government–funded but editorially independent broadcaster Radio Free Europe/Radio Liberty (RFE/RL), by sometimes confusing its own story lines. The same man in the same hospital bed in Odesa was cast on NTV as a foreign mercenary who brought 500,000 Euros from Germany to stir up trouble on behalf of Western powers, and then on Rossiya One, he was suddenly a local pro-Russian protester attacked by Euromaidan "fascists." Once an exposé on the dual-hatted "man on the scene" started racking up thousands of online views in Russia, NTV was forced to come out with a new explanation for the debacle—the man was now a schizophrenic with multiple personalities, and they apologized for getting duped by the wily lunatic who was so conveniently useful to both networks.

Meanwhile, in Crimea, tensions continued to run high. According to press reports, Ukrainian major Stanislav Karachevsky was packing up his belongings from his officer's quarters barracks room, preparing to leave Crimea, when a fight broke out between him and a junior sergeant of the Russian Armed Forces. The Russian officer opened fire on Karachevsky with an AK-47, hitting him in the chest with one bullet, and near the eye with another. According to the Ukrainian military, Karachevsky's friend, Captain Yermolenko, was then savagely beaten and arrested by Russian soldiers.

While focused on the brutal destabilization of the east, at the Embassy we also tried to return to our usual business that could no longer be postponed. That week, it was finally calm enough in Kyiv to hold my much delayed World Trade Organization (WTO) program for international trade students. The program assembled fifty students from all over Ukraine to hear from US and Ukrainian trade experts and stage a model WTO session to prompt discussion of Ukraine's bizarre recent WTO actions. We had planned the event long before Euromaidan, and it seemed a little out of place given burning concerns over whether Ukraine would remain whole and sovereign. At one point, I asked a student from an eastern Ukrainian town threatened by separatist violence whether she was worried about the future.

"Of course," she answered. "But coming here, I can forget about all of that for a few days. I've always wanted to represent my country, Ukraine, and try to get us the best trade deals I could to bring us some prosperity. That's my ambition. This event helped me for a few days not to think about the fact that I might not have a country when I graduate." Like so many of her fellow Ukrainians, she was living simultaneously in the problematic present and an even more fraught future.

In Donetsk, separatists encountered a roadblock when the press section of the self-styled Committee of Donbas Patriotic Forces issued a statement calling for the cancellation of any independence vote or referendum in Donetsk region without proper legal authority. In Kharkiv, Ukrainian government security forces retook the regional administration building and arrested seventy separatists. But just when the tide seemed to be shifting a bit away from the pro-Russian separatists, stark news came from Lugansk—the pro-Russian forces seized the local SBU building and its large weapons cache, although it was mined. According to an interview with a state security officer published by *Ukrainian Week* a year and a half after the incident, while the crowd was fronted by "drunken proletarians, women, and even children," several known Russian military intelligence (GRU) representatives were among the militants standing behind. He stated that the attack appeared to be retribution for the arrest of a number of separatist militants by the Lugansk SBU in recent days, including the self-declared separatist "People's Governor"—a development that was a fly in the ointment of Russian/separatist plans to stage attacks on the regional administration buildings of all regional capitals in the so-called Novorossiya zone on a single day. Minister of Internal Affairs Avakov promised to resolve the situation within forty-eight hours, either peacefully or by force. The following day, acting President Turchynov offered amnesty to the militants if they laid down their arms. On April 9, the Ministry of Defense's Crimea spokesman Seleznyov told the press that many of the same individuals who had seized military facilities in Crimea were capturing buildings in eastern Ukraine—essentially putting the lie to the propaganda line that all those involved were locals.

While US security contractor Greystone, another firm affiliated with Blackwater, denied that it had any personnel in Ukraine or any plans to send anyone, Russia's Rossiya One channel claimed, without any supporting evidence, that residents of Donetsk have found "proof" of their presence and that "similar reports are also coming from Kharkiv" regarding the involvement of "outside forces." We still have no idea what that "proof" might have been—none ever surfaced. Most likely, merely planting the lie guaranteed a bumper harvest of fear and anxiety among Rossiya One's viewers.

As acting Prime Minister Yatsenyuk visited Donetsk and Dnipropetrovsk to call for dialogue and constitutional reform, Ukraine's SBU announced the detention in Chernihiv of a Russian citizen trying to enter Ukraine while carrying communications equipment, flares, and the telephone number of a Russian Federal Security Service (FSB) official. The SBU stated that the individual confessed to working for Russian security services and sought to destabilize the situation in the southern regions of Ukraine. On Friday, April 11, Russian Foreign Minister Lavrov, reciting from a well-worn script, flatly denied that there were any Russian troops or agents in eastern Ukraine—exactly the same line as the Russian government had regarding Crimea recently. He also employed the "mirror of Maidan" strategy, adding, "There are Russian citizens there. But that is not surprising, since on the Maidan there were all kinds of people." Therefore, as the "Maidan mirror" logic chain dictated, Western nations who were supportive of the pro-reformist messages of Maidan but critical of the direct Russian military and intelligence incursion in Crimea and eastern Ukraine are simply hypocrites who only invoke their supposed values as tactics for their own benefit. Another example came that same day as the Russian Foreign Ministry announced that Lavrov had urged Kerry to put pressure on Kyiv "in order to avoid the use of force and to push [the government in Kyiv] to a dialogue with representatives of the regions to create conditions allowing for fully fledged constitutional reform." This closely resembled language that the United States used months earlier asking Russia to intercede with Yanukovych to avoid a brutal crackdown on Maidan. Of course, this was an attempt to create a false equivalency between the organic Ukrainian protest movement on Maidan and the Russian instigated and funded (and sometimes just plain Russian) separatists in the east. To be sure, there really was some local discontent with Kyiv among many local inhabitants in eastern Ukraine and skepticism toward the new government. But the overriding threat to the east's stability was Russia's efforts to inflame the situation and deny the new government in Kyiv any chance to build trust there as part of the Kremlin's plan to rip apart its insubordinate neighbor.

On Saturday, April 12, separatist militants seized the police station and SBU headquarters in the eastern city of Slovyansk. Pictures on social media from Slovyansk showed "little green men" in camo uniforms without insignia—a striking similarity to the forces that swept Crimea. Reuters quoted one of the "green men" in Slovyansk as saying "We don't want to be slaves of America and the West.... We want to live with Russia." Then, men in similar flagless outfits seized a police station in Donetsk. On that Saturday, new light board advertisements around that city showed a previously unseen tricolor flag—black, blue, and red—with the two-headed Russian tsarist eagle in the center below the words "Donetsk Republic." The Ukrainian government warned its Border Guard to be ready for "action at the border."

The situation looked increasing like Crimea. We had already seen this stealthy "hybrid war" unfold once before, and the patterns were now familiar. The Political Section was working overtime to decipher what was going on in the rapidly changing environment. The Political Section's Liz Zentos wrote in: "My contact confirmed that these are definitely Russian GRU [military intelligence] actions. He relayed that local security forces have been infiltrated by GRU and FSB and hence are not being cooperative. Russia's immediate priorities for the next 24 to 48 hours, he commented, are Donetsk and Luhansk, followed by Kharkiv." Tim Piergalski of the Embassy's Political Section followed up: "Social media speculation, confirmed by a contact in the FDPM's [first deputy prime minister's] office, is that the location of [building] seizures is not random. Slovyansk sits on the highway (M3) connecting Donetsk and Kharkiv. Krasnoarmiyska sits on the Dnipropetrovsk–Donetsk highway (M4). This is an attempt to surround Donetsk with pro-Russian roadblocks, preventing Kyiv from sending in additional troops to dislodge the Donetsk-based separatists. Blocking Donetsk would also block Luhansk, as the major highway to Luhansk goes through Donetsk. There do not (yet) appear to be blockades on the other minor roads connecting Zaporizhzhya (H15) and Mariupol (H20) to Donetsk. Separatists have also attempted to block troops in Donetsk from leaving their base." Automaidan activists reported that they were beaten as they tried to stop seventy armed Russian citizens in ten buses at a border crossing in eastern Ukraine. The gathering clouds of war continued to flash with lightning.

On Sunday, April 13, that war arrived in eastern Ukraine. Missile-carrying Ukrainian military helicopters flew low over the center of the small town of Slovyansk, while local residents reported hearing automatic gunfire and explosions. It was a large show of force designed to intimidate and dislodge the pro-Russian and Russian forces. As the Ukrainian government and armed forces had assiduously avoided any military confrontation in Crimea only to see it swiftly annexed after hoping for decisive international support that never came, they would not repeat the same strategy in the east. They would fight. Ukrainian armored personnel carriers moved in on separatist roadblocks outside of town. Within hours, media posted news of the first casualties of this new conflict. Unlike the grinding humiliation that Ukraine consciously resolved to suffer in Crimea, this situation was suddenly kinetic. This would be different.

Large new protests took place in Kharkiv, and armed men seized the city council building in the strategic port city of Mariupol. Dozens of other public buildings were attacked throughout the east. In order to provide firsthand observations, the Embassy's Defense Attaché Office once again dispatched observers. Staff Sergeant Shane Parlow wrote in at about 2:00 p.m. from Kharkiv as pro-unity and pro-Russian protesters clashed:

> Kharkiv battle starts. Home-made grenades. Both sides confronting. . . . Not good. . . . Weapons include wooden sticks, chains. . . . Smoke filling street, pro-Russians provoked everything. Hear what may be less than lethal shots. Not close enough. They are all chanting death to Pravyi Sektor. . . . Pro-Russian forces appear to be creating unorganized chaos, trying to locate pro-Ukrainian ralliers who quickly dispersed. Pro-Russians also attack police, and a homemade device just injured a policeman. . . . Pro-Russians still openly display weapons (sticks/chains/rocks). Many of their fighters have stuffed their jackets for padding and wear gloves/masks (maybe 75–100). . . . This all was obviously planned. The pro-Russian medics moved the opposite direction of the march to where the pro-Russian and pro-Ukrainian marchers would meet. As the march passed this intersecting street, all pensioners and women continued away while the young males massed. A few minutes later, the pro-Russians pushed toward the Ukrainian rally. Pro-Ukrainians smartly dispersed while being chased by pro-Russians with bats, chains, and homemade flashbangs. Pro-Russians seemed to want a strong police response.

Within hours, some pro-Russian demonstrators had broken into Kharkiv's city government building. It seemed that Kharkiv, Ukraine's second-largest city with a population of some 1.4 million persons, was in serious jeopardy.

Not all Russians swallowed the Kremlin's line about a fascist takeover in Kyiv. In Moscow, between one and five thousand people participated in a peaceful protest on Sakharov Avenue dubbed "The March of Truth" against propaganda in the Russian media regarding Ukraine. By Moscow standards, it was a pretty small rally that posed no threat to Putin's iron-handed grip on the media narrative. Meanwhile, the pro-Russian demonstrations in Ukraine without the benefit of the participation of Russian "tourists" or armed "little green men" were floundering. One example was in Zaporizhzhya, where about

5,000 locals pelted a gathering of 200 pro-Russian activists with eggs that Sunday. In the strategic port city of Mariupol in eastern Ukraine, on April 15, the important metal workers union issued a statement against the separatists: "The future of Ukraine is at stake today. Every day there is a growing wave of protests, seizures of administrative buildings, and attacks on offices and people. All of this is an attempt to drag as many Ukrainians as possible into a violent confrontation. . . . Those who today, under the guise of patriotic slogans, participate in unlawful and provocative actions play into the hands of the separatists. . . . Fellow countrymen, do not let anyone drag you into political 'disputes.' Do not be enticed by manipulators or provocateurs."

Images of sidelined former President Yanukovych popped up again like indigestion from a half-forgotten bad meal. On Sunday, April 13, he took to the airwaves, this time to accuse the United States directly of plotting death and destruction in Ukraine. The longer he spent in Russia, the more convinced he seemed that the West was the enemy. After calling on the Ukrainian military not to participate in any action against armed separatists in eastern Ukraine, he said, "According to information I received from the Ukrainian security bloc and from other government bodies, Kyiv was visited by CIA Director [John] Brennan. He held meetings with illegally appointed security chiefs, including Avakov, Nalyvaichenko, [Foreign Intelligence Service Head Viktor] Hvozd, and [First Deputy Prime Minister Vitaliy] Yarema, as well as so-called acting President [Oleksandr] Turchynov. It was precisely after these meetings that the decision to launch a military operation in the east of Ukraine was taken. Mr. Brennan in effect authorized the use of weapons and provoked bloodshed. Therefore the USA bears its share of responsibility for unleashing a civil war." The next day, the Russian newspaper *Vzglyad* falsely claimed that twenty American mercenaries disappeared in Ukraine and that Brennan visited Kyiv to help locate the men. CIA Director Brennan had in fact just been in Kyiv as part of a longer trip to Europe to discuss intelligence sharing. Intelligence sharing with Ukraine was a complex issue—many in Congress and the US military were pushing for more intelligence sharing with Ukraine to counteract Russian aggression, but Ukraine's SBU had been so penetrated by the Russian FSB for so many years that the wisdom of such sharing was not obvious. The trip was secret only insofar as the CIA never publicly discloses its director's travel schedule. And as the CIA is an intelligence organ that requires secrecy to fulfill its mandate, the Russian government could claim just about anything regarding Brennan's visit, and a sizable chunk of the world's population would believe it. A little secrecy in a tense environment inevitably creates an information vacuum for the propagandist's pen to fill, and then wallow around inside for as long as anyone will pay attention.

The Russian claim that Director Brennan somehow "authorized" the use of force was patently false, as the White House would say publicly several days later. But again, the damage was done. Like the claims that the United States gave $5 billion to Euromaidan (which was actually the total amount of development aid funding given to Ukraine since its independence in 1991) or that the new Ukrainian government dispatched American mercenaries to Donetsk, the goal was not to prove anything. It was just meant to cast enough shade and innuendo at the United States and others to demonize us in the aggregate and cast aspersions on all our motives. Having sat in numerous meetings where teams of US government lawyers argued over whether we had sufficient evidence to accuse another country of something, I was very accustomed to the idea that a government would never want to make an accusation that was false, sloppy, or disprovable because it would impact our long-term credibility. But what we were seeing from Russia was something quite different. Like Dr. Frankenstein in Mary Shelley's famous novel, they were adept at constructing their own monstrous simulacrum of reality from alternative facts and narratives, and sending it marching out into the world. To change the metaphor, in this narrative construction, when accusing others, it was fine to throw a bunch of sloppy propaganda spaghetti against the wall just to see what sticks. If someone contradicts you, just flatly deny the truth and call them a foreign agent or anti-Russian zealot. Then lob another handful of propaganda spaghetti. The next toss at the wall will distract everyone from the previous batch of invented tales that made everyone indignant yesterday. Amazingly, it works more often than not.

The State Department spokesperson's statement on April 13 was an example of the US approach, every word examined by lawyers, intelligence analysts, and policy experts who demanded certainty that we could prove each clause uttered if needed:

> On April 12, armed pro-Russian militants seized government buildings in a coordinated and professional operation conducted in six cities in eastern Ukraine. Many of the militants were outfitted in bullet-proof

vests and camouflage uniforms with insignia removed and carrying Russian-origin weapons. . . . Even more so than the seizure of main government buildings in Ukrainian regional capitals Donetsk, Luhansk, and Kharkiv last weekend, these operations bear many similarities to those that were carried out in Crimea in late February and culminated in Russia's illegal military intervention and purported annexation of Crimea. In the earlier Crimean case, highly organized, well-equipped, and professional forces wearing Russian military uniforms, balaclavas, and military gear without identifying insignia moved in first to take control of Crimean government and security facilities before being later replaced by regular Russian military forces. . . . In an indication that the April 12 operations were planned in advance, the takeovers have occurred simultaneously in multiple locations in eastern Ukraine: Donetsk, Slovyansk, Lyman, Kramatorsk, Chervonoarmiysk, and Druzhkivka. There are reports that additional attempts to seize buildings in other eastern Ukrainian towns failed. Inconsistent with political, grassroots protests, these seizures bear the same defining features and tactics across diverse locations, including takeover of government administration buildings and security headquarters, seizure of weapons in the targeted buildings, forced removal of local officials, rapid establishment of roadblocks and barricades, attacks against communications towers, and deployment of well-organized forces. In Slovyansk, armed units have now also moved beyond the seized buildings to establish roadblocks and checkpoints in the nearby area. . . . The Ukrainian government has reporting indicating that Russian intelligence officers are directly involved in orchestrating the activities of pro-Russian armed resistance groups in eastern Ukraine. In addition, the Ukrainian government detained an individual who said that he was recruited by the Russian security services and instructed to carry out subversive operations in eastern and southern Ukraine, including seizing administrative buildings. All of this evidence undercuts the Russian government's claims that Ukraine is on the brink of "civil war." In each of these cases, independent media have been harassed and excluded from covering the seizures, while pro-Russian media were granted special access and used to broadcast the demands of these armed groups. . . . The events of April 12 strongly suggest that in eastern Ukraine Russia is now using the same tactics that it used in Crimea in order to foment separatism, undermine Ukrainian sovereignty, and exercise control over its neighbor in contravention of Russia's obligations under international law.

Quite unlike the Kremlin's fables, each of the points in this detailed statement were grounded in demonstrable facts. Suspicions or innuendo didn't make the cut for this kind of official statement. We had the goods to back up every word. Every word. This was not a case of two sides both spinning the facts with their own gloss. It was an unfair fight because only one side even cared what the facts were. But our factual, lawyered statements were never going to capture the imagination and kick the brain's fear center like the Russian press screaming that American mercenaries are on their way to your house to kill you.

On Monday morning, April 14, acting President Turchynov agreed to a key demand of the separatists and announced that he would not oppose a referendum in eastern Ukraine on regional autonomy in conjunction with the May 25 presidential election. A majority of eastern Ukrainians would vote for a united Ukraine, he said. He had grounds for this confidence—recent polls had found that in Donetsk, a majority still supported a whole Ukraine and opposed secessionism. Crimea was the only Ukrainian region with a majority Russian population. While the east had a much greater number of ethnic Russians and Russian speakers than the west, they were only about 40 percent of the population—and this group was highly integrated into Ukrainian society. The Donbas was not Crimea.

Meanwhile in the Black Sea, an unarmed Russian jet made close passes above the American Navy's *USS Donald Cook* for nearly ninety minutes in international waters. A Pentagon spokesman called the incident a "provocative and unprofessional Russian action." Ukraine's SBU released tapes of Donetsk separatists receiving instructions from pro-Kremlin PR figure Aleksandr Boroday, a man known to Embassy Kyiv for a propaganda video in which he blamed the US State Department for Euromaidan. Meanwhile, Ukrainian social media circulated photos of "little green men" in Crimea and Donetsk carrying the same military-grade radios. In Dnipropetrovsk, Governor Kolomoyskyi issued a clear warning on social media: "I want to warn all the little green men that unlike others, we are not timid, and when you are trying to capture SBU and Interior Ministry buildings we will immediately shoot to kill. Anyone who wants to arrange a war in the region needs to know that Dnipropetrovsk will be their second Stalingrad, only in this battle the Ukrainian people will win." A few days later, Kolomoyskyi raised the stakes again, putting up ads offering $1,000 for each machine gun turned in, $2,000 for every bomb thrower, $10,000 for each Russian military "little green man" turned in, and most enticingly, $200,000 for each liberated administrative building turned over to his Dniepr Detachment. Predictably, Russia's vilification of him reached new heights of hysterics.

On Tuesday, April 15, evidence of the direct involvement of Russian military personnel in eastern Ukraine continued to mount. Ukraine's SBU identified the leader of the Russian military and paramilitary forces in Slovyansk as Russian military intelligence officer Igor Girkin (famous under his pseudonym Strelkov). Girkin was already notorious for his participation in Russian military and intelligence actions in Georgia and involvement in the recent seizure of the Crimean parliament. The day before, a Russian military lieutenant colonel was videotaped introducing himself as the new police chief in the eastern Ukrainian town of Horlivka. Slovyansk mayor Nelya Shtepa, who earlier had publicly declared her support for the separatists while surrounded by a group of armed men, withdrew her "support" stating that all of the pro-Russian forces in Slovyansk at that time were from Russia or Crimea, not Slovyansk. She then disappeared into prison.

Social media posts claimed that Russian troops were patrolling the occupied town of Slovyansk carrying RPG-30 rocket launchers, which were put into active service in 2012–2013 and were only available to the Russian army. In Slovyansk and other occupied cities, nearly all separatist groups appealed to Putin for Russian military action, or rather, *overt* Russian military action. These appeals were very useful to the Russian Federation insofar as they served to support the Kremlin's false assertion that Russian troops were not already militarily engaged in eastern Ukraine and enabling Moscow to claim it was exercising restraint by not responding to these "calls for fraternal help."

Then, fighting erupted at the Kramatorsk military airfield south of Slovyansk. Ambassador Pyatt wrote to the Kyiv Task Force: "SBU Deputy Nayda just stated at an MFA [Ministry of Foreign Affairs] briefing that the violence we're seeing at the Kramatorsk airfield resulted from a Russian-supported attack on Ukrainian forces. The Ukrainian forces were in a defensive mode against thirty men with automatic weapons demanding that the installation be abandoned early this a.m. At 3:00 p.m., thirty well-armed men with automatic weapons attacked again. Ukrainian officers repulsed the attack."

On Wednesday, April 16, Odesa's anti-Maidan group announced online the formation of the Odesa People's Republic, mirroring the illegal pseudo-states declared by "separatists" in Donetsk and Lugansk. In Kramatorsk, Ukrainian military from Dnipropetrovsk abandoned at least five armored personnel carriers after pro-Russian crowds surrounded them, and photos of men brandishing Russian or separatist flags driving the vehicles then quickly splashed across the Ukrainian internet. On the other side of the equation, Donbas miners declared Tuesday evening that they were prepared to take up arms to defend Ukraine against a Russian invasion.

On April 17, there was a new shootout in Mariupol. Ambassador Pyatt wrote to the Task Force: "Social media saying three dead, thirteen wounded. Moscow's *Life News* says their reporter is missing. Greek Ambo (they have a consulate in Mariupol) says the Greeks there are reporting an increasing atmosphere of fear and worry. Don't know who to support. Manufactured reality with false rumors of Pravyi Sektor coming. Interior Min Avakov says on his FB [Facebook] that Russian operators directed last night's attack on the Ukrainian facility."

Later that day, Russian President Putin held a nearly four-hour "Direct Line" question-and-answer program on live Russian television. In answering a question on whether Russia and the United States could compromise on Ukraine, Putin went out of his way to question whether eastern Ukraine was really part of Ukraine, calling it by its old Tsarist name: "I would like to remind you that what was called Novorossiya (New Russia) back in the Tsarist days—Kharkov, Lugansk, Donetsk, Kherson, Mykolaiv, and Odesa—were not part of Ukraine back then. These territories were given to Ukraine in the 1920s by the Soviet government. Why? Who knows. They were won by Potomkin and Catherine the Great in a series of well-known wars. The center of that territory was Novorossiysk, so the region is called Novorossiya. Russia lost these territories for various reasons, but the people remained." The statement, reminiscent of his declarations about Crimea being historically Russian, was alarming. It also lumped in a huge amount of territory, not just land on Russia's immediate border, into lands which he did not consider "really Ukraine."

In the same program, a questioner asked Putin about the identity of the "little green men" who fanned out across Crimea prior to the referendum. In a remarkable statement for someone who had consistently denied for months that Russian special forces were deployed in Crimea, he stated, "Of course, Russian servicemen did back the Crimean Self-Defense Forces. They acted in a civil but a decisive and professional manner, as I've already said. . . . It was impossible to hold an open, honest, and dignified referendum and help people express their opinion in any other way." However, he continued to insist that Russian servicemen were not deployed in eastern Ukraine, just as he had previously strenuously denied the deployment of Russian troops outside of their bases in Crimea up until the moment when he didn't.

On April 17, Secretary Kerry, Russian Foreign Minister Lavrov, acting Ukrainian Foreign Minister Andrii Deshchytsia, and EU Foreign Affairs Chief Catherine Ashton met in Geneva to try to negotiate an end to the crisis in eastern Ukraine. After a tense eight hours, they agreed to a statement noting that "all sides must refrain from any violence . . . all illegal armed groups must be disarmed; all illegally seized buildings must be returned to legitimate owners. . . . Amnesty will be granted to protestors and to those who have left buildings and other public places and surrendered weapons. . . . The OSCE Special Monitoring Mission should play a leading role in assisting Ukrainian authorities and local communities in the immediate implementation of these de-escalation measures. . . . The announced constitutional [reform] process will be inclusive, transparent, and accountable. It will include the immediate establishment of a broad national dialogue, with outreach to all of Ukraine's regions and political constituencies, and allow for the consideration of public comments and proposed amendments." Denis Pushilin, the self-appointed leader of the Donetsk People's Republic, immediately declared that he and his group were not bound by the Geneva statement and that the separatists would not leave Donetsk public buildings until a referendum on independence was held or until the "illegal government" in Kyiv departed. More building take-overs followed within hours, and two days after the agreement was signed the Polish Consul General in Donetsk told us that no buildings had been given up by the separatists. The Russian Federation had no interest in pulling back their surrogates, and the de-escalation promised by the Geneva statement was stillborn.

Even though the Geneva statement was brief and straightforward, the Russian and Ukrainian governments sparred over its meaning hourly. The statement said that "all illegally occupied streets, squares, and other public places in Ukrainian cities and towns must be vacated," which Russian foreign minister Lavrov asserted meant that the Ukrainian government must remove the protesters still encamped on Maidan. Acting Ukrainian Foreign Minister Deshchytsia countered that a protest permit had been issued to the protesters on Maidan so they were there legally, and the Geneva statement did not apply to them.

In reality, the Maidan had changed a lot since the new government took power nearly two months before. Most students had returned to school, executives returned to their jobs, family members returned to their families. These people represented the bulk and backbone of Maidan until February 21. Many of those remaining months later either did not have anywhere to go back to or held sufficiently radical political views to believe that the Maidan should be permanent in case the new government "betrayed them." It was no longer representative of Ukraine as it had been before. Most Ukrainian politicians knew that some ways had to be found to deal with the issue, such as finding jobs for those left on the Maidan. But it would be politically impossible for the new government to suddenly demand that everyone there go home. In the coming weeks, municipal workers would start removing some of the concrete barricades—a first step to returning downtown Kyiv to what it was before Maidan.

Meanwhile, in an attempt to sow fear and confusion among Jewish residents of eastern Ukraine, an unknown party circulated a flier calling for all Jews to register with the Donetsk People's Republic under threat of having their property confiscated. *Vice News's* reports from Ukraine's east were a visceral illustration of how rough things were getting. Ambassador Pyatt distributed one of these reports, noting, "Lots of military in this edition from the east—shots of the general in Kramatorsk being roughed up and some reminders of why the [alcohol] prohibition on the Maidan was so exceptional. And how wasted some of the People's Republicans are."

On Orthodox Easter Sunday, April 20, Russian news claimed that Pravyi Sektor nationalists had attacked separatists at a roadblock in Slovyansk, killing three. Reporting on the event, Russian television claimed that a large amount of Ukrainian army firearms, plastic explosives, smoke pellets, US-made night vision devices, and maps based on aerial photographs were found in the attackers' cars. But the flaming red arrow pointing to Pravyi Sektor was the business card of the group's leader, Dmitry Yarosh, found at the scene and shown on camera to the Russian television audience. Within hours, claims that this was indeed a Pravyi Sektor attack appeared on a Kremlin-controlled twitter feed, and the Russian Ministry of Foreign Affairs issued a statement claiming that the attack was evidence that the Ukrainians were not living up to their side of the Geneva deal. Details on the attack were murky, as only Russian media outlets could gain access to the area. Then, the story began to disintegrate. *Forbes* magazine and other media outlets noticed that the original news report on the attack aired by Life News, an outlet closely associated with the Kremlin, was uploaded to YouTube on April 19—the day before the incident allegedly occurred. Days later, the bodies of the alleged Pravyi Sektor members killed in the shootout were still missing. Pravyi Sektor representatives denied any involvement in the attack, calling it Russian provocation, and ridiculed the fact that Yarosh's business card somehow was found at the scene—a comically bad frame-up. And really, who leaves their business card at a murder scene? Ukrainian intelligence (SBU) also publicly called the event a Russian provocation and stated that Pravyi Sektor was not in the area at that time. Yet the affair was used to validate one of Russia's main propaganda claims aimed at eastern Ukrainians, that the "fascists and banderovsti" were roaming around with weapons in their hometowns, coming to get them.

On Monday, April 21, Vice President Biden was scheduled to arrive in Kyiv. Biden's involvement in Ukraine issues was long-standing, and his eight phone calls to Yanukovych had likely been key in persuading the then president not to deploy Ukrainian military against Kyiv's protesters. In Washington, the State Department spokesman issued pages of photographs of identified Russian special forces soldiers in eastern Ukraine. Ambassador Pyatt was busy that morning attending briefings, and wrote to the Task Force: "Just left our third meeting of the Geneva parties. Foreign Minister [Deshchytsia] pressed hard on lack of any Russian public support for agreement implementation. Contrasted this with strong Ukraine effort over holiday weekend. Russian rep (not chargé d'affaires this time—guess he was busy) had no answer. Ukraine asked for Lavrov condemnation of the Slovyansk journo hostage taking. (See horrible pictures on twitter.) Includes two Italians. One journo who was released says his captors were Russian. . . . SBU deputy joined. He and Interior Ministry rep said numbers of Russian intel operatives in the east growing. Said law and order situation getting out of control. One bank robbery in east today. Said Russians who took the Donetsk TV tower brought in digital equipment and are now transmitting Russian material (can't we confirm that somehow?).

Said a civilian Mi-8 helo was fired on over Slovyansk on the 19th when it was distributing copies of the Geneva agreement." From Washington, Director of the State Department's Ukraine, Moldova, and Belarus Office Michael Scanlon responded: "We have heard reports from Western investors on Ukraine's Volia cable [TV] that armed militants have entered some of their offices in the east demanding that the packaging of channels be switched to show Russian channels. Their staff accommodated out of concern for their personal safety."

Crimea was relatively quieter, but that did not mean that it was calm—especially not for the Crimean Tatars. A Russian-affiliated militia stormed the Crimean Tatar Mejlis, where I had met Majlis chairman Refat Chubarov two months before, demanding that they remove their Ukrainian flag and hoist the Crimean Republic colors. Several women were injured in the subsequent fight. Russia banned Mejlis head and Ukrainian Rada deputy Mustafa Dzhemilev from entering the Russian Federation for five years, now including Crimea, while *Ukrayinska Pravda* reported that Crimean authorities told local papers not to quote or mention Dzhemilev and other Mejlis leaders. They were being written out of the new history of Russian Crimea. According to the new authorities, their story wasn't to be told.

Although the separatists in eastern Ukraine had refused to comply with the Geneva statement, the Organization for Security and Cooperation in Europe (OSCE) still sent observers into eastern Ukraine in accordance with that agreement to report on the situation and ask for the release of hostages and the handover of seized buildings. On April 21, the OSCE team in Slovyansk saw the stolen Ukrainian Armed Forces armored vehicles alongside dozens of men armed with sniper rifles and other weapons. They also visited two of this group's hostages—Ukrainian journalist Irma Krat and Slovyansk mayor Shtepa.

Russian "mirroring" of US accusations continued. That the US accusations were evidence-based and the Russian ones concocted was again beside the point. After the United States released photographs of Russian soldiers and weapons in eastern Ukraine, the Russian Foreign Ministry revived baseless accusations of US "Greystone" mercenaries and weaponry in Ukraine. When the United States stated that Russia was making no effort to get separatists to comply with the Geneva statement, Russian officials publicly accused the United States of not pressuring the Ukrainian government to comply. As Russia was amassing intimidating military force on its border with Ukraine, the Russian Foreign Ministry on April 28 said that they were "deeply concerned" by the Ukrainian military supposedly amassing troops and military equipment at its border with Russia. This strategy diluted the effectiveness of US statements, but it could have other purposes as well. If a random Russian accusation about the US introduction of a certain type of weapon or tactic into Ukraine seemed really off the wall, it could be because this was the exact move that the Russian Federation was about to make. By going first and accusing the United States of some alleged misconduct, this tactic would then make our accurate but later claim of Russian transgressions appear like the kind of unfounded tit-for-tat accusation that they made constantly. The upshot was to make even basic facts seem unknowable to ordinary consumers of the news, leading them to conclude that they were lost in a world of smoke and mirrors, claims and counterclaims. It ushered people into a world where they had to question every development: "Is this what I really think, or is it rather what they want me to think?" This insidious mind game left people in eastern Ukraine, and everywhere else, most vulnerable to adopting a conspiracy-oriented mindset, which was the favorite playground of Russian propagandists. We weren't even contestants on this particular playing field. Our heavily lawyered statements were always solid, always provable. While we had facts on our side, they had the advantage of not needing to remain tethered to reality when spinning elaborate webs of lies and falsehoods. They used that advantage to great effect.

On Tuesday, April 22, in an ominous foreshadowing of far worse things to come, a Ukrainian military Antonov An-30 turboprop plane on a reconnaissance flight over Slovyansk was hit by several bullets. It was damaged but able to land safely. Unfortunately, the separatists would soon get better anti-aircraft weapons. Two bodies were found near Slovyansk, one of which was missing local Batkivshchyna council member Volodymyr Rybak. Investigators said that his body, bearing signs of torture, had been floating in a nearby river for several days. Acting President Turchynov immediately called for renewed "anti-terrorist operations" in eastern Ukraine after the murder. The following day, Russian Foreign Minister Lavrov accused Biden of ordering the renewed military operation, telling the press, "I have no grounds not to think that Americans direct this show in the most hands-on manner." State Department spokesperson Jen Psaki called these comments from Lavrov "ridiculous."

As the separatist power grab intensified, Russian journalists were honored guests while Western journalists found it a very dangerous place to practice their profession. "Separatists" kidnapped Italians Pal Gagaue and Cassimo Atanasio and Belarussian journalist Dmitry Galko on April 21, and *Vice News* reporter Simon Ostrovsky was taken in Slovyansk the following day and held for three days. Despite his captor's claims that Ostrovsky was treated as a "guest," on his release he said that he was tied and beaten during his captivity, perhaps an expression of the "separatists'" concept of hospitality.

Tension increased yet further when the Russian military began a fresh, large-scale training exercise on the Ukrainian border on April 24. Posts on Ukrainian social media claimed that Russian troops on the Lugansk border were close enough to be fully visible to Ukrainian border guards. The Ukrainian Foreign Ministry gave us an alarming nonpaper, that is, a document on plain paper without any indication of its author: "According to preliminary data obtained and under review, we are witnessing significantly intensified action of units of the Russian Armed Forces at the Ukrainian-Russian state border area, especially in the Donetsk and Lugansk areas." The paper described the activities of columns of armored vehicles, infantry equipment, helicopters, and troops on the other side of the border across from seven Ukrainian military installations. We could no longer rule out a direct conventional military clash between Russia and Ukraine. If that actually were to happen, the Russian military might not stop until it reached Kyiv and dealt with those it couldn't stop calling "fascists." Russian UN Ambassador Vitaly Churkin even informed his country's journalists that a military invasion of Ukraine could be justified by Article 51 of the UN charter, which guaranteed states the right to self-defense. During just the preceding twenty-four hours, Russian fighter aircraft had entered Ukrainian airspace seven times.

Also on April 24, Ukrainian intelligence posted to YouTube an intercepted audio recording, which they claimed demonstrated the involvement of Russian military intelligence officers in the murder of Slovyansk council member Rybak. In part of the recording, a man they identified as a Russian military intelligence officer orders the kidnapping, and in another, what was identified as the voice of Russian military intelligence colonel Igor Girkin (aka Strelkov) is heard telling self-proclaimed Slovyansk mayor Vyacheslav Ponomaryov to "come and pick up the body because it is starting to stink." This was incredibly dark stuff. We were no longer in the world of the mid-December Maidan street party. Margarita Semonyan, the editor-in-chief of Russia Today, sent a simple tweet: "Ukraine. R.I.P." In a truly outrageous statement, Sergei Lavrov told a forum of young diplomats in Moscow on April 25 that "all the power of American propaganda is being used to represent the Russian-speaking population of Ukraine as enemies who need to be killed." In an official statement, Secretary Kerry bluntly accused Russia of "deception and destabilization" in Ukraine and warned that further meddling would be an "expensive mistake." The Kremlin shrugged off the warning.

On Friday morning, April 25, separatists used antitank weapons to destroy a Ukrainian MI-8 helicopter and an AN-2 propeller plane on the ground during another attack on the Kramatorsk airfield. In Odesa, the State Security Service of Ukraine (SBU) announced that they had arrested members of a radical group that planned to carry out an attack on World War II veterans during their upcoming traditional May 9 parade celebrating Nazi Germany's surrender in 1945. According to the SBU press release, a Russian TV channel paid the group to conduct the attack, which they could film for television and blame publicly on Ukrainian nationalists. The details of the story itself were somewhat murky, but it was certain that such a film would have huge propaganda value in Russia. The image of Ukrainian nationalists attacking elderly Russian war veterans would make the average Russian's blood boil, and now Ukrainian intelligence was claiming that Russian intelligence was trying to engineer those images just for that reason. My colleagues took notice of the fact that Russia Today, Life News (Russian news website), and other Russian media outlets seemed to have an uncanny ability to be on the scene before big events would happen, such as the attack on a pro-Russian roadblock in the eastern city of Soledar on April 27. It inspired some dark humor. Our Public Affairs Officer Eric Johnson suggested, tongue-in-cheek, a new slogan for Russia Today's operations in eastern Ukraine: "Russia Today—We Make Sure Tomorrow's News Happens Today!" Every claim was suspect, every accusation met a counter accusation. When Russia accused Ukraine of cutting off water supplies to Crimea, anonymous hackers posted documents online stating that the cutoff was on the Russian side and done specifically to be able to blame the Ukrainians for the cutoff. The volleys of accusations went on and on.

It had been several days since anyone had heard from an OSCE observation group in eastern Ukraine. On Sunday, April 27, separatists in Slovyansk marched the OSCE team out in front of TV cameras to state that they were being detained but not mistreated. German Foreign Minister Steinmeier said in a statement, "The public parading of the OSCE observers and Ukrainian security forces as prisoners is revolting and blatantly hurts the dignity of the victims." They were far from the only prisoners in Slovyansk. The separatists detained various others whom they accused of being foreign spies or Ukrainian intelligence agents. These pro-Russian separatists released a Swiss member of the OSCE Vienna Document military observation team that day, while new, self-proclaimed Slovyansk "mayor" Ponomaryov declared the German-led team of seven internationals and their Ukrainian escorts to be "NATO spies" and said their release depended on whether Ukrainian authorities set free arrested separatists. The legitimately elected Slovyansk mayor, who had declared that the military forces which swept Slovyansk were foreigners, was still in jail. It was now obvious that the OSCE team members were hostages. Media reported that police found another body bearing signs of torture in the river near Slovyansk close to where the bodies of Horlivka city councilman Rybak and Kyiv university student Popravko had been discovered a week before. Ukrainian intelligence (SBU) confirmed that pro-Russian separatists in Kramatorsk captured three of their officers on April 27. In online videos, the three heavily bloodied, bound, and blindfolded prisoners stated that they were captured while on a mission to apprehend a separatist leader in Horlivka. Donetsk separatists seized the city's television broadcast center that day stating that they would only broadcast Russian TV channels, but the Ukrainian Ministry of Interior announced a few hours later that they had cleared that building of separatists. In the strategic port city of Mariupol, an arson attack burned a local court building to the ground. The following day, another eastern Ukrainian town, Kostyantynivka, fell to the separatists.

The United States took notice and responded at the highest level. While traveling in Manila, President Obama announced that his administration would sanction additional Russian officials in connection with the infiltration and destabilization of eastern Ukraine. The administration banned seven Russian government officials, including two members of President Putin's inner circle, from entering the United States, and the Treasury Department froze their US assets. The order also froze the assets of seventeen companies linked to Putin's inner circle. According to a White House statement on the action, "Since April 17, Russia has done nothing to meet its Geneva commitments and in fact has further escalated the crisis. Russia's involvement in the recent violence in eastern Ukraine is indisputable." Within hours, Russian deputy foreign minister Sergey Ryabkov told the press that "the statement by the White House press secretary prompts disgust" and "demonstrates a complete lack of understanding among our colleagues in Washington about what is happening in Ukraine." On the contrary, the West now understood Moscow's new style of warfare—which arrives in a package with the return address smudged out—better than during the Crimea invasion. The EU also issued a travel ban on an additional fifteen Russian officials on the same day. A very different response came from Beijing. Chinese Foreign Ministry spokesman Qin Gang announced his country's opposition to sanctions against Russia, calling them "not conducive to the issue's resolution." The Russian officials who ordered their neighbor's invasion, and those officials' cash, were still welcome in Beijing.

In Kharkiv, Ukraine's second city, Mayor Gennady Kernes was an elusive figure. Pro-Euromaidan figures labeled him and Kharkiv region governor Mykhailo Dobkin "the gruesome twosome" for their use of paid muscle to harshly repress protest activity. Kernes took the lead in pushing pro-Yanukovych propaganda and labeling the protesters as "fascists." He often posted pictures of himself online working out in the gym. But after the change in power, Kernes quickly started singing a different tune, saying that he would work with the new government and that Ukraine was indivisible. His uncompromisingly tough pro-Yanukovych position quickly morphed into antiseparatism in recent weeks. On April 28, Kernes took a morning swim at his usual spot. As he was leaving, an unknown assailant with a sniper rifle shot him in the back and critically injured him. He was immediately rushed into surgery with life-threatening wounds. Kernes survived and was soon transported to a hospital in Israel for further treatment, but the assassination attempt was further evidence of the ongoing breakdown of order in the eastern part of Ukraine, a country under attack from without and within.

14

THE LIE METASTASIZES

When we served in Beijing, Natalya and I became good friends with another State Department "tandem couple," James and Katie Hallock. We hadn't seen them in a few years and were really excited when they were assigned to Kyiv, although we would only overlap for a month or so. Via email we hammered home one constant message—Kyiv is a great place to work, calm and livable.

James arrived first, and we took him to dinner at a brewpub on Kreschatyk on his first night in town, just a block or so from Maidan. During training in Washington for the last year, James had been looking at images of people throwing Molotov cocktails and dodging bullets on the square. On this warm spring evening, we sat down outside the restaurant, ordered some food and a few beers, and began to catch up. Suddenly, out on the street an oddly familiar sight from a few months before materialized—a torch-lit procession with flags, Nazi symbols, other heavy right-wing iconography, and most importantly, a TV crew getting everything on tape as proof that Kyiv remained under "fascist control." The procession marched past us toward Maidan, and a few minutes later, we heard several loud blasts. Ducking into the restaurant from our outside table, we saw a young man running down the street brandishing a machete. I had never before seen a machete in Kyiv. It all seemed very artificial and bizarre. What was going on? We actually had a pretty good idea.

Eric Johnson in Public Affairs sent out a message: "*Ukrayinska Pravda,*

Hromadske, and Euromaidan are reporting a massive fight [involving] the fringe SNA (Socialist Nationalist Assembly) . . . Euromaidan is calling the SNA provocateurs." Then he wrote what we were all thinking: "Right-wing Ukrainians disturbing the peace on the streets of Kyiv is right out of Kremlin central casting."

Greg Pfleger from the Political Section secured some more details: "The SNA were stopped at the entrance to the Maidan tent city and asked to extinguish their torches. . . . At this point SNA took offense and began the conflict. SDF and so-called free sotnyas (unaffiliated sotnyas) contained the situation as best they could, and say all is calm now."

But just who were the SNA? As Eric put it, "In all the many hours I clocked on Maidan between November 21 and February 21, not once do I remember seeing SNA's colors, symbols, flags, or armbands." It was obvious that the images would be used in Russia as fresh evidence that Euromaidan, and by extension the new government, were neo-Nazis. Naturally, there would be no mention of the fact that this group had nothing to do with Euromaidan and appeared from nowhere to fight with Euromaidan. But the images of swastikas in downtown Kyiv with a provocative voice-over was a heat-seeking propaganda missile that would always reach its target.

"Just some street theater," I told James. That was the most accurate description I could conceive—it wasn't representative of what Kyiv was at the time, and it had a "play acting" sort of feel. But the scene certainly didn't help us give James the comforting welcome we had intended.

Meanwhile, Russian maneuvers around and within Ukraine were jangling nerves in Poland and the Baltic countries, where Putin's use of history as a justification for hybrid warfare felt like a direct threat. On April 28, the latest of 600 US troops and twelve American and British fighter aircraft arrived in the region as NATO's answer to the constant Russian military drills on their side of the border. UN Secretary General Ban Ki-moon condemned the detention of Organization for Security and Co-operation in Europe (OSCE) monitors in eastern Ukraine. While Russia's OSCE ambassador tried to transfer blame for the situation to the OSCE by calling the dispatch of the observers to eastern Ukraine "extremely irresponsible," the US OSCE delegation criticized Moscow for not condemning their abduction. Russia and the West's views of the evolving conflict forced upon Ukraine increasingly bifurcated. There wasn't even superficial rhetorical overlap, and certainly no agreement on what peace should look like.

Without providing any evidence or even explanation, on April 28 the Russian Foreign Ministry issued a statement that it was "extremely concerned" by reports that the Ukrainian government was creating "Nazi-style" concentration camps for the citizens of eastern Ukraine. The images shown were actually of a detention center east of Donetsk built for illegal migrants, with construction dating back to a contract awarded in 2010. Several days later, on May 1, Russian state television channel Rossiya One amazingly reported on "the Third Reich's influence on White House policies," claiming that World War II–era Ukrainian war criminals were influencing "Washington's tolerant attitude toward nationalist movements in Ukraine." While such reports were merely malicious fantasy, much more reliable reports were coming from Slovyansk and other cities that separatists were terrorizing non-Russian communities, especially Ukrainian and Roma populations, which had begun to flee. A well-played fictional menace could justify creating terror in the real world.

Pro-Russian titushky armed with pipes and clubs attacked pro-Ukrainian demonstrators in Kharkiv on April 28, seriously injuring at least fifteen and seizing seven hostages who were released later that night. Gunmen kidnapped the head of an anti-terrorist police unit in Luhansk and held him hostage in the separatist-occupied State Security Service of Ukraine (SBU) building. One Ukrainian serviceman was killed and another wounded in a bomb blast in Donetsk Oblast. The following day, Lugansk separatists added to their collection of occupied buildings by storming the regional administration building, then the TV center, then the local prosecutor's office. Video of the seizures indicated that the "little green men" were in charge, with local recruits following their directions.

While seriously wounded Kharkiv mayor Kernes was in Israel for further medical treatment, Russian media shifted into overdrive trying to blame Kyiv/Maidan–aligned forces for the nearly successful assassination attempt. They emphasized Kernes's past as a Yanukovych ally who fled briefly to Russia following the collapse of the Yanukovych government as the "fascists'" reason for trying to kill him. Naturally, these reports omitted the most relevant information—that since his return to Kharkiv, Kernes had become a supporter of the Kyiv government and a harsh critic of separatism. At the time he was shot, he was one of the strongest voices against the separatists. His past history as a Yanukovych loyalist actually made him more effective in delivering this message to those whom Kyiv found difficult to reach, and thus even more objectionable to those who wanted to fracture the new Ukraine.

On April 29, US media quoted Secretary Kerry, speaking to an unidentified group behind closed doors, as saying that the United States had signals intelligence definitively proving that intelligence operatives in eastern Ukraine were "taking their orders from Moscow." As if in response to seeing just how effective its own destabilization tactics had been in eastern Ukraine, Russia's Federation Council on the same day passed new laws stiffening the penalty within Russia for organizing mass unrest and terrorism, giving Russia's Federal Security Service (FSB) new search and detention authorities. Russian authorities didn't want anyone doing at home what they were fomenting in Ukraine.

The situation in the east remained fluid. News poured in hourly on the violent jockeying for position in tiny towns few of us had heard of before. Our Defense Attaché Office wrote on the morning of April 30, "From contacts out east: Horlivka is completely taken by pro-Russian forces, backed by twenty little green men. They are moving fast. Kostyantynov has some serious looking barricades going up." Even as Ukrainian forces cleared three separatist roadblocks outside of Slovyansk, acting President Turchynov told the press that Ukraine's military was largely helpless to resolve the situation in Donetsk and Luhansk regions. Violent pro-Russian extremists shot and seriously wounded Kharkiv lawyer and pro-European activist Ihor Chudovsky in a botched kidnapping attempt, while other pro-Russian extremists kidnapped local elected officials in Kostyantynov and Krasnoarmeysk. On May 1, the town of Alchevsk in Lugansk region fell. Militants seized the city hall building and kidnapped the mayor. This was not an eastern version of Euromaidan. The attackers were heavily armed, operated with military efficiency, and had no compunction about violence. There were no Gandhi banners hanging over this crowd of largely imported professionals.

During the spate of murders and kidnappings of local officials in eastern Ukraine, the Russian media most often referred innocuously to the "separatists" backed by undeclared Russian military forces as "advocates of federalization." That was like referring to Mafia enforcers as Salvation Army Santa Clauses collecting donations for Christmas dinners. In fact, the new government in Kyiv had been open to various proposals for constitutional reform and decentralization since the outbreak of the Crimea crisis. They had also been open to various types of polling and referenda to guide this process, as the gun-toting "advocates of federalization" had demanded. After some initial missteps, such as putting forward a draft language law that would have diminished the status of the Russian language in Ukraine had it passed, the Turchynov government recognized the necessity of giving more authority over such cultural and educational issues to the regions. The Ukrainian government convened a series of constitutional reform meetings, such as one held in the Rada on April 29, which included hundreds of parliamentarians, local government representatives from across Ukraine (including the east), judges, NGOs, and the media. Yet, despite the broad participation in this process, the Russian media continued to cast this process as closed and conspiratorial as it included reasonable voices from the east rather than from the armed militant groups that the Russians themselves supported.

The type of radical federalization advocated by the Russian Federation for Ukraine was something the Kremlin leadership would never have accepted for itself. Indeed, Putin quickly reversed the trend toward decentralization of power in Russia after he succeeded Boris Yeltsin in 2000. Were Ukraine to enact this type of decentralization, it would arguably have been even more advantageous for Moscow than either eastern Ukraine's independence or its annexation by Russia. Under Moscow's plan, federalization would amount to eastern Ukraine's de facto independence from Kyiv. Even better, it would come with an additional benefit. In this version of radical decentralization, all major Ukrainian foreign policy initiatives, including signing an agreement like the EU Association Agreement, could be vetoed by any of the regions. So if Moscow exercised de facto control over the authorities in eastern Ukraine, as it already did by this time, it could permanently undermine Ukraine's ability to chart its own foreign policy course. Kyiv was actually willing to grant wide latitude to the east on issues such as language, culture, and education. These were the substantive matters that Ukrainians in the east actually cared most about, not whether Moscow held veto power over Ukraine's foreign policy decisions as the Kremlin desired. So even when Kyiv basically offered eastern Ukrainians what they said they wanted, as articulated by a wide range of stakeholders in the full glare of the local and international press, Moscow was dissatisfied. It wanted much more—a silent controlling hand. That is why the Kremlin continued to insist that the Ukrainian constitutional reform process was nonrepresentative and nontransparent and constantly disparaged it. That is why the Russian media, the Putin administration's collective mouthpiece, tried so hard to convince many eastern Ukrainians that participating in this process was the moral equivalent of sitting at a table with Hitler talking casually over tea about how to best spit on your grandfather's grave.

Meanwhile, life in the east was getting even more dangerous. We received a message from an American-invested cable television and media company in Donetsk: "Armed men tried to enter the Donetsk offices of their cable company to force them to broadcast Russian television. They held them off yesterday. . . . I just spoke to our CEO regarding the situation in Donetsk. He said it was horrible. He tried to get authorities there and in Kyiv to help. There is no authority, he said. CEO is going to Donetsk now to try and ensure the safety of the employees. He refused to talk to me anymore on the mobile phone. Said it was too dangerous."

Donetsk separatists announced that they were preparing to hold a referendum on May 11 with a single question, "Do you support the creation of the Donetsk People's Republic?" There was no clarity about whether this was a "republic" within Ukraine, as the "Crimean Republic" had been for many years within Ukraine, something more independent, or just a pit stop on the road to Russian annexation. The complete lack of clarity about the goals of the separatists also pertained to the other great question about them: Who the hell were they? These were not even marginal political figures; they were not political figures at all on the local scene. People such as self-declared "Donetsk people's mayor" Denis Pushilin and his counterpart in Slovyansk Vyacheslav Ponomaryov had never even been players in local politics before. They materialized out of nowhere with the help of the anonymous but heavily armed "little green men." Without their foreign military backers, it would be doubtful that anyone would ever have heard of them.

Despite the turmoil and violence in substantial swaths of Donetsk and Lugansk regions, much of eastern Ukraine remained relatively calm even though the separatists and their state sponsors to the east doubtless wanted to see the entire region erupt in flames. Despite dueling rallies in Odesa, the Kyiv government's authority there remained intact. Kolomoyskyi's flamboyant and controversial style in Dnipropetrovsk seemed to be effective in keeping things from spinning out of control, and the attempted assassination of Mayor Kernes had failed to ignite the Kharkiv tinder keg. A member of the Defense Attaché Office visiting Zaporizhzhya wrote in on May 1: "No public display of St. George's ribbons, no Russian flags . . . all appears normal, inclusive of the new standard of seeing pro-Ukraine Self-Defense Forces (SDF) guarding government buildings, weaponless and coordinated with the mayor and police . . . overall a quiet day in Zap, many people are probably on the river enjoying shashlik [meat kabob] and the cool breeze." Overall it was a very mixed picture—calm prevailing in some places, chaos in others.

As the International Monetary Fund board in Washington, D.C., approved a two-year, $17 billion loan plan for Ukraine, authorities in London agreed to help Ukraine track down what could be tens of billions more in Yanukovych-era stolen funds. Meanwhile, the Russian government held its first May Day parade in Red Square since the Soviet era, an unsubtle reminder of Russia's burgeoning military power. Already engaged on its own territory in an undeclared war with its giant neighbor, Ukraine's acting President Turchynov signed a decree on military conscription for men between eighteen and twenty-five years old. Then, in the early morning hours of Friday, May 2, the Ukrainian military launched a large-scale offensive against separatists in Slovyansk. This was not a negotiation tactic, a PR ploy, or mere intimidation—this was the first real Ukrainian attempt during the most recent crisis to retake lost ground by force. There was a real risk of major retaliation, so Turchynov put the Ukrainian armed forces on high alert for a possible massive Russian invasion in response. Russian media soon reported that two Ukrainian helicopters were shot down, but sorting fact from propaganda was difficult since only Russian media were reporting from Slovyansk, a town of over 100,000 in the north of the Donetsk region. Ukrainian intelligence soon confirmed that one helicopter had been shot down by "foreign military experts" near the city. It was obvious that the separatists had acquired considerable ground-to-air anti-aircraft rocket equipment and the capability to use it in very short order. One Ukrainian pilot was dead, more were wounded. Separatists called on Slovyansk residents via ham radio to come to the central town square to make a video appealing to Putin for direct Russian military invasion. Meanwhile, Donetsk separatists seized control of the railway control center and cut electricity for regional rail transit.

Journalists from CBS, SkyNews, and Buzzfeed were all reported temporarily missing or detained in eastern Ukraine. Russia's Ministry of Foreign Affairs (MFA) called Ukraine's military operations in eastern Ukraine "destructive" and "punitive," blaming Ukraine for trashing the principles of the Geneva statement and claiming that Western countries were preventing a peaceful resolution of the crisis by continuing to back Kyiv. That much was expected, of course, but the Russian statement further stated, without any evidence of course, that their favorite bogeyman, Pravyi Sektor, was involved in attacks on Slavyansk and that "in the course of the punitive operation of the Ukrainian Army and the illegal ultranationalist formations, the English language was heard in the ether, and the attackers of Slovyansk included English-speaking foreigners." More shade and baseless innuendo, intended only for a certain population predisposed to believe. This accusation mirrored numerous Western statements of fact, backed by actual photos and other evidence, that Russian forces were active in the area. In quick response, Ukrainian diplomats called the Russian allegations "cynical and baseless," stating that, with the exception of Russian commandos, no foreigners took part in the clash.

On May 2, tragedy and horror hit Odesa, Ukraine's third-largest city, which had been largely spared from upheaval to that point but was part of what Russian President Putin included in his "Novorossiya" zone during his April 17 call-in show two weeks earlier. During the day, clashes broke out between pro-Russia and pro-unity demonstrations. While Odesa was a largely Russian-speaking city, pro-Ukraine sentiment remained strong and few wanted to see the chaos unfolding in Donetsk and Lugansk spill over into their beautiful city on the northern coast of the Black Sea. While several days before a website announced the creation of the "Odesa People's Republic," the town's prominent anti-Maidan leaders denied having anything to do with the internet manifesto, saying that they supported a looser Ukrainian federation rather than independence or secession.

After a pro-unity march was attacked by about three hundred anti-Maidan protesters, a running street battle involving Molotov cocktails, rocks, and air pistols rolled through downtown Odesa. Images of the body of Euromaidan activist Ihor Ivanov, shot in the street, were soon posted on social media, leading both sides to bring firearms downtown. The fighting intensified. Witnesses told journalists and our contacts that pro-Russian forces fired at pro-unity protesters from behind police lines and from the rooftop of a local shopping mall. The press quickly reported three deaths and fifteen injuries. By most accounts the pro-Russian groups were greatly outnumbered, and by evening, they were pushed back to their encampment outside the Odesa Trade Union Building. As the pro-unity groups began destroying their camp, pro-Russian activists retreated inside the building. The warring sides continued to exchange

Molotov cocktails. Then, a fire between the second and third floors began to envelop the building. Horrifying images of people jumping out of windows to escape the flames shocked the country, then the world. The death count was horrific: forty-two people died at the building—thirty-two from smoke inhalation, and ten while jumping to escape the flames. Apart from the sniper murders on Maidan, it was the largest loss of life of the crisis. Graphic video released the next day showed charred bodies on the main staircase inside the building. The Ukrainian government declared two days of mourning to start the following day, and acting Prime Minister Yatsenyuk called it "a tragedy not only for Odesa, but a tragedy for all Ukraine." State Department spokesperson Marie Harf expressed condolences on behalf of the United States: "The United States today mourns with all Ukrainians the heartbreaking loss of life in Odesa. Today the international community must stand together in support of the Ukrainian people as they cope with this tragedy."

Our Defense Attaché Office was also working with their contacts to pin down exactly what had happened: "We received some more info this morning on the clashes as relayed by the local police. 43 dead, over 200 injured, 50 of those seriously. The majority of the dead seem to be pro-Russians who were holded [sic] up in the Trade Union Building. According to police, the pro-Russians set the entrance on fire to keep pro-Ukrainians and police at bay, but the fire spread quickly through the building. The surviving pro-Russians that were captured claimed they were all local Odesa residents. However, seized passports and other documents indicated they were mostly from Transnistria and [other parts of] eastern Ukraine. Also seized were automatic weapons, smoke grenades, flash bangs, and machetes. Despite being well organized and supplied, the pro-Russians were not prepared for the anger of the overwhelming pro-Ukrainian crowd."

The Embassy tried to make sense of the horrific events in a city that had seemed calm. Our Public Affairs Section had only just finished our regular "America Days" event in Odesa several days before. During this program, which included documentary film showings, jazz guitar, and Frank Sinatra music, Odesa did not appear to be a city on edge. No one at the Embassy had forgotten SBU reports about a cynical effort by a Russian television station, broken up several weeks earlier, to stage an attack on World War II veterans during Victory Day celebrations on May 9 in order to destabilize the region. Ambassador Pyatt wrote to the Task Force: "Tragic day in Odesa . . . at least

30 killed. I'm convinced based on what I saw there three weeks ago that none of this could have happened without outside provocation. Indeed, most of the violence seems to have been a result of Odesans responding to the provocative violence of armed separatists who were shooting at crowds. We'll learn more in the days ahead. Photos appearing online of both Odesa police and pro-Russian terrorists in Odesa wearing matching red armbands—just like the matching yellow armbands of the police and titushky in Kyiv when the killings started on Maidan in February. . . . Definitely a coordinated operation." Public Affairs's Andrew Paul responded: "Could not agree more. Today's news is really shocking after spending three days in Odesa this week. Monday–Wednesday we had eleven staff at twenty-five separate public events, workshops, or meetings in multiple locations for America Days in Odesa. The city was calm and had a friendly, comfortable feel; our local partners and local audiences were all welcoming, appreciative, and even expressed cautious optimism for the future, or echoed the idea that Odesa was too cosmopolitan to fall victim to mass violence—by itself. Those who expressed fears about the future explained how outsiders were the source of their fear."

Russia's spin doctors leaped onto the Odesa tragedy. The Russian Presidential Administration website sent condolences to the families of those killed in Odesa "as a result of the punitive actions of the Kyiv authorities"—portraying the deaths as somehow a result of the Ukrainian military's actions to reclaim other parts of the Black Sea coast far east of Odesa. The Russian Foreign Ministry also stated that the Odesa tragedy would make it impossible to hold a presidential election in Ukraine on May 25, something they were already unenthusiastic about. Odesa governor Volodymyr Nemyrovskyy blamed local cops for selling out Ukraine to Russia: "Today's casualties in Odesa could have been avoided. To have done that, the police should not have sold out their country or their consciences, and should have followed their oath to the Ukrainian people. . . . Shame on them." On Facebook, a widely shared post from "Odesa Doctor" Ihor Rozovskyy stated that he was stopped from assisting fire victims by "Nazi radicals." Ukrainian blogger Maksym Savenevskyy noted that the photo used for "Dr. Rozovskyy" was actually that of a Russian dentist with a different name, and that the posting came from an account that was only one hour old. An editorial in Russia's *Komsomolskaya Pravda* called for Russia to punish the "fascists" who "restored Holocaust ovens in the middle of Odesa." The greater the barrage of lies, the better. Some at least would find their targets.

On the morning of Saturday, May 3, pro-Russian militias in Slovyansk finally released the OSCE observers they had kidnapped. The Russian government portrayed this as a humanitarian gesture while continuing to deny their own influence over the separatists. Official Russian public enthusiasm for the armed militants who were seizing swaths of eastern Ukraine swelled. Russian Deputy Prime Minister Dmitriy Rogozin tweeted, "Hey, guys. I would exchange everything I have right now, without thinking about it for an instant, for the happiness of being together in a trench with the defenders of Slovyansk!" Showing admirable self-restraint, Rogozin denied himself the happiness he imagined and remained at his post in Moscow. Were he serious, there was certainly enough fighting in the east to grant Rogozin's wish to join his separatist brothers-in-arms. Heavy combat was taking place around Kostyantynivka in Donetsk region, and skirmishes were breaking out at multiple roadblocks. Meanwhile, in Odesa, in the aftermath of fresh tragedy, pro-Russian groups attempted to seize a local police station, forcing the police to release sixty-seven people arrested during the previous night's clashes. The separatists also hung a large Russian flag from the charred Trade Union Building. On Monday, May 5, four Ukrainian servicemen were killed and thirty wounded during fighting around Slovyansk in which they claimed to have killed over thirty separatists.

That same day, Russian authorities continued to keep Crimean Tatar leader Mustafa Jemiliev from entering Crimea despite the protests of his community. Russian Crimea's prosecutor general, the thirty-four-year-old Nataliya Poklonskaya, meanwhile threatened to ban Crimean Tatar Mejlis chairman Chubarov's organization for "extremist actions." Observers expected Putin to travel to Crimea for the World War II "Victory Day" celebrations, and no one would be allowed to rain on that parade.

Later on Monday, the SBU released an unusual statement, announcing that 1.5 kilograms of a radioactive substance possibly containing U-235 was seized from a group of eight Ukrainians and one Russian citizen crossing into Ukraine on April 30. The SBU stated that the material was intended for use in a "dirty bomb" to destabilize southeast Ukraine. The following day, an interesting posting was removed from the Russian President's Council on Civil Society and Human Rights website, as *Forbes* magazine put it, as if it were radioactive waste. According to the official results of the Crimea referendum, out of the 83 percent of registered voters who cast a ballot, 97 percent favored annexation. Putin's own Human Rights Council's report, written on the basis of polling and other independent research in Crimea, concluded that outside of Sevastopol, home to the Russian-leased naval base where support for Russia was unusually strong, the turnout was likely between 30 and 50 percent with between 50 and 60 percent voting for annexation under the watchful eyes of the Russian military. That would have meant victory anyway, so what was the purpose of the blatant lying? Indeed, with many groups such as Ukrainians and Crimean Tatars refusing to participate in the referendum, the claimed 83 percent voter turnout had always appeared suspect. Now an official Russian government website was validating these suspicions and essentially calling the official results fraudulent. Even credulity has its limits.

Through our Embassy's election monitoring efforts over the years, our local staff had a good network of friends and contacts at district election commissions (DECs) and local polling stations throughout Ukraine, including in the east. One of our local staff members received a harrowing report from DEC 108 in Luhansk region: "On May 6 at 18:00, four masked people entered DEC 108 in the local culture center (5 Lenin Square, Krasnodon), blocked the entrance, and demanded DEC members to stop preparations for the [May 25] presidential election and prepare for the referendum on May 11 instead. They said to Head of DEC . . . that their legal grounds for the May 11 referendum was 'a bullet in the head.' They left after agreeing to meet next day at 8:00 a.m. DEC members appealed to the police to provide them with a security guard. The police didn't want to accept the official statement until the DEC lawyer addressed the head of Krasnodon MOI [Interior Ministry] department. At 22:00, up to ten armed masked people came inside the DEC when the head and two women were working there. They locked women in a separate room, and beat up the DEC head for 40 minutes demanding lists of the voters (which were not in the DEC at that time). They scattered and destroyed part of the documents and left. The terrorists' spokesperson was a PoR [Party of Regions] city council member, who came with them unmasked." Indeed, when the plaintiff's legal argument is 'a bullet to the head,' who really has time to go back and consult the latest statutes? What would you do in that situation? Stand up for the law on principle and receive your deserved congratulations from the grave?

Publicly released intercepted phone calls had become a regular feature of the information war. On Wednesday, May 7, the SBU released a recording of a call between Dmytro Boytsov, a leader of the separatist "Orthodox Donbas" group, and his controller, Alexander Barkashov of the far-right, neo-Nazi "Russian National Unity" party in Moscow. The recording (translated as follows from some salty Russian in press reports) starts with Boytsov telling Barkashov that the activities of the Ukrainian military "cocksuckers" would force them to cancel the planned May 11 referendum on the establishment of the Donetsk People's Republic:

Barkashov: "Dima, Dima, Dima, there is no way that you cancel it. It will mean that you got scared."

Boytsov: "No, we are not scared at all. We simply can't hold it, we're not ready."

Barkashov: "Dima, just flog whatever you want. Write something like 99 percent down. . . . Are you going to walk around and collect papers? Are you fucking insane? Forget it, fuck them all."

Boytsov: "Got it."

Barkashov: "Write that 99 percent . . . well, not 99 percent . . . let's say 89 percent voted for the Donetsk Republic. And that's it, fucking shit."

So, needless to say, at US Embassy Kyiv we were expecting an electoral process of the highest integrity on the eleventh.

Also on May 7, the Ukrainian cabinet moved its daily meeting to Kharkiv in order to continue its dialogue with the regions on constitutional reform as spelled out in the Geneva statement. Putin then publicly called on the separatists to delay their referendum and said that he might back Ukraine's May 25 national presidential elections, leaving observers to wonder if he really meant it or was just cagily distancing himself from his real positions. The militants announced the following day that they would proceed with the referendum regardless of Putin's statement. According to fresh polling by the Pew Research Center, 70 percent of all Ukrainians, including 58 percent of Russian speakers, desired Ukraine to remain a single, unified state. But no one expected the separatist polls to show this reality. After all, who actually shows up to be closed in a box by violent, heavily armed extremists at an illegal, hastily contrived election? It's not likely that a broad cross section of the peace-loving electorate would. But no matter. To paraphrase Stalin, it is not he who votes that counts, but he who counts the votes.

Meanwhile, in my own bailiwick, the date of the much-delayed intellectual property rights concert was drawing near regardless of what was happening elsewhere in the country. We had several popular bands lined up, and our original idea to give away tickets to those answering a few basic questions about intellectual property rights in Ukraine still seemed sound. I met with our partners, including Ignat, Dmytro who had led me on a tour of the Maidan those months ago, and ticket seller Karabas and PR firm Ahead. We had reserved the city's biggest indoor rock venue, StereoPlaza, which could accommodate about 5,000 people. Everyone was nervous about the big upcoming event, but their anxiety wasn't limited to relevant topics discussed in our cramped meeting room. During a break, Dmytro went outside to smoke a cigarette. Ignat and I followed to keep him company. The conversation inevitably turned to the situation in Ukraine.

"But really," Dmytro offered. "If things get really bad here, like if we get well and truly invaded, I'm sure that the United States would help us out. . . . I mean, we're a massively strategic country, right? Heart of Europe and all that crap, right?" He took a drag on his cigarette. "Am I right?" He asked, hoping to reassure himself.

I didn't know how to answer. Dmytro was a friend, and I had to be honest with him. "Ukraine's not a NATO member. There's no alliance." I began.

Dmytro cut me off. "That's not what I asked. My question was simple. Yours is the most powerful country in the world, and we are looking at getting invaded by a foreign military. Would you guys help us?"

There was a long pause. I couldn't lie to him. "As far as the military goes, I wouldn't plan on it," I said, looking back at him. He seemed sad but not surprised. He finished his smoke in silence. "OK," he said after a long pause. "Let's go back inside. We've got a concert coming up, you fuckers."

Late on Thursday, May 8, the SBU announced that it had blocked the transfer of 100 million rubles from the Russian Ministry of Defense in Sevastopol to a firm in Donetsk. Ukrainian Prime Minister Yatsenyuk already said that his government would be on high alert for provocations on May 9, World War II Victory Day. That day a heavy police presence blanketed Kyiv. Following a night in which forty pro-Russian separatists attacked and burned down a border post in Lugansk region and also ambushed an Interior Ministry convoy transporting captured separatists, there was no reason for anyone to let their guard down. Apart from the military and security forces, mass media were the primary target of the militants who desperately wanted to replace Ukrainian TV and radio with Russian broadcasts. Unknown saboteurs even attempted an attack on the Kyiv TV tower, disrupting transmissions for a short time in the middle of the night. As Putin presided over a large Victory Day celebration in Red Square, Prime Minister Yatsenyuk, acting President Turchynov, and three former presidents of Ukraine laid wreaths at the World War Victory Park in Kyiv. Russian media focused nearly exclusively on a group of Communists booing Yatsenyuk at the event, not the fact that the Kyiv government they insisted were "fascists" was completely unified in celebrating the historic victory over actual fascists.

It was becoming increasingly difficult to keep tabs on what was happening in eastern Ukraine, other than that it was terrifying. While the east had a greater percentage of Russian speakers and those who sympathized with Russia on the global stage than elsewhere in Ukraine, it was always a diverse region. Before the crisis, although city councils and local administrators were largely run by Yanukovych's Party of Regions, opposition parties also had seats and spoke up loudly about local affairs. Opposition newspapers and websites had flourished in the east. Their problem was convincing locals to care about their views or feel that their community's problems were actually fixable. They had not been subjected to intimidation or oppression. Separatism was never part of that local conversation any more than residents of Florida's Key West were serious about an armed uprising to make the Jimmy Buffet–loving "Conch Republic" an actual independent nation. However, there was no doubt that the unease of many in the east with the new government in Kyiv was real. In normal times, the new central government would have the opportunity to sort through these issues and prove to the easterners that Kyiv was working for their interests too. But outside interference denied the new Kyiv government this opportunity. The relentless slander campaign by the Russian media, so influential in eastern Ukraine, branding the new government as fascists who burn their critics in ovens, was only the most visible part of the effort. Other parts were even more sinister and distressing. Moderate local political voices and media outlets in the east disappeared through a coordinated campaign of kidnappings and armed attacks. Those who disagreed with the separatists and their well-armed "little green men" were in physical danger. In accordance with their goals, the diversity of opinion that long characterized the east was being snuffed out as it gradually was in Russia itself.

Our Embassy followed events as closely as possible, as always trying to enable Washington to make its best and most well-informed decisions. Situation report #284: "Shots fired in Mariupol. At least four people taken to hospital with gunshot wounds. Approximately thirty people have seized two floors of the police HQ. Also reports that pro-Russian groups are attempting to seize nearby military base. Mariupol City Hall on fire." After so many similar situation reports, it was hard to avoid becoming numb to the ugly brutality that the words depicted. "Euromaidan activist Valeriy Salo burned alive in his car in Donetsk oblast. . . . Luhansk: A man is shot dead in his car on the road to Kyiv." Self-proclaimed Slovyansk mayor Ponomaryov stated that his forces would no longer take prisoners, but would kill all Ukrainian soldiers immediately. Eastern Ukraine was turning before our eyes into a battlefield of neighbors. Suddenly, it was an artificial conflict zone where one side was instigated by, supplied, and abetted by Ukraine's Slavic "Big Brother," intent on sowing chaos and reaping the whirlwind.

None of us knew the ultimate Russian strategy in the east—whether they would take the Crimea route of annexation, attempt to create another Transnistria-style "frozen conflict" zone, or continue until they had installed another compliant regime in Kyiv. The first and last options risked major international condemnation and military conflict, but it was a risk that the Kremlin had already taken in Russia's "near abroad" (*blizhnee zarubezh'e*) more than once since the breakup of the Soviet Union. The first "frozen conflict" zone in Transnistria was one likely accidental outcome of that breakup. The Soviet 14th Army was orphaned in a tiny sliver of Moldova after the USSR dissolved in late 1991, and despite being a largely Russian force, it was slated to become part of the military in Moldova—a new state with a predominantly ethnic Moldovan/Romanian population to which those soldiers felt no allegiance. After brief fighting, Transnistria declared its independence in 1992, though it was recognized by no one, not even by Russia. Russian troops remain in Transnistria to this day, and Russia is seen as the one player that could resolve the situation but has chosen not to. After the 2008 Russian invasion of Georgia, Russia carved off two "frozen conflict zone" pseudo-states from Georgian territory, South Ossetia and Abkhazia. It seemed entirely possible that the eastern Ukrainian self-declared "People's Republics" might be added to this collection of poor, tiny, isolated, and unrecognized microstates cut off from most of the world, granted permanent misery and economic desolation in a state of suspended animation as a sacrifice to the geopolitical goals of the Russian Federation.

Mariupol was an important place to watch. Situated in southeastern

Ukraine on the Sea of Azov, the city of some 450,000 persons, almost evenly divided between ethnic Ukrainians and Russians, was an important regional administrative and economic center. Gauging how much emphasis the Russians placed on wresting it from Ukrainian control could be an important clue to their strategy. On May 9, unidentified kidnappers grabbed Mariupol's police chief as a major attack on a police station left one Ukrainian soldier and scores of separatists reported dead. If Russia's goal was the creation of a land bridge between Russia and Crimea, Mariupol, the next major coastal city west of Russia on the Sea of Azov (just north of the Black Sea), was the obvious target. Full control over the Ukrainian land that Putin referred to as Novorossiya would complete this land bridge to Crimea, with the added bonus of a land link to the spot where the post-Soviet "frozen conflict" was born, Transnistria. However, no one in our Embassy or in Washington knew what Russia's plan was, or indeed, if any existed other than opportunism.

For months, the Russian media had portrayed Russia's actions in Ukraine as a fight against "fascists," as a kind of final chapter to the Second World War. It was in that frame of mind that Putin flew from the annual May 9 Victory Day parade in Moscow to Crimea. At the Crimean Victory Day ceremony, Putin noted, "Sevastopol showed the whole world that when people are determined to fight for their native land, dignity and freedom, the enemy cannot pass. . . . I am sure that 2014 will also become part of [Sevastopol's] chronicle and of that of our entire country, as the year in which the peoples here expressed their firm desire to be together with Russia. In this decision they have shown that they remain true to the historic truth and our forefathers' memory." It was his first visit since the annexation. Less than two years earlier, Putin had left Yanukovych cooling his heels for hours at a palace in Yalta while he—Russia's biker-in-chief—unexpectedly toured the peninsula with his favorite Night Wolves motorcycle gang. Now he returned to Crimea with that very palace, and everything else in Crimea, under his firm control. The United States, EU, UK, and NATO quickly condemned his visit. It's doubtful that Putin even bothered to shrug.

It was a heady time for Russian officials as their country was literally on the march, and it induced among some of them a kind of threatening bluster to match the times. After Romania denied clearance for Russian Deputy Prime Minister Rogozin's aircraft on its way to breakaway Transnistria, he tweeted in response, "Ukraine does not allow me to pass through again. Next time I'll fly on board TU-160." The Romanian Foreign Ministry immediately asked for clarification regarding whether Russia's deputy foreign minister was actually threatening to violate their airspace in Russia's largest strategic bomber. The Ukrainian Foreign Ministry denied that they refused Rogozin's overflight rights, calling his statement "cheap propaganda." As Rogozin left Moldova/ Transnistria, Moldovan authorities reported confiscating a local petition he was carrying calling on Moscow to recognize Transnistria's statehood.

An internet video posted on May 10, the day before the illegal referenda in eastern Ukraine, purported to show tens of thousands of ballots already marked "yes," ready for use the following day. Meanwhile, self-proclaimed "People's Governor of Luhansk" Valeriy Bolotov predicted the turnout for the referendum would be as high as it was in Crimea. Other reports coming in the east were confused. Though the Donetsk City Council banned the use of its facilities for the referendum, now municipal employees were "encouraged" to cast votes. At around 10:10 a.m., foreign journalists stated that two men, armed with a sawed-off shotgun and a pistol, arrived at school number one in Donetsk and demanded that they stop filming or taking photographs. In Mariupol, social media showed long lines of people outside makeshift voting facilities. Human Rights Watch issued a report declaring that the Ukrainian military may have used excessive force in Mariupol resulting in needless deaths. In Lugansk region's town of Bryansk, *Ukrayinska Pravda* reported that two pro-Ukrainian youth were shot dead, and two more were wounded after yelling "Glory to Ukraine!" at a pro-Russian checkpoint. On "Referendum Day," the body of the Mariupol police chief Valeriy Androshchuk, kidnapped by pro-Russian separatists on May 9, was found hanged in the woods outside of the city. Murders like this showed with gruesome precision the antidemocratic nature of the illegal referenda, an integral component of the hybrid war to dismember Ukraine. It was polling in the midst of a terror campaign manufactured to ensure the preordained outcome.

In Russia, not surprisingly, the news sounded much different. On referendum day, the Russian press focused on reports that a child was critically injured in Slavyansk by right-wing forces for wearing a St. George's ribbon— the symbol of the Soviet Union's World War Victory that had recently been co-opted as a separatist and anti-Maidan symbol. Were such reports true, it would have greatly concerned the US government as well, and the Embassy would raise our concerns directly and forcefully with the Ukrainian government. The problem was that so much of this type of information only appeared in propagandistic Russian press releases and couldn't be verified. In this case, for example, the allegedly victimized child could not be found. In another case, many analysts suggested that horrifying images of mutilated bodies broadcast in the Russian media, accompanying claims of Ukrainian military brutality around Slovyansk, appeared to be photos from Russia's conflict in Chechnya years before. Had these accusations originated from reliable interlocutors, we would have had more to go on, and if the accusations turned out to be well-founded, we would have been just as critical of Ukraine as we were of Russia. But given the jaw-droppingly unreliable track record of Russian media reporting in Ukraine, there was good reason to doubt their veracity.

Similarly, on May 14, we received a report that miners in the vicinity of Mariupol were worried about lawlessness in Ukraine's National Guard. This was a serious accusation, and it was something we would publicly condemn were it true. Ambassador Pyatt sent a message to the Kyiv Task Force asking for additional investigation. The following day, he wrote again to the group:

> I've poked around a bit more on this. It's clear that law and order evaporated in Mariupol on Saturday after the army and militia retreated. ATMs burned, gun shops looted, etc. etc. I talked last to a young woman I trust whose family is from Mariupol. . . . She reported that things stabilized yesterday after Yatsenyuk implemented his plan to use Akhmetov's security folks to restore law and order. They and local police are now patrolling jointly—not/not a Slavyansk situation of a "liberated" zone. She said the main problem she hears about is criminality among the Donetsk Republic folks. . . . Also voiced concern about the pending refugee crisis as Ukrainians flee Donbas if Putin takes the land grab.

Elizabeth added:

> [My contacts also] seriously questioned the reporting that miners were complaining about National Guard lawlessness. He said there was a general worry, especially among Mariupol steel workers (presumably the same crew doing the patrols), that the government cannot protect the population and had lost control of law and order. But that was

not a fear of National Guard. And he noted that law enforcement is thought to be loyal to Oleksandr Yanukovych—hence the fears of criminal gangs taking over. Further, our contact from Independent Miner's Union made a strong statement in the press that miners did not support separatism.

A report on May 16 that separatists had seized a private bank vehicle carrying money for the wages of miners, teachers, and doctors seemed unlikely to make the militants any more popular.

But if the miners would not come to separatism, separatism would come to them. Chris Greller wrote in: "We received notice from union contacts that a group of armed men have seized the administration building and trade union office at the Donbasantratsyt mine complex near Krasny Luch, Lugansk. This is a large complex managing seven nearby coal mines. The Confederation of Free Trade Unions (KVPU) has 2,500 members at the mining complex, out of a workforce of 9,000. The enterprise is publicly owned. So far, mines continuing to operate and the armed separatists have issued no demands. . . . Given the stated position of the miners' union to defend mines from outside interference and separatists, the situation could be quite volatile."

The referendum voting in the east was a tragicomedy presented by amateur actors whose incompetence, as we knew very well, really didn't matter because they came on stage armed with real guns. The separatists were not the only ones holding referenda that day. The principled jokesters holding a mock poll asking whether Donetsk should join the UK and Kolomoyskyi's allies asking if locals wanted to join Dnipropetrovsk were also out and about doing their thing. The watchword for the separatists' referendum was "chaos." Social media reported that casting ballots at multiple separatist polling stations was just fine, and that one could cast a ballot regardless of whether one was from Donetsk, Kyiv, Moscow, or Havana. In any case, since the separatists did not have access to updated voter rolls, it would have been difficult for them to know who was authorized to cast a vote anyway. Not that they cared. Such were the day's events. None of this electoral street theater mattered anyway since everyone already knew what the result would hold; the theater reviews had been written long before the performance, and they were all enthusiastic. Separatist leader Denis Pushilin announced well before the polls closed that new "state bodies and military authorities" would be formed immediately after the election results were announced. Those results were never in question. In Moscow, city authorities thoughtfully even allowed a makeshift separatist polling station for Ukrainians temporarily abroad or working in the city where they could stop by and cast a vote in favor of the dismemberment of their nation. While the separatists had said they would wait until the next day to announce results, they apparently couldn't contain themselves. Shortly after midnight, the Donetsk People's Republic's self-styled elections chief Roman Lyagin announced that 90 percent of voters had chosen to establish a "republic." Voter turnout was close to 75 percent—a triumphant expression of the people's will. This was almost identical to the 89 percent victory ratio suggested as optimal in the intercepted intra-party Donetsk-Moscow phone call released recently by Ukrainian intelligence. But again, no one really doubted the outcome. Luhansk organizers said that 96.2 percent of its voters supported the loosely defined concept of autonomy. Later in the night, when "tainted ballots" were taken into account, it turned out that exactly 89 percent voted in favor of the formation of the Donetsk People's Republic. Rarely have politicians been able to read the mood of the public so accurately in advance of an election. Meanwhile, a discordant note was sounded by the Ukrainian Foreign Ministry that reminded everyone of the Pew Research Center poll finding that only 18 percent of those they questioned supported secession. But perhaps each of the armed men voted ten times, which would have been entirely possible in this jury-rigged referendum held under a cloud of violent menace. In any case, the men with the guns favored secession. That was all that mattered.

In the morning, Russian military intelligence officer Igor Girkin (aka Strelkov), though clearly a foreign citizen working for a foreign government, proclaimed himself commander-in-chief of the Donetsk People's Republic and ordered the "law enforcement organs" of his spanking new state to immediately prosecute the Ukrainian leadership as well US CIA Director Brennan, Assistant Secretary of State Nuland, and State Department spokesperson Jen Psaki. This might be considered a rather audacious start for an aspiring pseudo-state's faux-independent intelligence agency. On the other hand, Girkin/Strelkov was magnanimously sparing President Obama, Secretary of State Kerry, Senator John McCain, and others from the purview of his judicial vigilance. No doubt he saw that as a political winner.

That Monday morning, I flew from Kyiv to Geneva to attend a meeting of the General Council, the highest level body of the World Trade Organization.

This was not a normal part of my routine, so as the Ukraine trade specialist, it was a big day for me. I joined a small group of fellow American officials seated on the main floor behind the "United States" nameplate. It was an incredible thrill for a diplomacy geek like myself. The topic was how well had Russia fulfilled the obligations it had undertaken when it joined the WTO in August 2012, including removal of the bullying trade barriers it maintained toward its neighbors like Ukraine. Ten delegates spoke against the Russian position: Ukraine, the United States, Canada, Japan, New Zealand, Norway, the European Union, Korea, Taiwan, and Australia. One delegate spoke in defense of the Russian position: Russia. The Russian delegation had introduced an agenda item before the main topic, accusing the EU, the United States, and Canada of violating their own WTO commitments through the introduction of Ukraine-related sanctions. The accused, including the United States, simply stated that they respected their WTO commitments and left it at that.

After ten members criticized Russia's bad behavior, the Russian ambassador replied in a mocking tone, "Taking a lesson from other delegations, I'll just say that we respect our WTO commitments and have not violated them."

In Ukraine we had heard this snide Russian boomerang response many times: fling back others' accusations by accusing them of exactly what they are accusing you of, then mock your opponents and accuse them of hypocrisy. Short and indignant. No need to deal with the substance of the accusations.

Back on the home front, despite its opposition to Ukraine's military actions in the east and the Euromaidan movement, the remnants of Yanukovych's struggling Party of Regions were not taking kindly to the newcomers in its traditional home base of Donetsk. Likely most irritating was self-proclaimed "People's Governor" Pavel Gubarev's claim that Party of Regions (PoR) backer Rinat Akhmetov, Ukraine's richest man, had paid off two-thirds of Donetsk's separatists. After branding Gubarev an "impostor and swindler," Yanukovych's PoR, now out of Yanukovych's control, sharpened their tone even further: "To explain things clearly—this [situation] is like when a group of homeless persons from Tuapse beach brings their leader to the Krasnodar Duma and says, 'This is the people's governor.' In the best case, the whole of this group with its leader should be sent to the madhouse." This rather esoteric put down, at least for foreigners unfamiliar with the Black Sea resort of Tuapse and the southeastern Russian city of Krasnodar, was difficult for the BBC and other international news outlets to explain. They resorted to pointing out that Gubarev's most prominent prior work experience before becoming "People's Governor" was as a Santa-for-hire, doubtful preparation for the responsibilities he now supposedly shouldered. These were not actual local leaders, but nobodies from the local fringe backed by foreign firepower. That, and only that, now made them somebodies.

The new "People's Governor" must have been quite unhappy when even Russia stopped short of immediately recognizing the eastern referendum vote as legitimate. Instead of referring to it as a binding vote necessitating independence, Moscow merely said it was something which should "prompt a dialogue" between the eastern regions and Kyiv. This was considerably less than a ringing endorsement. Separatist leader Denis Pushilin asked the Russian Federation to consider Donetsk region's accession to Russia the day after the vote, but received no response from Moscow. The strong international response to the annexation of Crimea seemed to be having some impact on Russia's economy. Whether there was a connection between Western sanctions and Russia's apparent reluctance to go "full Crimea" in eastern Ukraine was still an open question.

Meanwhile, on May 14, the news from the east was grim—separatists reportedly killed six Ukrainian servicemen in fighting near Kramatorsk, and fifty-four "terrorists" were supposedly killed battling Ukraine's National Guard near Slovyansk. Self-proclaimed Lugansk People's Governor Valery Bolotov survived an assassination attempt. Gunmen forced the mayor of Horlivka to resign. In Kyiv, the Ukrainian government held a "National Roundtable" including a wide range of participants from the entire political spectrum. Only armed separatists were excluded. The purpose was to discuss constitutional and other reforms that would ease the crisis. Russian Foreign Minister Lavrov immediately downplayed the significance of the dialogue, telling Bloomberg news that he didn't "understand its composition." This was code for saying they wouldn't back talks without the "People's Republics" at the table. Though the Russian Foreign Ministry continuously called for dialogue, they seemed uniformly antagonistic to it in practice. Kyiv was engaging with traditional local leaders in Donbas, rather than recognizing Russia's armed stand-ins. Moscow seemed to perceive a quick peace that left Ukraine (minus Crimea) whole as against their interests. It's vital to remember that Kyiv's many attempts to engage the real local leaders of Donbas represented the "Maidan government" reaching out to the most stridently "anti-Maidan" elements of the recent conflict. This was indispensable to healing the country. The Russian government's every move seemed calculated to keep this from happening.

The National Roundtable was only one of many efforts to bridge the divide within Ukraine. The Ukrainian Catholic University started an exchange program to bring thousands of students from Ukraine's east to west and vice versa to help break down stereotypes. The National Roundtable moved to Kharkiv on May 17, again bringing the top levels of the Ukrainian government eastward to try to forge common ground. The Roundtable then moved to Mykhailov, another eastern city, on May 21.

On May 16, the Crimean Tatar community in Kyiv held a requiem at the National Opera House commemorating the seventieth anniversary of Stalin's cruel and arbitrary deportation of their parents' and grandparents' generations from Crimea to Soviet Central Asia and Siberia. Tatar leader Mustafa Dzhemilev told the Ukrainian press that Russian forces were bringing special vehicles to Crimea in preparation for arrests during protests related to the anniversary. Djemilev's wife had just been hospitalized after riot police cordoned off the block around her home in Crimea and conducted a snap search of her property. Why would the Kremlin object to the solemn commemoration of one of Stalin's innumerable crimes against humanity?

As always, Russian propaganda missed no opportunity to foment trouble. State-funded TV station Rossiya One reported that the snipers who killed protesters in February on Maidan "could have been" Georgians trained by the United States. Reading the ridiculous claim at my desk at work, just a few miles from the site of that massacre, I remember thinking that this would have been the perfect propaganda piece if they would have only remembered to mention Pravyi Sektor and NATO. Then I read deeper into the article. "These [snipers] are now in Kyiv, helping 'Pravyi Sektor' to conduct operations against the civilian population," said the former commander of the Avaza battalion Tristan Tsitelashvili. Well, still no mention of NATO, but blaming Georgia, the United States, and Pravyi Sektor for the deaths on Maidan was an impressive propaganda hat trick in itself. It didn't matter if these accusations really stuck. If even just a few people believed it, that was good enough. Just a few more small drops of poison in the well of truth. Tomorrow's outrageous lie would ensnare another few readers, as would the outrageous lie the day after that. Before long, reasonable people would simply say, "We just don't know what happened on Maidan." The cumulative effect of this gradual and purposeful perception poisoning was to place lies and conspiracy theory on the same plane as the truth even though the facts are actually perfectly clear. When the lies sufficiently muddy the truth, the perpetrators of the lies will have achieved the goal. John Stuart Mill, the British philosopher and avatar of liberalism, believed that truth would prevail against falsehood in an open marketplace of ideas. If only it were that easy in the internet age of systematic lies, bots, trolls, and alt-facts. In the oft told tale, when the French foreign minister asked Stalin about the plight of Catholics in the Soviet Union back in the 1930s, Stalin incredulously asked, "The Pope? How many divisions does he have?" Were Stalin around today, in the same spirit he might ask: "How many Twitter bots does the truth have? Who pays the trolls hyping the truth?"

On May 16, the separatists declared Russian citizen Aleksandr Boroday to be the "Donetsk People's Republic" prime minister. His main qualification seemed to be his close relationship with Russian intelligence agent Girkin/ Strelkov, the man who just named himself "Defense Minister." Ukraine's border guards briefly arrested Luhansk People's Republic head Bolotov as he arrived at a border checkpoint, presumably to cross into Russia. An estimated two hundred militants wielding automatic weapons and grenades then freed him.

Meanwhile, Ukraine's presidential election was approaching. Russian government spokespeople continued to claim that the upcoming polls would be illegitimate and that Russia would not recognize them despite Putin's occasional hints to the contrary. One unintended outcome of Russia's seizure of Crimea and its dispatch of destabilization agents threatening easterners who wanted to vote in the national elections was that the type of Russia-friendly coalition which had brought Yanukovych to power was no longer possible in Ukraine. Too many former Yanukovych voters were now excluded from the electorate by land grabs and the violent extremists' threats against potential voters in the east. Moreover, with good reason, many voters blamed the Party of Regions for Yanukovych's corruption and its failure to find a peaceful resolution to the Euromaidan crisis. Therefore, the victory of a pro-Western, pro-Maidan presidential candidate in the national election was nearly certain. Of course, the irony was that Russia itself was responsible for this situation. Yet the Kremlin's foreknowledge of this likely outcome meant that it was in Russia's interests to continue to argue that no outcome could be legitimate, and to continue to cast Ukraine as a lawless hellhole run by fascists.

On May 19, Assistant Secretary Toria Nuland wrote to all European Bureau ambassadors and Public Affairs Sections:

> As all of you know, just one week from today, Sunday, on May 25, Ukrainians will vote for a new President. It is a pivotal moment for the country and the region, and I want to ask all of you and your public diplomacy teams to seek opportunities to engage with key audiences (host government, opinion makers, think tankers, journalists, civil society leaders, and online) to amplify the simple message that we must do all we can to help Ukrainians exercise their right to choose their own future peacefully, freely and fairly through the ballot box. . . . Our goal is to support the Ukrainian government—directly and through the OSCE—to ensure that these elections meet the highest international standards and are a credible, free, and fair expression of the Ukrainian people's political will. These elections represent a stark contrast to the efforts of separatists who seek to impose their will through intimidation and the barrel of a gun. . . . Please also work quickly in your media market to counter false stories about the situation in Ukraine or the US role. Truth does not seem to be a requirement for Russia's propaganda machine or its proxies; for example, this weekend one of our posts had to battle a false story in a major European online daily alleging the arrest of CIA officers in eastern Ukraine. Please also let us know immediately if you pick up similar efforts to smear Ukraine or us.

Ukrainian intelligence (SBU) announced that they had arrested three men, employees of a local private security firm, who received money from separatist leaders in Luhansk to detonate a car bomb in a crowded area of Odesa in order to bring new panic and chaos to the area, which was still in mourning after the tragic May 2 fire deaths. While the Russian government accused Ukraine of harassing its journalists, the Ukrainian government stated that two Russian Life News journalists were presumed to be members of separatist militant groups because they were carrying mobile anti-aircraft missiles in their car. Indeed, Russia Today and Life News did have quite a penchant for being around when things blew up. A video appearing on YouTube a few days later appearing to show those Life News journalists ordering the separatists to fire a sophisticated anti-tank missile seemed to cross the line between documenting war and waging it.

Despite the grim situation in large swaths of Donetsk and Lugansk regions, it was increasingly clear that even larger chunks of the east were simply refusing to descend into chaos. Zaporizhzhya remained calm, and Odesa was returning to normality after mourning its own tragedy. Kharkiv and Dnipropetrovsk also didn't seem to be taking the bait. A professor in Mariupol described the situation there to our Public Affairs Section: "The environment is coming back to normal, people are still reluctant to participate in actions but are not afraid to walk in the streets, and students are coming back to lectures." She noted that the scariest days were May 9 and 10, when separatists were attacking administrative buildings. Our Public Affairs information officer remarked on what the professor told her: "In her opinion, lots of people from both sides are ready to talk with each other as everybody is really tired of fighting. She also mentioned that intellectuals are eager to participate in normalizing the situation but have lots of doubts about how to do it properly." Rinat Akhmetov, the east's most powerful and influential figure who seemed to perpetually play both sides, took to the airwaves to call for "Donbas with weapons! Donbas without masks!" Never showing his allegiance cards while the game's still in play was always Akhmetov's MO, but at least this was a call for peace. Good enough for today. While the violence in the east was horrific, it was limited to an area much smaller than the maps of "Novorossiya" circulating on Russian social media. Putin was not an infallible strategist—he seemed to be getting only about one quarter of the Ukrainian territory on fire that he wanted . . . at least judging by the map.

Now that the election was just days away, something resembling a charm offensive emanated from Moscow. The Russian military returned several Ukrainian Navy vessels seized in Crimea, and President Putin announced that he had ordered Russia's military to pull back from its front line positions against the Ukrainian border. Prime Minister Medvedev called the idea that Russia wanted to annex additional Ukrainian territory "propaganda," but this assurance was undercut by his assertion just a few days later that Russia was "under no obligation" to stay out of eastern Ukraine. Finally, just two days before the Ukrainian presidential election, Putin said at an investment forum that Russia would "treat the choice of the Ukrainian people with respect."

But even as these mollifying words were uttered, the situation on the ground in eastern Ukraine was getting rougher. In the stilted language of an official Ukrainian State Border Guard Service press release: "Since 10:00 p.m., May 21st, 2014, a rapid situation aggravation happened at the Lugansk detachment responsibility border sector." That night, border guards detected three Russian KAMAZ heavy duty cargo trucks escorted by one NIVA 4 × 4 passenger vehicle trying to make an illegal border crossing from Russia into Luhansk region. On the logical assumption that this was a delivery of men and material for the separatists, they fired warning shots, and when these were ignored, they opened fire at the vehicles' tires, forcing the mystery convoy to return to Russia.

Bureaucrats the world over, including myself I must confess, are remarkably similar in our practice of turning high human drama into the pablum of regularized situation reports and their dead language, in this case: "On this occasion information was sent to Russian officials stating that was the fourth case of unchecked cargo vehicles border violation from RF [Russian Federation] territory prevented by Ukrainian border guards."

Within a few minutes, a second attack erupted along another stretch of Russia's border with Luhansk region. According to the Border Service's antiseptic language, "The Stanichno-Lugansk State Border Guard Department in Lugansk area was attacked by an armed group. Hand grenades, grenade launchers, and other small arms were used." Suddenly, a major separatist goal appeared to be that of opening up a stretch of the Russia-Ukraine border which they controlled. One can only imagine what they expected to receive through such a portal once they wrested it from the Ukrainian Border Guard. Again, when reading the official language, one could almost forget the smell of gunpowder and fear on the ground: "After border guards refuse to perform ultimatum on 22nd, May, 2014, at 00.25 a.m. guerrillas assaulted the [Border Guards] using grenades, automatic and group firearms. Around 01:00 a.m. the attack was repelled."

That same night, Associated Press journalists bore witness to the aftermath of the violent deaths of eleven Ukrainians at a checkpoint near Volnovakha in the Donetsk region. One more Ukrainian serviceman died that day in Donetsk, making it the single deadliest day for the Ukrainian military in the east since the beginning of the conflict. According to the Ukrainian Elections Commission press secretary Kostyantyn Khivrenko, three more district election commissions in Luhansk and Donetsk regions were occupied that day, bringing the number seized by separatists to prevent them from participating in the national presidential elections to more than half of the total.

Meanwhile, the impact of the Crimea annexation on regular people's lives continued. Tamara Sternberg-Greller from the Consular Section wrote in: "We had a Summer Work Travel applicant today who went to university in Sevastopol at the National University of Nuclear Energy and Industry who told us that when the Russians arrived in Crimea, the president of the university declared that all students had to choose whether they wanted to be Ukrainian or Russian citizens. Those who chose to be Ukrainian were removed from the university and had to transfer elsewhere. This applicant was a straight-A student at that university. He is from Rivne and chose to be Ukrainian, and thus was kicked out. He says that he knows of at least one other person with the same story." A few weeks later, a violent attack on a Kyiv Patriarchy Ukrainian Orthodox church in Crimea's Perevalnoe showed just how much danger those in Crimea with ties to Kyiv faced—even holy men of a faith pretty much identical to Russia's own de facto state religion in all aspects except the location of its headquarters.

On Friday, May 23, Embassy Kyiv's election monitoring teams headed out into the field across Ukraine. It was too dangerous to post observers in Donetsk or Lugansk, but we had observers in other eastern and southern cities, such as Mykolaiv, Zaporizhzhya, Izyum, Kherson, Berdyansk, Odesa, Kharkiv, and Dnipropetrovsk in addition to several western cities. Throughout the day, the teams wrote to the Task Force, confirming the calm preparations for the election being held in all regions not under "separatist" control. Even places that had experienced some recent violence were doing okay, with 202 out of 216 polling stations open in Mariupol. Tim Piergalski wrote in from Lviv: "Very few campaign billboards. Tons of people outside on an absolutely gorgeous day, kids playing in fountains. Two old men playing electric guitars in the park (Beatles, CCR [Creedence Clearwater Revival], Eric Clapton, Ukrainian folk). . . . Some weird American drinking kvass in the park listening to them. Sampled the local chocolates to check for fascism, found none."

Not everything was so idyllic. That night, two Western journalists and their local translator, longtime local dissident Andrei Mironov, were hit by artillery fire near Slavyansk. The next day, Italian photojournalist Andrea Rocchelli was declared dead, as was Mironov.

If everything is working properly, election monitoring is about as exciting as sitting around watching strangers fill out any other standardized government forms. Reports from the field sent back to the Kyiv Task Force reflected this:

From Kherson: "Our first polling station (PEC no. 650630) in Kherson opened on time and without incident."

From Chernivsti: "No concerns to report. We will be moving shortly to nearby PEC 730186, which has 696 registered voters."

From Odesa: "PEC chair very eager to demonstrate to observers that PEC operates according to regulations. 2332 voters, 19 home voters. PEC opened on time, we've seen a steady flow of voters, we estimate by 8:30 approaching 50 voters. Calm situation."

From Zaporizhzhya: "An old woman asked for assistance in filling out the form and explaining the procedure. The head of the commission entered the booth and started explaining the ballot. The deputy, within seconds went over and told the head to get out of the booth and asked the friend who arrived with the elderly woman if she could assist. The deputy then assured the observers that the head of the commission did not observe the vote."

From Sumy: "In Vorozhba village smooth sailing. Steady stream of voters. Organized. Observers present. Mobile polling unit out and about. Everything looks great."

From Lutsk: "The only problem reported so far is the occasional pensioner who forgot their eyeglasses."

In Donetsk, however, separatists spent the day harassing polling stations that tried to open and seized the Hotel Victoria where Governor Taruta housed many of his temporary staff. The militants posted a picture on Twitter of a number of discarded ballot boxes sitting on the street outside the regional administration building. They scrawled the word *trash* on the ballot boxes. Indeed, in the areas they controlled, they themselves were responsible for trashing the election itself.

Meanwhile, Russian and Ukrainian social media seemed to be observing two different elections in different countries. On the Ukrainian net, the story was about the orderly opening of polling stations across Ukraine, enthusiastic participation, and long lines of people waiting to vote. This matched what we were seeing on the ground. Kremlin-controlled social media, however, posted photos of empty polling places and called the vote an empty exercise in choosing between various flavors of "fascism." One pro-Kremlin website noted that one polling station in Odesa had not opened and cited it as an example of anti-Russian bias in the administration of the vote.

Parts of eastern Ukraine remained a battleground. The words *Donetsk* and *rapidly deteriorating* seemed permanently linked in our Embassy situation reports. Journalists risking their lives to report from the city noted an increase in hired and foreign fighters, especially armed Chechens. Ukrainian social media was awash in photos of armed Chechen militias in Donetsk, arriving in Vostok Battalion trucks. Several weeks later, Putin-backed Chechen strongman Ramzan Kadyrov would tell the press that 74,000 Chechen "volunteers" were "willing to bring order to the territory of Ukraine." While out on election observation, a taxi driver told one US Embassy observer that his family in Slavyansk told him that armed groups of five to ten Chechens each arrived the previous week and were already operating there. For months, the Russian media had accused the Ukrainian government of bringing foreign mercenaries to the east. Now, foreign mercenaries were actually on the ground—Russian citizens from Chechnya, fighting on behalf of the "separatists." Such organized Chechen involvement would be unthinkable without Moscow's blessing or active promotion. One of our friends in Donetsk called Political Chief Sasha Kasanof, who updated the Task Force in the terse bullet points used for breaking information:

- "Situation in Donetsk is rapidly deteriorating.
- He's currently in Donbas palace hotel overlooking Lenin Square and said the 700+ strong rally includes about 100 armed men (who at one point yesterday shot their automatic weapons in the air over the crowd to 'celebrate'). (He didn't mention the hostage situation at Victoria.)
- Multiple reports from journos that things are incredibly tense and clashes at checkpoints in north of region. Much not being reported.
- He hosted OSCE team yesterday (they departed yesterday afternoon). Hard to access most DEC [District Election Commission] and other areas.
- Rumor that seps control area around airport.
- Citizens incredibly afraid. City is eerily empty and all his contacts staying inside at the moment.

■ He added that he came on Friday 'relatively optimistic' but is now very concerned about the next day or two."

Disturbing as this report was, at least there was more information coming out of Donetsk than Lugansk. According to one Electoral Commission member there, gunmen attacked one of the few open polling stations at 3:20 p.m. Eleven armed men seized the premises, smashed tables and ballot boxes, and took all election-related documents and ballots. A nearby precinct then closed polling and evacuated their ballots. The separatists correctly viewed the ballots of an actual democratic election as a threat to the bullets that were their currency in the battle for power.

In Kyiv, the Internet Party of Ukraine was running its perpetual candidate for office, Darth Vader. Dressed in a Hollywood-quality Darth Vader costume with impressive sound effects, he cut quite a figure registering his candidacy flanked on the streets of Kyiv by a phalanx of fully costumed and choreographed Stormtroopers. The parody was quite direct and effective—his presence ridiculed how voters accepted as normal some of the more malevolent figures on the ballot. The Internet Party plastered campaign billboards around town of Vader posing with cute kids, with slogans like "For the Children!" On Election Day, Vader himself was denied a ballot because he was wearing a mask. Rules are rules, after all.

That evening, our observers began reporting that their polling stations were having problems transmitting their results electronically back to Central Election Commission (CEC) servers in Kyiv. Observer Keri Robinson wrote in: "Our PEC [Precinct Election Commission] has been instructed not to bring ballots to the DEC [District Election Commission] because of hacking. They can't enter the data so they don't want PECs bringing their ballots to them. They are freaking out because they will need to wait with them here." Some observers saw similar problems, others didn't. No one could pinpoint the issue.

The digital chaos silently threatening crucial election infrastructure was no surprise to Nikolay Koval, chief of Ukraine's Computer Emergency Response Team (CERT-UA). He had barely slept recently, and his nimble mind was busy jumping between the solid bits and bytes of information at hand. It had all begun with a call from the CEC several weeks before: "Look, something weird is going on. Our personal computers aren't turning on and our servers are disabled." After investigating, Nikolay agreed that something was definitely happening. The Cisco ASA protective firewall was inexplicably turned off, leaving the system open to exploitation. He and his team looked at the logs and CM system, revealing suspect activity with outside private internet addresses. The admin accounts were compromised. In other words, they had been hacked. In coordination with Ukrainian intelligence and others, CERT-UA got to work.

They identified the IP addresses where the attacks originated. Hackers at those addresses began their initial reconnaissance incursions and system scans of CEC computers in mid-March, less than one month after the revolution in Kyiv. They were probing for vulnerabilities; weak spots for exploitation by sophisticated malware. But the activity was so robust and multifaceted that Koval came to believe that Ukraine was not up against one hacker or even one hacker group, but an ecosystem of organizations with the same general orders competing with each other for wins. Some seemed more interested in simply showing that Kyiv's election process was vulnerable, others more interested in causing generalized system damage. But each seemed backed up by sufficient resources to indicate that these were not lone actors. So-called zero-day exploits—new, previously unknown vulnerabilities—were increasingly the territory of well-resourced state actors. Some of this unique code employed pointed to a particular state actor in this ecosystem, APT28, a hacking arm of Russian military intelligence (GRU). In future years, APT28, also known as "Fancy Bear," CyberBerkut, or any of a dozen other names, would be associated with hacking of the US Democratic National Committee in 2016, the Bundestag, and the World Anti-Doping Agency. After analyzing hard drive images and servers, CERT-UA found fifteen computers infected with advanced cyber espionage malware connected to APT28, making this the most technically advanced attack they had ever investigated.

Then, two days before the election, hackers again compromised the CEC's servers, jeopardizing the critical election infrastructure in an obvious slash-and-burn style attack to sabotage the network. But the attack was immediately recognized and systems were restored. But why do this two days before the election and not on election night? Was the worst yet to come?

It was. As election night approached, more malware kicked in. For twenty hours, the software designed to show election results in real time stopped functioning. At small polling stations where the results were reported to the main server, suddenly they were being routed to an intermediate server. A malevolent digital hand had taken control. In this struggle, unknown and unseen outside of technical and intelligence circles, CERT-UA went into crisis response mode.

By late evening, the SBU reported that Ukraine's CEC servers were under a massive cyberattack emanating from Russia. The hacking was far more sophisticated than the simple Denial of Service attacks to which the CEC was well accustomed. Koval and CERT-UA knew that there were multiple issues—the vote tabulation system was down and the public website was compromised. Triaging the situation, they concentrated on the tabulation system—fixing the public-facing website would have to wait. After getting those systems restored that evening, Ukrainian officials, including Koval, returned to issues with the public website. They identified an incursion on CEC computers that placed an image on display. Instead of actual election results, the picture included fake election data erroneously claiming that Pravyi Sektor leader Dmytro Yarosh was winning the election with 37 percent of the vote. Yarosh's actual support was less than 1 percent. The election commission successfully removed the file, and the fake data was never posted to the public website in place of the real data. However, Russia's most watched news program, the regular evening news on *First Russian Channel (ORT)*, apparently somehow "expected" the erroneous data to appear and showed on television a screenshot of the fake outcome the virus was supposed to produce, claiming that Yarosh was winning the Ukrainian election. Again, Russian television displayed a screenshot of fake data that were never actually shown to the public, but would have been had the virus been successful. How did they get it? With a breathless report on the fake result already prepared?

The situation was remarkable, not only with regard to the exceptional coordination between Russian cyber warfare operations and the Russian press, prepared in advance to hype the fake results. At first glance, it might also seem surprising that the Kremlin would go to such lengths to fake a victory for someone they unreservedly regarded as a "fascist." One might think they would intervene to support a pro-Russian candidate, but they took the opposite tack. Their overriding goal was to support their false narrative that Ukraine was awash with fascists. A Yarosh victory, however improbable, would have validated the false narratives in the eyes of the Russian people that Ukraine was irredeemably in the grip of the far right, that its government was inherently illegitimate, and that the "organic uprising" in the east was a natural reaction to how the rest of Ukraine had succumbed to the menace of fascism.

To promote that outcome, they employed cyber warfare to intervene on behalf of the Ukrainian far right, the very force they so vilified. Despite all of their hatred spewed at Pravyi Sektor, a Pravyi Sektor victory would have been their ideal outcome because it would discredit Ukraine not only in Russia, but in the international community as well. But their malware was disabled, and the boldly dishonest gambit fell flat.

Koval knew that Russian citizens, conditioned by their media, were already scared of Yarosh as a model of the "fascist killers" from western Ukraine. For their perfect Ukrainian election victor, the Russian Federation had chosen their own image of evil carefully cultivated for many months in their domestic press. After his team and others defused the digital bomb sitting underneath the election, Koval had some time to reflect, writing: "I believe that we should not underestimate the ability of hackers—especially those that enjoy state sponsorship—to disrupt the political process of a nation. If CEC's network had not been restored by May 25, the country would simply have been unable to follow the vote in real time. However, to what extent would that have caused citizens to doubt the integrity of the entire process? It is hard to know."

National elections in Ukraine usually required a second runoff round given the multitude of candidates and Ukraine's legal requirement that the winner receive a majority of the vote. But by evening, with greater than a 60 percent turnout, it was clear that a runoff would be unnecessary. Petro Poroshenko, Ukraine's self-made chocolate king, former Yanukovych cabinet member, and early Euromaidan supporter, was crossing the finish line with a first-round victory. Poroshenko had entered the political arena early in the Euromaidan protests and often mixed it up with protesters and policemen on the square, suffering business losses in Russia due to his political positions. Achieving around 54 percent of the first-round vote, his support dwarfed that of the next ranking contender, newly freed former prime minister and "Gas Princess" Yuliya Tymoshenko, whose support was in the low teens. Tymoshenko graciously conceded, at least for the moment. Three-time former world heavyweight boxing champion, political party leader, and Maidan activist Vitali Klitschko was elected mayor of Kyiv. Voter turnout was high everywhere except Donetsk and Lugansk, where terrorist threats limited voter turnout to the teens. Surprisingly, various Russian authorities, and even former President Yanukovych, living in exile in Russia, stated publicly that they would respect the election results.

On the morning of May 26, Ukrainian air traffic control suspended all flights to Donetsk as masked gunmen seized the sleek, modern steel and glass Donetsk airport. In the middle of the night, Donetsk's armed separatists announced that they "were declaring martial law" in order to wage war against Ukrainian forces in the area. It was hard to imagine how this "martial law" would be any different from the "Donetsk People's Republic's" reign of terror over the last two months. Then, we received reports of Ukrainian attack helicopters using anti-tank guided missiles and an SU-27 fighter jet over the Donetsk airport against the group of armed Chechen pro-Russian fighters who had seized the airport. The airport, named after famed composer Sergei Prokofiev, suddenly became the focus of some of the most intense fighting of the conflict to date. The next day, one separatist told the media that the bodies of thirty of his fellow militants were stacked in a truck outside a local hospital. Attackers included Russian passport holders. Radio chatter in Donetsk indicated that these militants were especially well equipped, even having night vision goggles. Russia publicly called on Ukraine to withdraw its military from its own soil in the east and to "stop its war against its own people." The Ukrainian Foreign Ministry countered, releasing a statement asking the world community to pressure Russia to stop sending more "terrorists and weapons" into eastern Ukraine.

While the war of words raged on, the Ukrainian government was increasingly losing control over its border with Russia, and with it, its ability to prevent the inflow of men and material that sustained the Donetsk and Lugansk militants. On May 27, Ukraine's State Border Guard Service (SBGS) reported that it had encountered more border-runners overnight. While the SBGS captured two cars and a minibus loaded with weapons, more unidentified vehicles with armed men successfully entered Lugansk from Russia. President-elect Poroshenko later told Ambassador Pyatt that more separatist Vostok Battalion combatants and weaponry crossed the border illegally from Russia the following night to reinforce the separatists.

On May 29, separatists shot down another Ukrainian military helicopter outside of Slavyansk, killing fourteen Ukrainian soldiers. The downing of the helicopter again highlighted the separatists' increasing possession of, and ability to deploy, high-tech anti-aircraft weaponry not typically at the disposal of months-old, homegrown militant groups. Separatists also kidnapped more OSCE monitors. By May 30, the normally staid reports from Ukraine's SBGS were bearing more surreal headlines: "Separatist addressed to RF [Russian Federation] President with appeal 'to assist in fight against genocide of Russians in Donbas by official Ukrainian government'. . . . Ukrainian servicemen knocked off unmanned flying vehicle of Russian manufacture with container of unknown chemical liquid. . . . Accumulation of 500 people of Caucasus [Chechen] origin were noticed in Shyrokyi village of Lugansk region."

The next day, armed separatists stormed the border guard station near Dyakove, Luhansk region, claiming after the border guard fought them off that they had mined the area. On June 3, the Ukrainian military destroyed an ammunition storage facility in Slovyansk and cleared Krasyi Liman of separatists. The next night, former Minister of Internal Affairs Yuriy Lutsenko claimed on social media that fifteen trucks with gunmen illegally crossed the border from Russia into Lugansk after Ukrainian border guards abandoned their posts. With the seizure of two border posts in Lugansk region—Chervono-Partyzansk on June 3 and Dolzhanskyy on June 5—the separatists now controlled what they had long desired—a stable portal to Russia. Acting President Turchynov vowed a massive military operation to reclaim the border. By June 11, the so-called separatists' First Lugansk Kozak Brigade, which had captured the border post at Dolzhanskyy, claimed to control 200 kilometers along the Ukraine-Russia border, completely opening it to incursions from the Russian side.

Meanwhile, our family's scheduled departure date from Ukraine was edging closer, but with the Embassy operating in crisis mode for nearly six months, I hadn't had much time to think about life after Kyiv. On May 31, I had to make one of those calls that every husband hates to make to his wife. "Natalya," I started, trying to take a positive spin. "Looks like I've been given a great opportunity to be Toria Nuland's control officer during her visit."

"When?" she asked, unmoved.

"From next Friday to Tuesday," I trailed off.

"You mean our last weekend before packing out? When we'll be at home sorting through everything we own?"

"Yes," I said sheepishly. "That weekend."

Not surprisingly, the Regional Security Office had some reservations about assembling 4,300 people under the US Embassy seal on June 5 for the Intellectual Property Rights concert. I had a knot in my stomach as well. We had started planning for the concert a year earlier, before Maidan, before the sniper massacre, before the new government, before the invasion of Crimea and the east. It was a different country then. In the back of the Embassy van on the way to StereoPlaza with my wife and son, I had that flash of fear. Kyiv was peaceful, but there was tremendous violence in the east every day. If someone brought that kind of darkness to Kyiv, would our event have been a good target? The thousands of tickets we gave away online to raise awareness of intellectual property right issues had been snapped up within hours. For months, my biggest fear had been that no one would come to the show and it would be a flop. In that moment, sinking down into my seat in the van, no one coming seemed like the safest outcome.

As we pulled up to the venue, the lines for the front door wrapped all the way around the large building. The place would be packed. Ignat and Dmytro met me with big smiles. They had poured a tremendous amount of sweat into making this night a success, and now it was time to enjoy it.

"Young people in this town have been through a lot," Ignat said as we walked into the building. "Tonight, we'll get our message out. But we'll also give back a little and let them relax . . . and let them be in a country not at war for the night."

Dmytro's mood was ebullient. "Chris, you've seen me in conferences and on Maidan, but this is my real natural habitat—with the musicians, the lights . . . just relax. This is going to be great."

I went up to the balcony where David, Elizabeth, and most of the Embassy Economic Section was sitting, waiting for the show to start. Soon the crowd was swaying and chanting to the trippy stylings of Druha Rika and pumping their fists along with Ukrainian rock-rapper Tartak. Four other popular acts played, and then Ignat invited me to speak to the crowd before the last act came out. I brought along my son Andrew to see the massive crowd from the stage.

I hadn't prepared to speak that night. "Thank you so much for coming," I started, unused to the sound of my own voice booming out of Marshall stack amplifiers.

Downloading music legally supports Ukrainian artists, and that's important. The world needs Ukrainian voices. Your voices explain your country to the world. Modern Ukraine is just over twenty years old,

and much of the planet doesn't yet understand who you are or what
your struggles mean. They don't yet understand that you are the ones
fighting and sacrificing for the universal values that we all believe in—
democracy, anticorruption, and the right to live in peace. Your artists
and cultural figures can help them understand what Ukraine has to give
to the world, and what you can teach us. Please support them. Have a
great night.

On the ride home, the evening felt to me like a triumphant island of posi-
tivity and security in a turbulent ocean.

On June 6, a Ukrainian military AN-30 aerial photography plane was shot
down over Slavyansk, likely by a Russian-made MANPAD (man-portable
air-defense systems) "Igla" rocket. Only two of the seven-man crew survived.
In keeping with the east's newfound role as a setting for tragedy, the first provable child death from the ongoing fighting was recorded on June 9—that of
an eight-year-old girl. Each side blamed the other. Mariya Turchenkova from
Russia's Ekho Moskvy (Echo of Moscow) radio station reported on the home-
coming of the bodies of thirty-one Russian citizens killed fighting in eastern
Ukraine. Turchenkova claimed that one of the bodies belonged to Sergey
Zhdanovich, a retired FSB agent. Over the next week, KAMAZ trucks, anti-
aircraft weaponry, and small artillery pieces appeared on the streets of Horlivka
in Donetsk Oblast matching those that recently had crossed the border illegally
from Russia.

Saturday, June 7, the inauguration of Ukraine's first post-Euromaidan
president, Petro Poroshenko, temporarily suspended normal life in Kyiv. Vice
President Biden led the high-level US delegation, which included Senators
McCain and Murphy, Assistant Secretary of State Nuland, and others. Most,
like Biden, McCain, and Murphy, would only be on the ground for a few hours
to attend the inauguration ceremony. Nuland, however, would stay on, spending a day in Odesa before returning to Kyiv for several days of back-to-back
meetings. Planning her intensive schedule consumed my workdays for weeks.
Rather bizarrely, no issue consumed more time than whether or not a shipment
of "indestructible soccer balls" that Toria Nuland intended to donate to an
orphanage in Odesa could be sent to Ukraine aboard Air Force Two with Vice
President Biden. Getting permission entailed a stream of hundreds of emails

flowing back and forth from our Embassy to the National Security Council to the State Department's Educational and Cultural Affairs Office to the Office of the Vice President to the US Air Force. Scheduling a meeting with Ukraine's president was infinitely easier than getting a bunch of soccer balls onto Air Force Two, for which, I suppose, there was no precedent that could be cited. The effort failed, and I helped the balls find a less fancy ride to Ukraine.

In any case, our delegation to Poroshenko's inauguration went off without a hitch. Vice President Biden met with President Poroshenko and Prime Minister Yatsenyuk. Surprisingly, even Belarusian President Lukashenko, so often a dependable defender of the anti-Western Kremlin party line, stood to applaud Poroshenko's statements during his inaugural address that Crimea was part of Ukraine and Ukraine was part of Europe. Following the ceremony, Assistant Secretary Nuland flew to Odesa, where she met Odesa governor Ihor Palitsia and Dnipropetrovsk governor Kolomoyskyi in addition to Ukrainian Navy leadership and civil society representatives. The emotional highlights of her Odesa trip were visits to two churches to remember those who lost their lives during the May 2 fire at the local Trade Union Building. The US government properly felt the need to mourn the tragedy as well. Nuland also delivered the problematic "indestructible soccer balls" to a local orphanage. After returning to Kyiv, Nuland met Ukraine's top political leaders and businessmen, and also held a roundtable discussion with now out-of-power Party of Regions leaders. Russia's Ambassador Mikhail Zurabov canceled a meeting with her at late notice, a not unexpected snub. Just before her departure, freshly elected Kyiv mayor Klitschko took Nuland on a walking tour of Maidan to discuss his plans for the city. In a press conference at the Embassy, the assistant secretary reiterated strong US support for the new Ukrainian government and denied several Russia-spread rumors, including the assertion that the United States sought to deploy missile shield technology in Ukraine.

By early June, the separatists' "revolution" in the east was already beginning to eat its own children. On June 7, after an apparent argument between separatist factions, assailants shot and killed self-proclaimed People's Republic of Donetsk leader Denis Pushilin's assistant, Maksym Petrukhin, near a popular café on Pushkin Boulevard in Donetsk. A few days later, veteran Russian intelligence agent Igor Girkin (aka Strelkov) announced the arrest of self-proclaimed Slovyansk mayor Ponomaryov for obscure reasons. After more squabbling between the armed groups grappling for pieces of the east, one such group proclaimed the founding of the Lysychansk People's Republic on land already claimed by the Lugansk People's Republic. Evidently, there was money to be made by holding territory. One Ukrainian newspaper claimed that some local gunmen were charging $1,000 per adult and $500 per child for local residents to flee the conflict area. On June 13, Pushilin's bus exploded near the Donetsk Regional Administration Building while he was not on board, killing three others. What had first presented itself as the supposed embodiment of eastern Ukrainian patriotic politics had quickly degenerated into a species of gang warfare.

Meanwhile, it had been a busy time for former Ukrainian parliamentarian Oleh Tsaryov. He first came to the Embassy's attention for his unhinged accusations that the United States was supporting "color revolution" in Ukraine through TechCamp and his personalized slander of members of the US Embassy staff, including the public posting of their personal information. Now his true colors were flying high. After calling for the Maidan, which he labeled a Western-backed conspiracy, to be cleared by force in February, he launched a presidential campaign, which gained little traction. In April, he joined the separatists, telling Russian television that locals asked him to head up a united front in Ukraine's southeast in favor of "federalization." He then withdrew from the election and released a video calling for the creation of Novorossiya out of eight Ukrainian regions. Kyiv's Rada then withdrew his parliamentary immunity in order to prosecute him for treason, but by then he was beyond their reach as a supposed official in the Donetsk People's Republic. Tsaryov's political trajectory from a Russian media darling and anti-American conspiracy theorist to membership in a violent separatist faction tearing Ukraine apart was worth pondering. It validated our gut instinct that he, like some others of our sharpest critics who sprayed out falsehoods against the US Embassy, hardly had the best interests of Ukraine at heart. Their motivations were more primal and personal. In changing circumstances, they were happy to tear their own home country to shreds if they thought they could claim one of those shreds for themselves. That such people viewed us as enemies was an unwitting compliment. We stood with those who actually wanted the best for their own nation.

Several days later, on June 12, self-appointed Donetsk People's Republic leader Denis Pushilin surfaced in Moscow, asking the Russian government for additional support. An online photo showed the ultranationalist Russian politician cum provocateur Vladimir Zhirinovsky hosting him in his Duma (parliament) office with a tray of cookies. That same day, the Ukrainian Ministry of Defense published pictures of trucks, small arms, and other equipment provided by the Russian military to eastern separatists. In the Russian government's first official admission of contact with the armed separatists in eastern Ukraine, Foreign Minister Lavrov barefacedly stated that Russia would provide "humanitarian assistance" to the area through "militias because of Kyiv's refusal to work together on this issue." In Kyiv, about one hundred persons protested the SBGS's inability to seal the eastern border, thirty of them attempted unsuccessfully to force entry into the SBGS building.

The Ukrainian government, afraid that Russia would exploit the Kremlin's proffered "humanitarian corridor" from Russia to eastern Ukraine to deliver war material rather than humanitarian supplies, rejected the Russian plans. On June 12, Ukrainian Minister of Internal Affairs Avakov told the press that three T-64 tanks crossed the border into Ukraine from Russia. This was a further escalation in the lethality of military items that were finding their way from Russia into separatist hands. The militants, for their part, were clearly on high alert and exhibiting paranoid behavior. Near Snizhne, a small city in eastern Ukraine, they hijacked a bus carrying twenty-five orphaned children and their teachers from Dnipropetrovsk who were traveling for their summer vacation, kidnapping them for a day. The reason for their outrageous and otherwise inexplicable actions could have been nervousness about an expected big delivery of Russian weapons and supplies. Indeed, within a day, the State Department publicly confirmed that the three "tanks, several BM-21 'Grad' multiple rocket launchers and other military vehicles crossed the border near the Ukrainian town of Snizhne." The Russian press tried to debunk the story, claiming that the separatists had appropriated three tanks from the Ukrainian military. The problem with this particular falsehood was that the tanks in question had equipment not used by the Ukrainian armed forces. The following day, the Ukrainian military stated that they had destroyed two of the Russian tanks along with three armored personnel carriers and four other separatist vehicles at a cost of four servicemen killed and thirty-one wounded. This was a real war.

On June 14, separatists near the Lugansk airport demonstrated their terrifying new anti-aircraft capabilities by shooting down a Ukrainian military IL-76 transport aircraft, killing all forty Ukrainian servicemen and nine crew aboard. Luhansk People's Republic leader Bolotov publicly took "credit" for the deaths. In response to this latest act of aggression, about one hundred protesters attacked the Russian Embassy in Kyiv, overturning cars, throwing paint at the building, and taking down the Russian flag. Ukrainian foreign minister Deshchytsia arrived at the scene to calm the protesters. He was caught on film saying that while Putin was a Khuilo (roughy translated as "dickhead"), they shouldn't take violent action against the Russian Embassy. Even though he was actually trying to protect the Russian Embassy, his insult instantly galvanized the Russian media, which demanded his resignation. In Washington, State Department spokesperson Jen Psaki immediately condemned the attack on the Russian Embassy. On Monday, June 16, the Ukrainian government deployed a heavy contingent of security forces around the Russian Consulate in Odesa, demonstrating their seriousness not to allow a repetition of the events that had unfolded over the weekend in Kyiv.

In more disturbing news from the east, on June 14, Ukrainian intelligence arrested five men from an "illegal armed formation" near the Lugansk town of Dyakove, seizing maps, ammunition, rocket-propelled grenades, and, most disturbingly, MANPADS—shoulder-launched anti-aircraft missiles. By this time, eastern Ukraine was awash in Russian anti-aircraft weaponry, drifting across the border along with mass quantities of men and other war material, making the skies above treacherous in ways the world would soon discover.

Three days later, on June 17, Russian operative and Donetsk People's Republic Defense Minister Girkin/Strelkov, arguing the case for yet more Russian support, told Russian newspaper *Komsomolskaya Pravda* that the separatists would not last one month without major Russian aid. But that understated the case—it was obvious that without the dispatch of Russian men and material, the separatists wouldn't have ever existed in any organized form. Ukrainian National Security and Defense Council secretary Andriy Parubiy estimated the number of armed separatists in the east to be between fifteen and twenty thousand, with roughly half coming from Russia and its various regions, such as Chechnya. President Poroshenko announced a peace plan that would start with a unilateral Ukrainian ceasefire, but it was immediately rejected by the Russian-backed separatists. Roving battles in the countryside of Lugansk and Donetsk regions continued to produce nightly fatal casualties. On the night of June 18 alone, fifteen Ukrainian servicemen were killed and thirteen went missing. The BM-21 Grad rocket launchers from Russia were taking their toll on Ukrainian troops on the ground. Assessing the numbers of casualties on the separatist side was difficult or impossible because of lack of access by trained observers.

Immersed as we were in the daily updates, meetings with contacts, and meetings with friends, it did not seem possible for Natalya and I to remove ourselves from the flow of events in Ukraine. Of course, it would be delusional to believe that the situation had stabilized and achieved closure. It hadn't. Too much was still going on, in Kyiv and throughout the country, particularly in eastern Ukraine. Whether the reformist ethos of Maidan, foreign pressure, or the pull of the nation's old corrupt ways would become the dominant trend was still very much in play.

But life in the Foreign Service was full of bureaucratically determined beginnings and endings. Neither Natalya nor I felt ready to leave; we were emotionally invested in the ever-unfolding story of Ukraine. Our son Andrew was only nine but still had the images of Kyiv burning in February in his eyes, our daughter Elena could recite beautiful Ukrainian poetry. Ignat and Dmytro had become true friends, as had Ukrainian government officials like Mykola Kovinya and Svitlana Zaytseva. Our housekeeper Irina had spent nearly as much time with our children as we had, and they had become attached to her and she to them. We worried for Ukraine in the abstract, and we worried for our friends specifically. But the end date on our assignment orders arrived. It was time to go.

A good friend of ours, Serhiy Olkhovsky, had just arrived to begin his own foreign service Kyiv adventure and threw us a going away party. On June 16, we sent all of our worldly possessions away packed in boxes, and on June 20, we enplaned at Boryspol International Airport for the 900-mile flight to Hamburg where we would board a ship to New York. We wanted a period of relaxation and readjustment, and our good friends Luke Schtele (of TechCamp fame) and Ben Rafferty were also heading back by ship. It was a relaxing time, as were the weeks in Orlando with my parents once we made it back home. But letting go of Ukraine wasn't possible. We had witnessed too much struggle and change not to be changed ourselves by the experience, an experience that would stay with us no matter where our careers and lives took us.

I had just begun my new job at the State Department's Office of Taiwan Coordination when I saw news of the downing of Malaysian Airlines Flight 17 in the skies over Donetsk on July 17, just four weeks after we had left Ukraine. I cringed, immediately remembering the flood of Russian anti-aircraft weaponry that had washed over eastern Ukraine in the last six months. The flow of these high-tech death delivery systems was not a secret; it was widely reported. The Moscow-backed separatists had proudly acknowledged the downing of large Ukrainian military aircraft with grotesquely high death tolls in the past. We quickly learned what happened to MH17. The US government had the signals intercepts; we detected a surface-to-air missile launch from the conflict zone at that exact time. The US intelligence community, a cautious group that normally takes its time reviewing and parsing its information, was able to say within hours that the aircraft carrying 283 passengers and fifteen crew on board was struck by an SA-11 "Buk" missile fired from terrorist-controlled territory in Ukraine. The facts were perfectly clear. Over the coming months, true to form, the Russian press and government rolled out the most outlandish conspiracy theories involving the Ukrainian military, the CIA, NATO, or any combination of their favorite bogeymen to try to absolve their viciously barbarous clients of this heinous crime. That this involved denying justice to over three hundred murdered souls with no connection to the conflict, including eighty children, didn't change this cold-blooded calculus. In the West, too many observers and commentators tried to demonstrate their impartiality and lack of bias by giving equal weight to the truth and the lies. Such a stance is destructive of the commitment to truth that must be the bedrock of humane societies. The only reaction I could manage was nausea.

In the end, there is still truth. And truth must be disentangled from the cobweb of lies in which propagandists seek to envelop it. And when the truth is extricated, it must be proclaimed and assiduously defended from those who would deny it, reject it, or bury it for whatever reasons of partisanship, cynicism, or simply fatigue. Returning home from Ukraine, I was amazed and disheartened to discover how many Americans believed that the United States had sponsored Maidan, overthrown Yanukovych, or had otherwise been involved in some massive dark intelligence operation in Ukraine. This story, heavily promoted by the Russian media on orders from the Kremlin, is simply untrue. Moreover, this lie degrades the struggle and sacrifices made by Ukrainians for the future of their own country. This lie attempts to transform the Ukrainians from heroic defenders of their own future threatened by the corruption of their own rulers into merely the duped pawns of great powers and intelligence services. It is not fair, and more importantly, it is factually not true. During my time in Ukraine, my colleagues and I witnessed tremendous courage as the nation of Ukraine tried to reclaim its future, first against betrayal by domestic criminals in power and then against foreign invasion. It is an important piece of world history, and it must be defended against those who believe that the quantity and volume of their lies will outweigh that truth. These pages have been an effort to shed a bit more light on that history, and to show the work of US Embassy Kyiv at the time for what it was. We were there to witness, and at some critical moments, we were able to help by remaining true to our American ideals and promoting democratic compromise and peaceful conflict resolution. When we had the opportunity, we tried to save lives. But we at the US Embassy were not the stars or the prime movers of this story. That title will always belong to the Ukrainian people, no matter what lies are spun to attempt to obscure that truth. In the end, there is still truth. And as Americans, I firmly believe it is our duty to fight for that truth under all circumstances. Losing our way is not an option. For those who believe in human dignity, America remains the indispensable nation. There is no plan B. Either America and our allies lead or those who believe in the righteousness of strongman rule, mafia interests, and oppression of anyone who can be oppressed will. I pray we always remain up to the challenge.

EPILOGUE

So, what did it all mean? What does Ukraine's struggle continue to mean? Given all the propaganda and all the lies about our work at US Embassy Kyiv, what does it mean to have been an American diplomat in Kyiv during those momentous events? Everyone who was there has their own story. I can only tell mine. But when I try to put it in the larger context, to judge our own actions, I have to go back to the beginning of what it means to be an American.

Now that almost 250 years have passed since our own revolution and we are an unquestioned world power, we Americans sometimes forget how it all started. Now that the world has so many democratic nations and even the most oppressive are forced to give lip service to democratic principles, it is easy to forget how radical the notion of a people ruling themselves was in those days. The world was filled with monarchies, their oligarchic supporters, and state apparatuses unapologetically dedicated to supporting their own perpetual domination over their population. Many Old World elites regarded the American experiment as an ill-advised, mongrel threat that would collapse under the weight of the ignorance of the masses. But they were wrong. Those democratic ideas endured, expanded, and shaped our world.

The United States was not born as an expression of ethnicity or religion, nor of cultural or partisan political identity. It was born of the acceptance of the ideas in our foundational documents. Some of those ideas included a rejection of tyranny and autocracy, a respect for an individual's right to improve their own life, and the idea that people should have equal opportunity and enjoy as much freedom as possible unless they impinge on the freedoms of others. We have never been perfect in the implementation of these ideas. But that doesn't change the fact that our founding fathers, with all of their own moral contradictions, laid out an amazingly farsighted system under which we could strive to gradually take these ideas from the pages of the Declaration of Independence and the Constitution and, step by sometimes painful step, make them real.

Most Americans remember Thomas Jefferson as the third president or as the drafter of the Declaration of Independence. But at the State Department, he will always be our first Secretary, or "S." At his second inauguration in 1805, S #1 said, "We are firmly convinced, and we act on that conviction, that with nations as with individuals, our interests soundly calculated will ever be found inseparable from our moral duties, and history bears witness to the fact that a just nation is trusted on its word when recourse is had to armaments and wars to bridle others." These words are simple, but living by them is tough. For me, these words mean that America's long-term interests are always represented best when we stand up for our country's values, when we do our moral duty. Always. Any short-term benefit that we might consider grasping by selling out an ally, bullying a trading partner, or making it easier to forget about those suffering most in the world is always, in the long run, against our "interests soundly calculated." When we stoop below our values, we are failing to soundly calculate our own long-term interests. We damage American power.

We are powerful when we have influence. Our influence comes from the fact that we are an example. Our influence comes from the fact that, for all of our flaws, we never stop trying to improve our own society. Our influence comes from a free press, which demonstrates daily that we are strong enough to withstand holding a spotlight to our most embarrassing problems. And most importantly, our international influence has historically come from the fact that we have tried to build a world that others want to be a part of; a fair world where even the largest powers play by rules that everyone understands. A world in which the big do not prey on the small just because they can. This stance has allowed us a unique chance to shape the world, and Americans at home have profited from the peace and business opportunities that flow from that. This allows us to be powerful, wealthy, and successful through fulfilling our moral duties. Thomas Jefferson was right.

What threatens our adversaries the most? In the early days of our republic, our tiny military wasn't a threat to anyone; in modern times, most adversaries would never dream of confronting us on the battlefield because of our military superiority. But what truly threatens autocrats is the universal appeal of our values, and the fear that these ideas can convince their own populations that they deserve better. This is what happened in Ukraine. When one looks at the amount of time that RT and other Russian media outlets spend on the single message that the United States is irredeemably corrupt and our democratic system is a fraud, one cannot escape the conclusion that their systemic smearing of us is a vital self-defense mechanism. No one can see the light from the shining city on a hill if it is covered in mud.

So, did we fulfill our goals in Ukraine? How can we make a reasonable assessment? Some might be tempted to make a "scorecard." On the negative side, Ukraine is no longer whole—part of it annexed, another part forcibly destabilized and suffering. On the positive side, most of Ukraine today is at peace and looking toward the future. Yanukovych did not use the military to order a larger bloodbath after heavy US and EU pressure. Only a fraction of Putin's so-called Novorossiya zone in Ukraine was actually destabilized.

But trying to draw up a "scorecard" is a fundamentally wrong approach as it fosters the dangerous illusion that the world is some giant chessboard in which some are born kings and others born pawns to be toyed with. Given our ideas about equality and self-determination, this notion of "geopolitics" is un-American at its core. Ukraine is no one's to play with; it belongs only to the Ukrainian people. They are the only ones with the right to keep score, and the only score that matters is whether they've managed to improve their own lives.

A better way for us to judge ourselves would be to use the standard of S #1—Thomas Jefferson. Did we fulfill our moral duty, which is by nature inseparable from our own long-term interests? At the Embassy, we worked night and day to clarify the situation on the ground, getting the latest, most accurate information back to Washington. When we could make meaningful interventions, the vice president, the ambassador, the assistant secretary, or someone else did it. When the thinly disguised Russian machinery of war rolled in across the border, we showed it to the world for what it was and implemented sanctions to deter even worse behavior. There will always be some regrets, and I wish that earlier action could have deterred even more theft and destruction. But I did leave Ukraine believing that we fulfilled our moral duty. And in doing so, we made America just a bit more influential, a bit stronger, and a bit more secure.

We must remain true to our principles not only because it is right, but because it is our strategic edge. Our principles are why others want us to lead. That world leadership, founded on a values-based foreign policy, is not some burden to endure—it is the core of our strength. To abandon this now would be giving up the greatest gift and wisdom of those who launched our nation into the world. America is still an experiment, as is Ukraine. As Ukraine struggles with its own demons to bring the ideas of its revolution into reality, we should do the same. History goes on. The struggle never ends.

INDEX